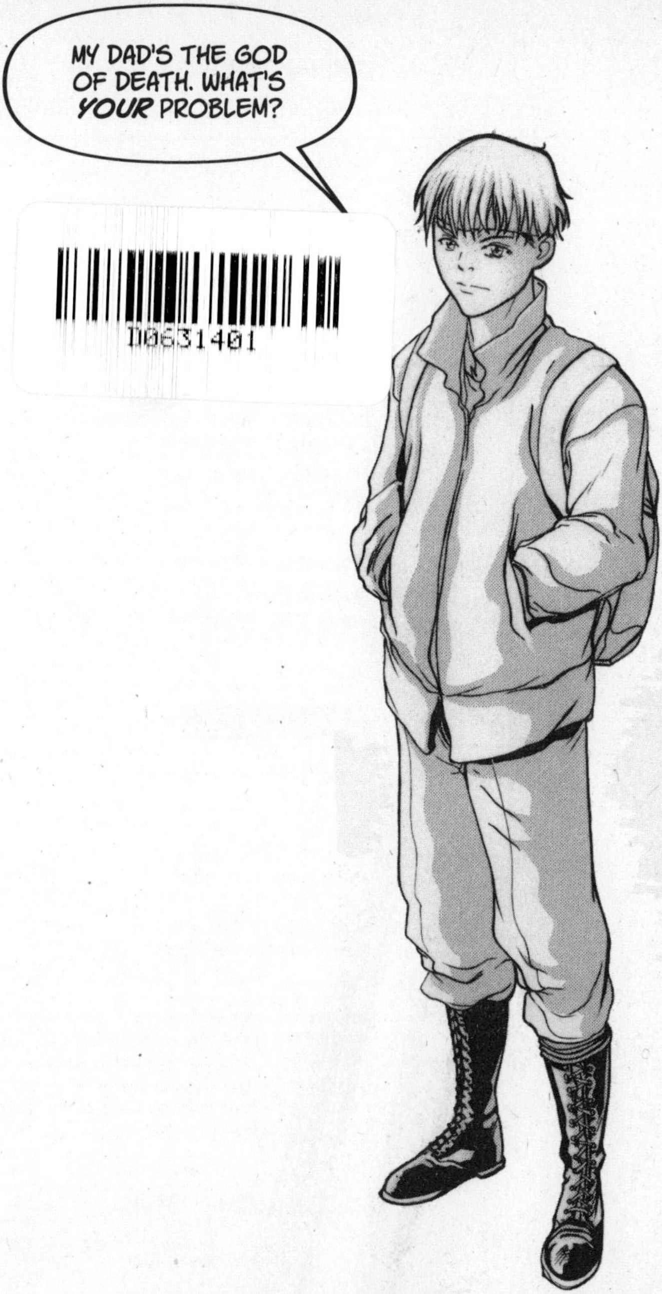
MY DAD'S THE GOD OF DEATH. WHAT'S *YOUR* PROBLEM?

Pantheon High Vol.1
Created by Paul Benjamin and Steven Cummings

Lettering - Lucas Rivera
Cover Art - Steven Cummings
Cover Design - Fawn Lau

Editor - Paul Morrissey
Digital Imaging Manager - Chris Buford
Pre-Production Supervisor - Erika Terriquez
Art Director - Anne Marie Horne
Production Manager - Elisabeth Brizzi
Managing Editor - Vy Nguyen
VP of Production - Ron Klamert
Editor-in-Chief - Rob Tokar
Publisher - Mike Kiley
President and C.O.O. - John Parker
C.E.O. and Chief Creative Officer - Stuart Levy

A  Manga

TOKYOPOP and 🐸 are trademarks or registered trademarks of TOKYOPOP Inc.

TOKYOPOP Inc.
5900 Wilshire Blvd. Suite 2000
Los Angeles, CA 90036

E-mail: info@TOKYOPOP.com
Come visit us online at www.TOKYOPOP.com

ISBN: 978-1-59816-734-4

First TOKYOPOP printing: February 2007
10 9 8 7 6 5 4 3 2 1
Printed in the USA

VOL. 1

WRITTEN BY
PAUL BENJAMIN

ART BY
STEVEN & MEGUMI CUMMINGS

TOKYOPOP®

HAMBURG // LONDON // LOS ANGELES // TOKYO

CONTENTS

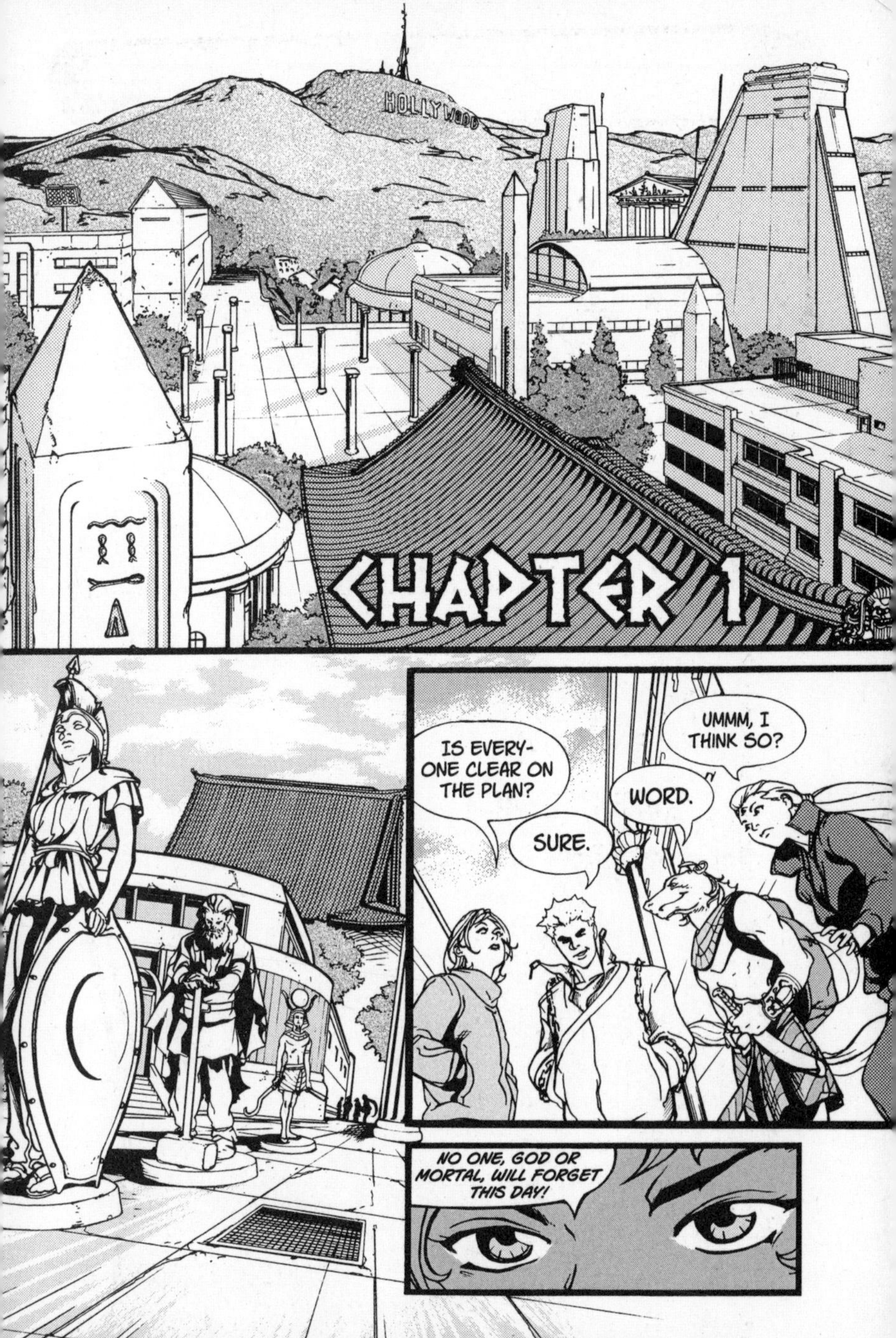
HOLLYWOOD
CHAPTER 1
IS EVERY-ONE CLEAR ON THE PLAN?
SURE.
WORD.
UMMM, I THINK SO?
NO ONE, GOD OR MORTAL, WILL FORGET THIS DAY!

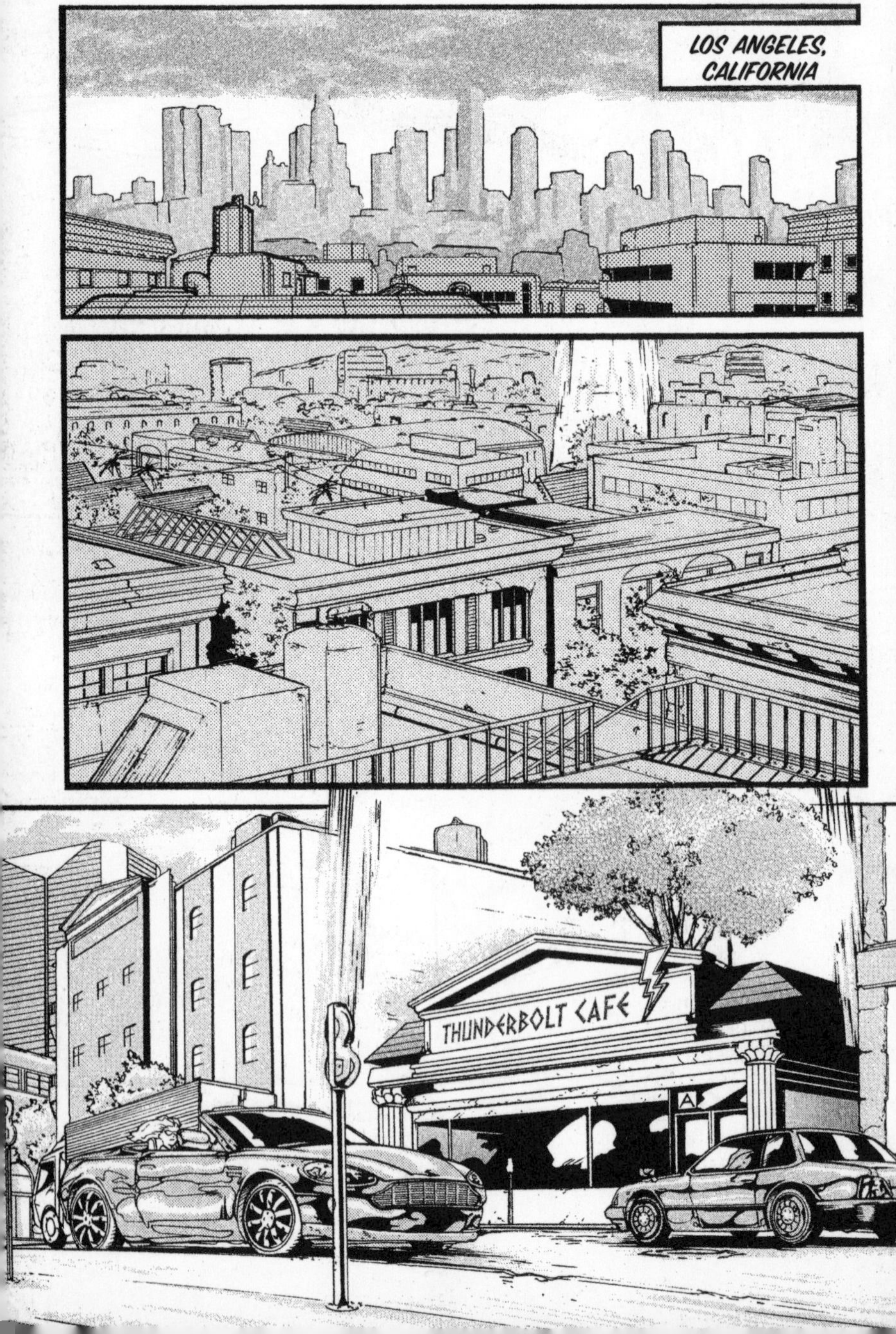
LOS ANGELES, CALIFORNIA
THUNDERBOLT CAFE

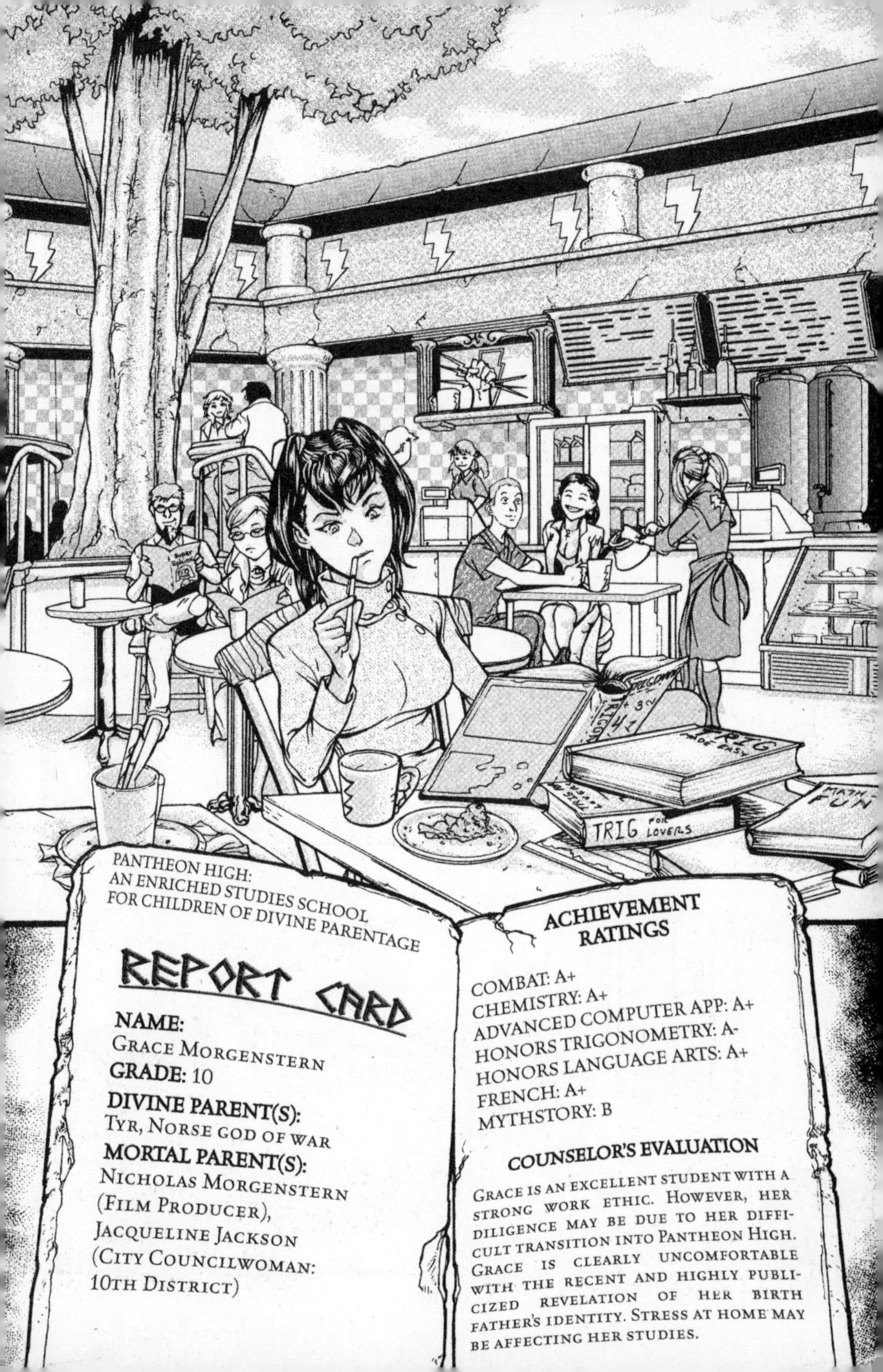
TRIG MADE EASY
TRIG FOR LOVERS
MATH FUN
PANTHEON HIGH:
AN ENRICHED STUDIES SCHOOL
FOR CHILDREN OF DIVINE PARENTAGE
REPORT CARD
NAME:
Grace Morgenstern
GRADE: 10
DIVINE PARENT(S):
Tyr, Norse god of war
MORTAL PARENT(S):
Nicholas Morgenstern (Film Producer), Jacqueline Jackson (City Councilwoman: 10th District)
ACHIEVEMENT RATINGS
COMBAT: A+
CHEMISTRY: A+
ADVANCED COMPUTER APP: A+
HONORS TRIGONOMETRY: A-
HONORS LANGUAGE ARTS: A+
FRENCH: A+
MYTHSTORY: B
COUNSELOR'S EVALUATION
Grace is an excellent student with a strong work ethic. However, her diligence may be due to her difficult transition into Pantheon High. Grace is clearly uncomfortable with the recent and highly publicized revelation of her birth father's identity. Stress at home may be affecting her studies.

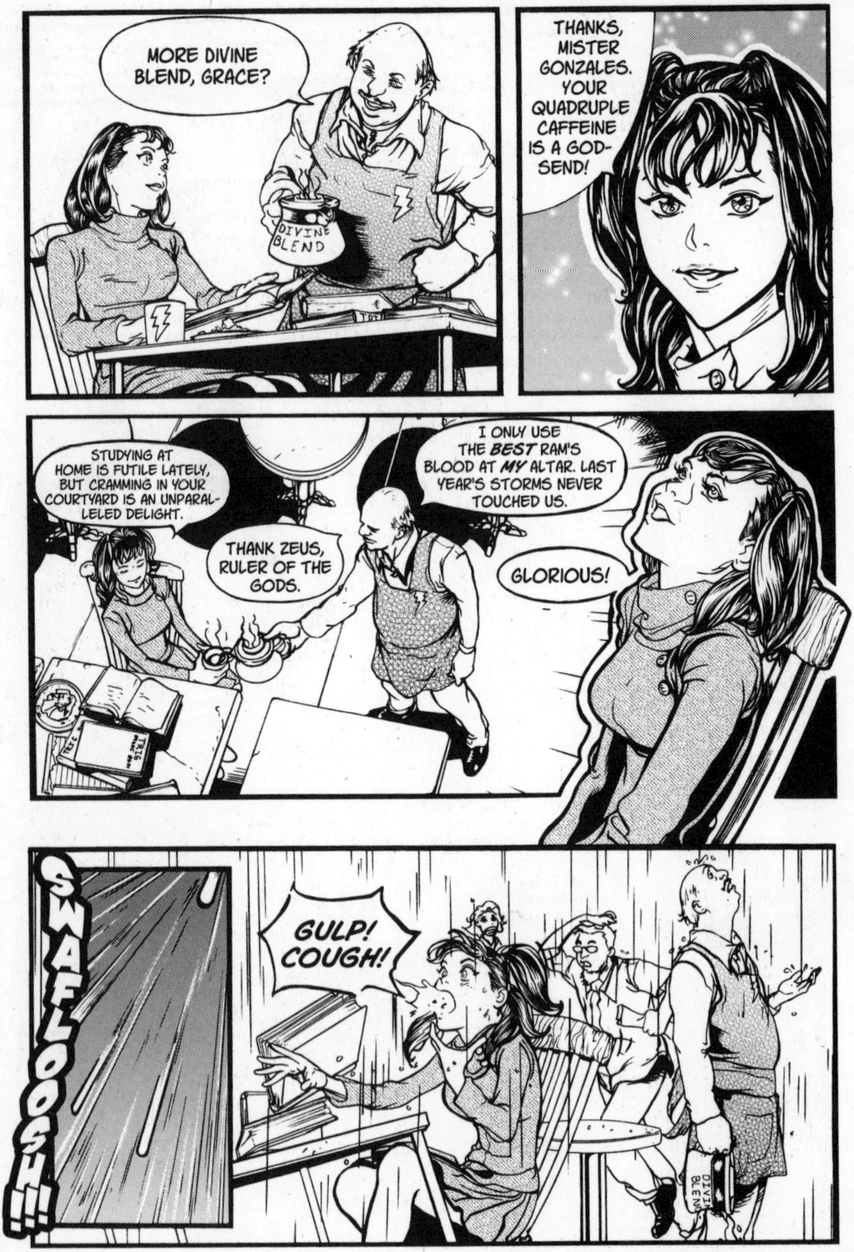
MORE DIVINE BLEND, GRACE?
DIVINE BLEND
THANKS, MISTER GONZALES. YOUR QUADRUPLE CAFFEINE IS A GOD-SEND!
STUDYING AT HOME IS FUTILE LATELY, BUT CRAMMING IN YOUR COURTYARD IS AN UNPARALLELED DELIGHT.
THANK ZEUS, RULER OF THE GODS.
I ONLY USE THE BEST RAM'S BLOOD AT MY ALTAR. LAST YEAR'S STORMS NEVER TOUCHED US.
GLORIOUS!
SWAFLOOOSH!!!
GULP! COUGH!
DIVINE BLEND

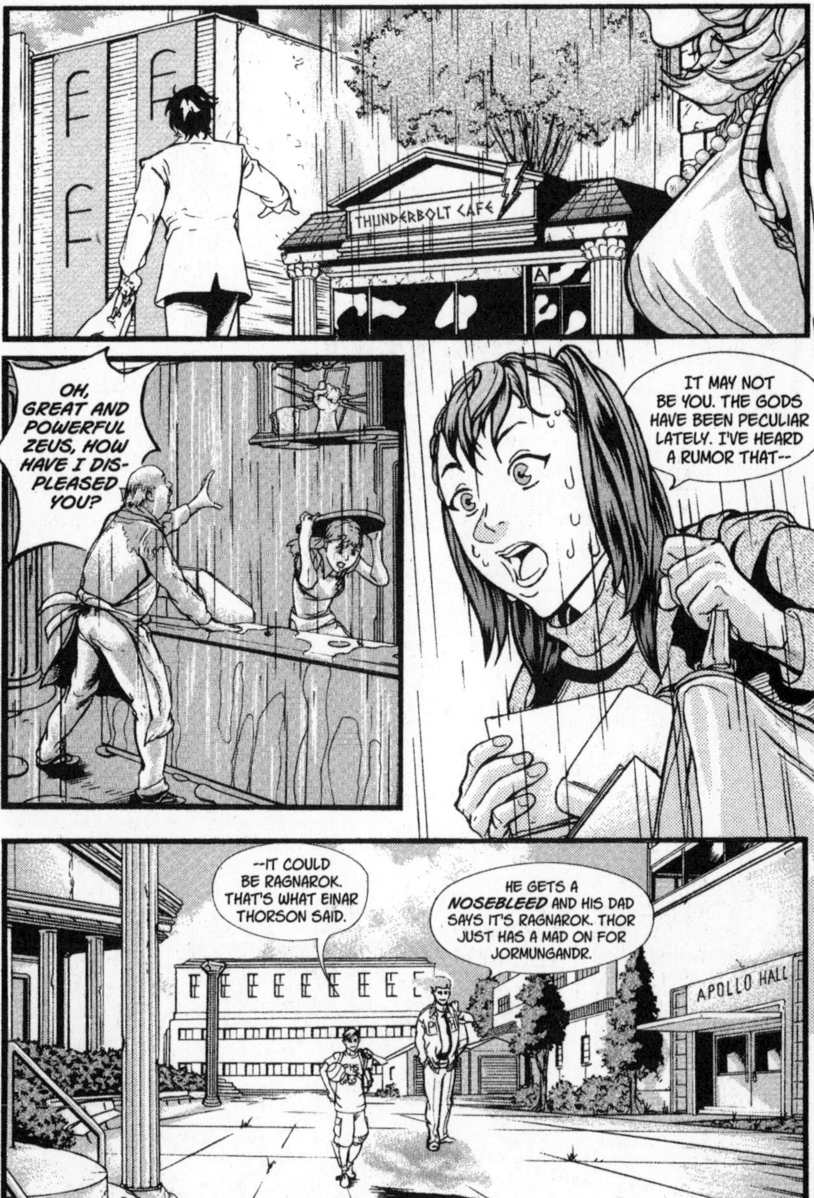
THUNDERBOLT CAFE
OH, GREAT AND POWERFUL ZEUS, HOW HAVE I DIS-PLEASED YOU?
IT MAY NOT BE YOU. THE GODS HAVE BEEN PECULIAR LATELY. I'VE HEARD A RUMOR THAT--
--IT COULD BE RAGNAROK. THAT'S WHAT EINAR THORSON SAID.
HE GETS A NOSEBLEED AND HIS DAD SAYS IT'S RAGNAROK. THOR JUST HAS A MAD ON FOR JORMUNGANDR.
APOLLO HALL

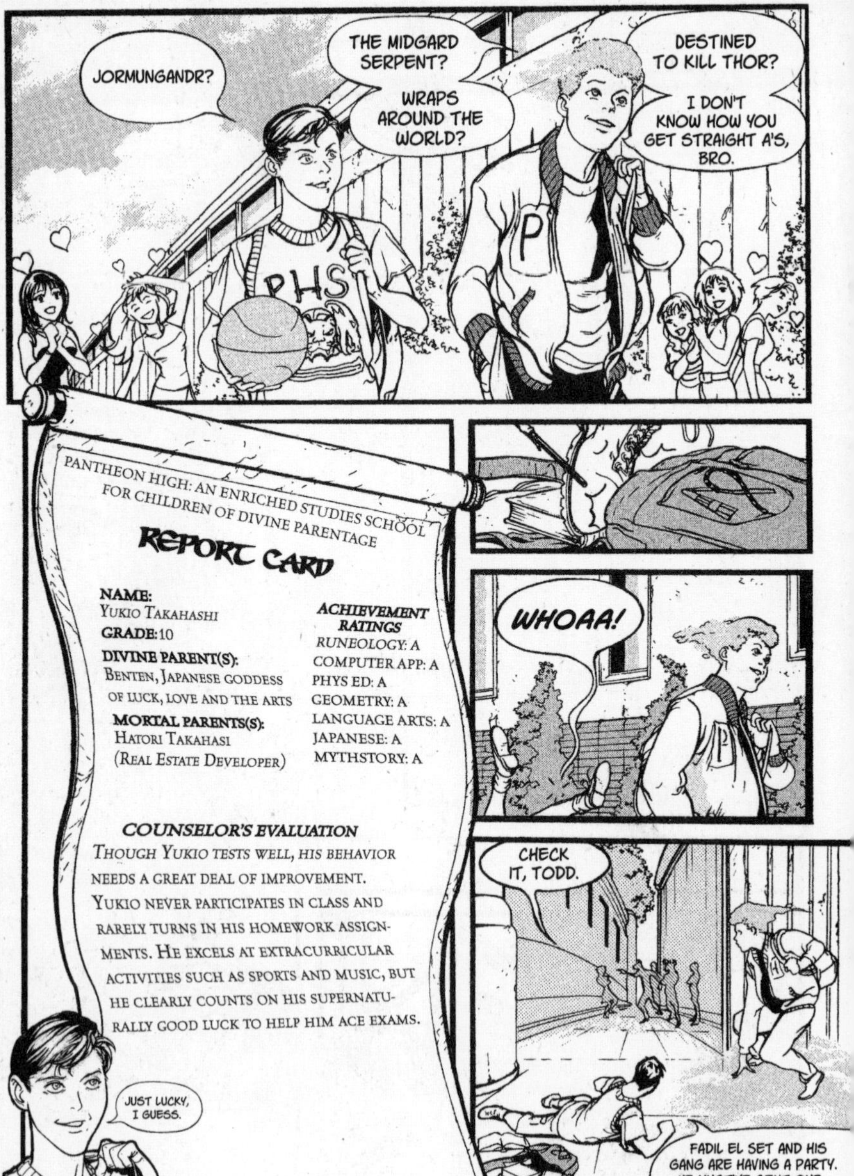

JORMUNGANDR?
THE MIDGARD SERPENT?
WRAPS AROUND THE WORLD?
DESTINED TO KILL THOR?
I DON'T KNOW HOW YOU GET STRAIGHT A'S, BRO.
PHS
P
PANTHEON HIGH: AN ENRICHED STUDIES SCHOOL FOR CHILDREN OF DIVINE PARENTAGE
REPORT CARD
NAME:
YUKIO TAKAHASHI
GRADE: 10
DIVINE PARENT(S):
BENTEN, JAPANESE GODDESS OF LUCK, LOVE AND THE ARTS
MORTAL PARENTS(S):
HATORI TAKAHASI
(REAL ESTATE DEVELOPER)
ACHIEVEMENT RATINGS
RUNEOLOGY: A
COMPUTER APP: A
PHYS ED: A
GEOMETRY: A
LANGUAGE ARTS: A
JAPANESE: A
MYTHSTORY: A
COUNSELOR'S EVALUATION
THOUGH YUKIO TESTS WELL, HIS BEHAVIOR NEEDS A GREAT DEAL OF IMPROVEMENT. YUKIO NEVER PARTICIPATES IN CLASS AND RARELY TURNS IN HIS HOMEWORK ASSIGNMENTS. HE EXCELS AT EXTRACURRICULAR ACTIVITIES SUCH AS SPORTS AND MUSIC, BUT HE CLEARLY COUNTS ON HIS SUPERNATURALLY GOOD LUCK TO HELP HIM ACE EXAMS.
JUST LUCKY, I GUESS.
WHOAA!
CHECK IT, TODD.
FADIL EL SET AND HIS GANG ARE HAVING A PARTY. HE MUST'VE SENT OUR EVITES TO THE WRONG ADDRESSES.

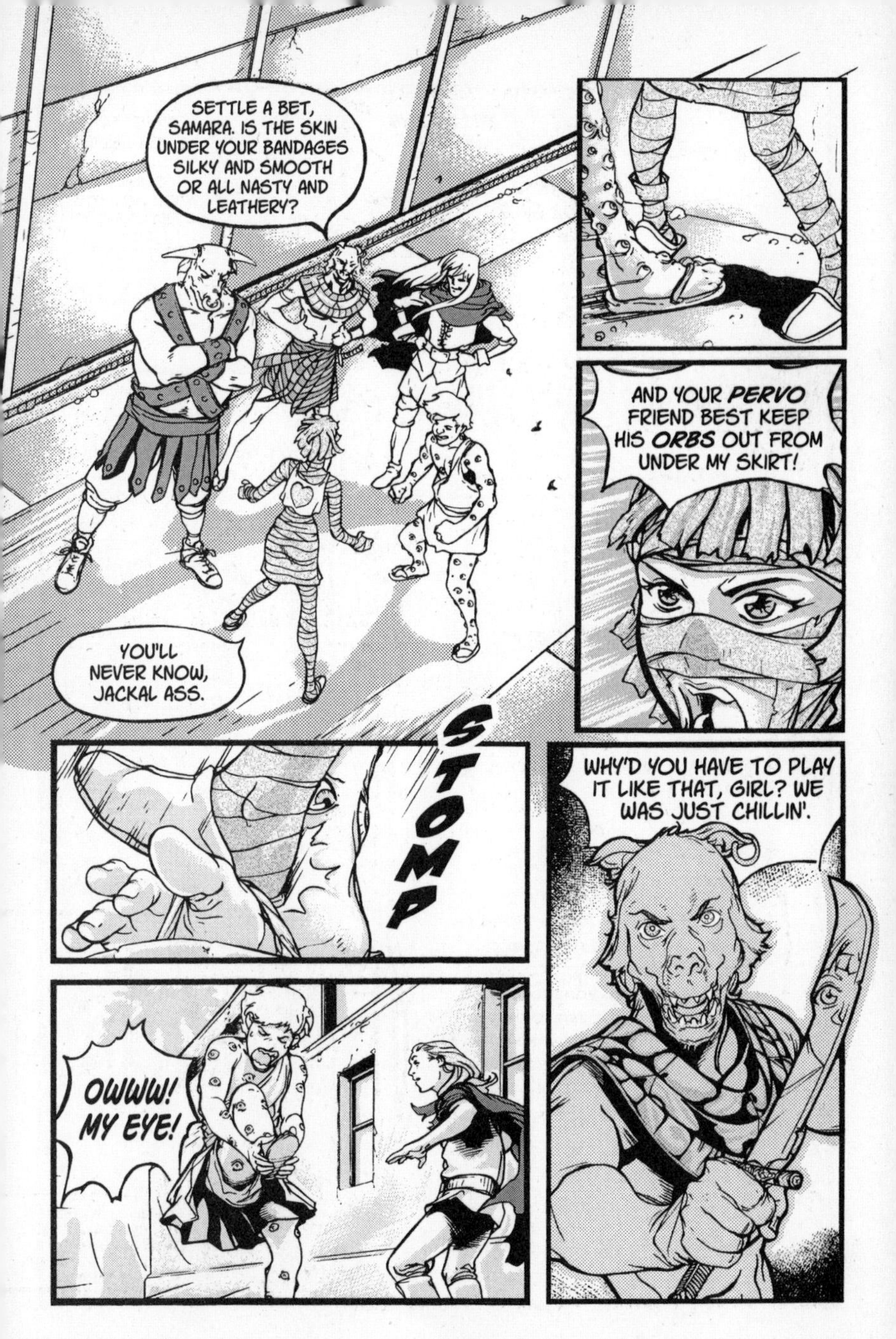
SETTLE A BET, SAMARA. IS THE SKIN UNDER YOUR BANDAGES SILKY AND SMOOTH OR ALL NASTY AND LEATHERY?
YOU'LL NEVER KNOW, JACKAL ASS.
AND YOUR *PERVO* FRIEND BEST KEEP HIS *ORBS* OUT FROM UNDER MY SKIRT!
STOMP
OWWW! MY EYE!
WHY'D YOU HAVE TO PLAY IT LIKE THAT, GIRL? WE WAS JUST CHILLIN'.

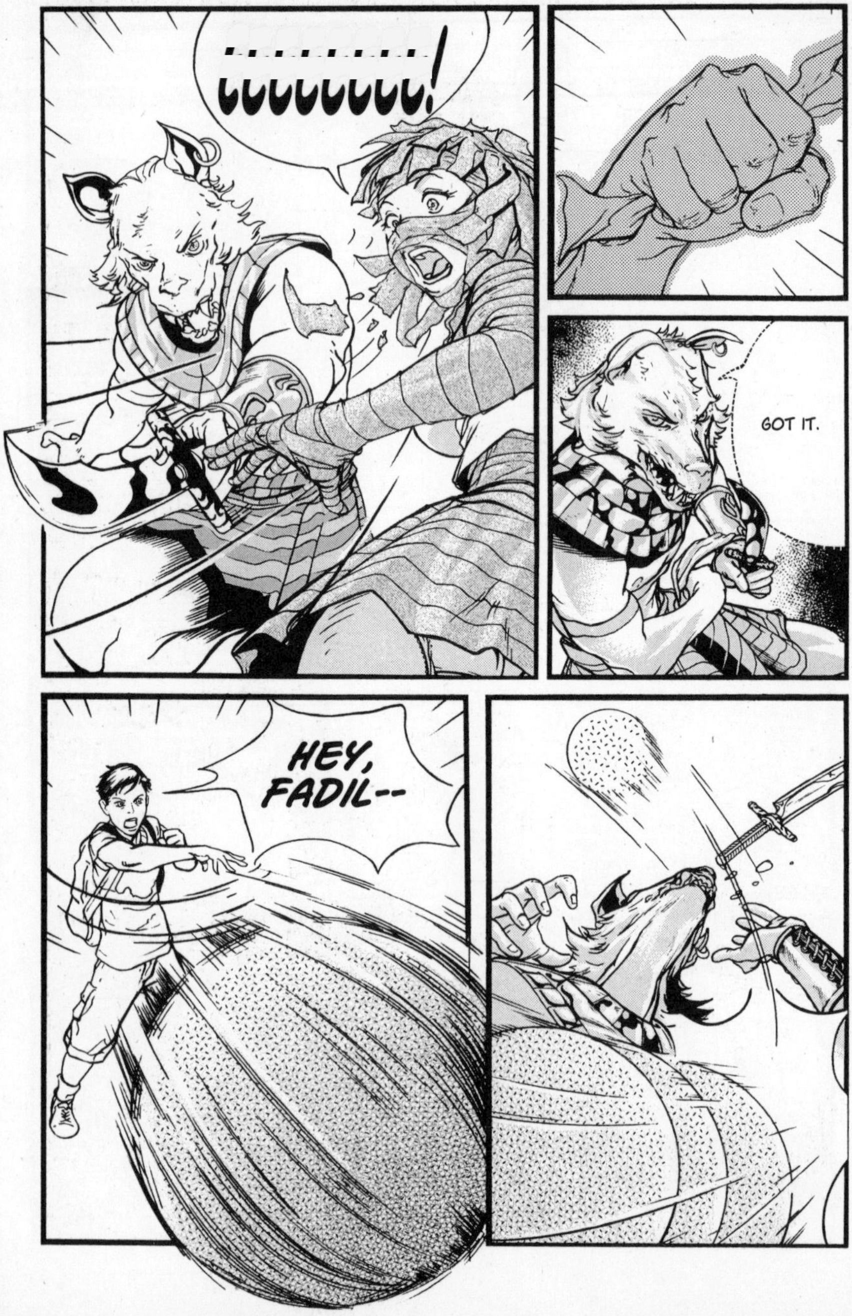
GOT IT.
HEY, FADIL--

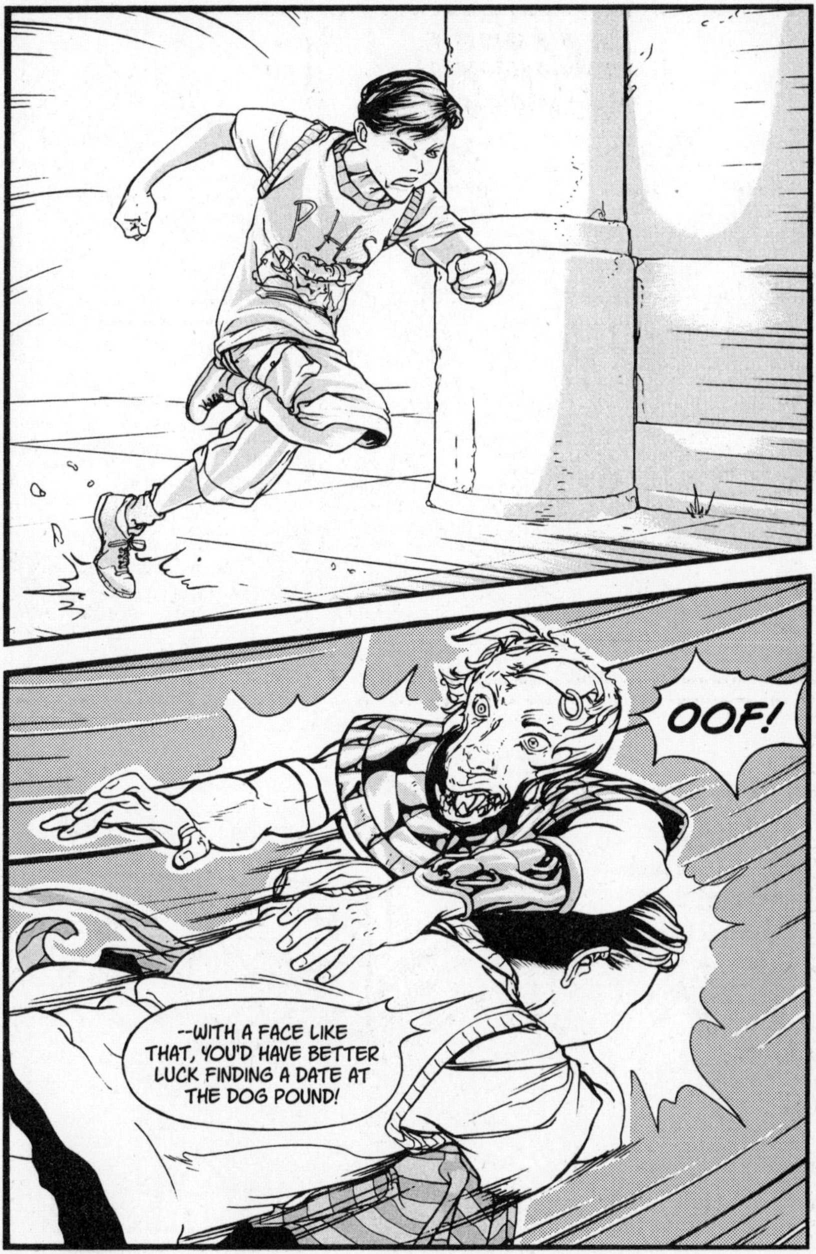
OOF!
--WITH A FACE LIKE THAT, YOU'D HAVE BETTER LUCK FINDING A DATE AT THE DOG POUND!

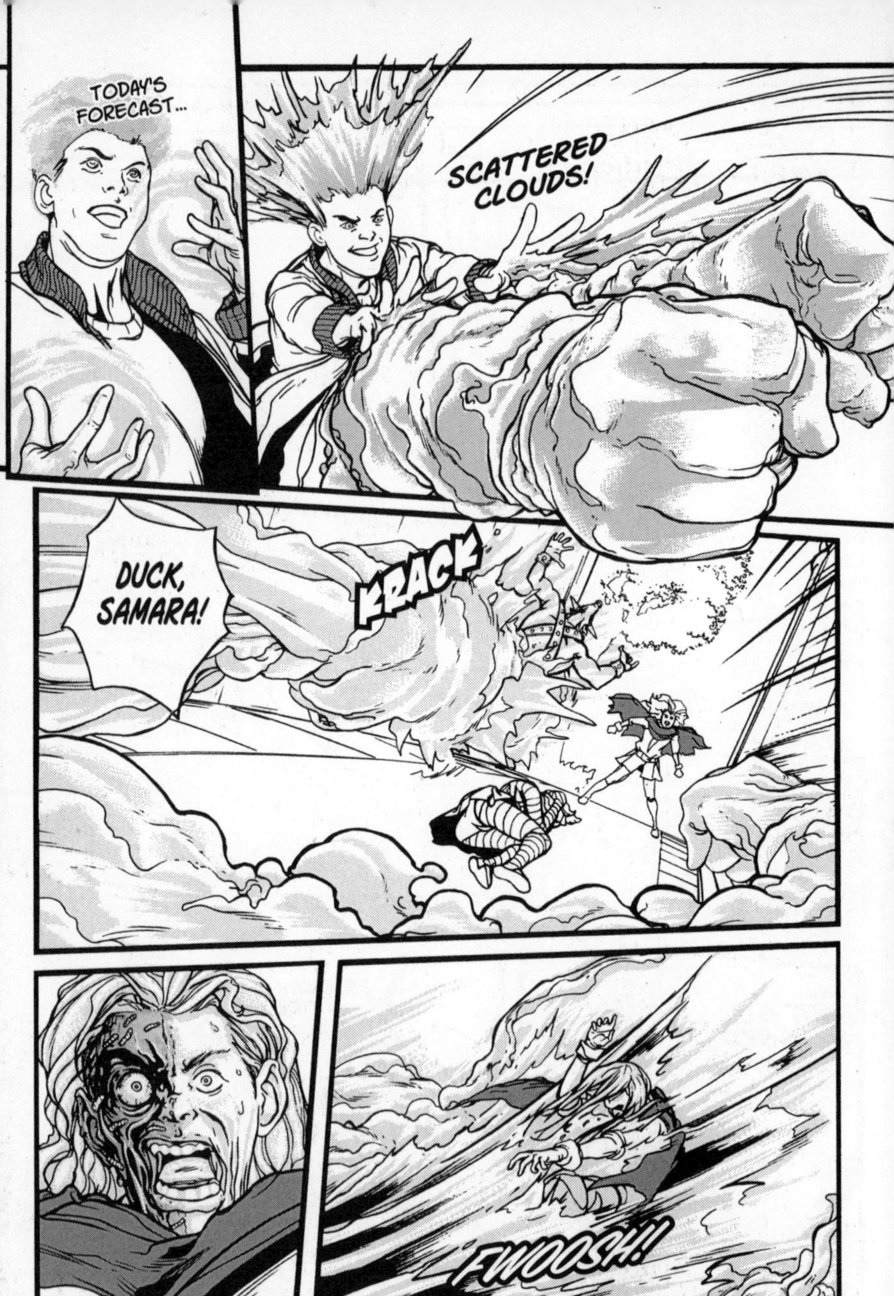
TODAY'S FORECAST...
SCATTERED CLOUDS!
DUCK, SAMARA!
KRACK
FWOOSH!

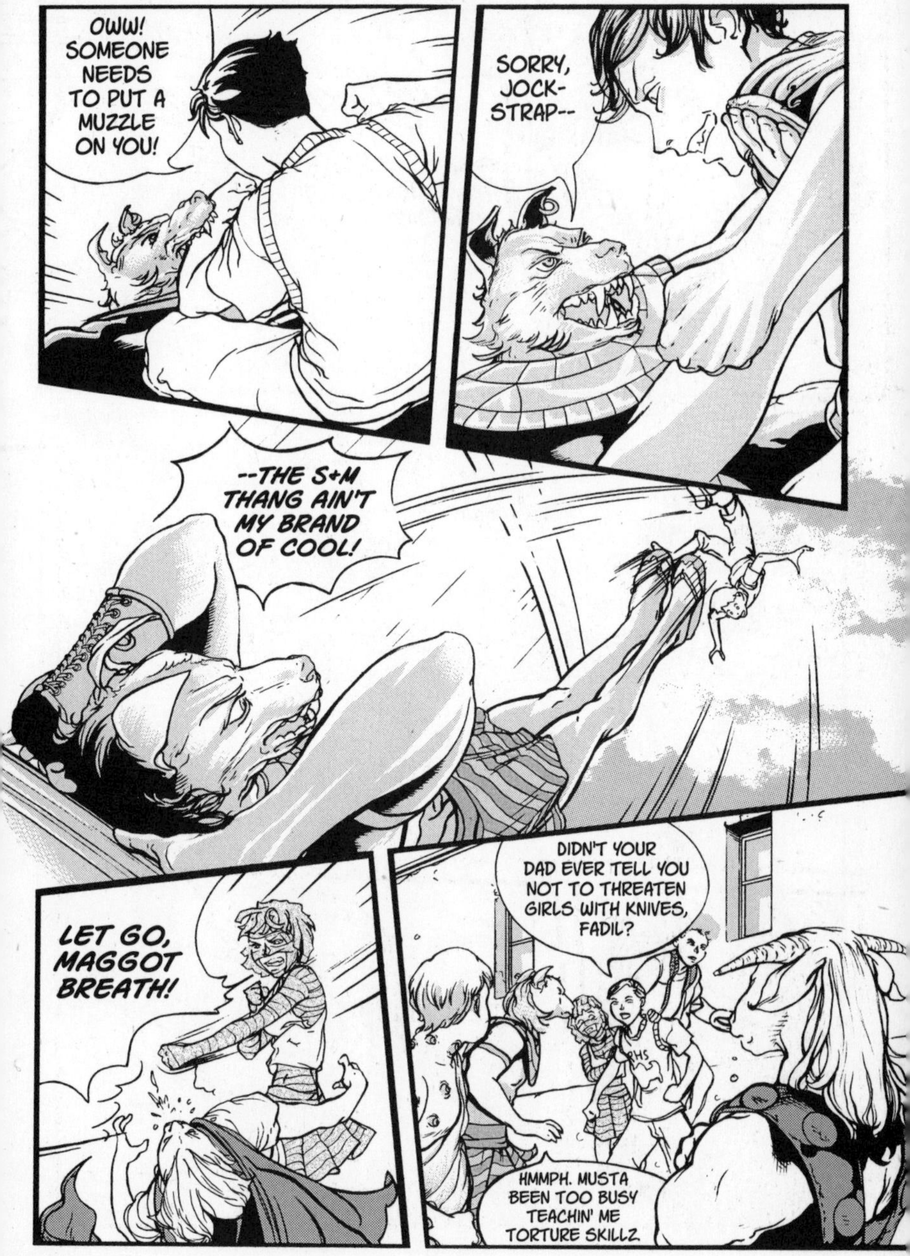
OWW! SOMEONE NEEDS TO PUT A MUZZLE ON YOU!
SORRY, JOCK-STRAP--
--THE S+M THANG AIN'T MY BRAND OF COOL!
LET GO, MAGGOT BREATH!
DIDN'T YOUR DAD EVER TELL YOU NOT TO THREATEN GIRLS WITH KNIVES, FADIL?
HMMPH. MUSTA BEEN TOO BUSY TEACHIN' ME TORTURE SKILLZ.

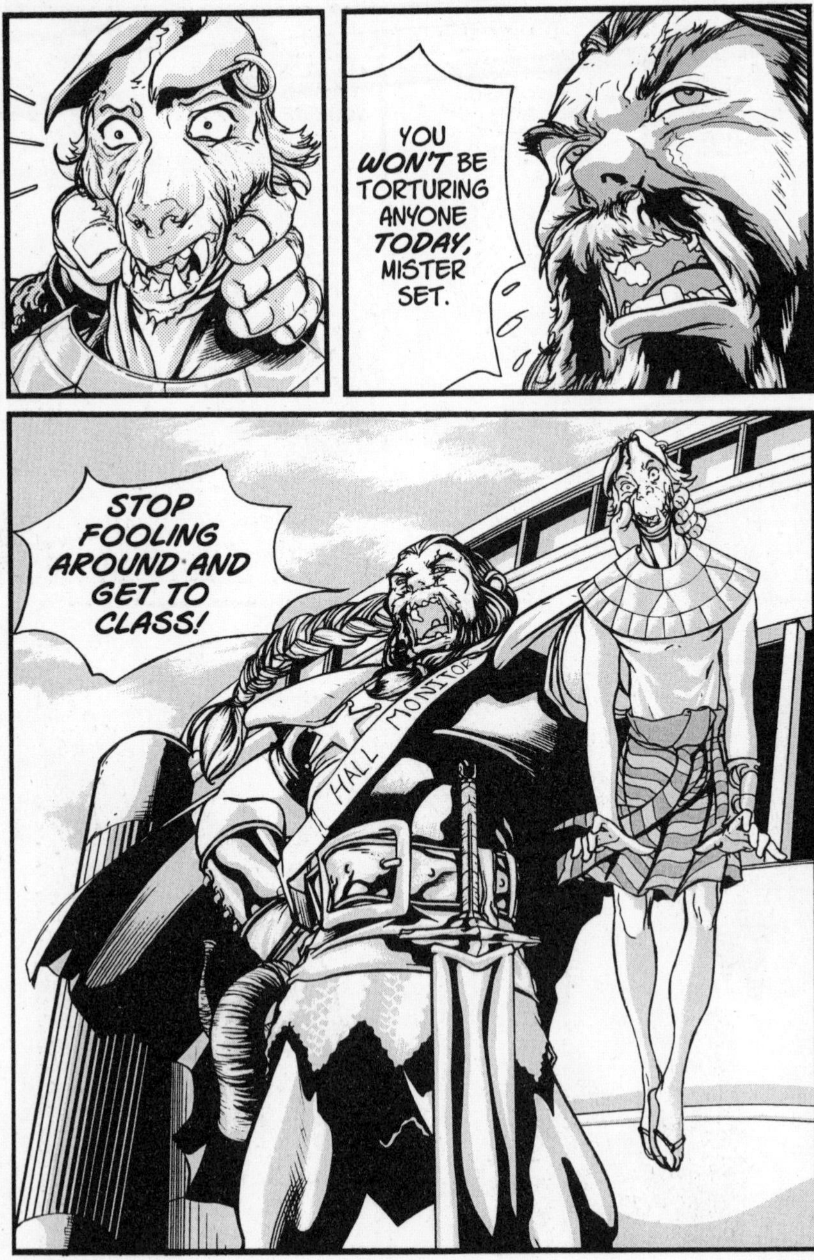
YOU WON'T BE TORTURING ANYONE TODAY, MISTER SET.
STOP FOOLING AROUND AND GET TO CLASS!
HALL MONITOR

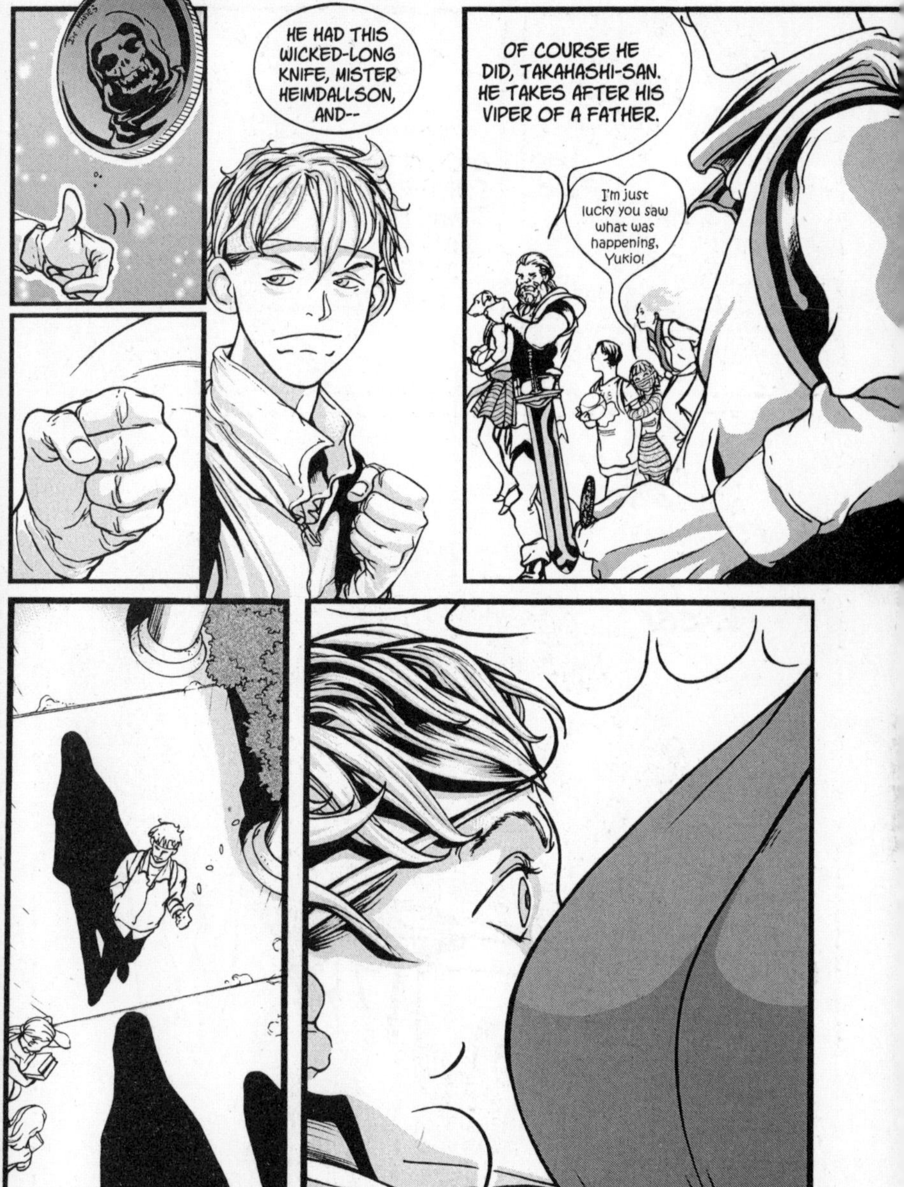
HE HAD THIS WICKED-LONG KNIFE, MISTER HEIMDALLSON, AND--
OF COURSE HE DID, TAKAHASHI-SAN. HE TAKES AFTER HIS VIPER OF A FATHER.
I'm just lucky you saw what was happening, Yukio!

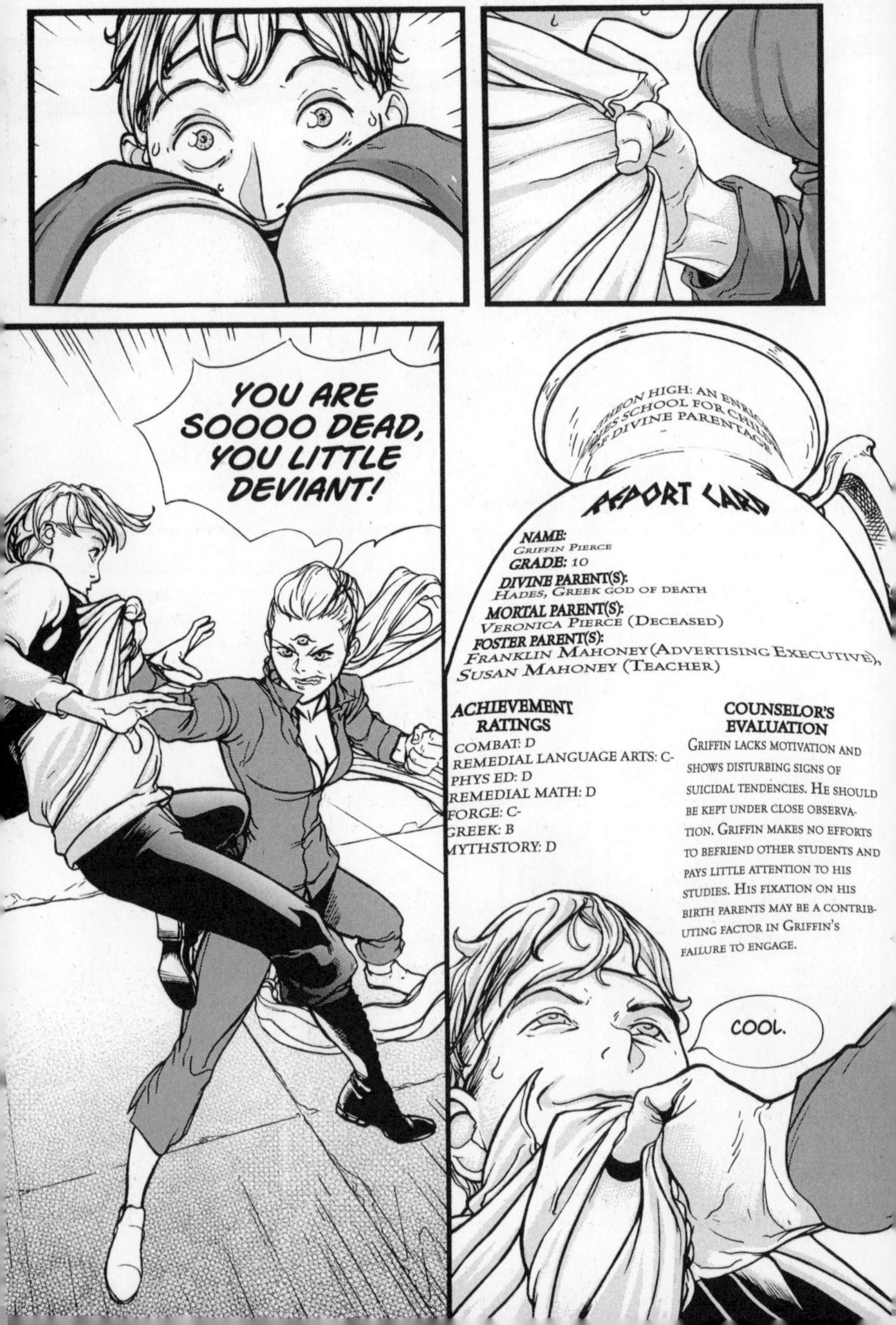
YOU ARE SOOOO DEAD, YOU LITTLE DEVIANT!
REPORT CARD
NAME:
GRIFFIN PIERCE
GRADE: 10
DIVINE PARENT(S):
HADES, GREEK GOD OF DEATH
MORTAL PARENT(S):
VERONICA PIERCE (DECEASED)
FOSTER PARENT(S):
FRANKLIN MAHONEY (ADVERTISING EXECUTIVE),
SUSAN MAHONEY (TEACHER)
ACHIEVEMENT RATINGS
COMBAT: D
REMEDIAL LANGUAGE ARTS: C-
PHYS ED: D
REMEDIAL MATH: D
FORGE: C-
GREEK: B
MYTHSTORY: D
COUNSELOR'S EVALUATION
GRIFFIN LACKS MOTIVATION AND SHOWS DISTURBING SIGNS OF SUICIDAL TENDENCIES. HE SHOULD BE KEPT UNDER CLOSE OBSERVATION. GRIFFIN MAKES NO EFFORTS TO BEFRIEND OTHER STUDENTS AND PAYS LITTLE ATTENTION TO HIS STUDIES. HIS FIXATION ON HIS BIRTH PARENTS MAY BE A CONTRIBUTING FACTOR IN GRIFFIN'S FAILURE TO ENGAGE.
COOL.

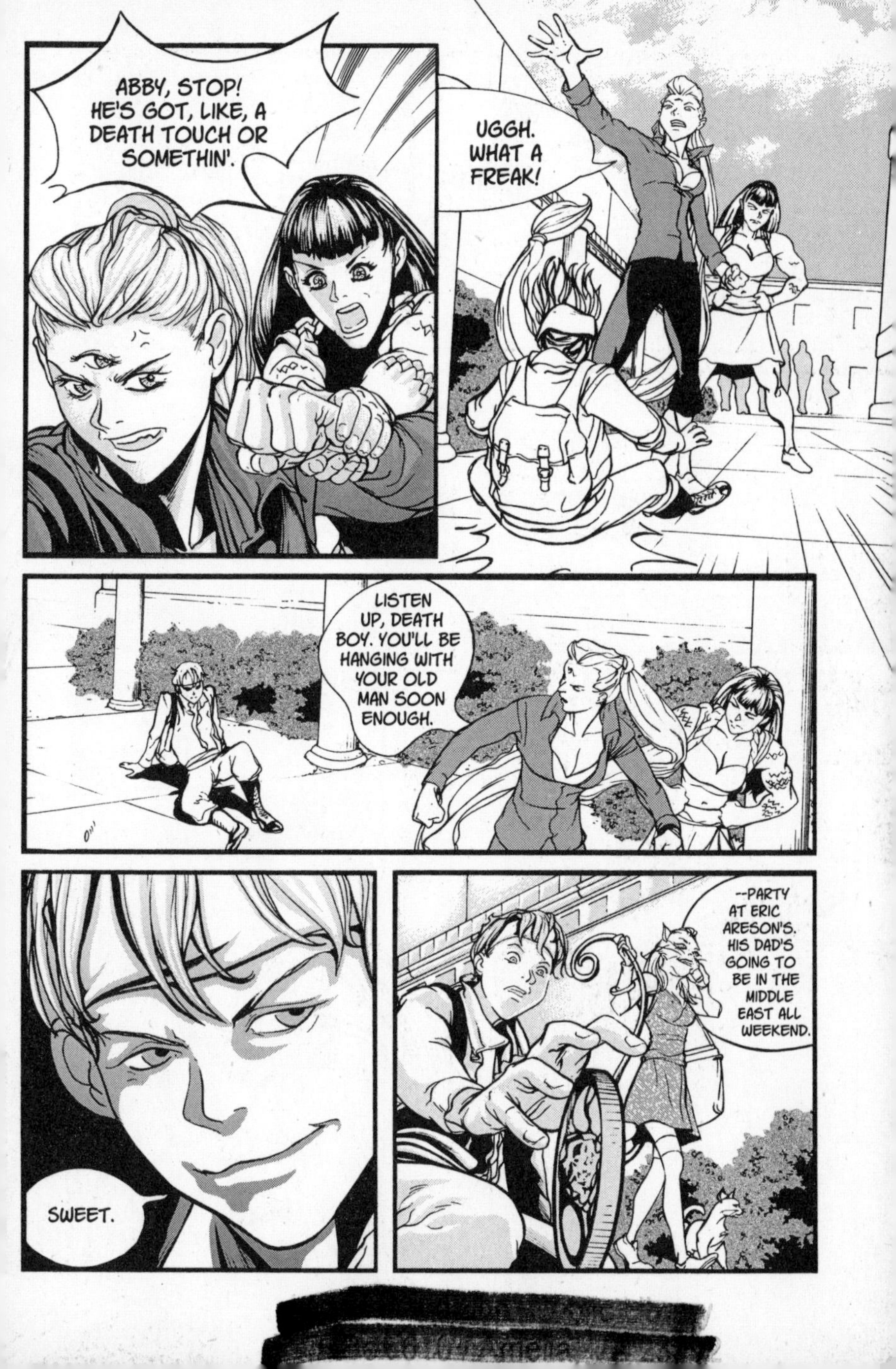
ABBY, STOP! HE'S GOT, LIKE, A DEATH TOUCH OR SOMETHIN'.
UGGH. WHAT A FREAK!
LISTEN UP, DEATH BOY. YOU'LL BE HANGING WITH YOUR OLD MAN SOON ENOUGH.
SWEET.
--PARTY AT ERIC ARESON'S. HIS DAD'S GOING TO BE IN THE MIDDLE EAST ALL WEEKEND.

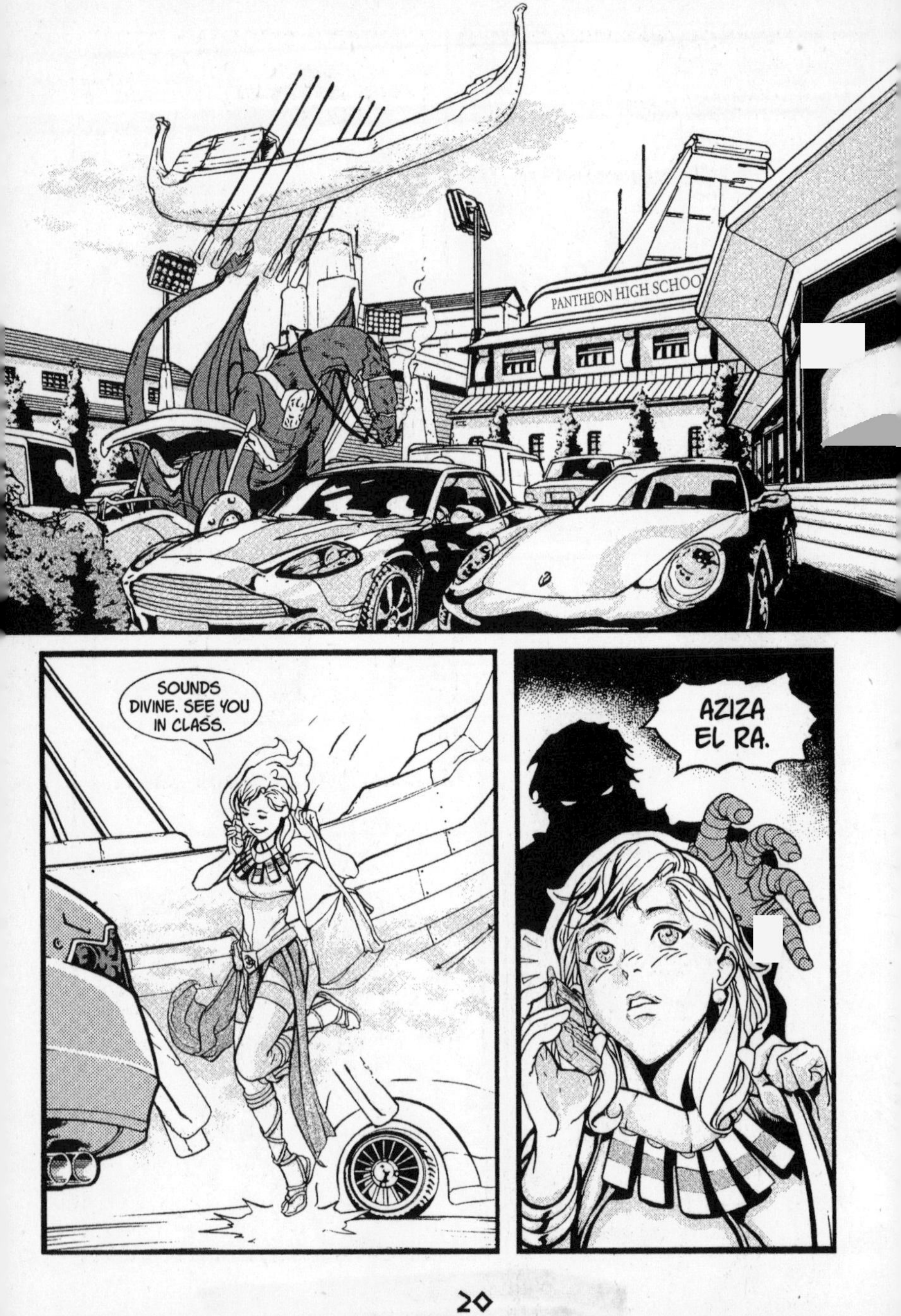
PANTHEON HIGH SCHOO
SOUNDS DIVINE. SEE YOU IN CLASS.
AZIZA EL RA.

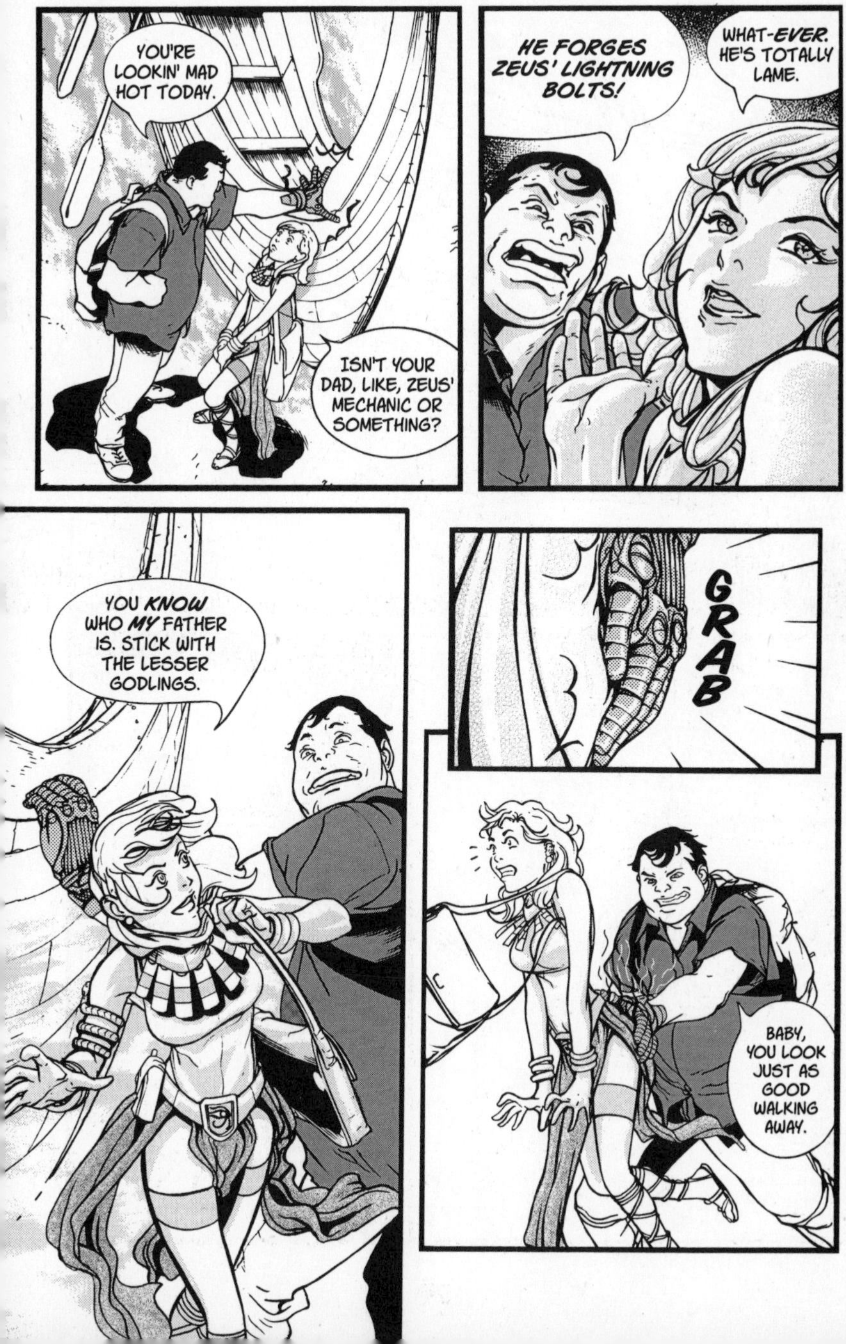
YOU'RE LOOKIN' MAD HOT TODAY.
ISN'T YOUR DAD, LIKE, ZEUS' MECHANIC OR SOMETHING?
HE FORGES ZEUS' LIGHTNING BOLTS!
WHAT-EVER. HE'S TOTALLY LAME.
YOU KNOW WHO MY FATHER IS. STICK WITH THE LESSER GODLINGS.
GRAB
BABY, YOU LOOK JUST AS GOOD WALKING AWAY.

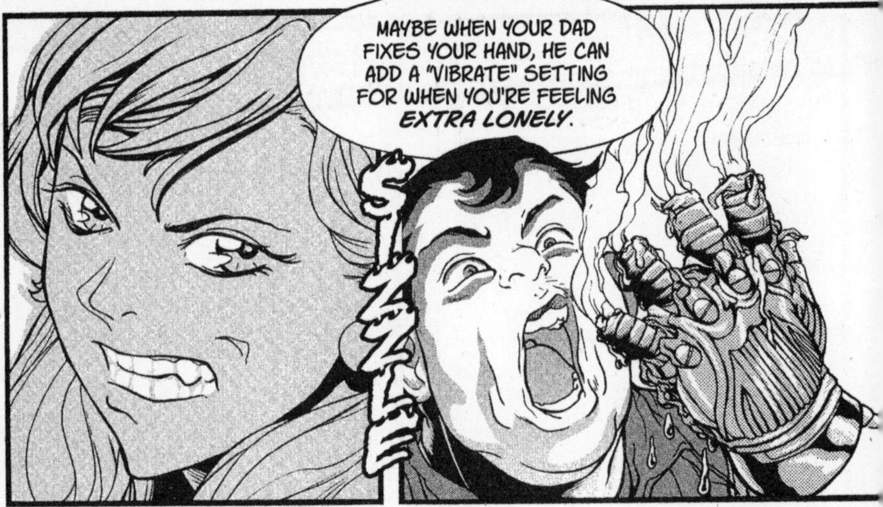
MAYBE WHEN YOUR DAD FIXES YOUR HAND, HE CAN ADD A "VIBRATE" SETTING FOR WHEN YOU'RE FEELING *EXTRA LONELY*.
SIZZLE

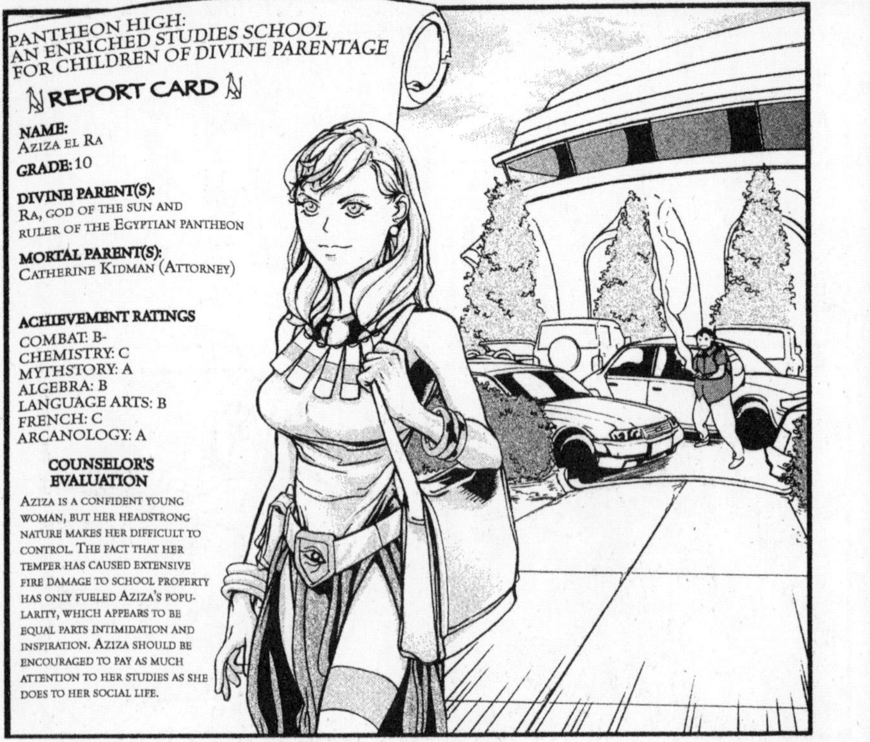
PANTHEON HIGH:
AN ENRICHED STUDIES SCHOOL
FOR CHILDREN OF DIVINE PARENTAGE
REPORT CARD
NAME:
Aziza el Ra
GRADE: 10
DIVINE PARENT(S):
Ra, god of the sun and ruler of the Egyptian pantheon
MORTAL PARENT(S):
Catherine Kidman (Attorney)
ACHIEVEMENT RATINGS
COMBAT: B-
CHEMISTRY: C
MYTHSTORY: A
ALGEBRA: B
LANGUAGE ARTS: B
FRENCH: C
ARCANOLOGY: A
COUNSELOR'S EVALUATION
Aziza is a confident young woman, but her headstrong nature makes her difficult to control. The fact that her temper has caused extensive fire damage to school property has only fueled Aziza's popularity, which appears to be equal parts intimidation and inspiration. Aziza should be encouraged to pay as much attention to her studies as she does to her social life.

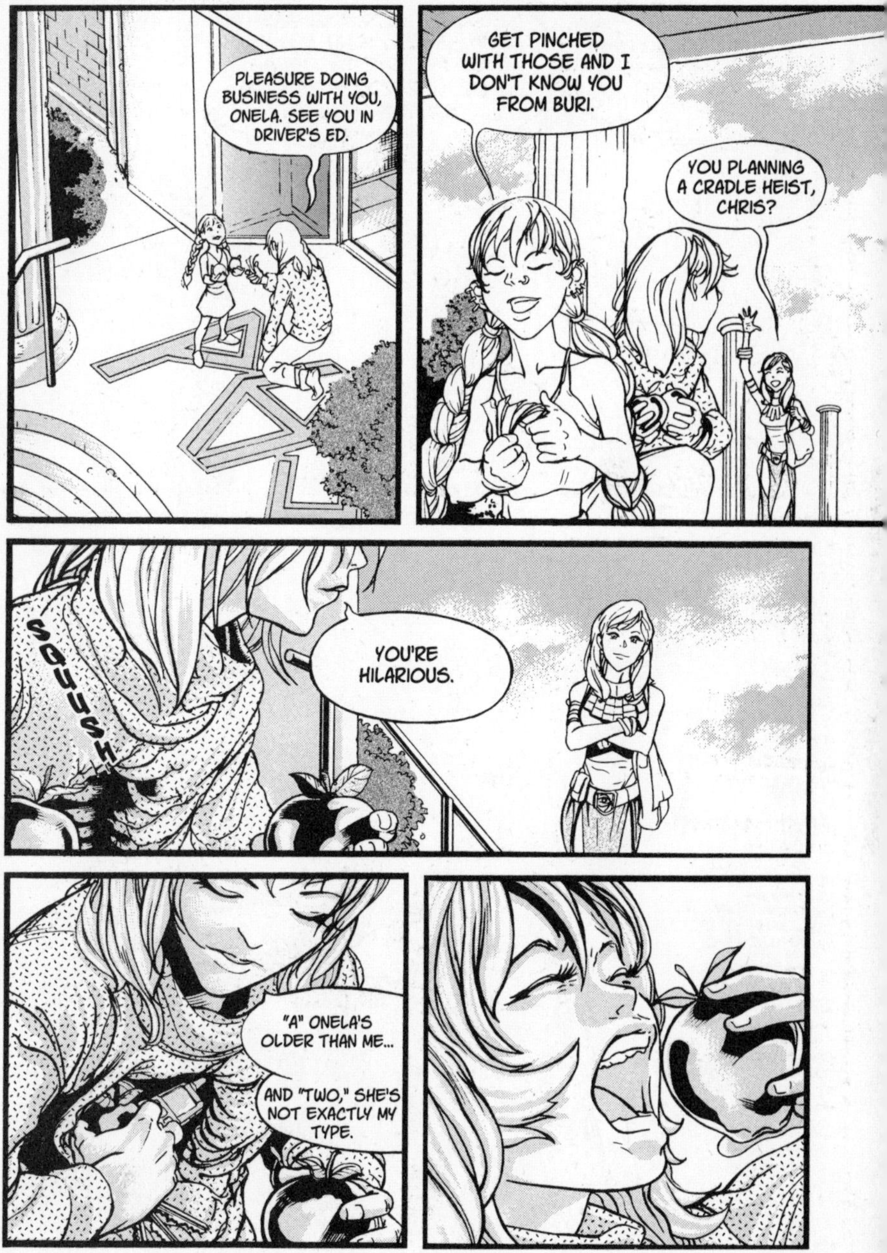
PLEASURE DOING BUSINESS WITH YOU, ONELA. SEE YOU IN DRIVER'S ED.
GET PINCHED WITH THOSE AND I DON'T KNOW YOU FROM BURI.
YOU PLANNING A CRADLE HEIST, CHRIS?
SQUUSH
YOU'RE HILARIOUS.
"A" ONELA'S OLDER THAN ME...
AND "TWO," SHE'S NOT EXACTLY MY TYPE.

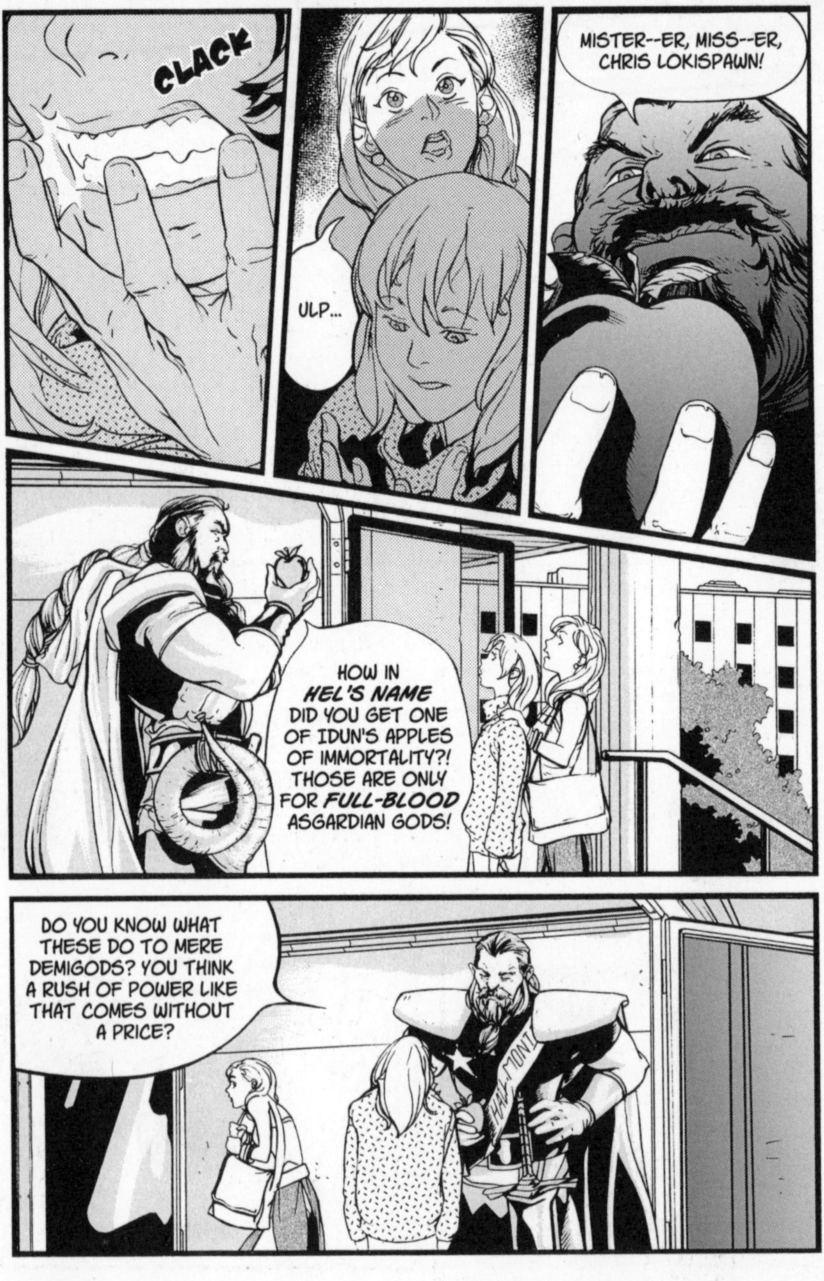
CLACK
ULP...
MISTER--ER, MISS--ER, CHRIS LOKISPAWN!
HOW IN HEL'S NAME DID YOU GET ONE OF IDUN'S APPLES OF IMMORTALITY?! THOSE ARE ONLY FOR FULL-BLOOD ASGARDIAN GODS!
DO YOU KNOW WHAT THESE DO TO MERE DEMIGODS? YOU THINK A RUSH OF POWER LIKE THAT COMES WITHOUT A PRICE?

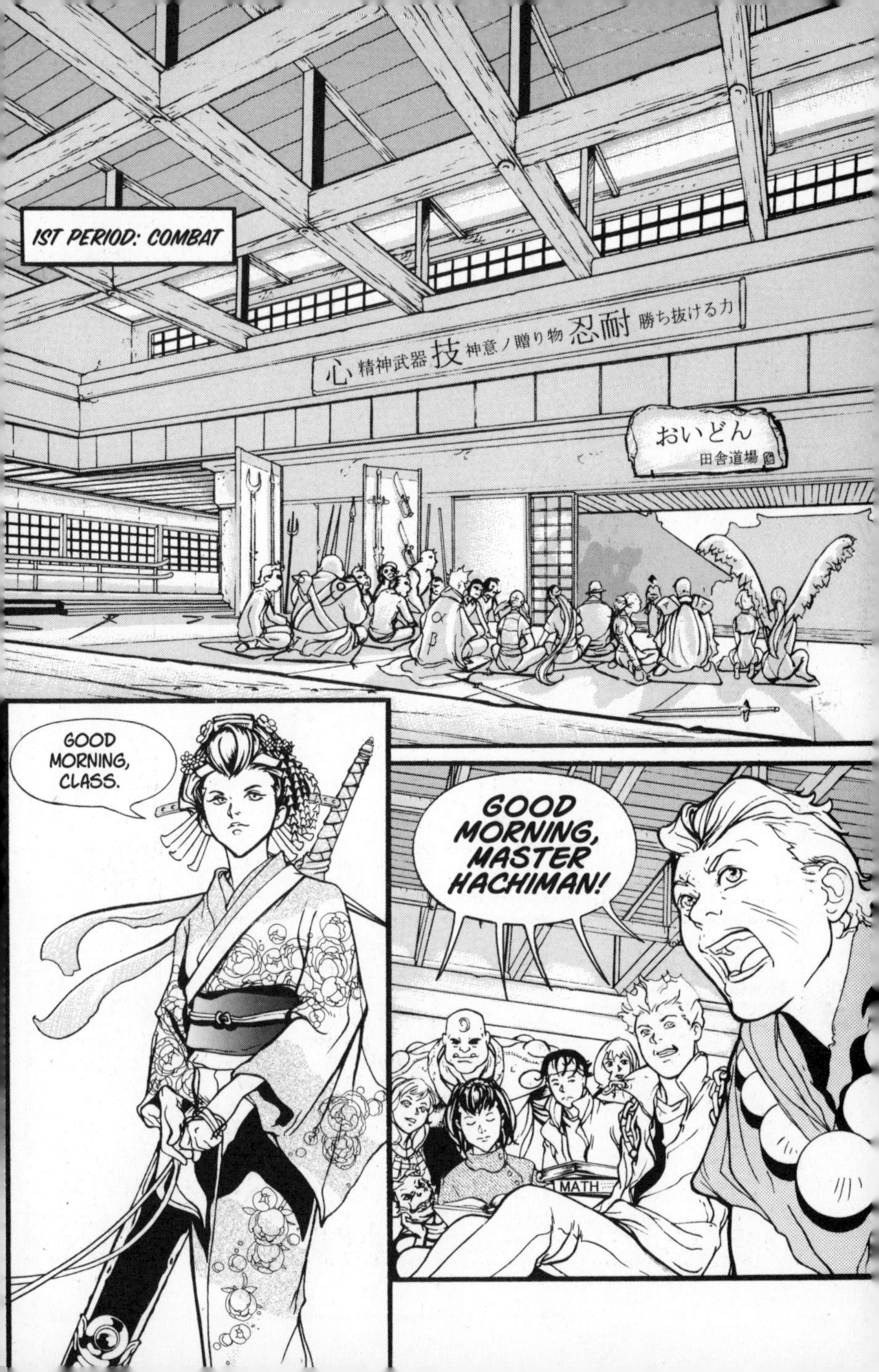
1ST PERIOD: COMBAT
心 精神武器 技 神意ノ贈り物 忍耐 勝ち抜ける力
おいどん
田舎道場
GOOD MORNING, CLASS.
GOOD MORNING, MASTER HACHIMAN!
MATH

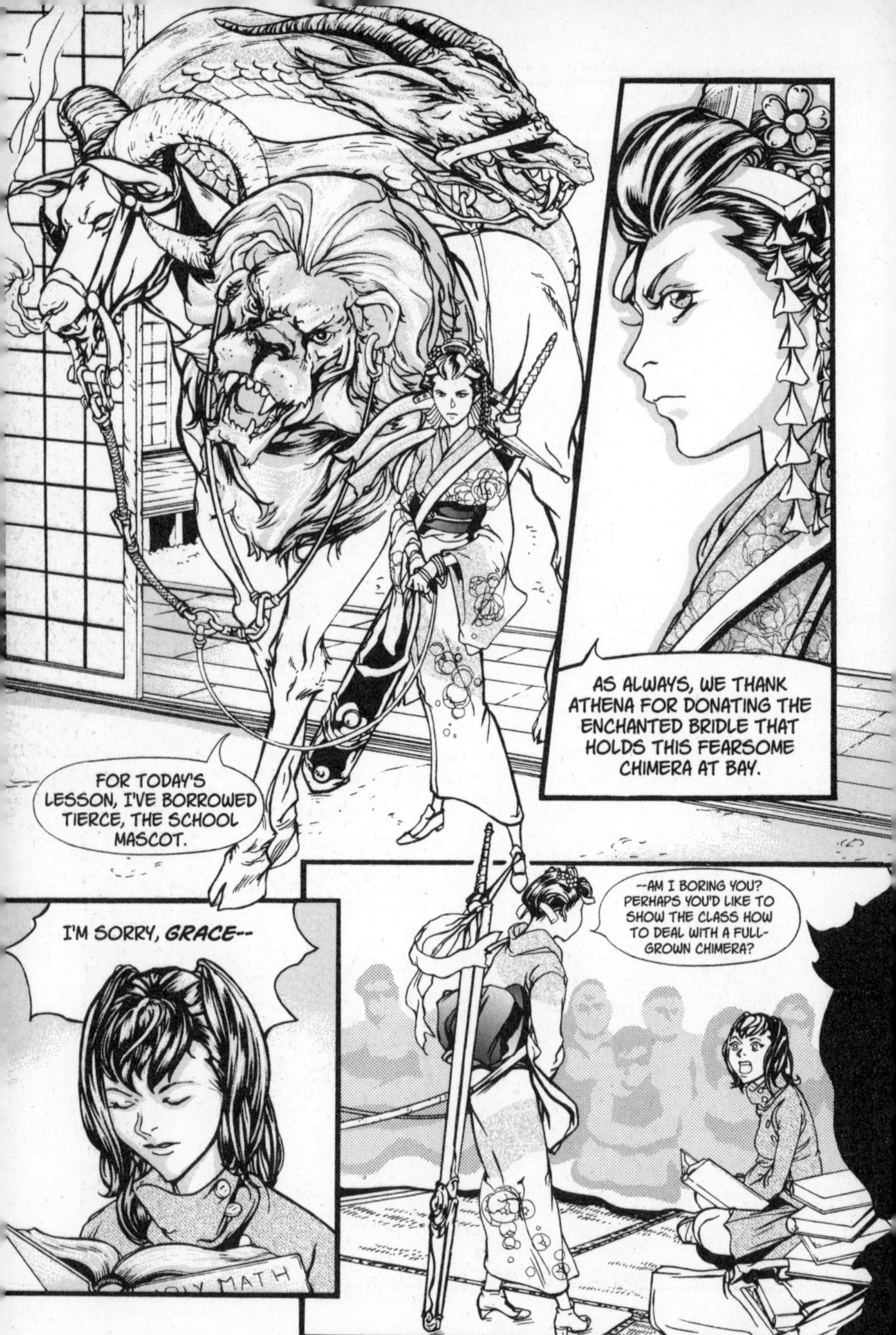
FOR TODAY'S LESSON, I'VE BORROWED TIERCE, THE SCHOOL MASCOT.
AS ALWAYS, WE THANK ATHENA FOR DONATING THE ENCHANTED BRIDLE THAT HOLDS THIS FEARSOME CHIMERA AT BAY.
I'M SORRY, *GRACE*--
--AM I BORING YOU? PERHAPS YOU'D LIKE TO SHOW THE CLASS HOW TO DEAL WITH A FULL-GROWN CHIMERA?

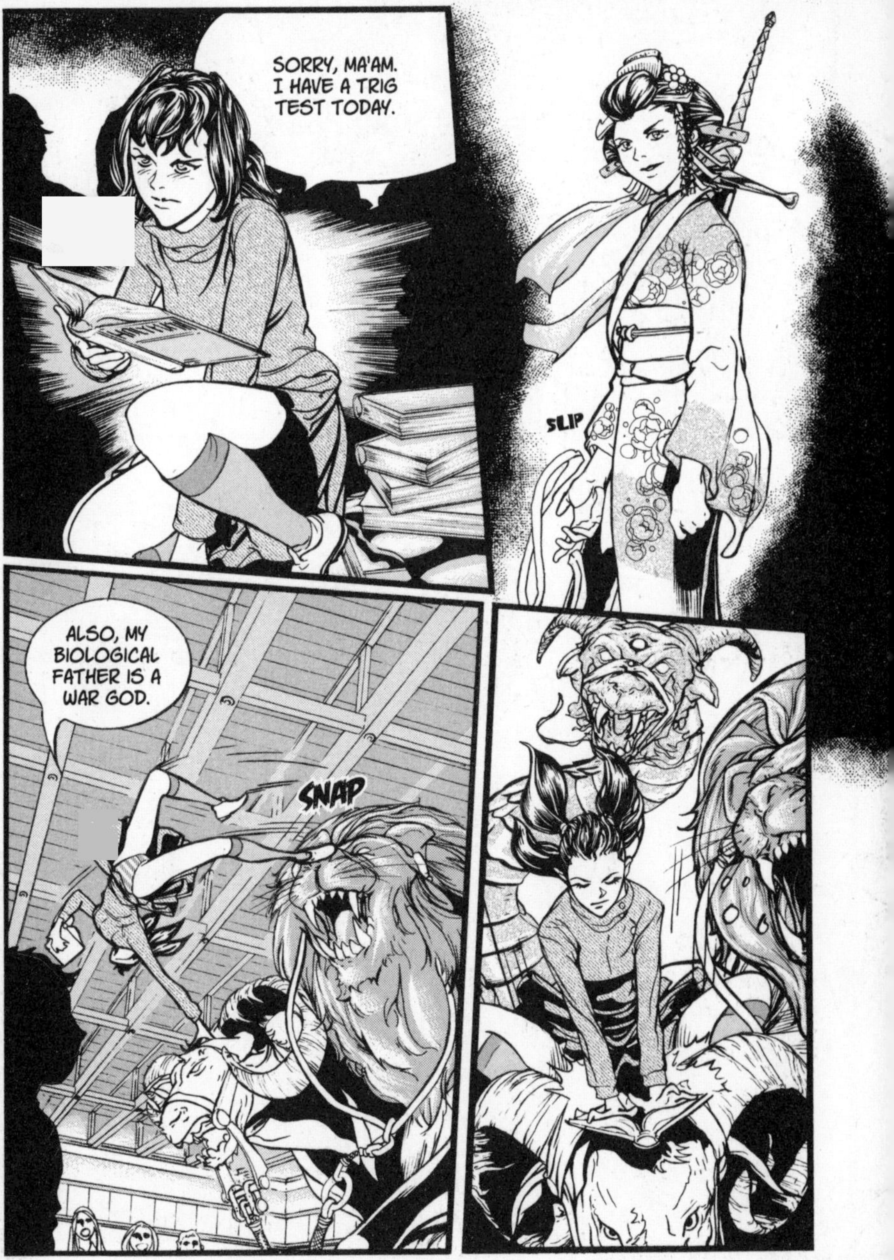
SORRY, MA'AM. I HAVE A TRIG TEST TODAY.
SLIP
ALSO, MY BIOLOGICAL FATHER IS A WAR GOD.
SNAP

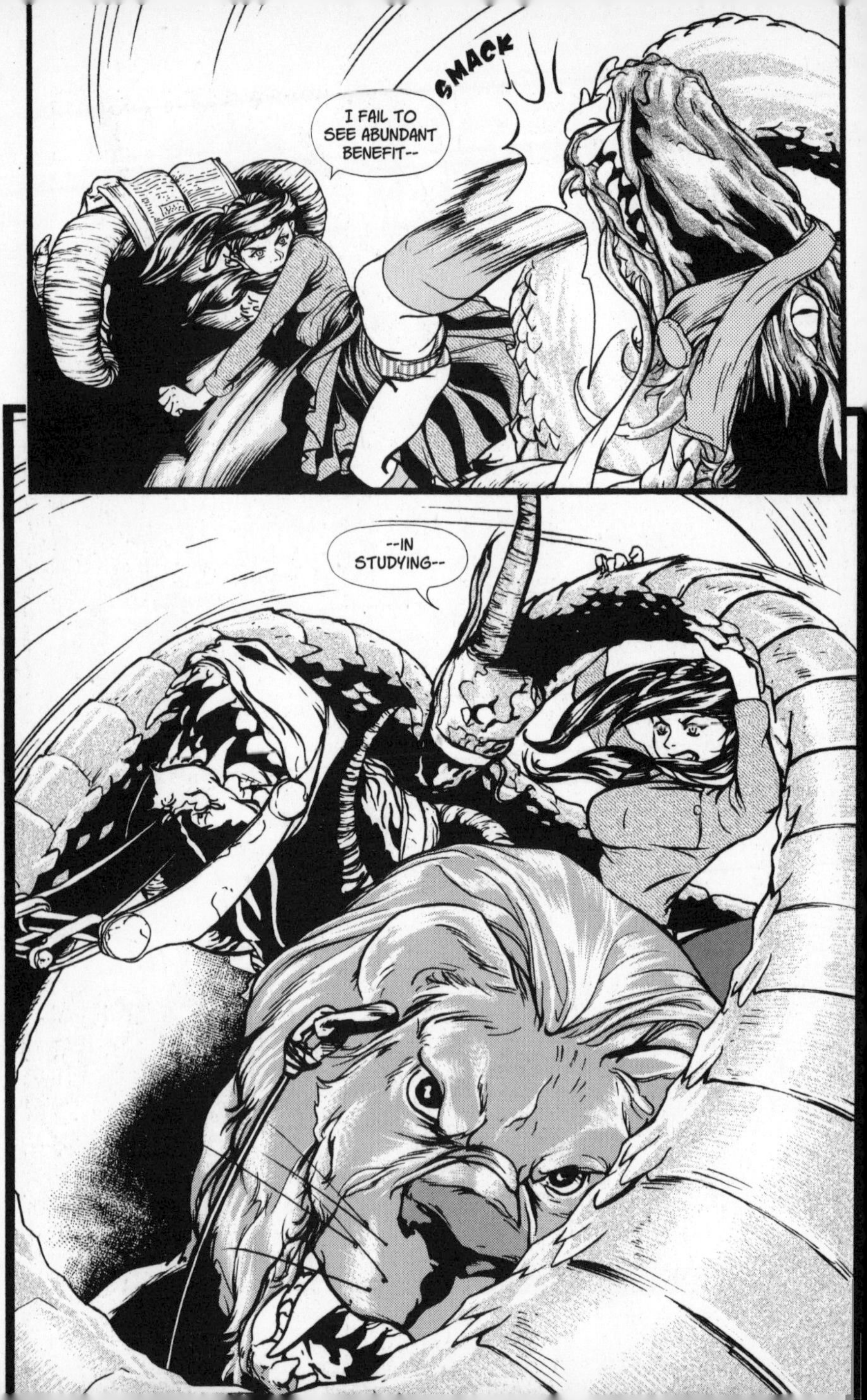
I FAIL TO SEE ABUNDANT BENEFIT--
SMACK
--IN STUDYING--

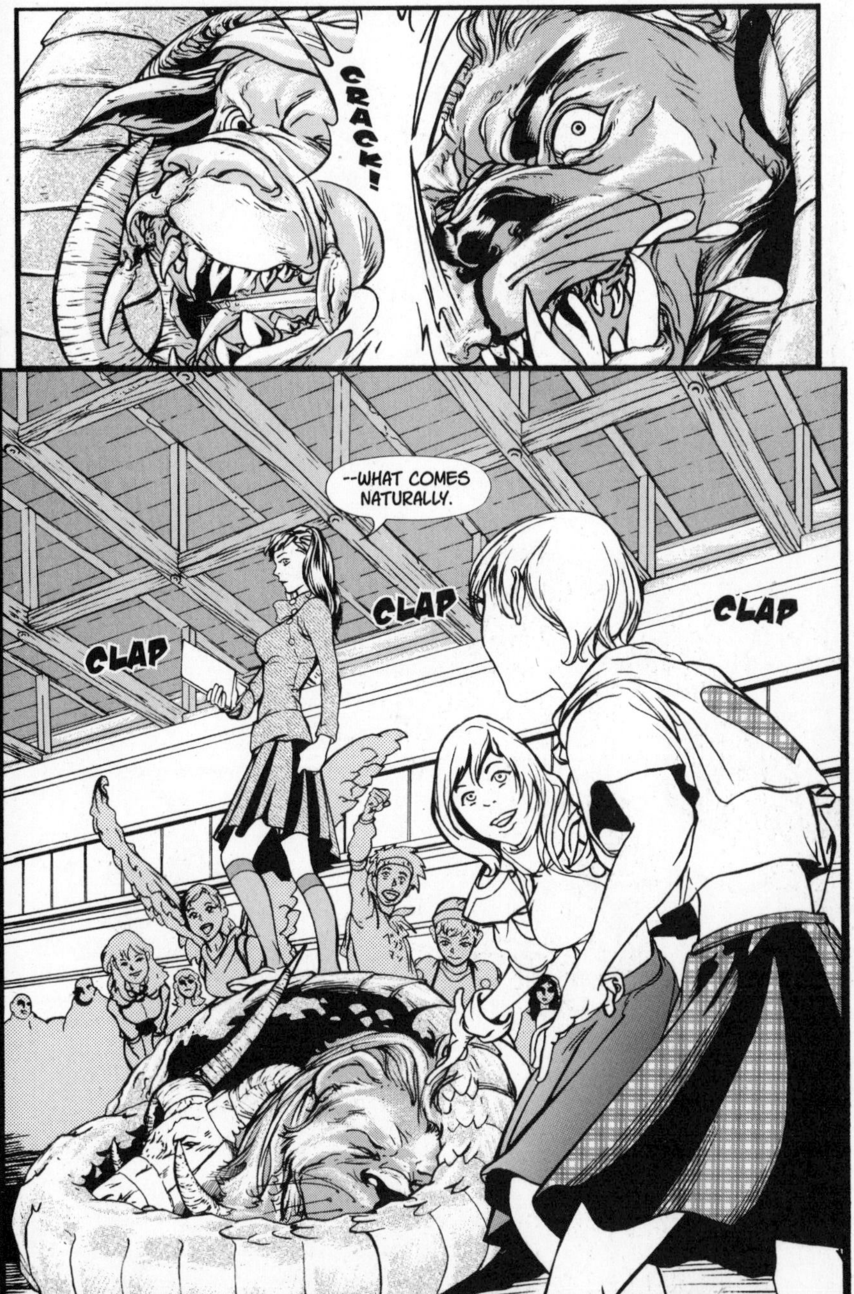
CRACK!
--WHAT COMES NATURALLY.
CLAP
CLAP
CLAP

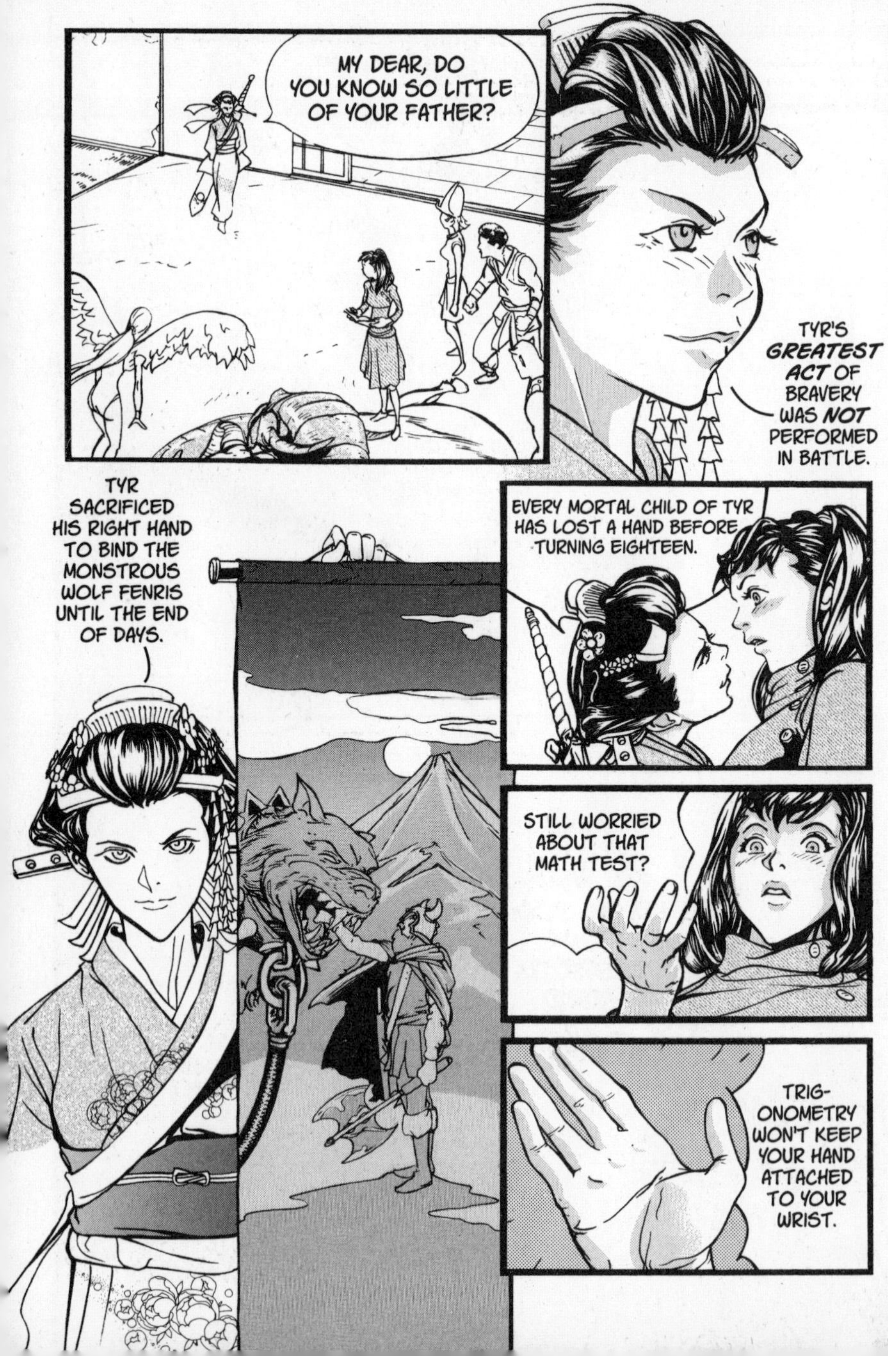
MY DEAR, DO YOU KNOW SO LITTLE OF YOUR FATHER?
TYR'S **GREATEST ACT** OF BRAVERY WAS **NOT** PERFORMED IN BATTLE.
TYR SACRIFICED HIS RIGHT HAND TO BIND THE MONSTROUS WOLF FENRIS UNTIL THE END OF DAYS.
EVERY MORTAL CHILD OF TYR HAS LOST A HAND BEFORE TURNING EIGHTEEN.
STILL WORRIED ABOUT THAT MATH TEST?
TRIG-ONOMETRY WON'T KEEP YOUR HAND ATTACHED TO YOUR WRIST.

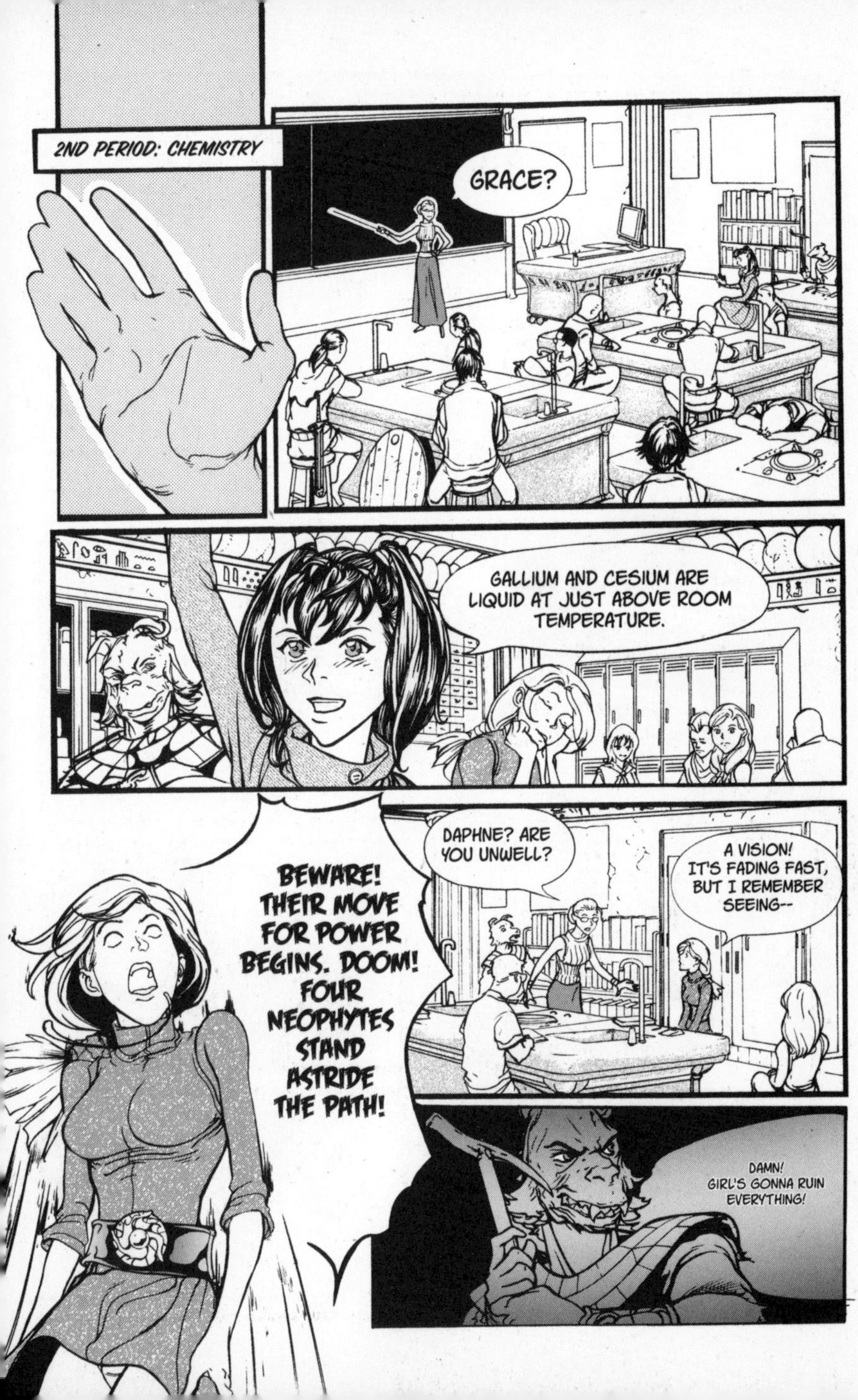
2ND PERIOD: CHEMISTRY
GRACE?
GALLIUM AND CESIUM ARE LIQUID AT JUST ABOVE ROOM TEMPERATURE.
BEWARE! THEIR MOVE FOR POWER BEGINS. DOOM! FOUR NEOPHYTES STAND ASTRIDE THE PATH!
DAPHNE? ARE YOU UNWELL?
A VISION! IT'S FADING FAST, BUT I REMEMBER SEEING--
DAMN! GIRL'S GONNA RUIN EVERYTHING!

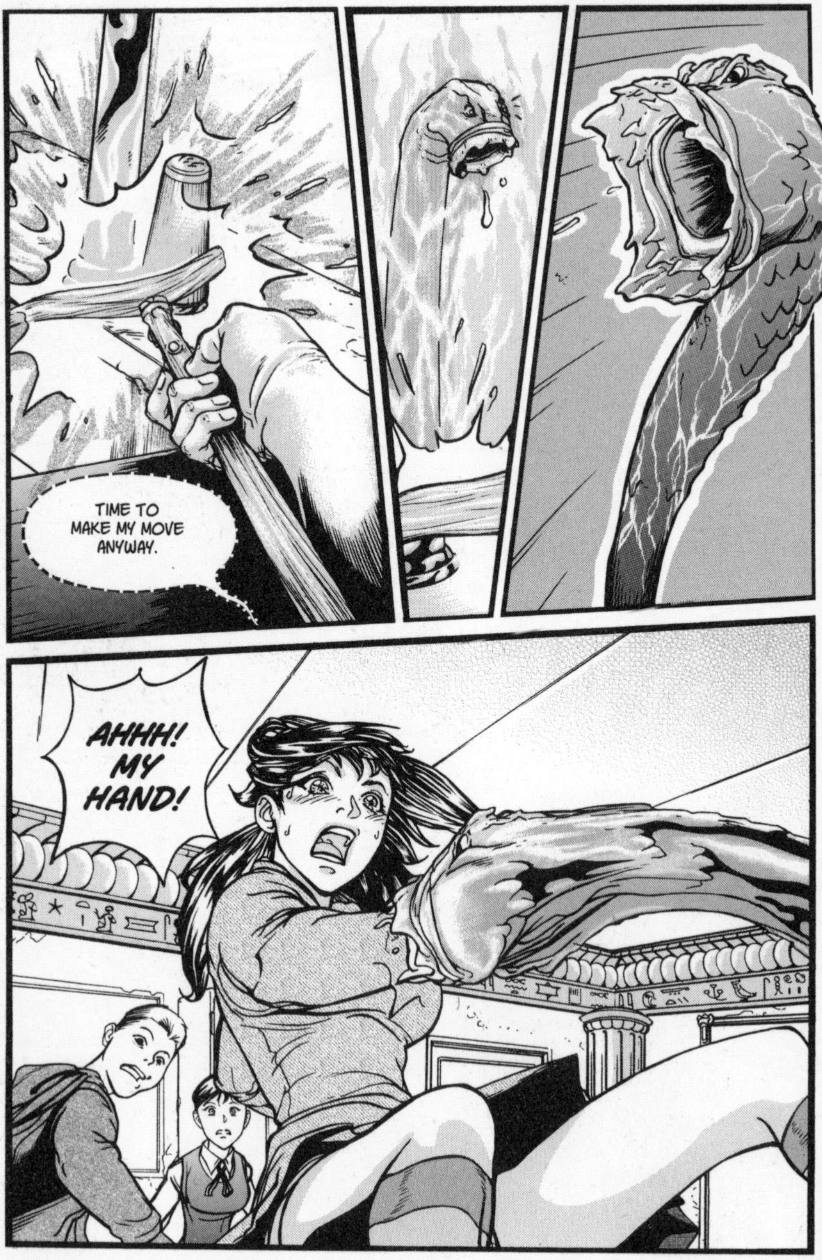
TIME TO MAKE MY MOVE ANYWAY.
AHHH! MY HAND!

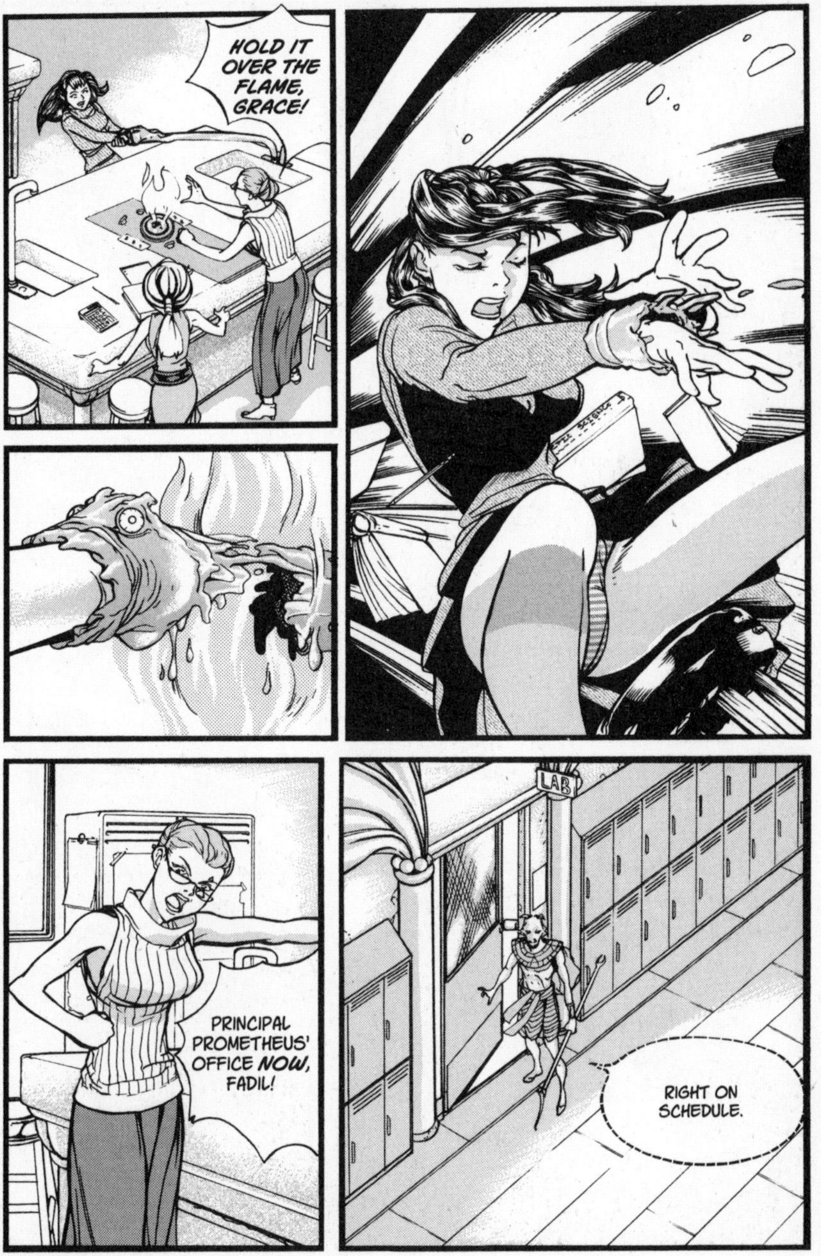
HOLD IT OVER THE FLAME, GRACE!
PRINCIPAL PROMETHEUS' OFFICE NOW, FADIL!
LAB
RIGHT ON SCHEDULE.

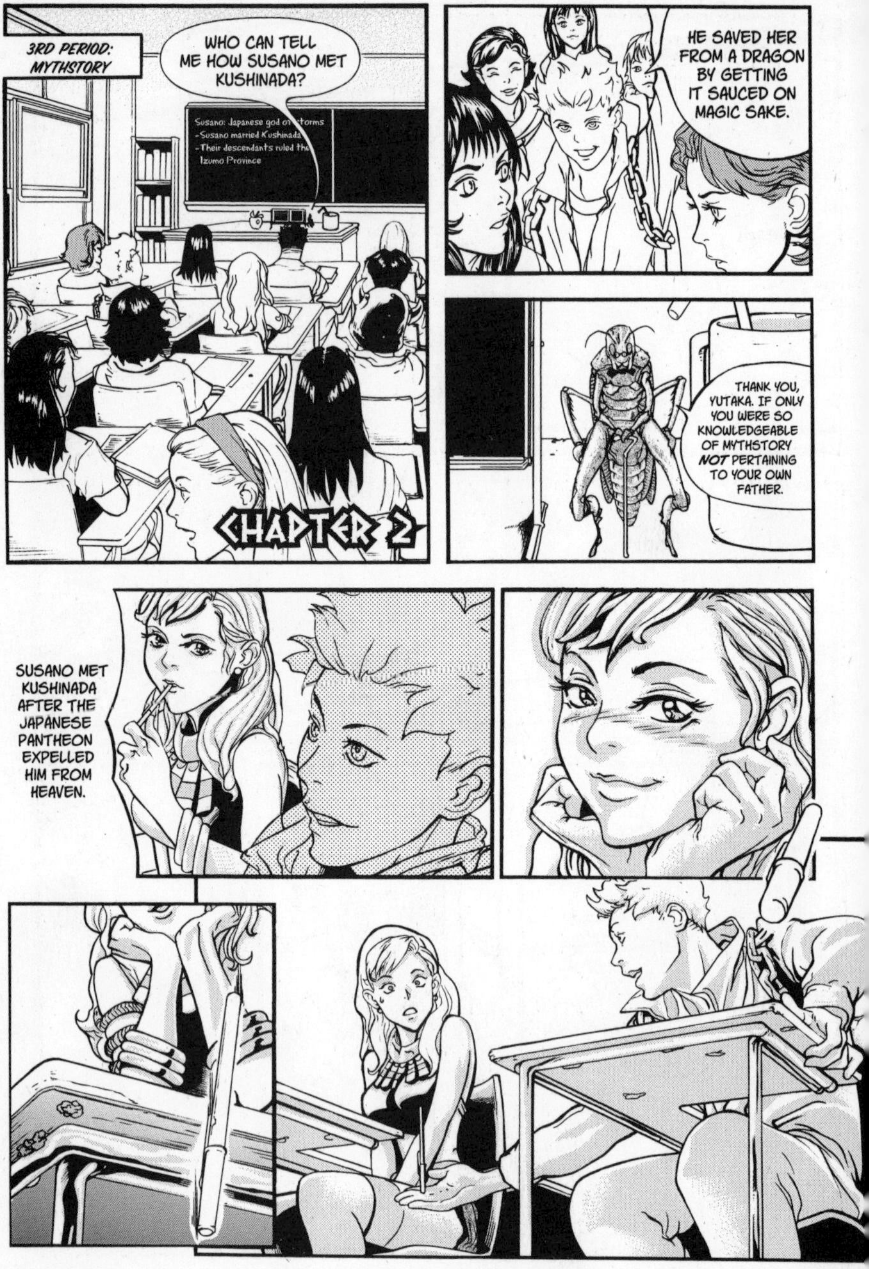
3RD PERIOD: MYTHSTORY
WHO CAN TELL ME HOW SUSANO MET KUSHINADA?
Susano: Japanese god o torms
-Susano married Kushinada
-Their descendants ruled the Izumo Province
CHAPTER 2
HE SAVED HER FROM A DRAGON BY GETTING IT SAUCED ON MAGIC SAKE.
THANK YOU, YUTAKA. IF ONLY YOU WERE SO KNOWLEDGEABLE OF MYTHSTORY ***NOT*** PERTAINING TO YOUR OWN FATHER.
SUSANO MET KUSHINADA AFTER THE JAPANESE PANTHEON EXPELLED HIM FROM HEAVEN.

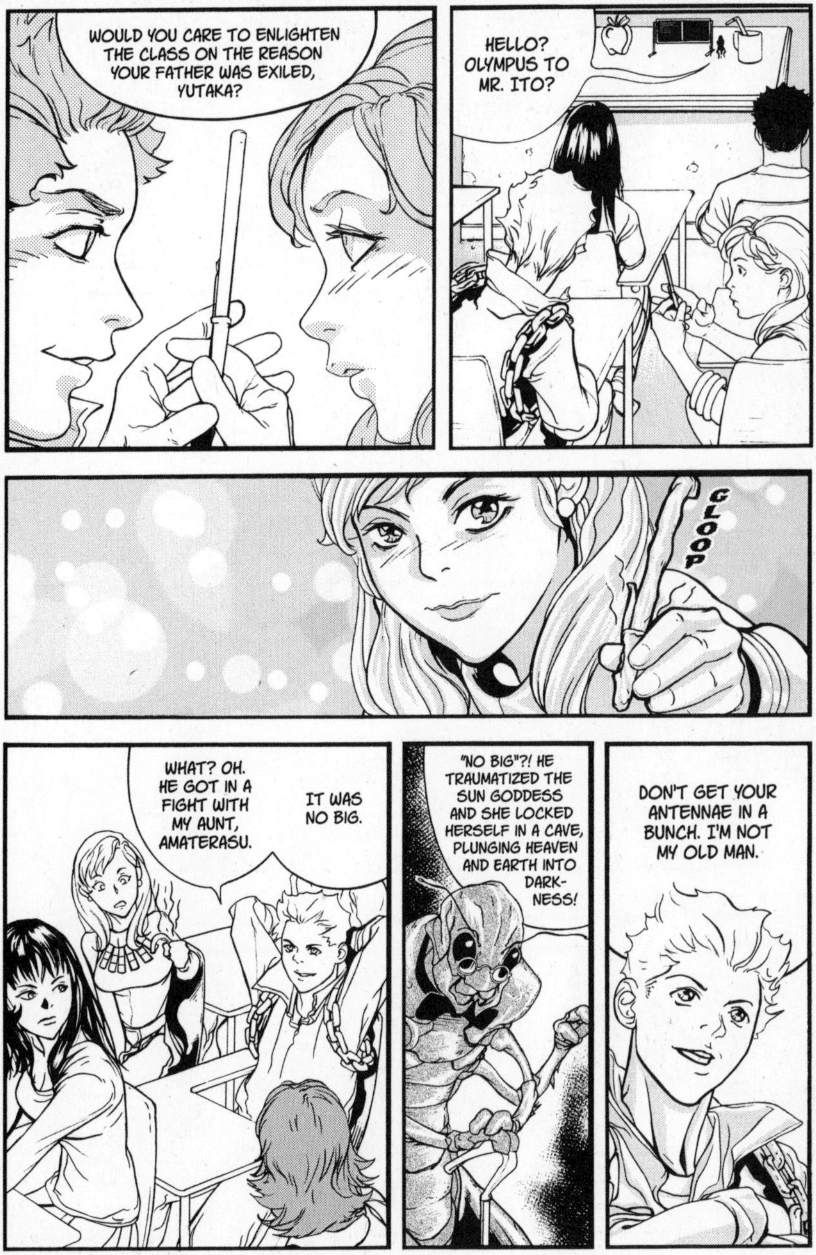
WOULD YOU CARE TO ENLIGHTEN THE CLASS ON THE REASON YOUR FATHER WAS EXILED, YUTAKA?
HELLO? OLYMPUS TO MR. ITO?
GLOOP
WHAT? OH. HE GOT IN A FIGHT WITH MY AUNT, AMATERASU.
IT WAS NO BIG.
"NO BIG"?! HE TRAUMATIZED THE SUN GODDESS AND SHE LOCKED HERSELF IN A CAVE, PLUNGING HEAVEN AND EARTH INTO DARK-NESS!
DON'T GET YOUR ANTENNAE IN A BUNCH. I'M NOT MY OLD MAN.

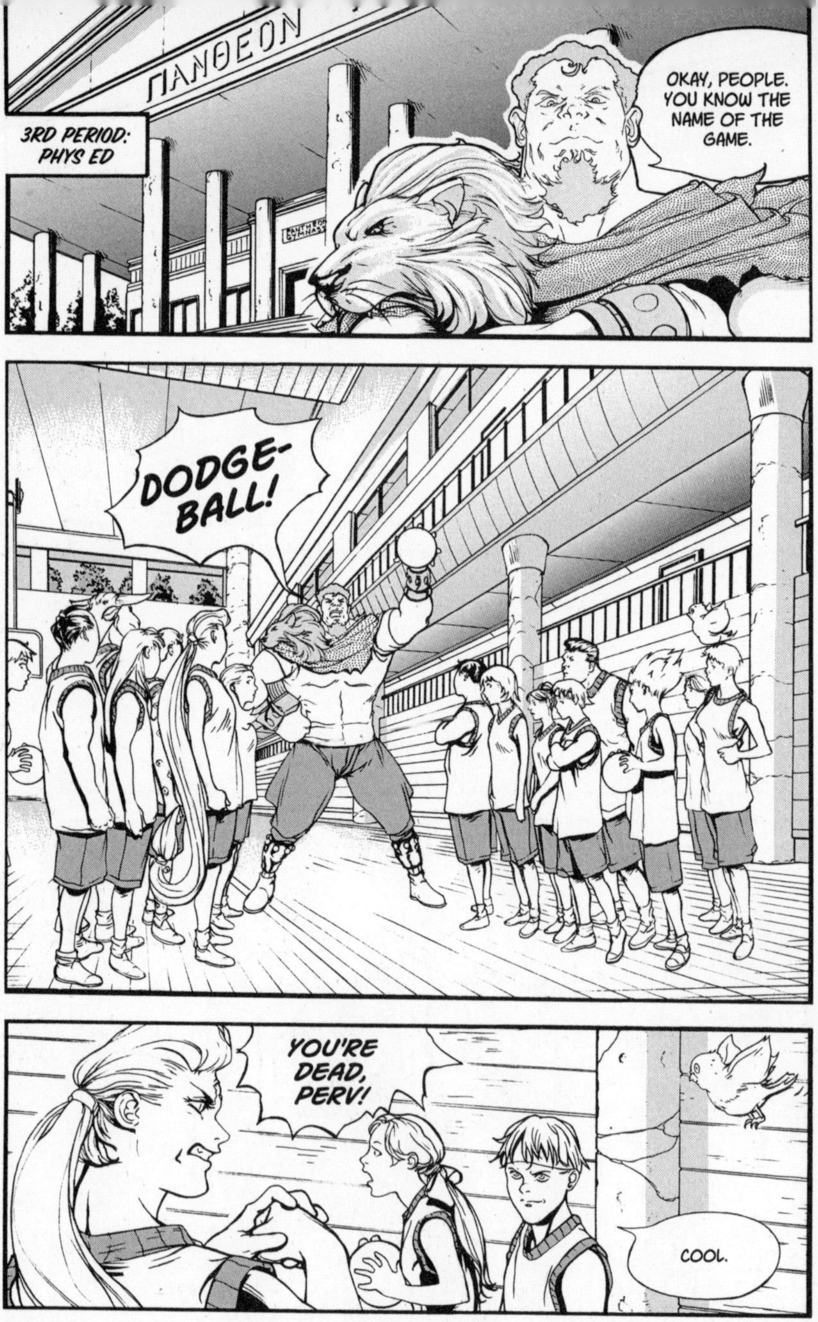
ΠΑΝΘΕΟΝ
3RD PERIOD: PHYS ED
OKAY, PEOPLE. YOU KNOW THE NAME OF THE GAME.
DODGE-BALL!
YOU'RE DEAD, PERV!
COOL.

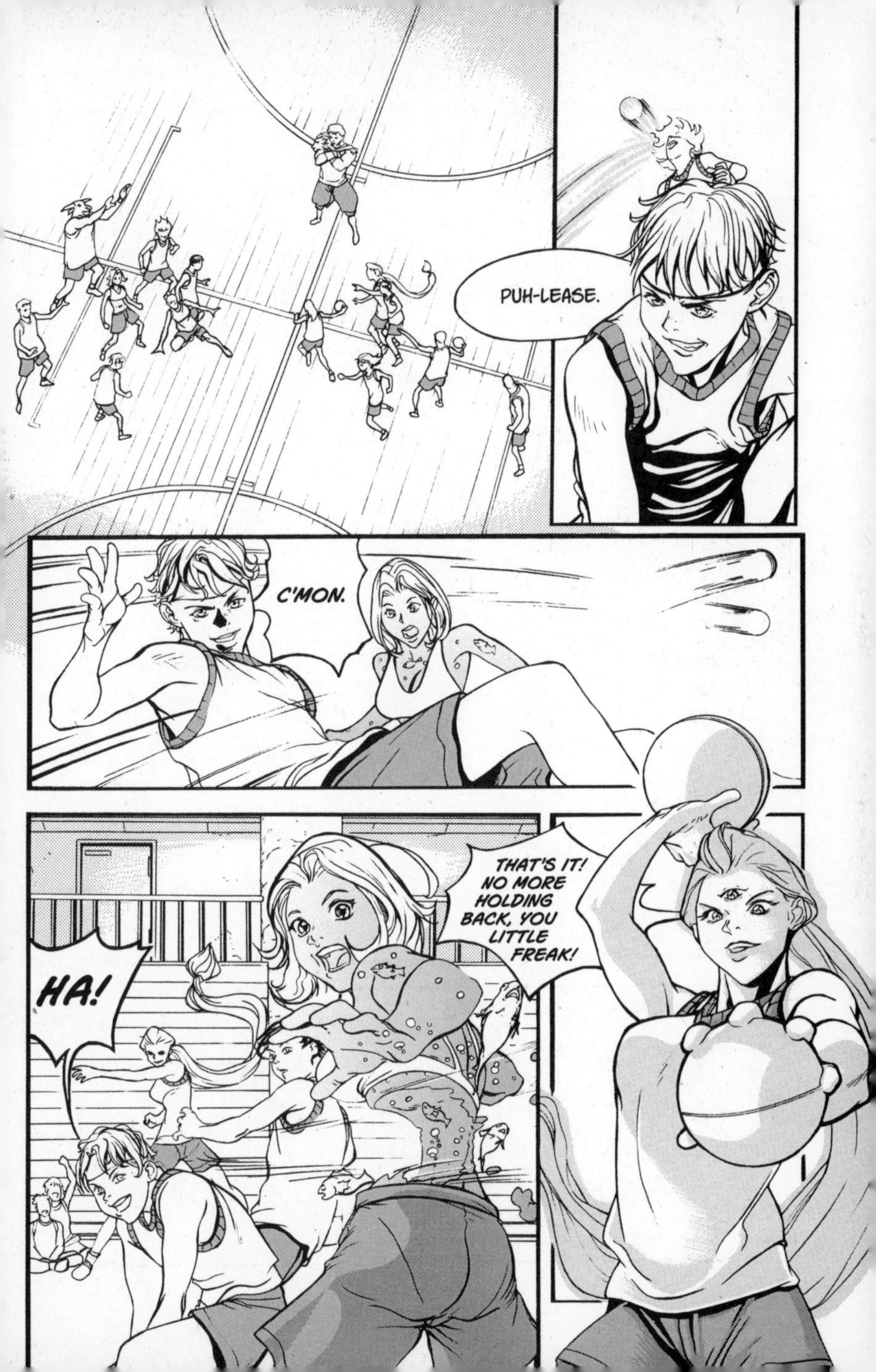

PUH-LEASE.
C'MON.
HA!
THAT'S IT! NO MORE HOLDING BACK, YOU LITTLE FREAK!

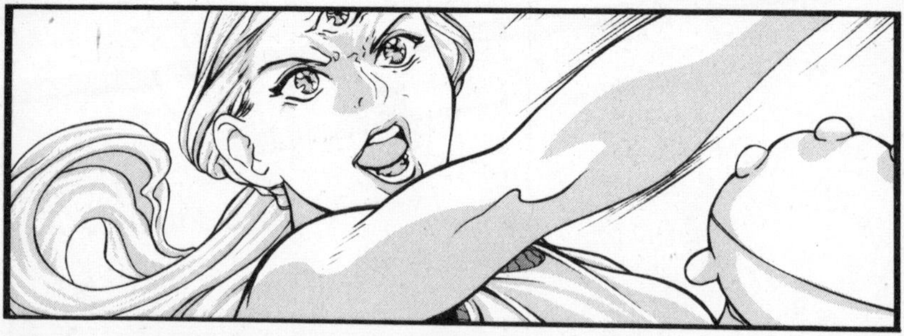
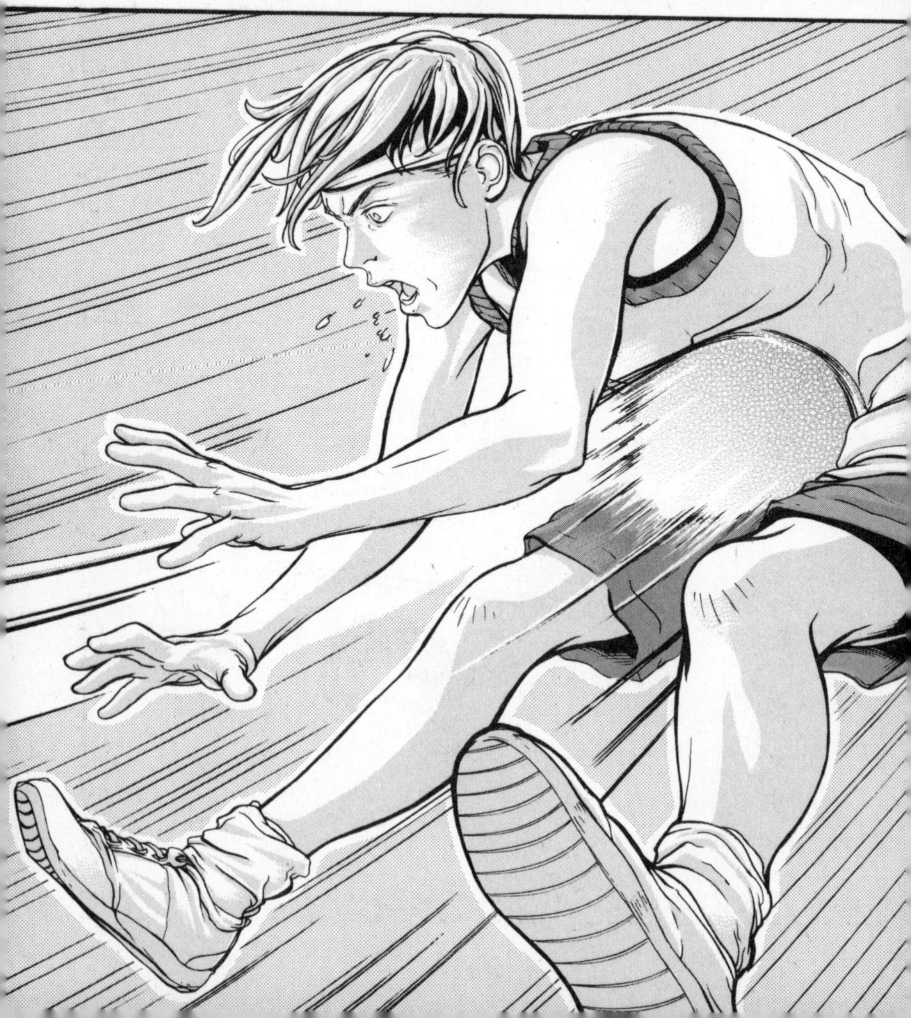

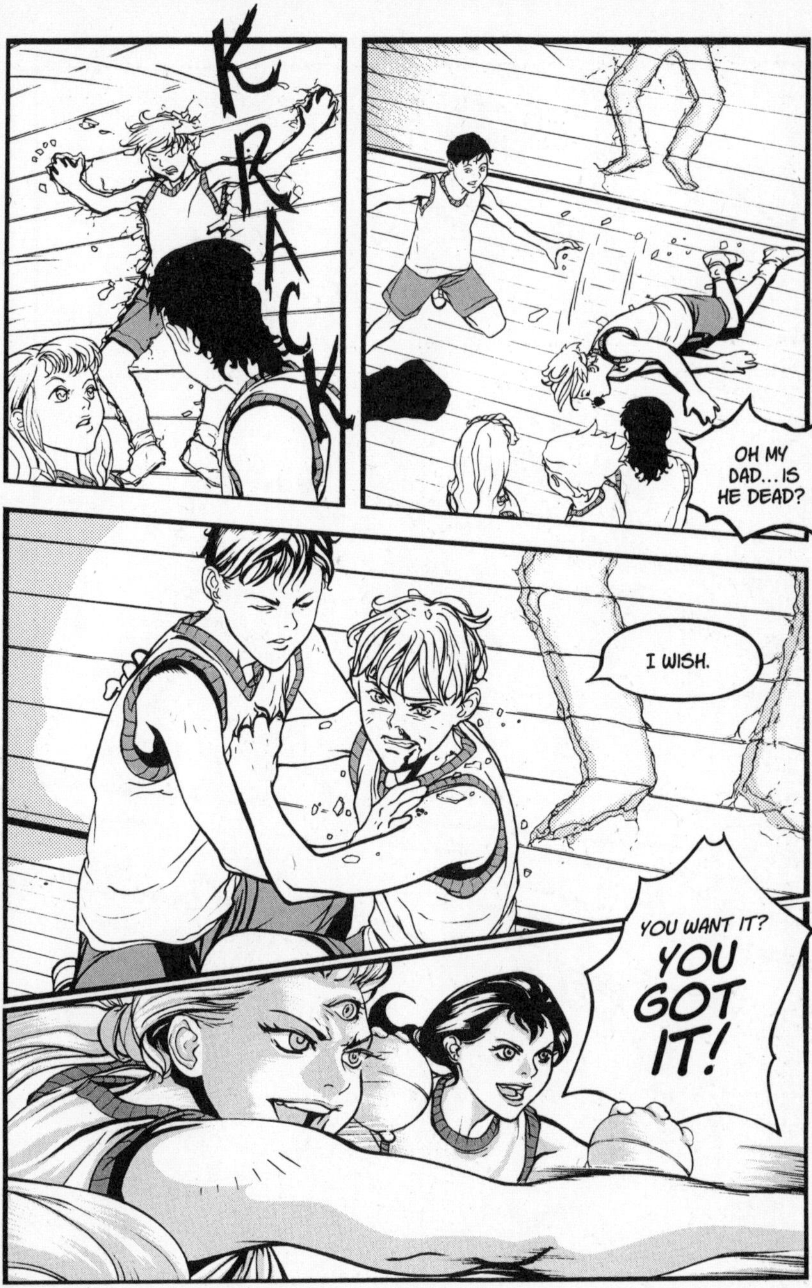
KRACK
OH MY DAD... IS HE DEAD?
I WISH.
YOU WANT IT? YOU GOT IT!

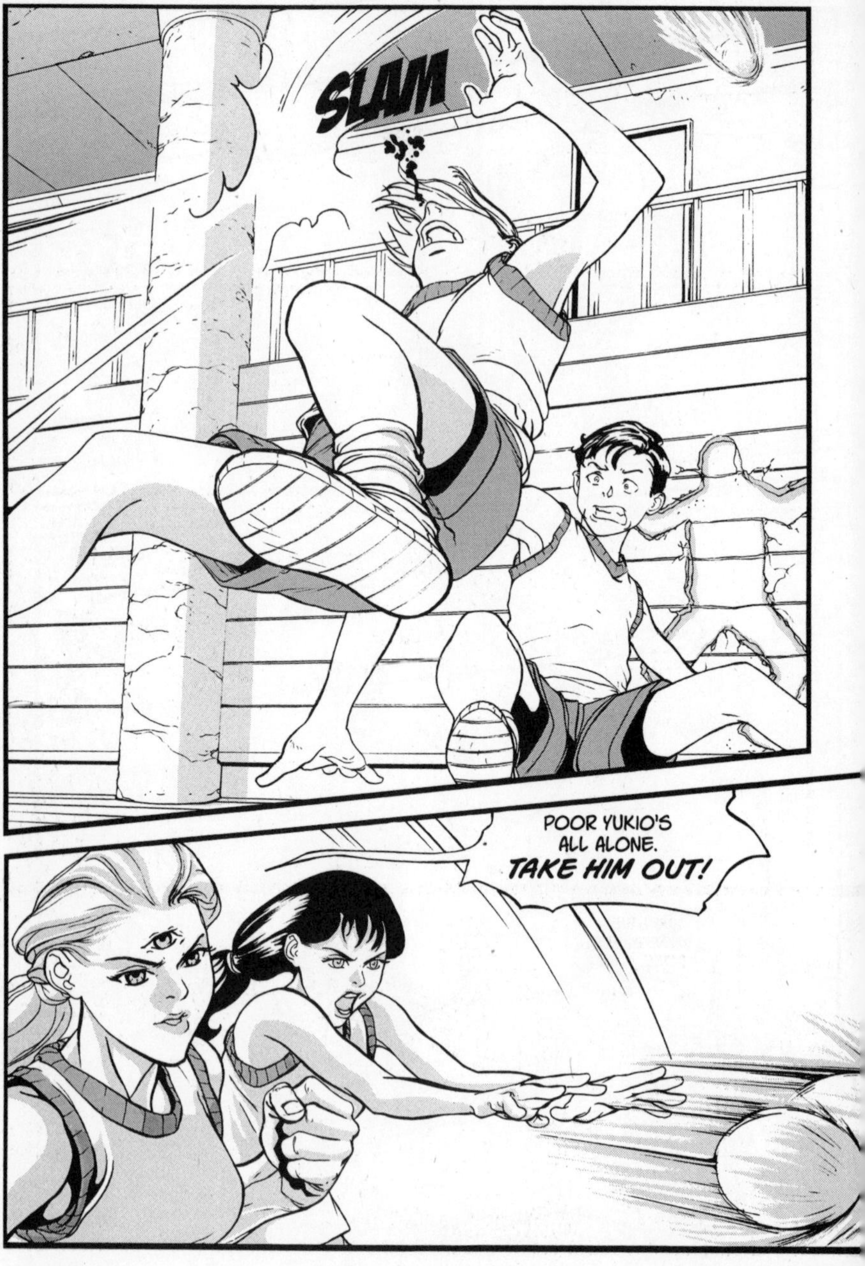
SLAM
POOR YUKIO'S ALL ALONE. TAKE HIM OUT!

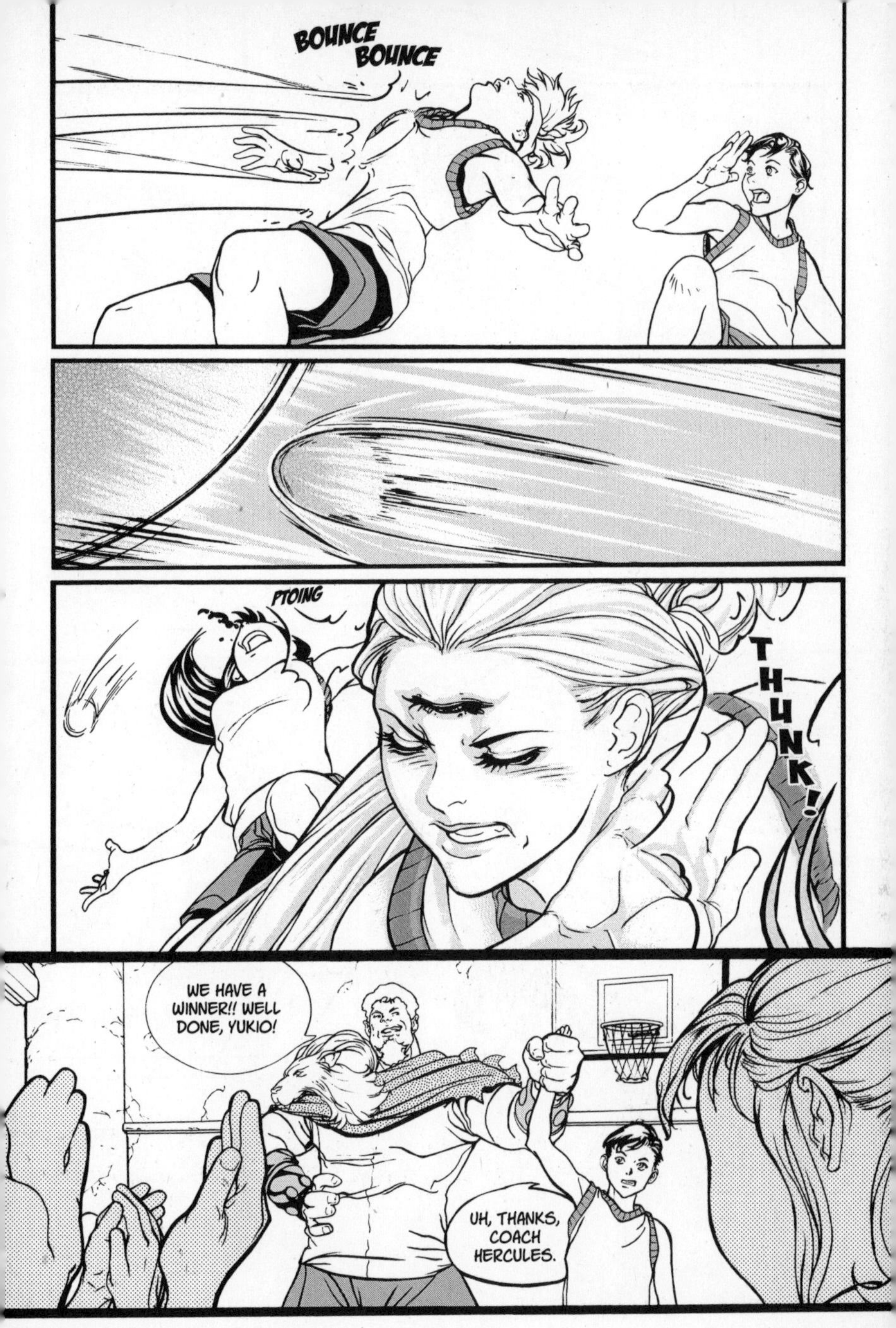
BOUNCE BOUNCE
PTOING
THUNK!
WE HAVE A WINNER!! WELL DONE, YUKIO!
UH, THANKS, COACH HERCULES.

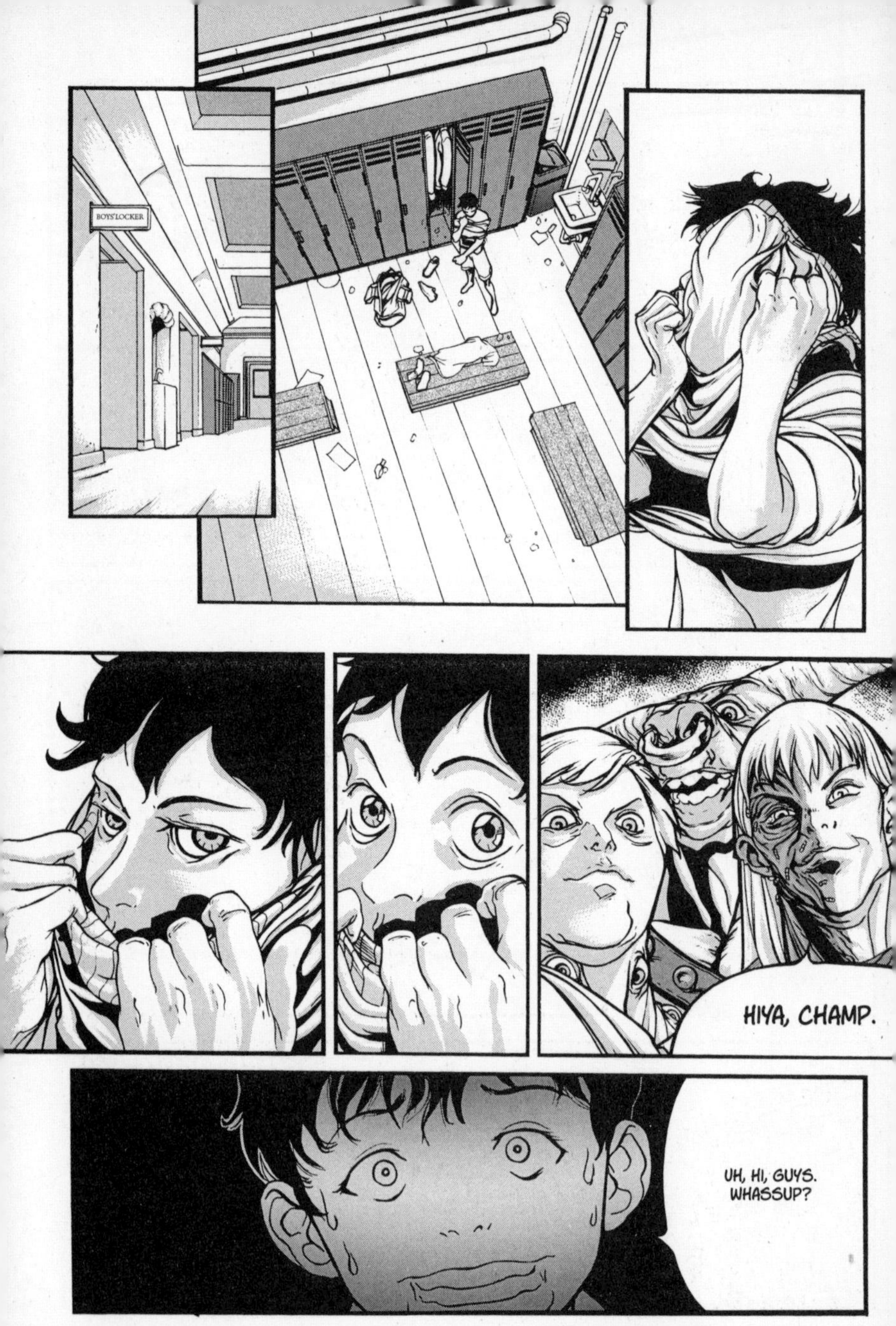
BOYS' LOCKER
HIYA, CHAMP.
UH, HI, GUYS. WHASSUP?

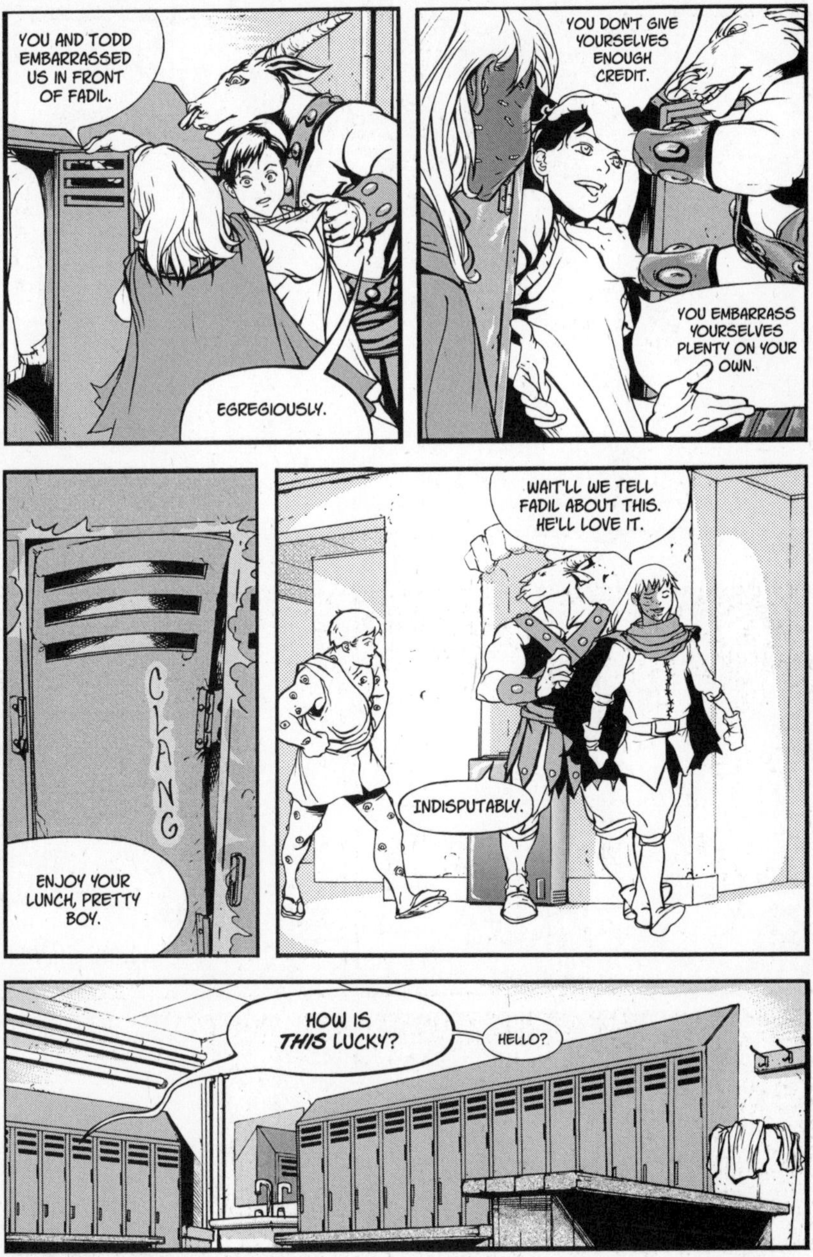
YOU AND TODD EMBARRASSED US IN FRONT OF FADIL.
EGREGIOUSLY.
YOU DON'T GIVE YOURSELVES ENOUGH CREDIT.
YOU EMBARRASS YOURSELVES PLENTY ON YOUR OWN.
CLANG
ENJOY YOUR LUNCH, PRETTY BOY.
WAIT'LL WE TELL FADIL ABOUT THIS. HE'LL LOVE IT.
INDISPUTABLY.
HOW IS *THIS* LUCKY?
HELLO?

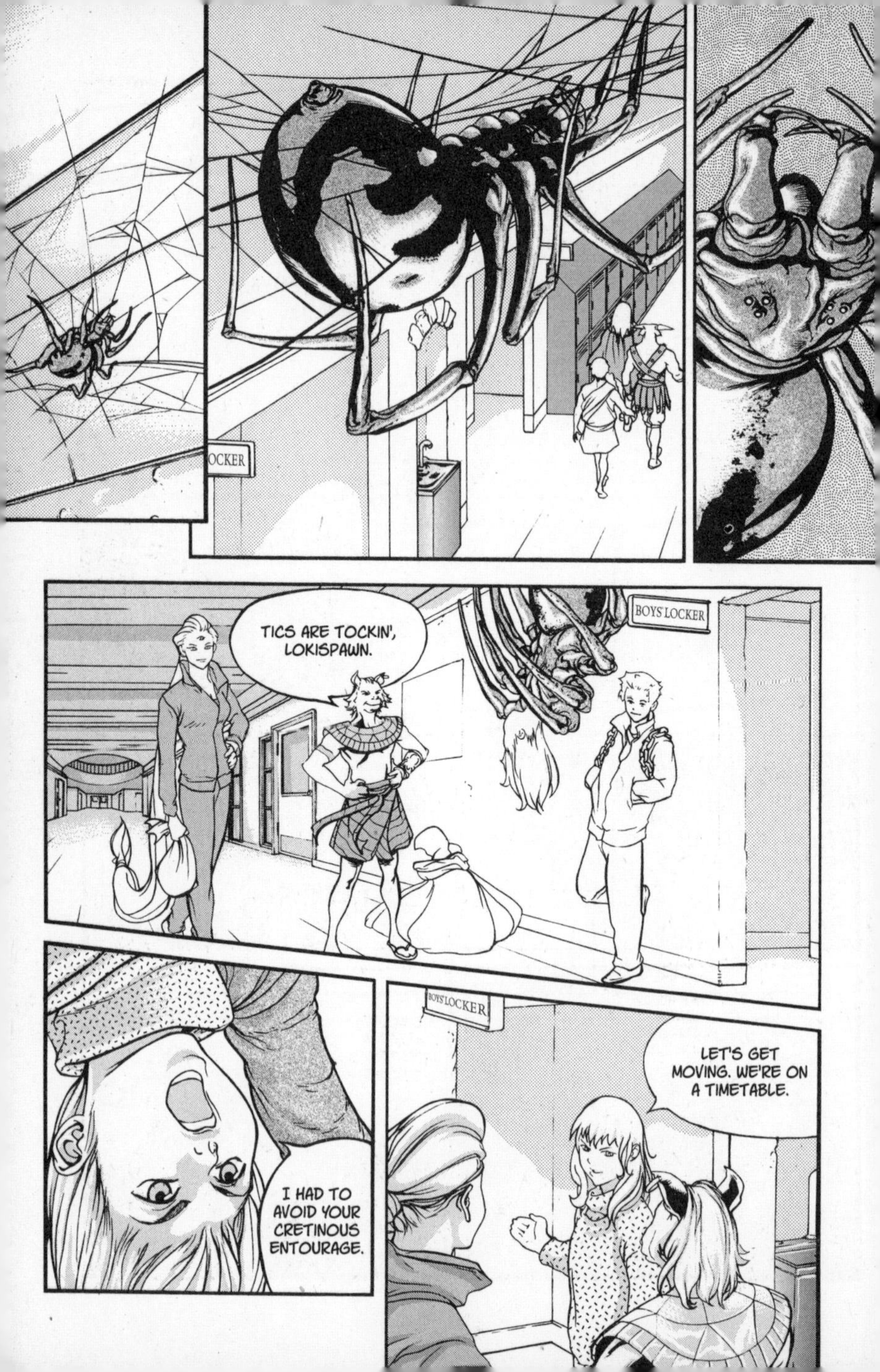
OCKER
BOYS' LOCKER
TICS ARE TOCKIN', LOKISPAWN.
I HAD TO AVOID YOUR CRETINOUS ENTOURAGE.
BOYS' LOCKER
LET'S GET MOVING. WE'RE ON A TIMETABLE.

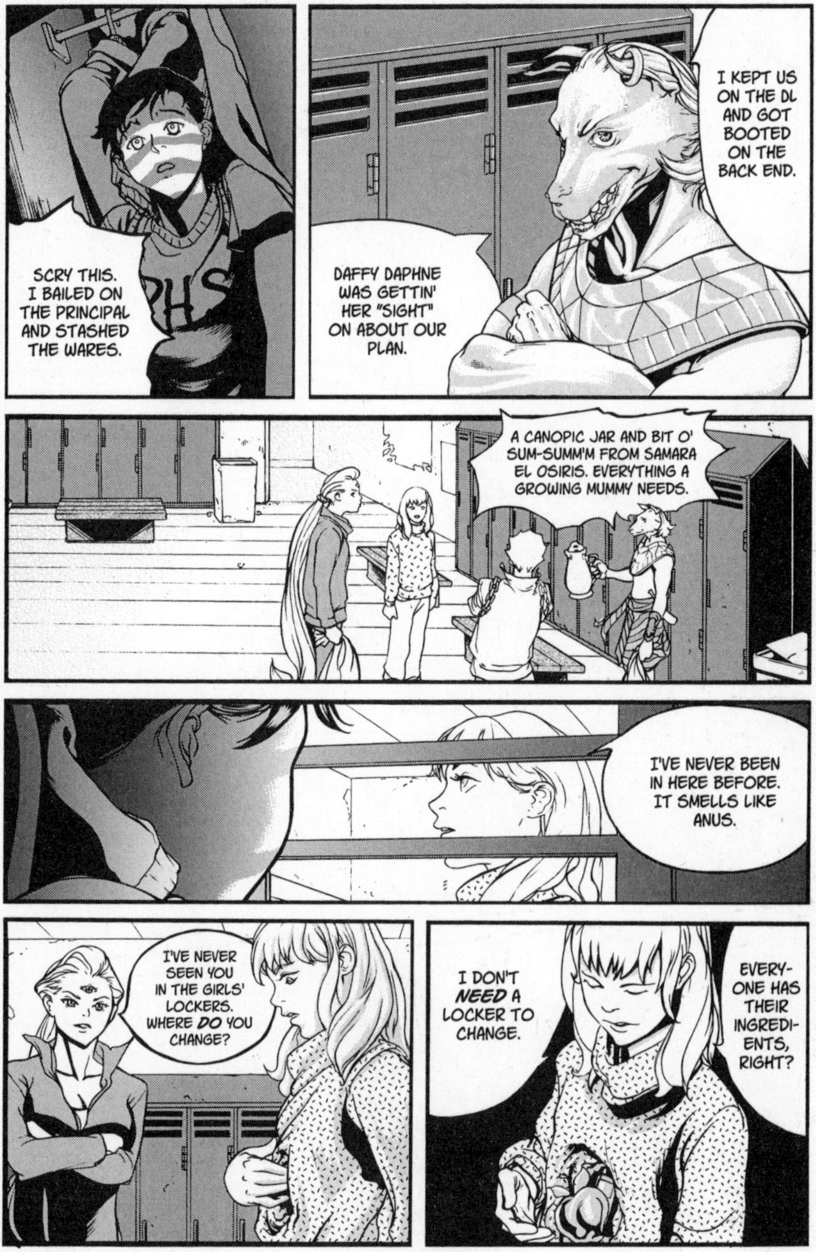
SCRY THIS. I BAILED ON THE PRINCIPAL AND STASHED THE WARES.
DAFFY DAPHNE WAS GETTIN' HER "SIGHT" ON ABOUT OUR PLAN.
I KEPT US ON THE DL AND GOT BOOTED ON THE BACK END.
A CANOPIC JAR AND BIT O' SUM-SUMM'M FROM SAMARA EL OSIRIS. EVERYTHING A GROWING MUMMY NEEDS.
I'VE NEVER BEEN IN HERE BEFORE. IT SMELLS LIKE ANUS.
I'VE NEVER SEEN YOU IN THE GIRLS' LOCKERS. WHERE ***DO*** YOU CHANGE?
I DON'T ***NEED*** A LOCKER TO CHANGE.
EVERY-ONE HAS THEIR INGREDI-ENTS, RIGHT?

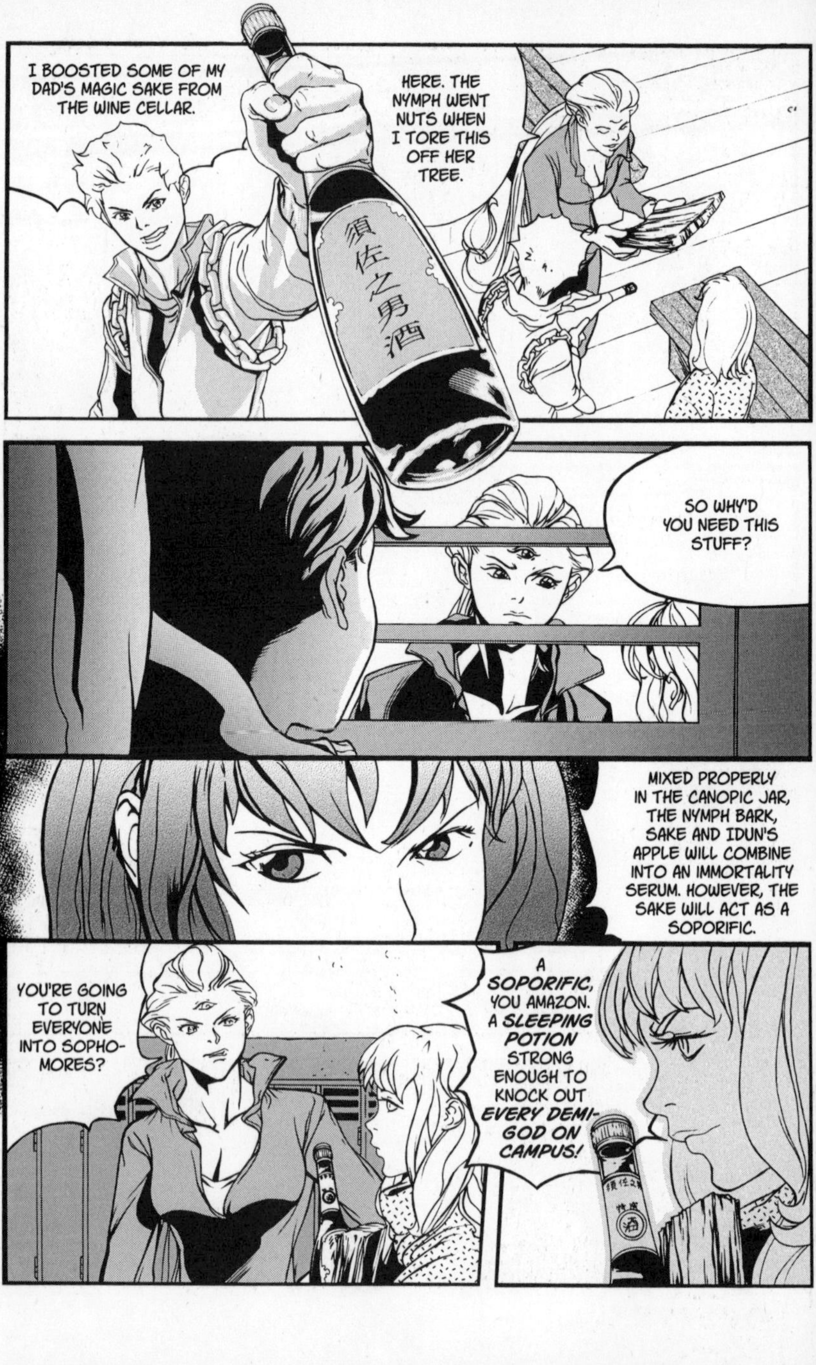
I BOOSTED SOME OF MY DAD'S MAGIC SAKE FROM THE WINE CELLAR.
須佐之男酒
HERE. THE NYMPH WENT NUTS WHEN I TORE THIS OFF HER TREE.
SO WHY'D YOU NEED THIS STUFF?
MIXED PROPERLY IN THE CANOPIC JAR, THE NYMPH BARK, SAKE AND IDUN'S APPLE WILL COMBINE INTO AN IMMORTALITY SERUM. HOWEVER, THE SAKE WILL ACT AS A SOPORIFIC.
YOU'RE GOING TO TURN EVERYONE INTO SOPHO-MORES?
A *SOPORIFIC,* YOU AMAZON. A *SLEEPING POTION* STRONG ENOUGH TO KNOCK OUT *EVERY DEMI-GOD ON CAMPUS!*

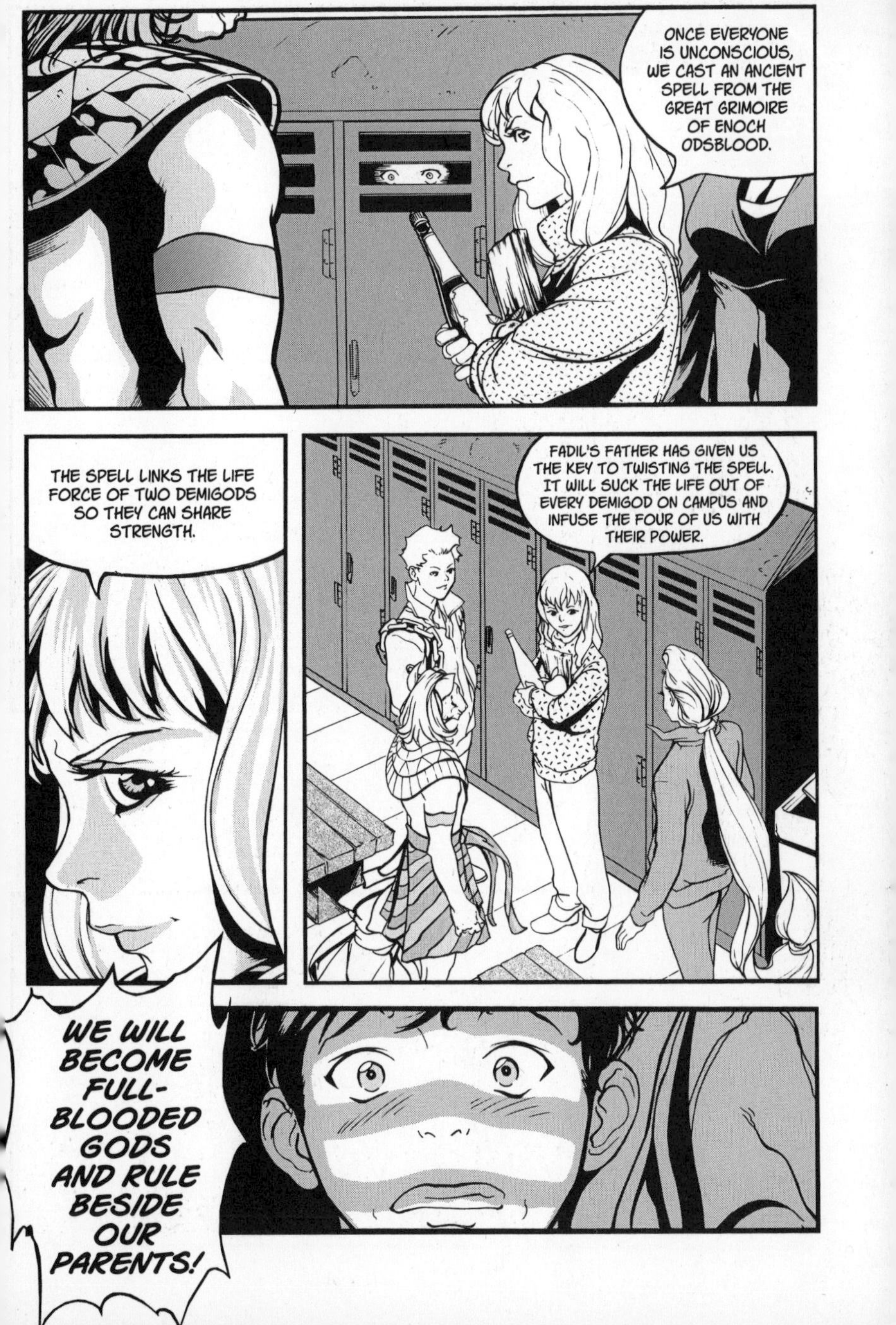
ONCE EVERYONE IS UNCONSCIOUS, WE CAST AN ANCIENT SPELL FROM THE GREAT GRIMOIRE OF ENOCH ODSBLOOD.
THE SPELL LINKS THE LIFE FORCE OF TWO DEMIGODS SO THEY CAN SHARE STRENGTH.
FADIL'S FATHER HAS GIVEN US THE KEY TO TWISTING THE SPELL. IT WILL SUCK THE LIFE OUT OF EVERY DEMIGOD ON CAMPUS AND INFUSE THE FOUR OF US WITH THEIR POWER.
WE WILL BECOME FULL-BLOODED GODS AND RULE BESIDE OUR PARENTS!

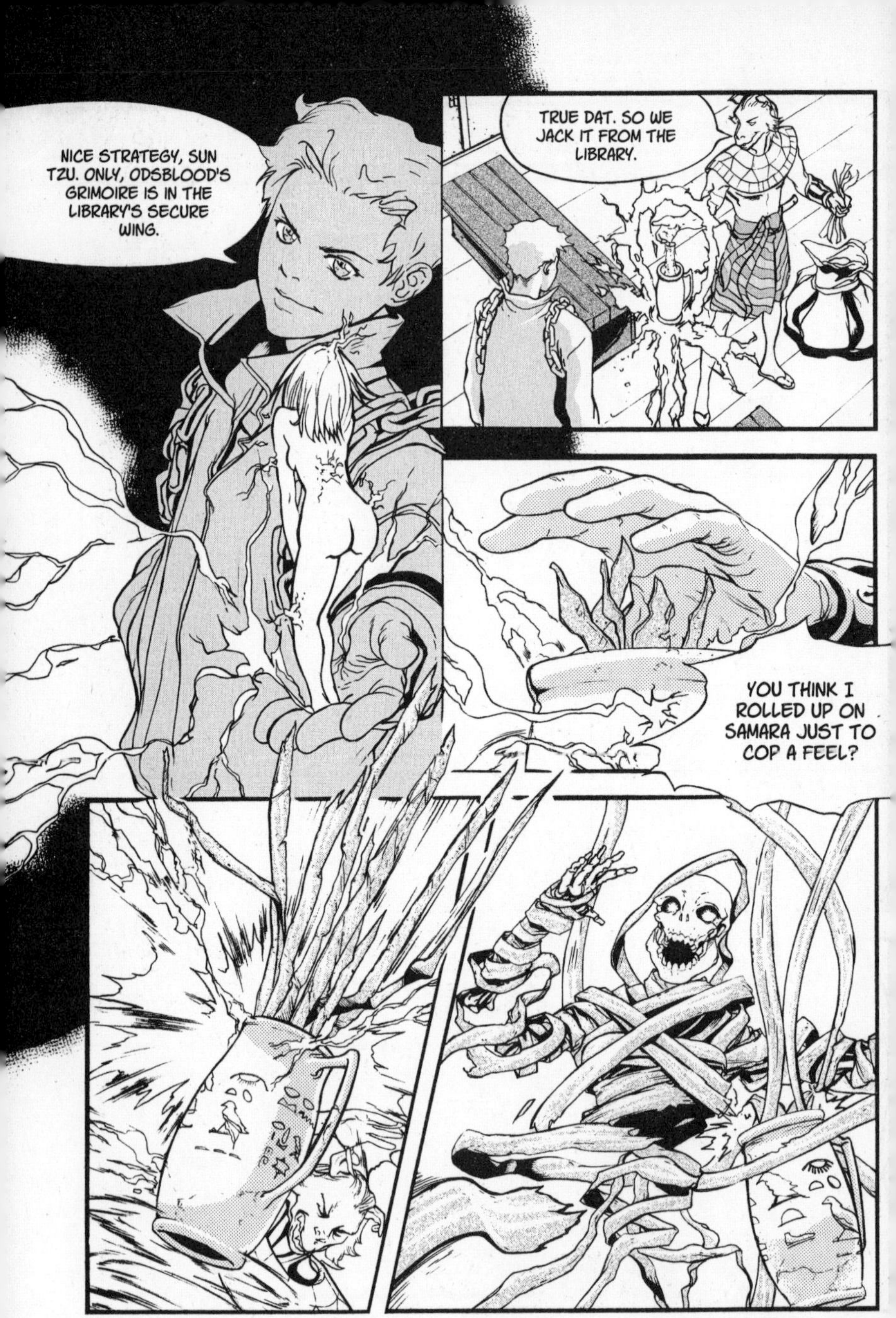
NICE STRATEGY, SUN TZU. ONLY, ODSBLOOD'S GRIMOIRE IS IN THE LIBRARY'S SECURE WING.
TRUE DAT. SO WE JACK IT FROM THE LIBRARY.
YOU THINK I ROLLED UP ON SAMARA JUST TO COP A FEEL?

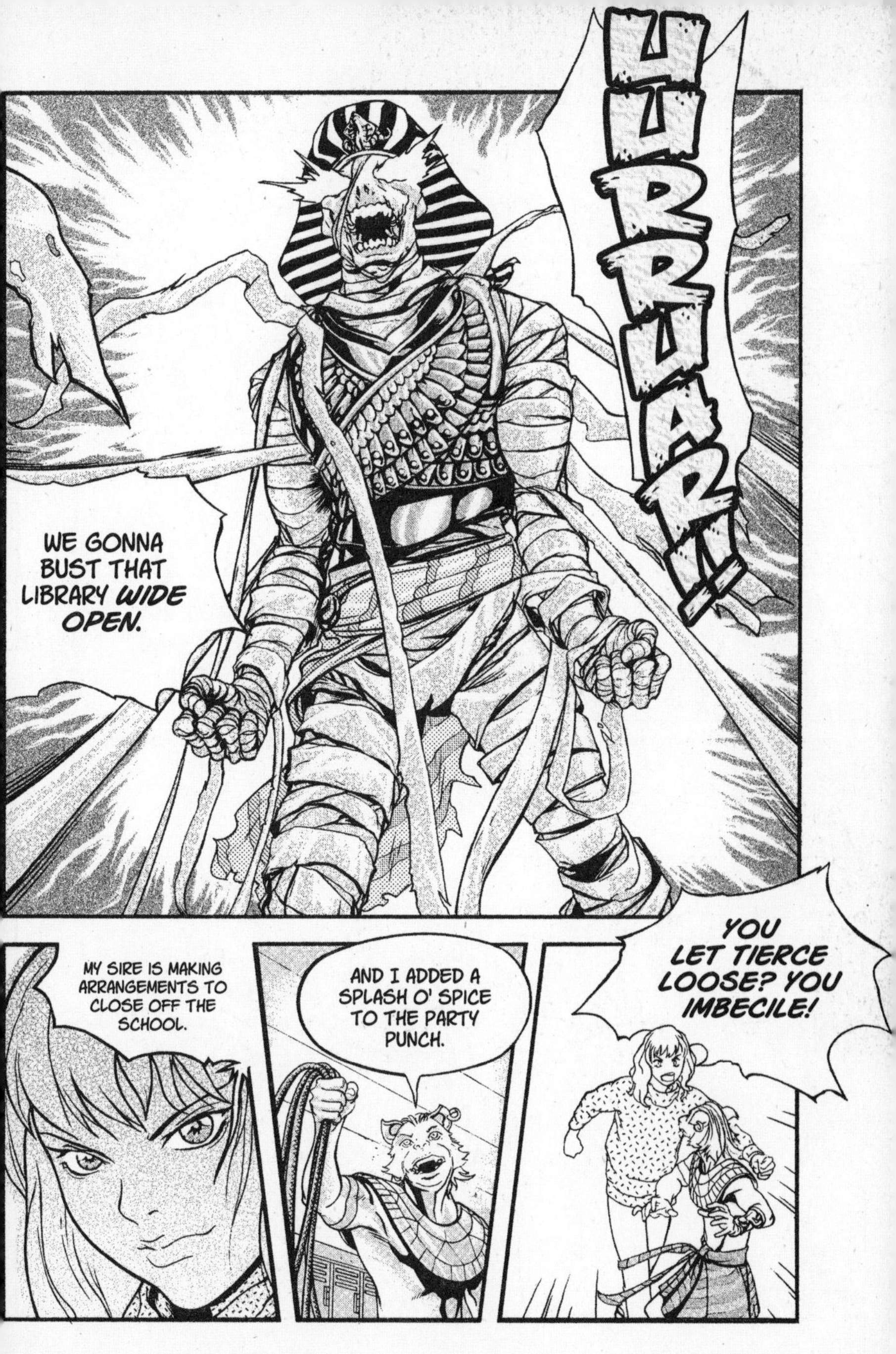
UURRUAR!
WE GONNA BUST THAT LIBRARY *WIDE OPEN.*
MY SIRE IS MAKING ARRANGEMENTS TO CLOSE OFF THE SCHOOL.
AND I ADDED A SPLASH O' SPICE TO THE PARTY PUNCH.
YOU LET TIERCE LOOSE? YOU IMBECILE!

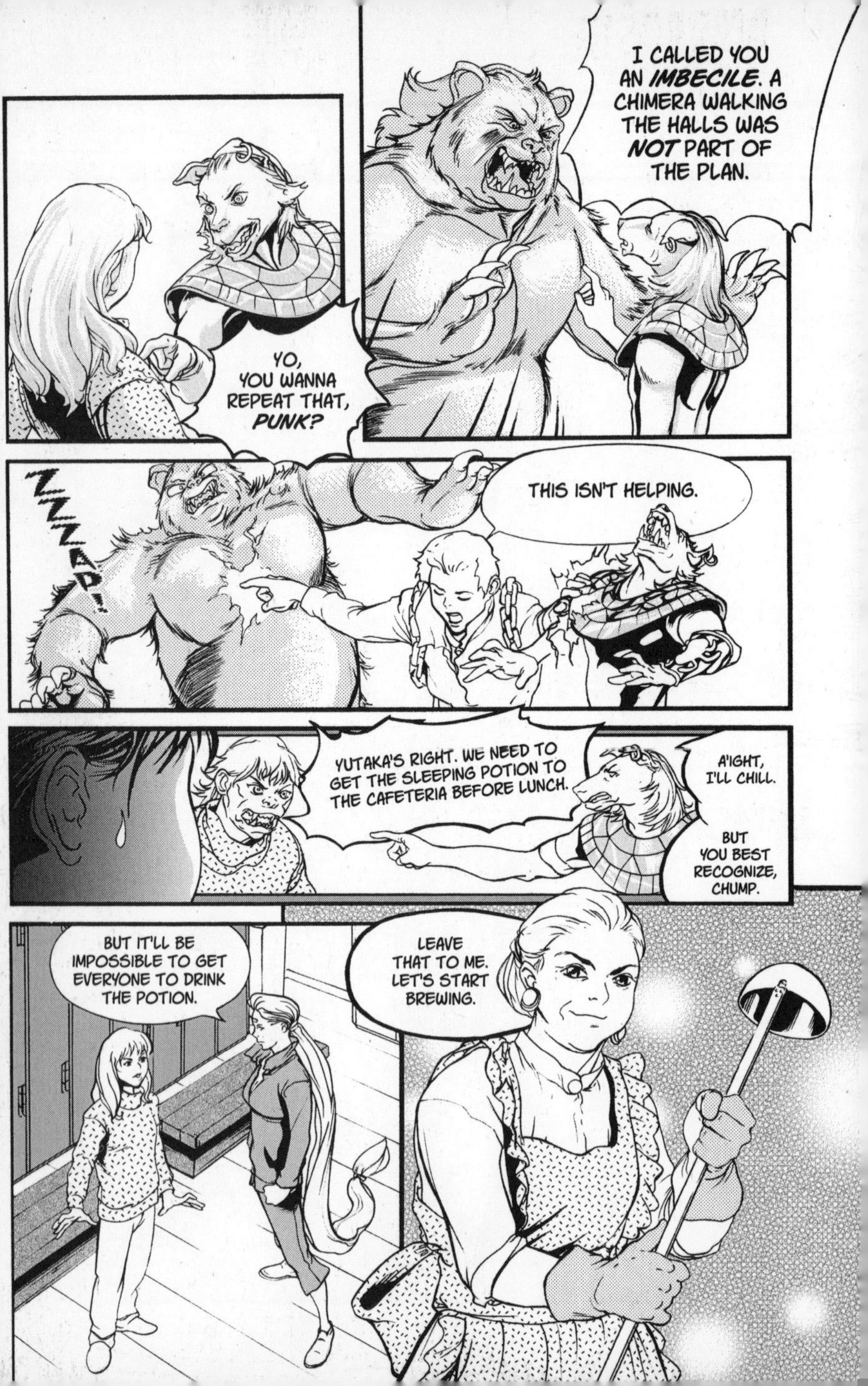
YO, YOU WANNA REPEAT THAT, PUNK?
I CALLED YOU AN IMBECILE. A CHIMERA WALKING THE HALLS WAS NOT PART OF THE PLAN.
ZZZAP!
THIS ISN'T HELPING.
YUTAKA'S RIGHT. WE NEED TO GET THE SLEEPING POTION TO THE CAFETERIA BEFORE LUNCH.
A'IGHT, I'LL CHILL.
BUT YOU BEST RECOGNIZE, CHUMP.
BUT IT'LL BE IMPOSSIBLE TO GET EVERYONE TO DRINK THE POTION.
LEAVE THAT TO ME. LET'S START BREWING.

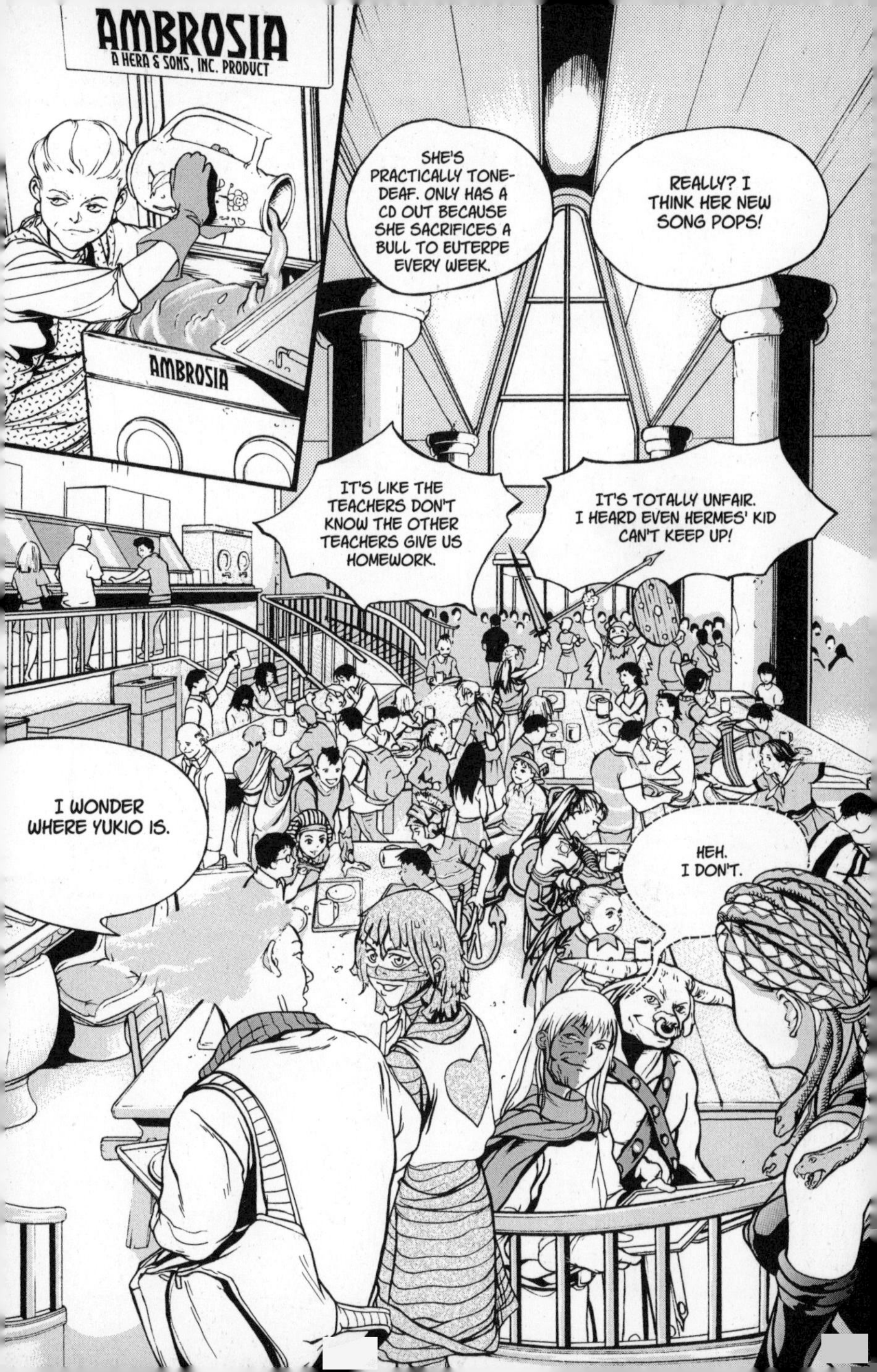
AMBROSIA
A HERA & SONS, INC. PRODUCT
AMBROSIA
SHE'S PRACTICALLY TONE-DEAF. ONLY HAS A CD OUT BECAUSE SHE SACRIFICES A BULL TO EUTERPE EVERY WEEK.
REALLY? I THINK HER NEW SONG POPS!
IT'S LIKE THE TEACHERS DON'T KNOW THE OTHER TEACHERS GIVE US HOMEWORK.
IT'S TOTALLY UNFAIR. I HEARD EVEN HERMES' KID CAN'T KEEP UP!
I WONDER WHERE YUKIO IS.
HEH. I DON'T.

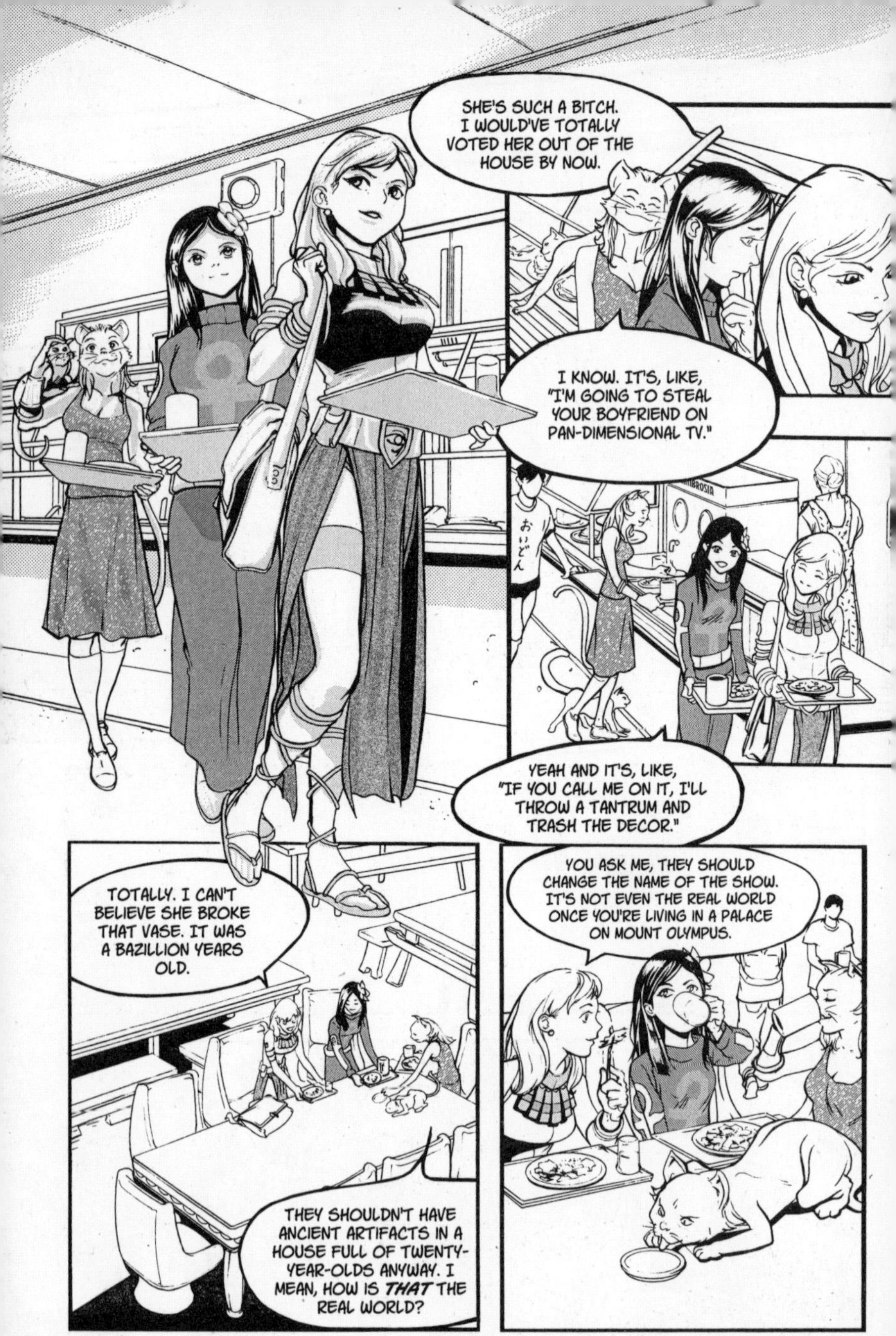
SHE'S SUCH A BITCH. I WOULD'VE TOTALLY VOTED HER OUT OF THE HOUSE BY NOW.
I KNOW. IT'S, LIKE, "I'M GOING TO STEAL YOUR BOYFRIEND ON PAN-DIMENSIONAL TV."
おいどん
YEAH AND IT'S, LIKE, "IF YOU CALL ME ON IT, I'LL THROW A TANTRUM AND TRASH THE DECOR."
TOTALLY. I CAN'T BELIEVE SHE BROKE THAT VASE. IT WAS A BAZILLION YEARS OLD.
THEY SHOULDN'T HAVE ANCIENT ARTIFACTS IN A HOUSE FULL OF TWENTY-YEAR-OLDS ANYWAY. I MEAN, HOW IS *THAT* THE REAL WORLD?
YOU ASK ME, THEY SHOULD CHANGE THE NAME OF THE SHOW. IT'S NOT EVEN THE REAL WORLD ONCE YOU'RE LIVING IN A PALACE ON MOUNT OLYMPUS.

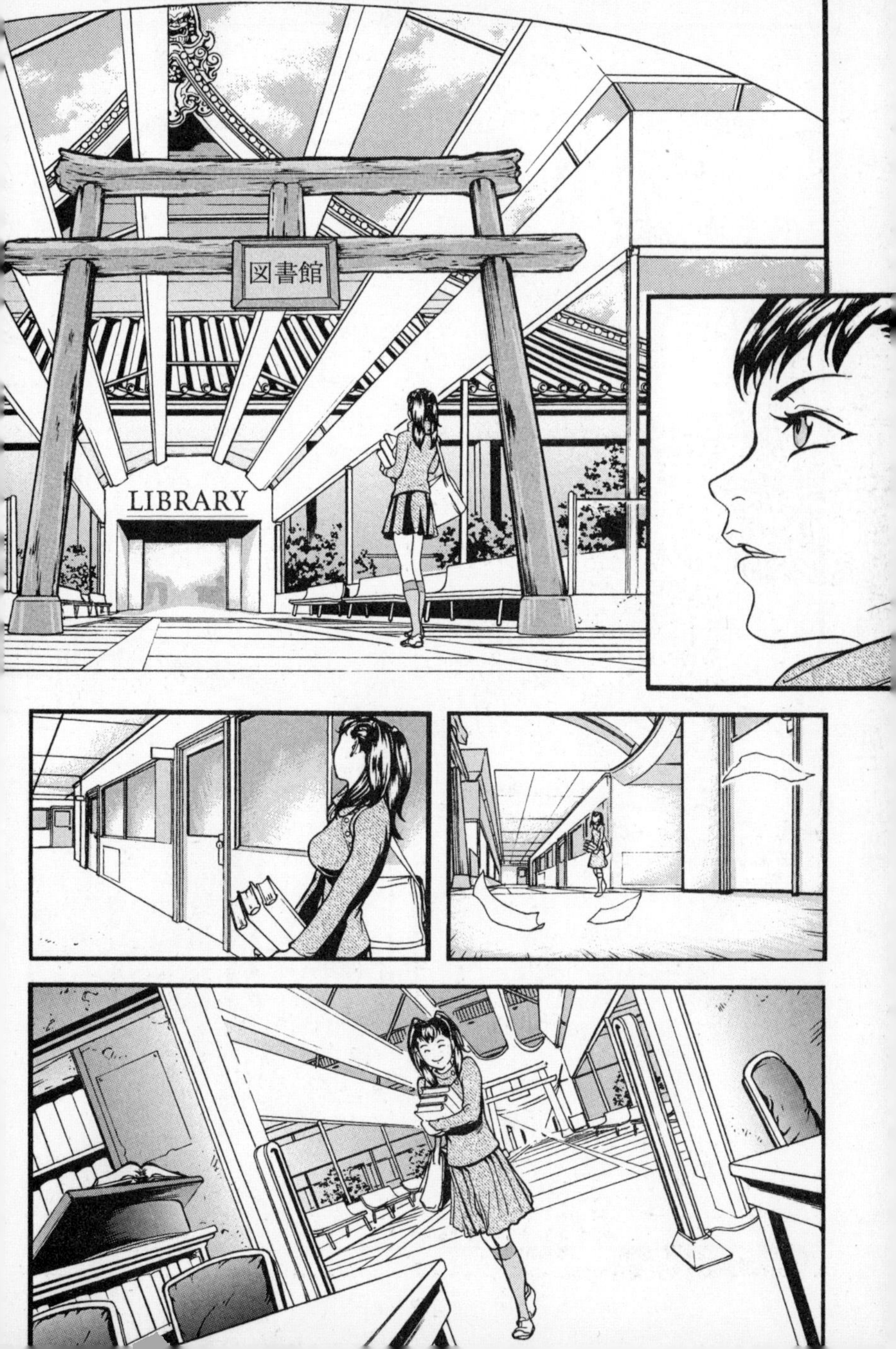
図書館
LIBRARY

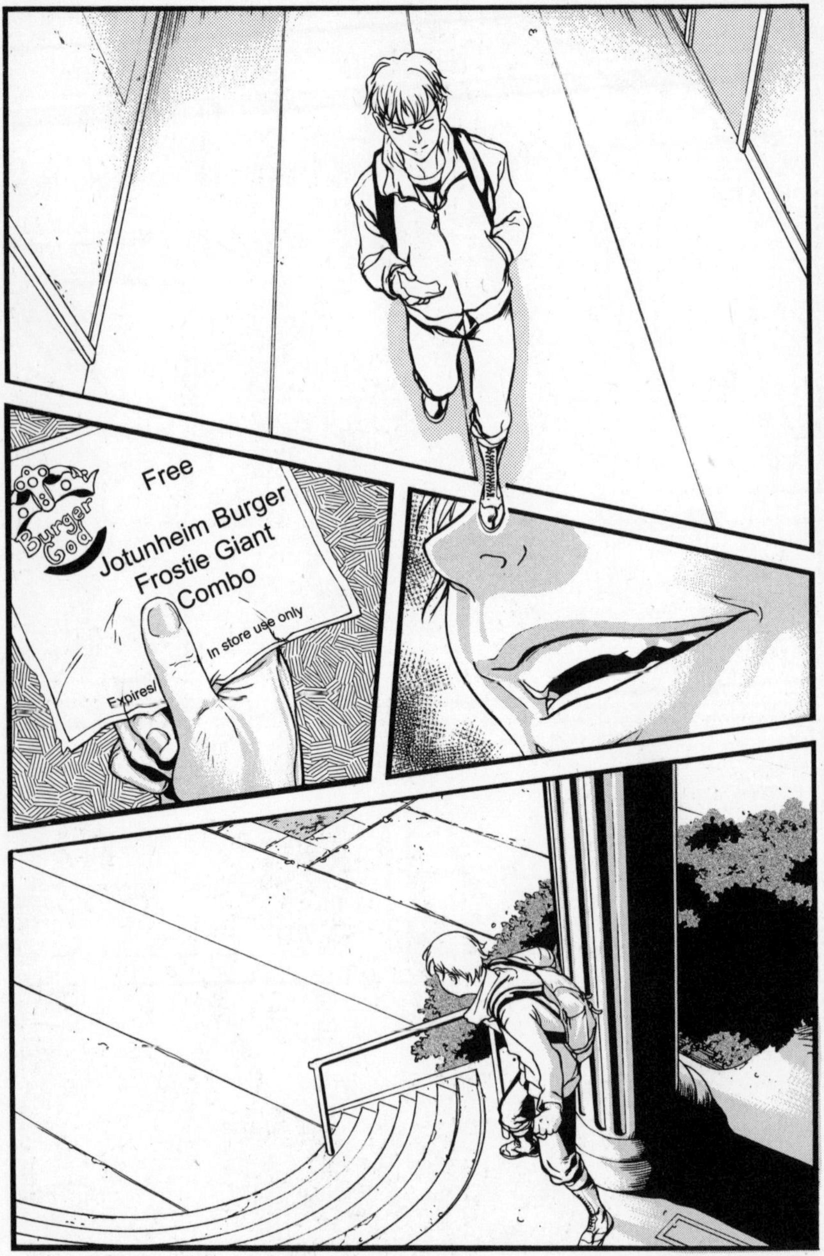
Burger God
Free
Jotunheim Burger
Frostie Giant
Combo
In store use only
Expires/

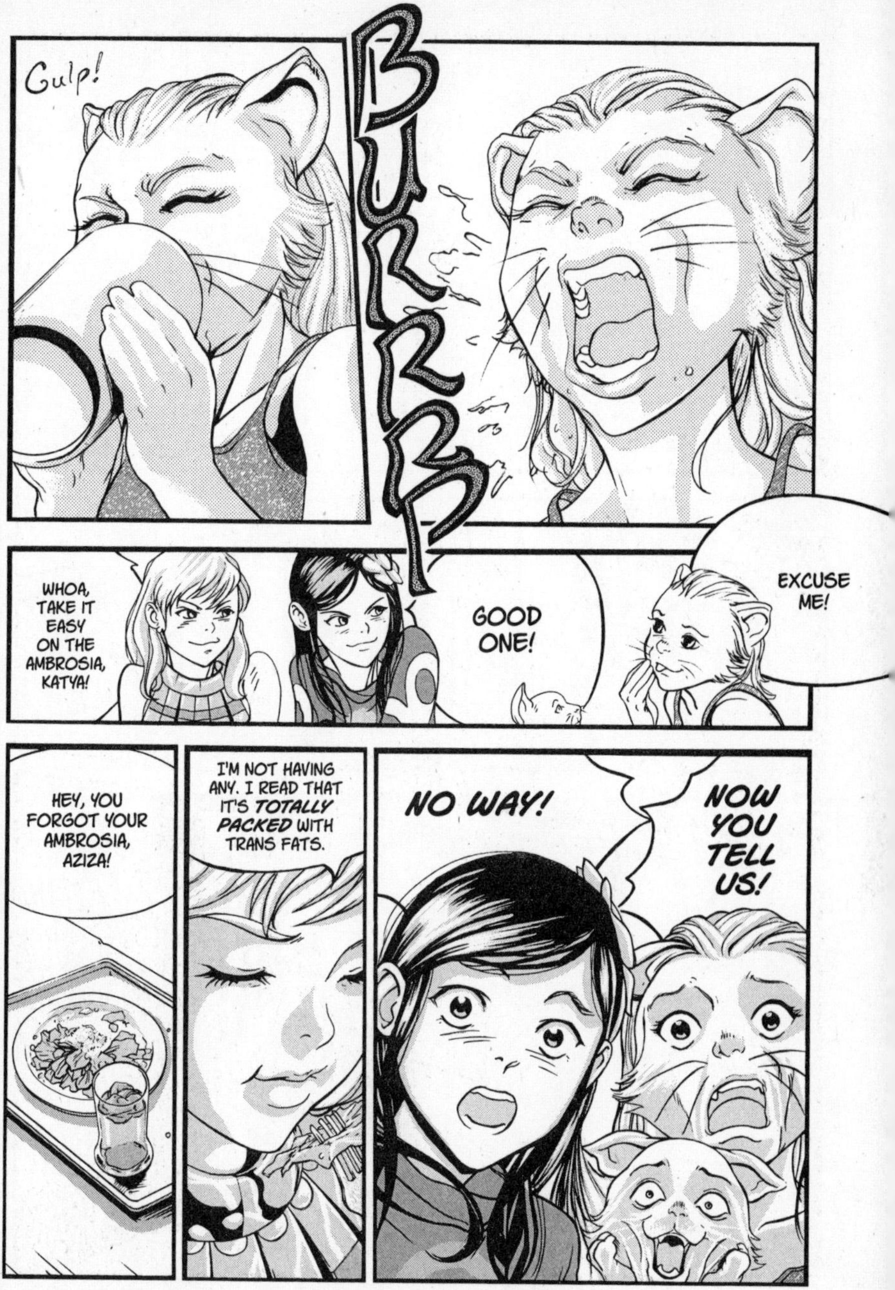
Gulp!
BURRRP!
WHOA, TAKE IT EASY ON THE AMBROSIA, KATYA!
GOOD ONE!
EXCUSE ME!
HEY, YOU FORGOT YOUR AMBROSIA, AZIZA!
I'M NOT HAVING ANY. I READ THAT IT'S *TOTALLY PACKED* WITH TRANS FATS.
NO WAY!
NOW YOU TELL US!

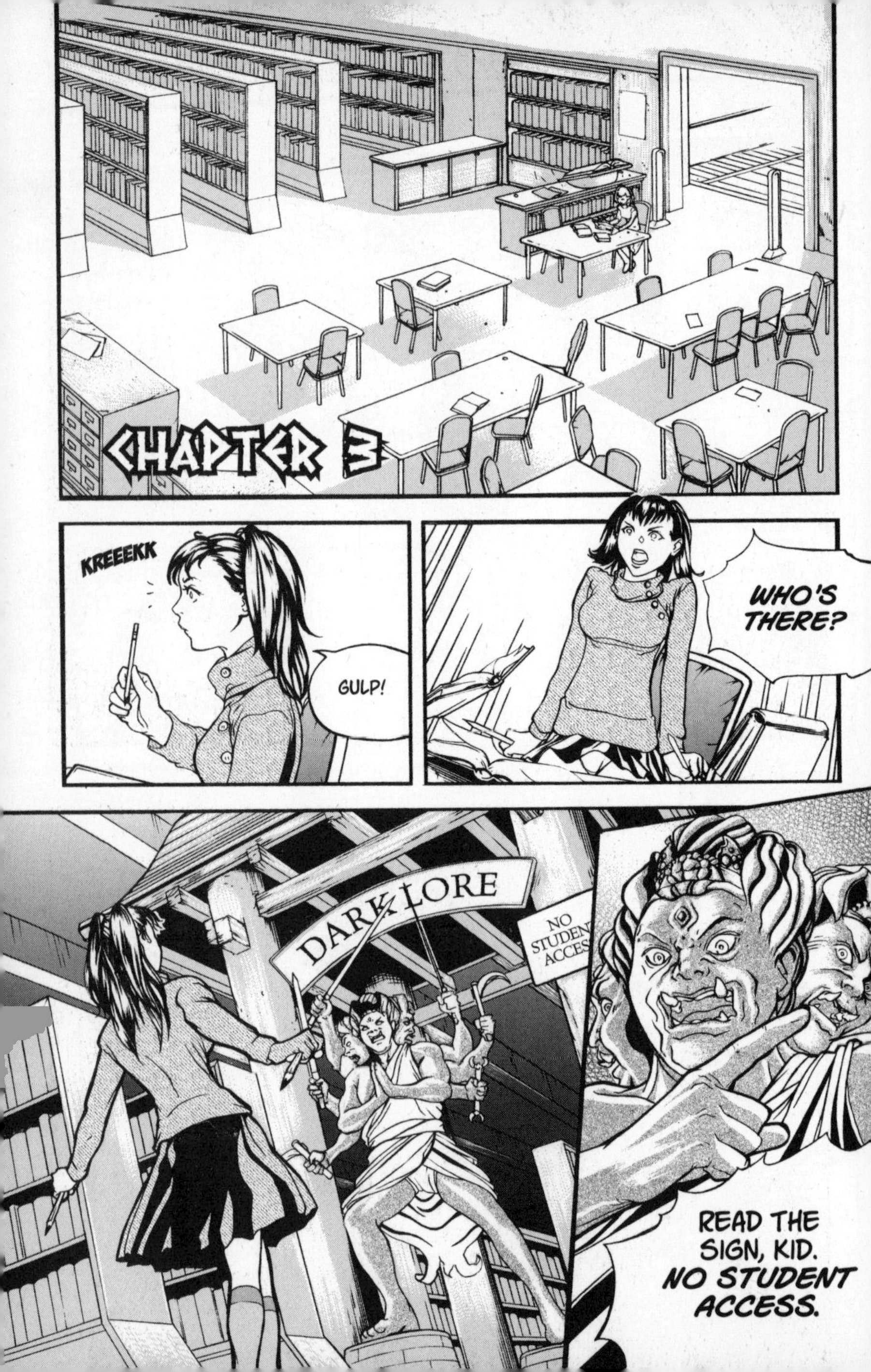
CHAPTER 3
KREEEKK
GULP!
WHO'S THERE?
DARK LORE
NO STUDEN ACCES
READ THE SIGN, KID. NO STUDENT ACCESS.

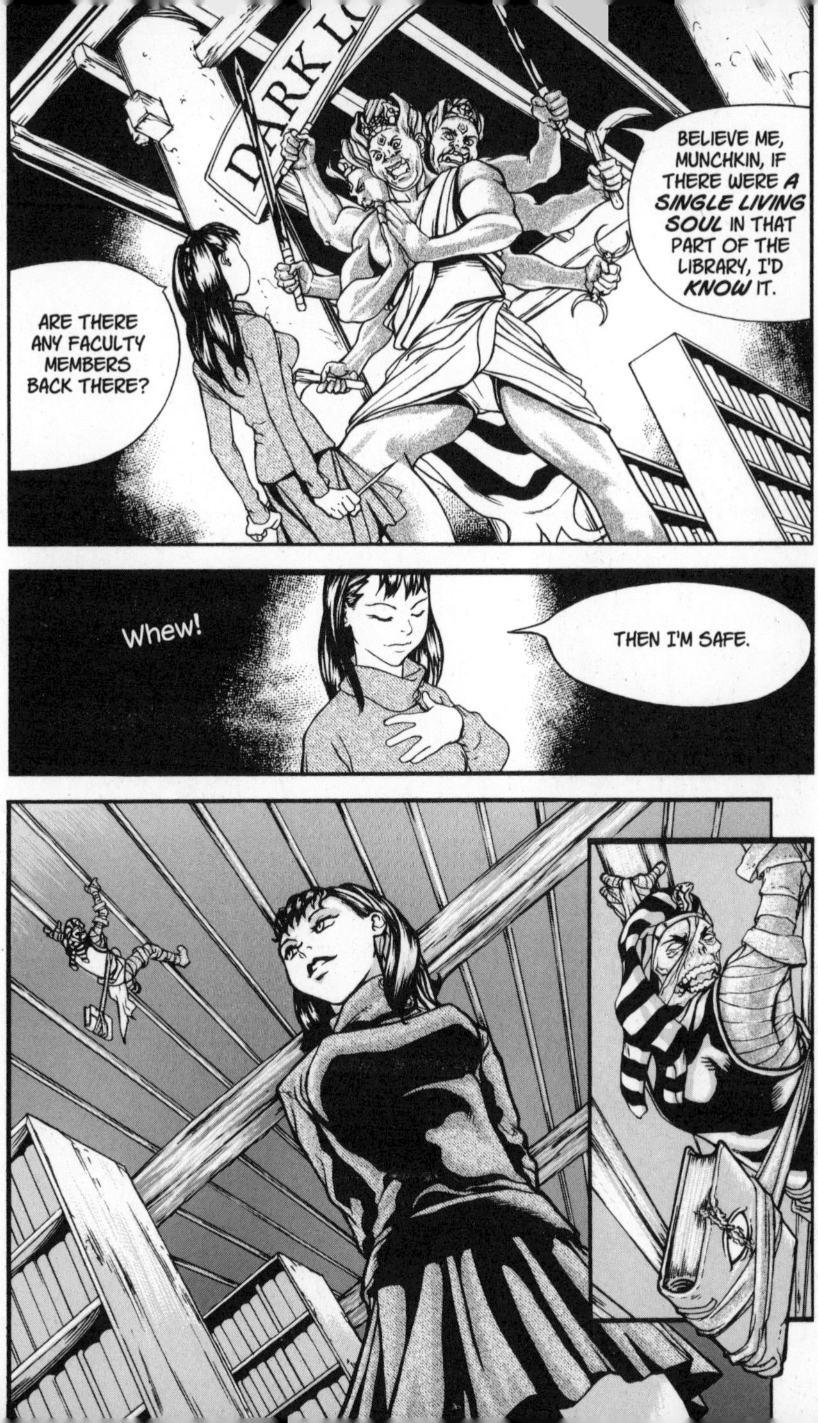
DARK L
ARE THERE ANY FACULTY MEMBERS BACK THERE?
BELIEVE ME, MUNCHKIN, IF THERE WERE A SINGLE LIVING SOUL IN THAT PART OF THE LIBRARY, I'D KNOW IT.
Whew!
THEN I'M SAFE.

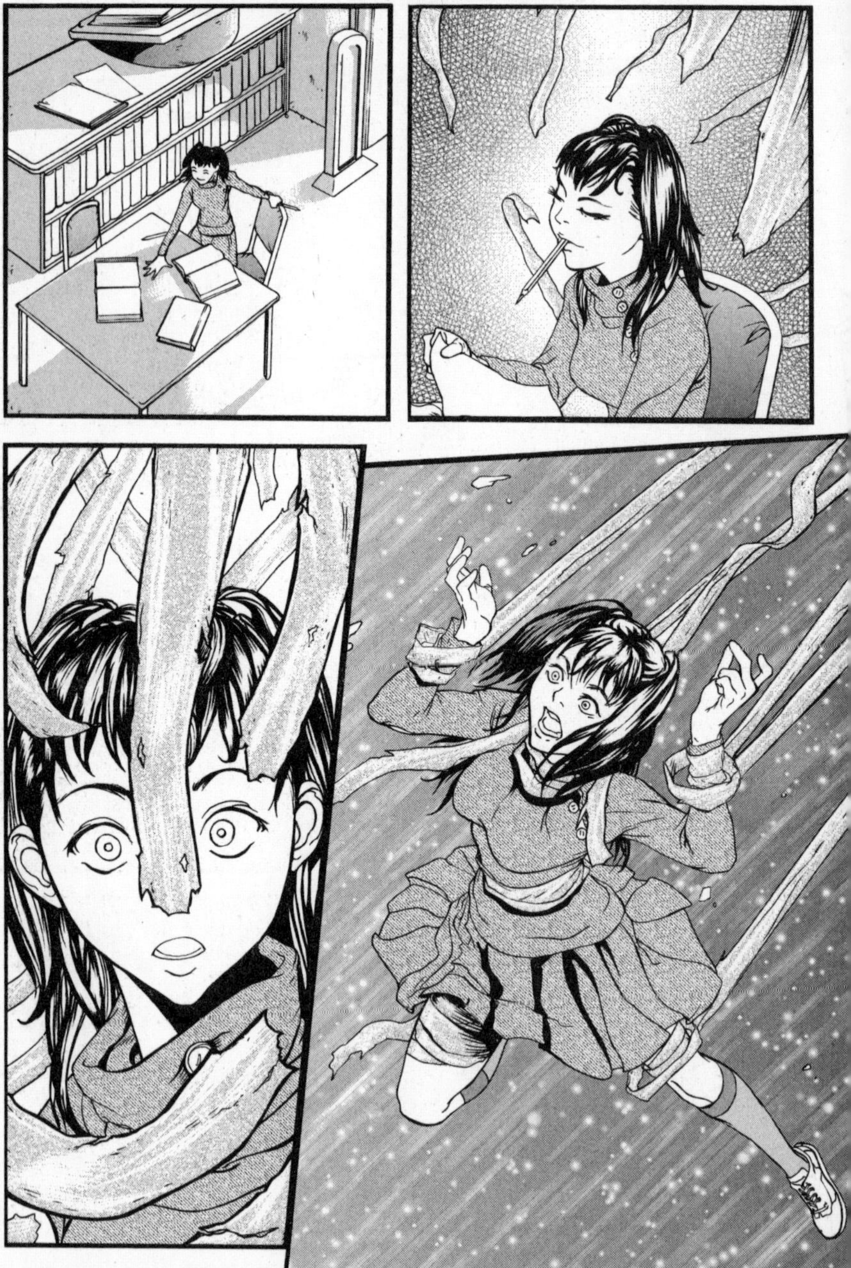

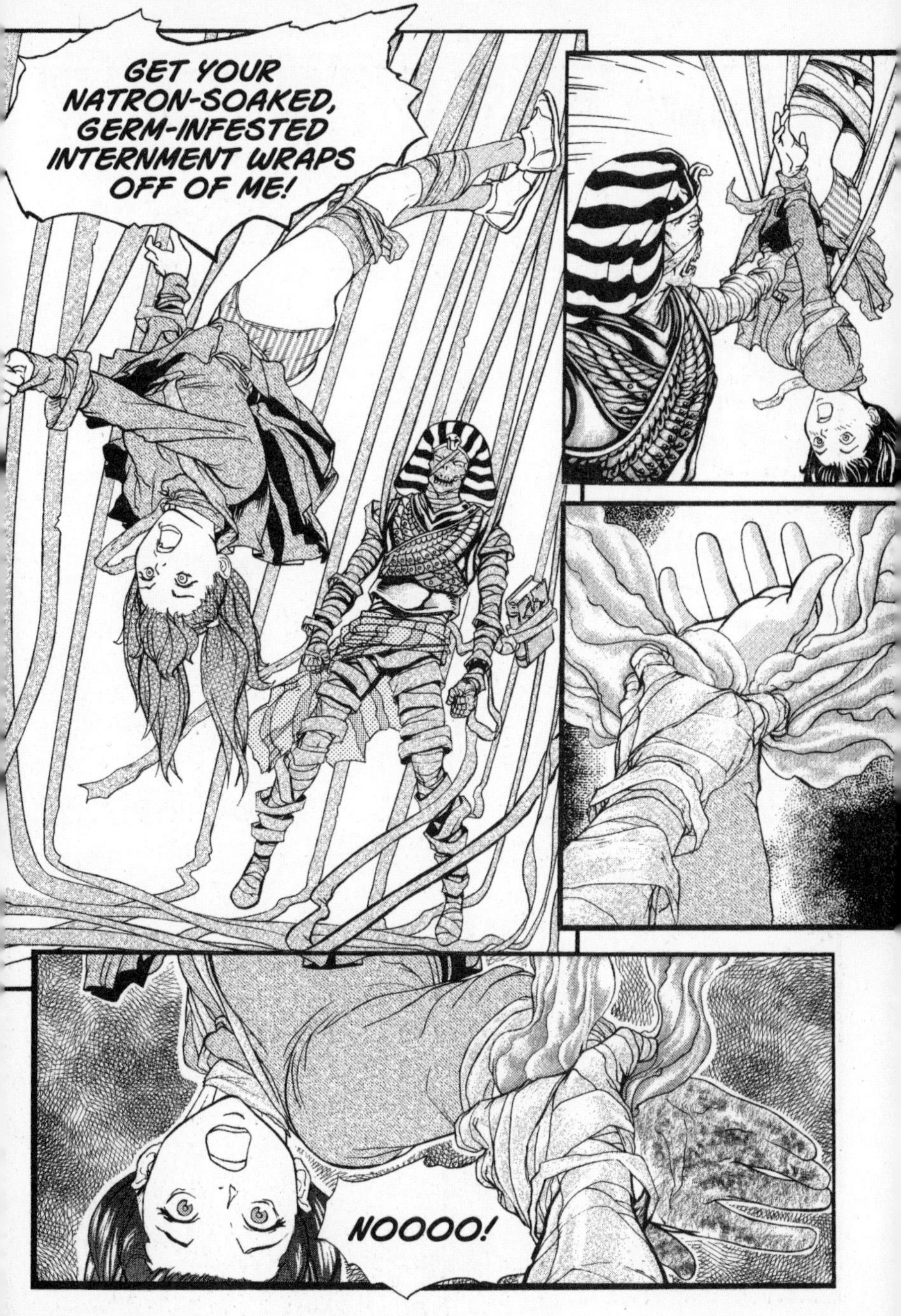
GET YOUR NATRON-SOAKED, GERM-INFESTED INTERNMENT WRAPS OFF OF ME!
NOOOO!

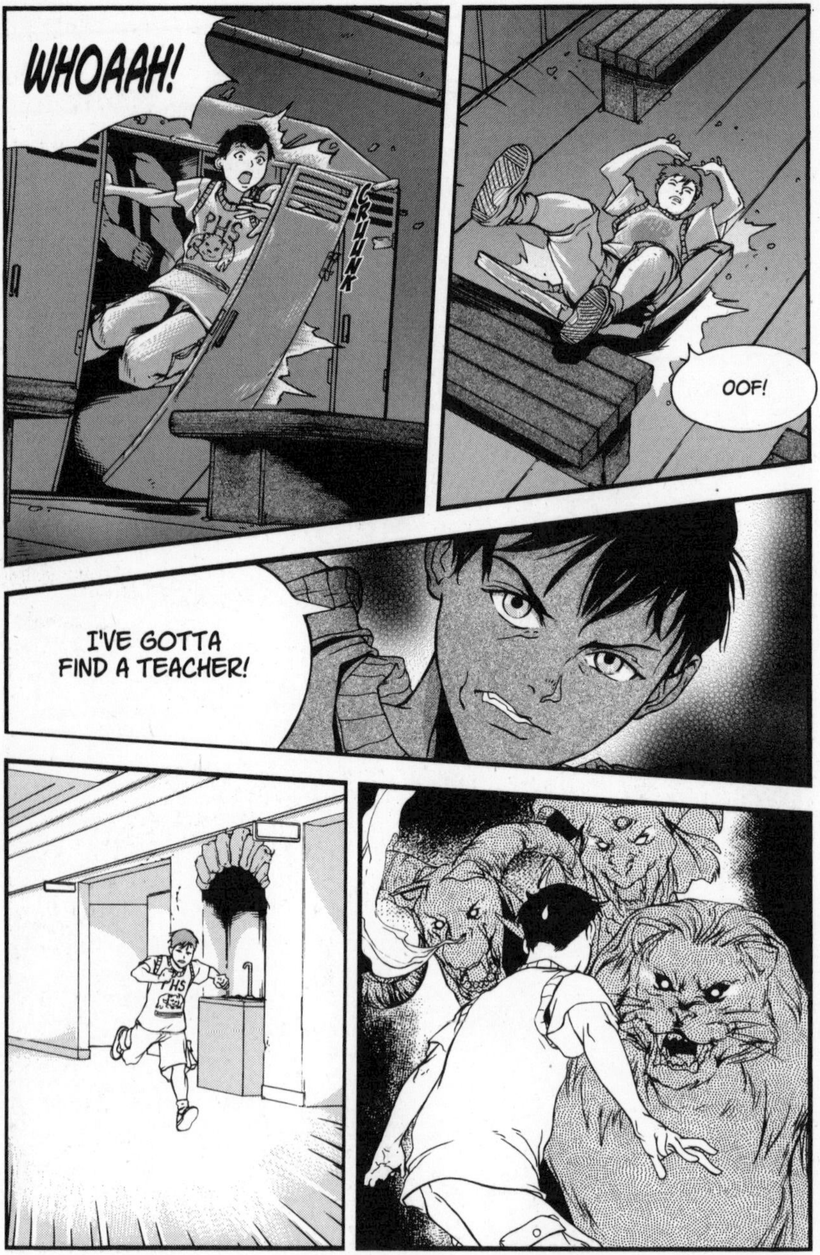
WHOAAH!
CRUUNK
OOF!
I'VE GOTTA FIND A TEACHER!

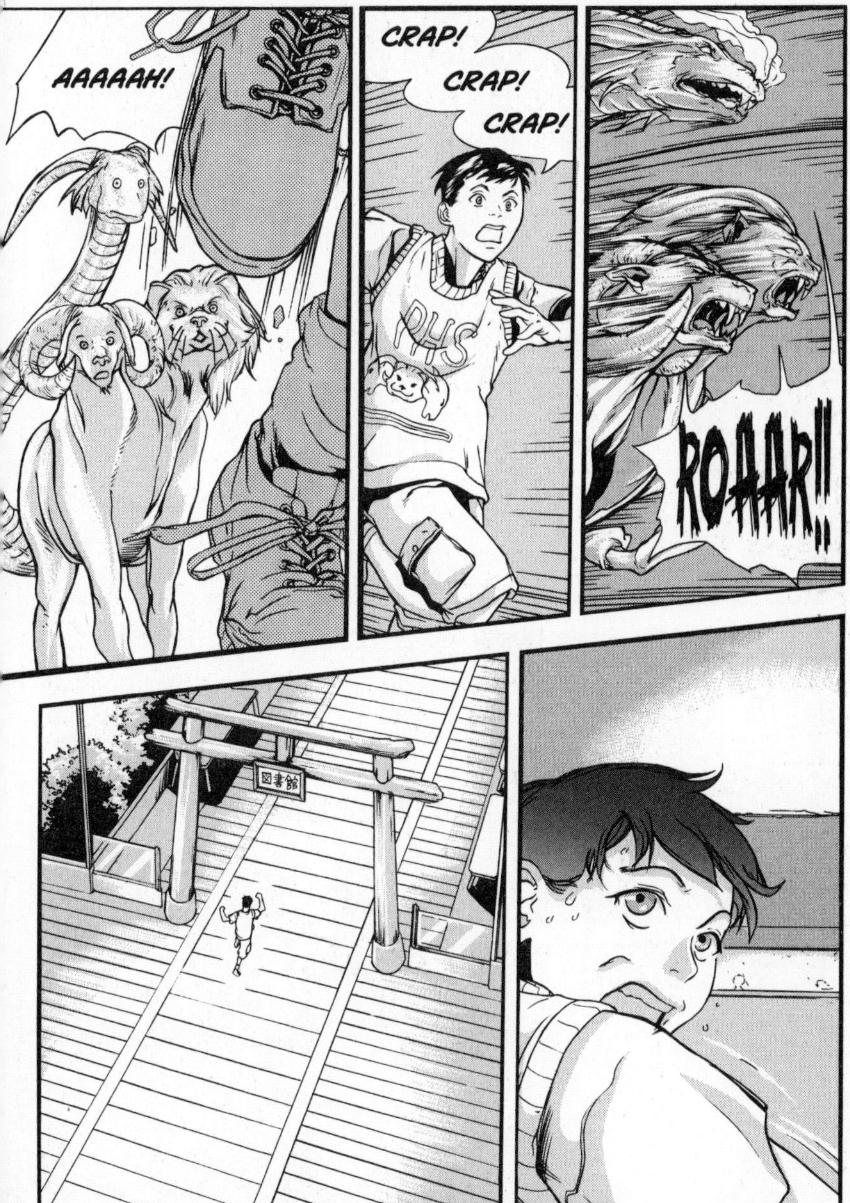
AAAAAH!
CRAP!
CRAP!
CRAP!
ROAAR!!
図書館

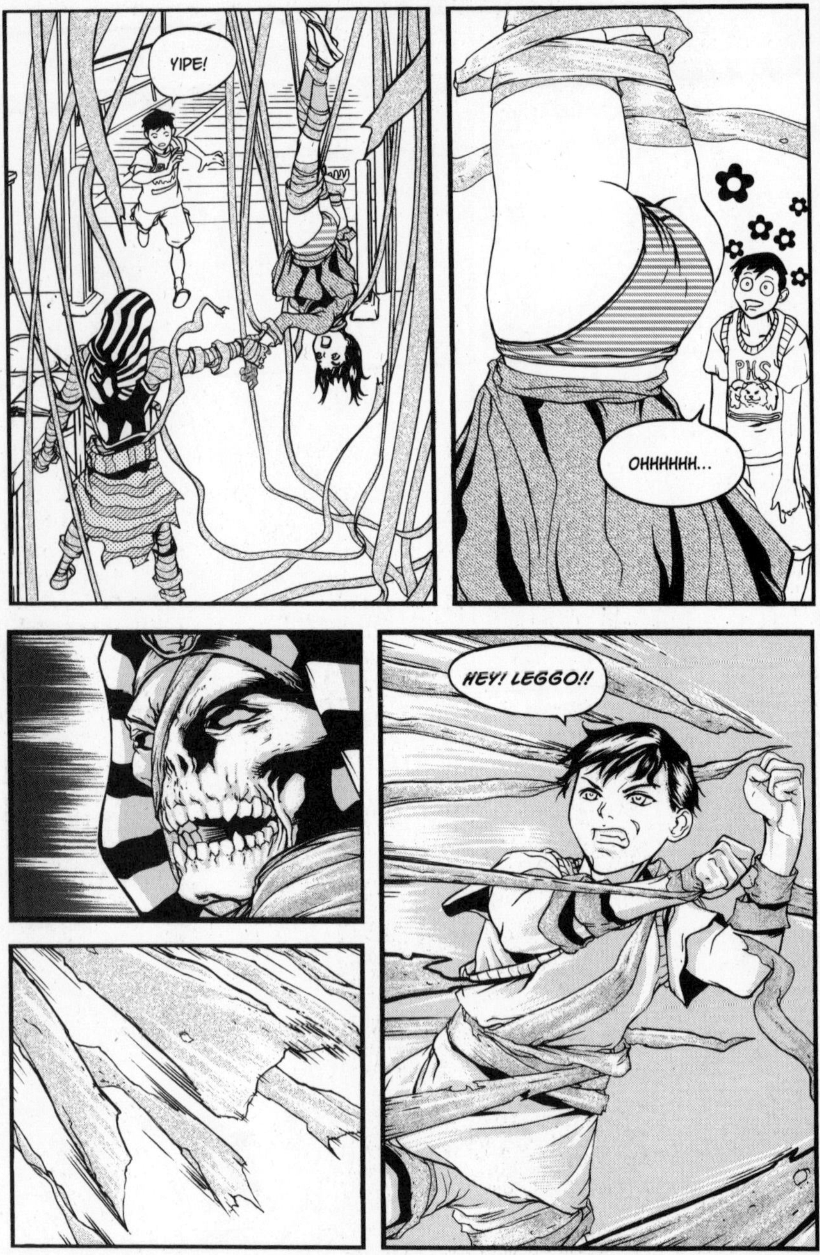
YIPE!
OHHHHHH...
HEY! LEGGO!!

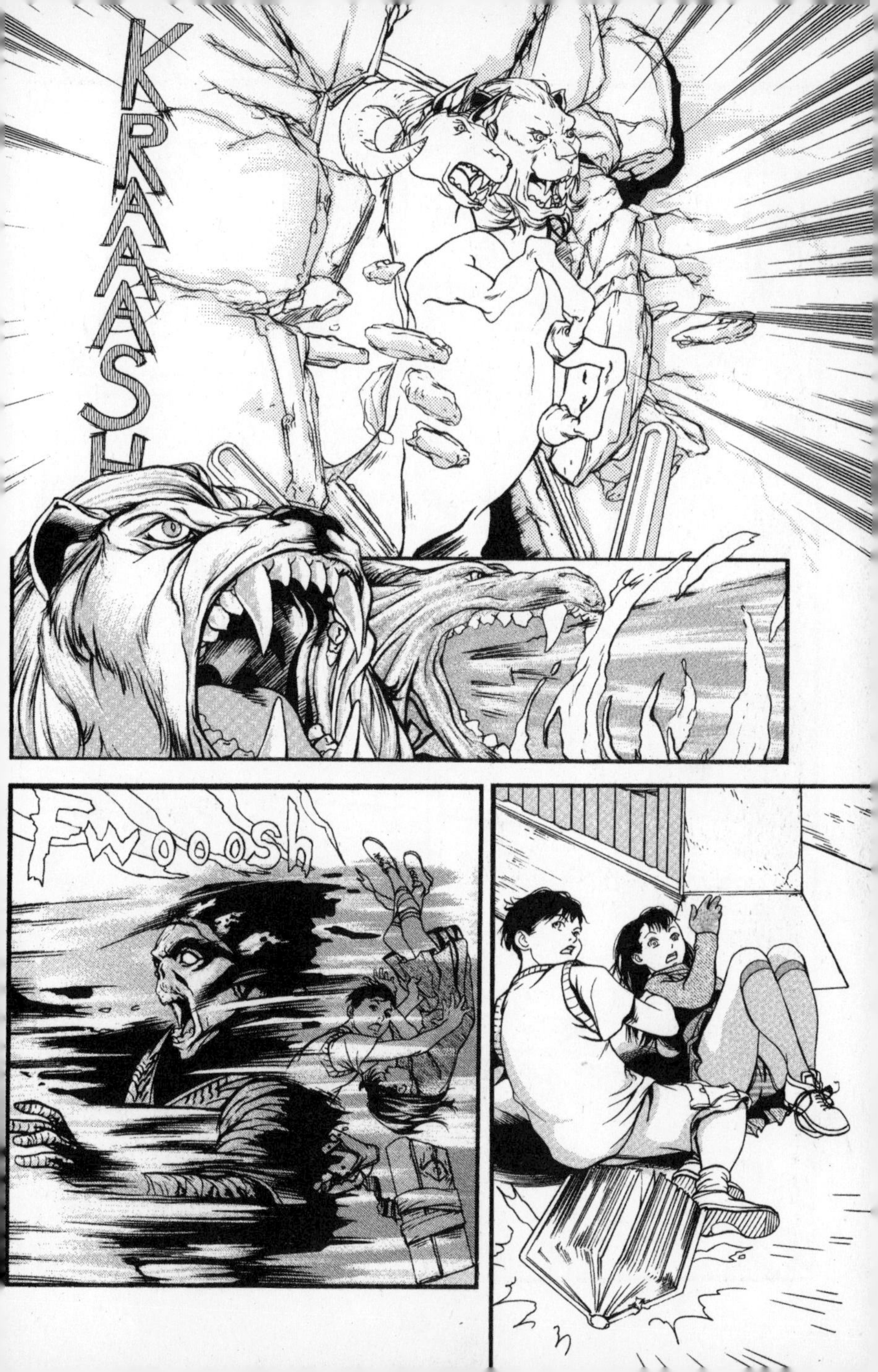
KRAAAASH
Fwooosh

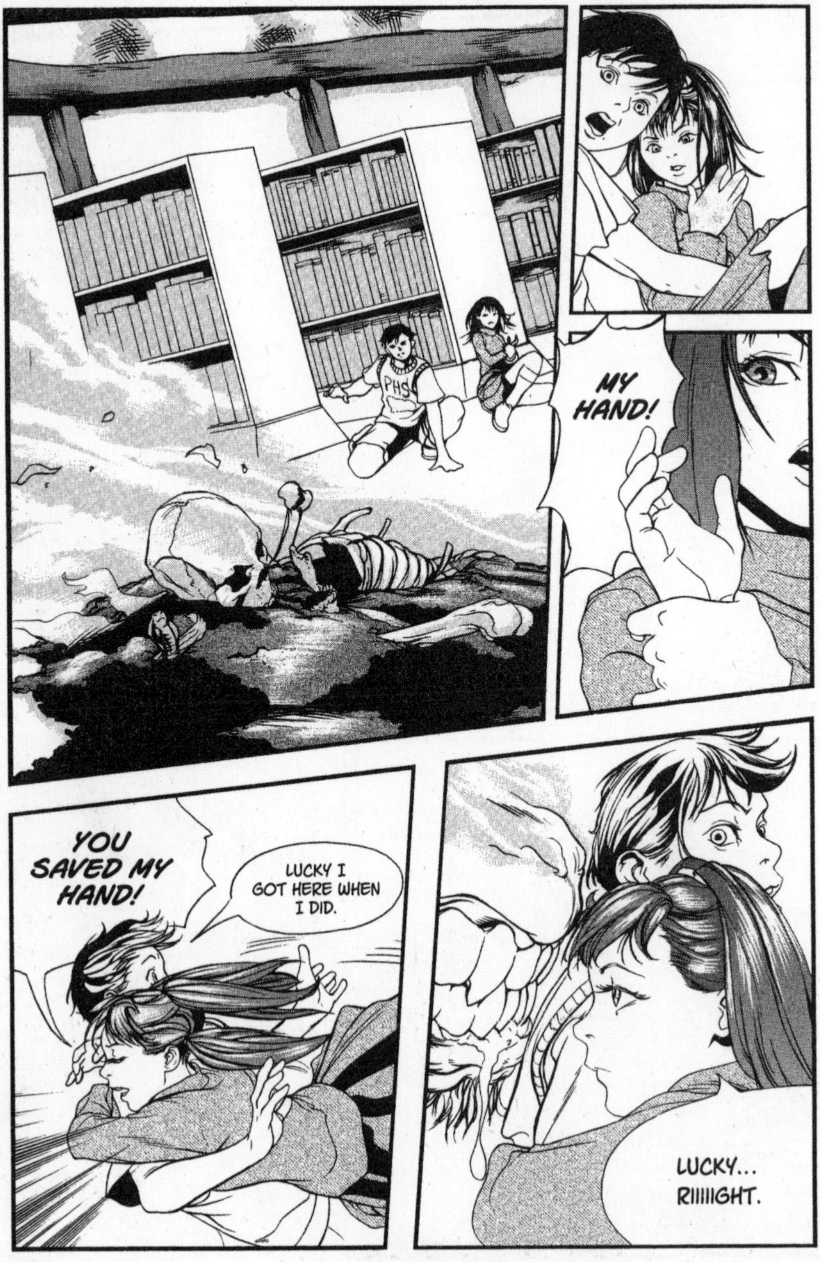
MY HAND!
YOU SAVED MY HAND!
LUCKY I GOT HERE WHEN I DID.
LUCKY... RIIIIGHT.

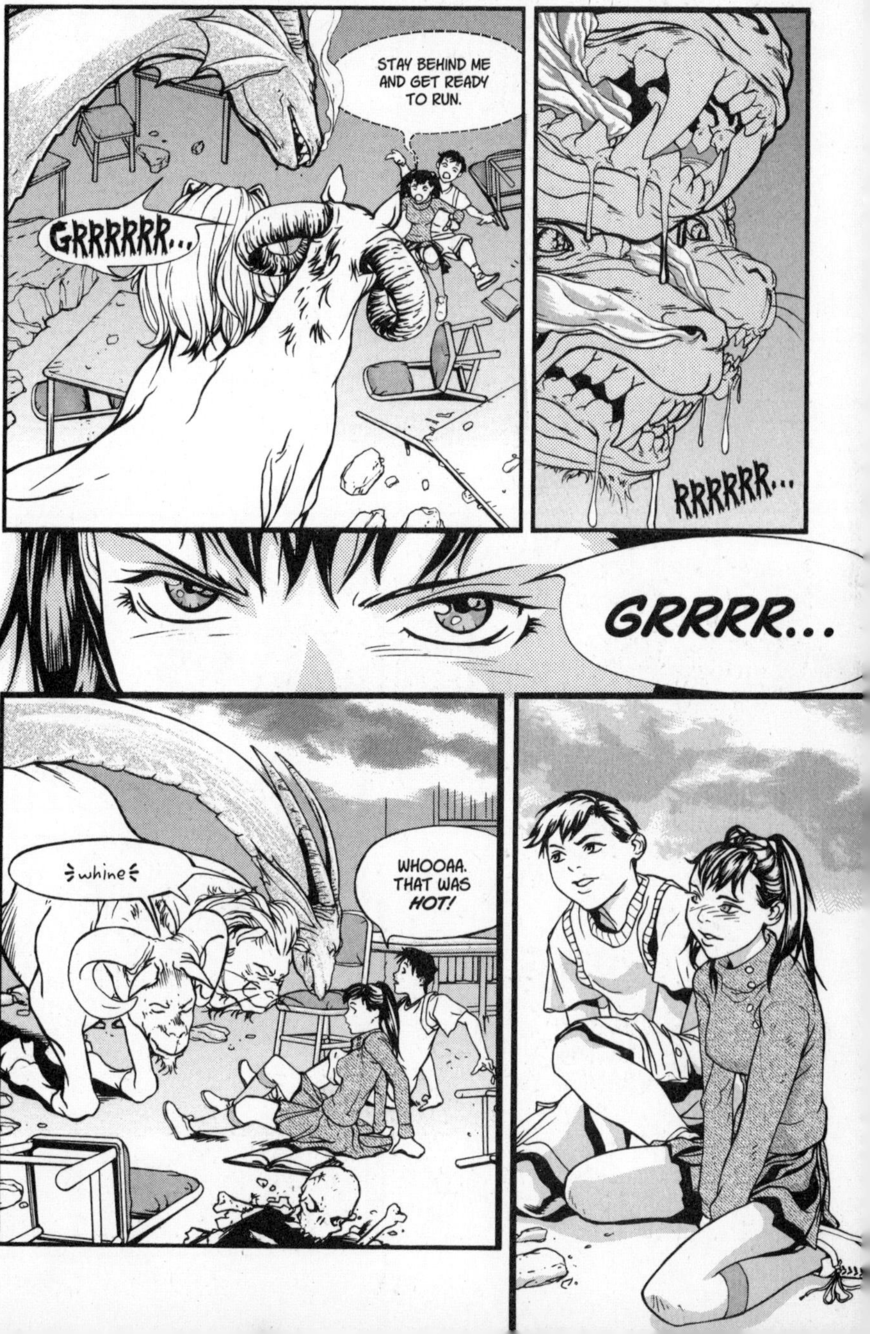
STAY BEHIND ME AND GET READY TO RUN.
GRRRRRR...
RRRRRR...
GRRRR...
whine
WHOOAA. THAT WAS HOT!

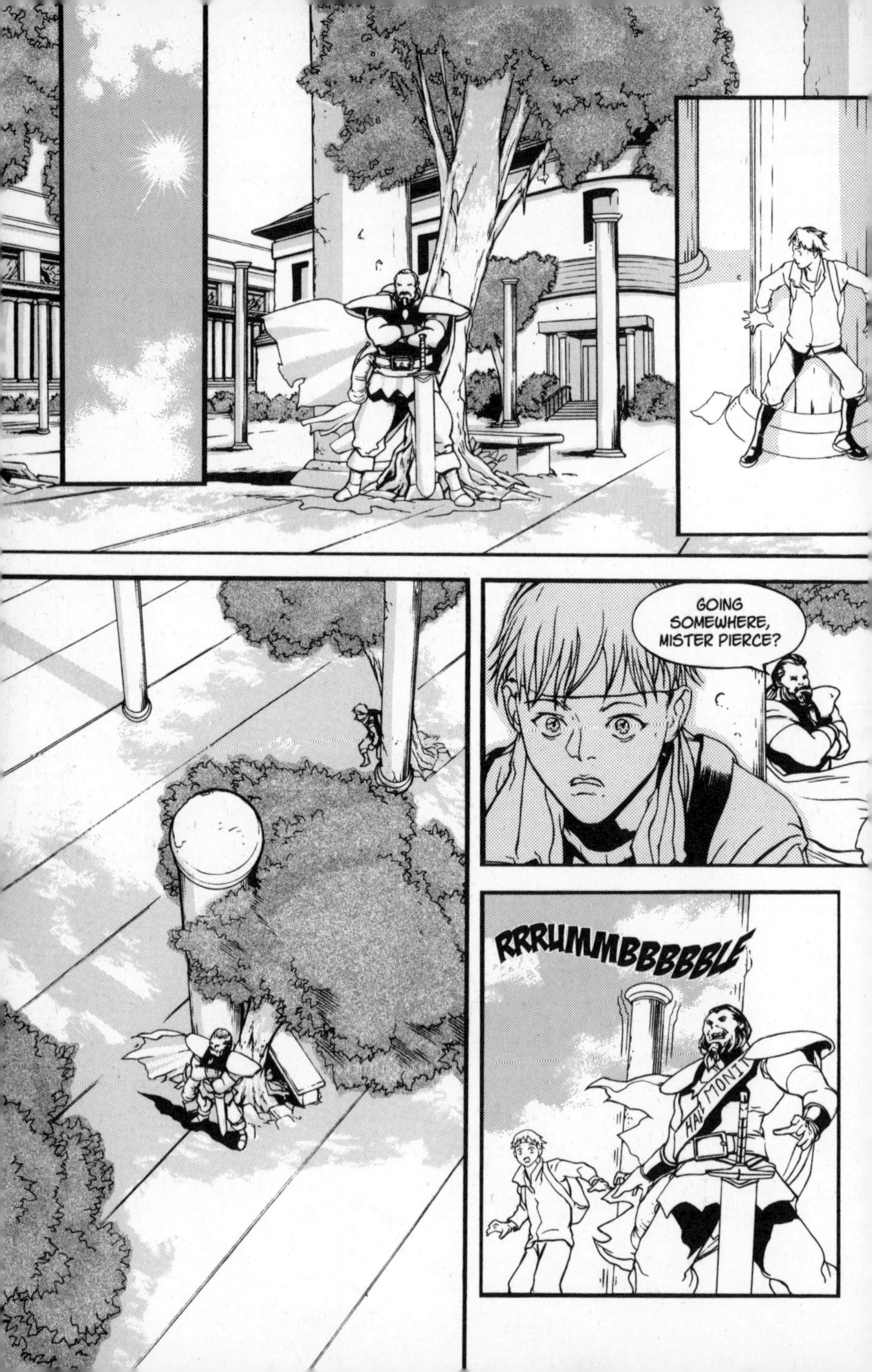
GOING SOMEWHERE, MISTER PIERCE?
RRRUMMMBBBBBLE

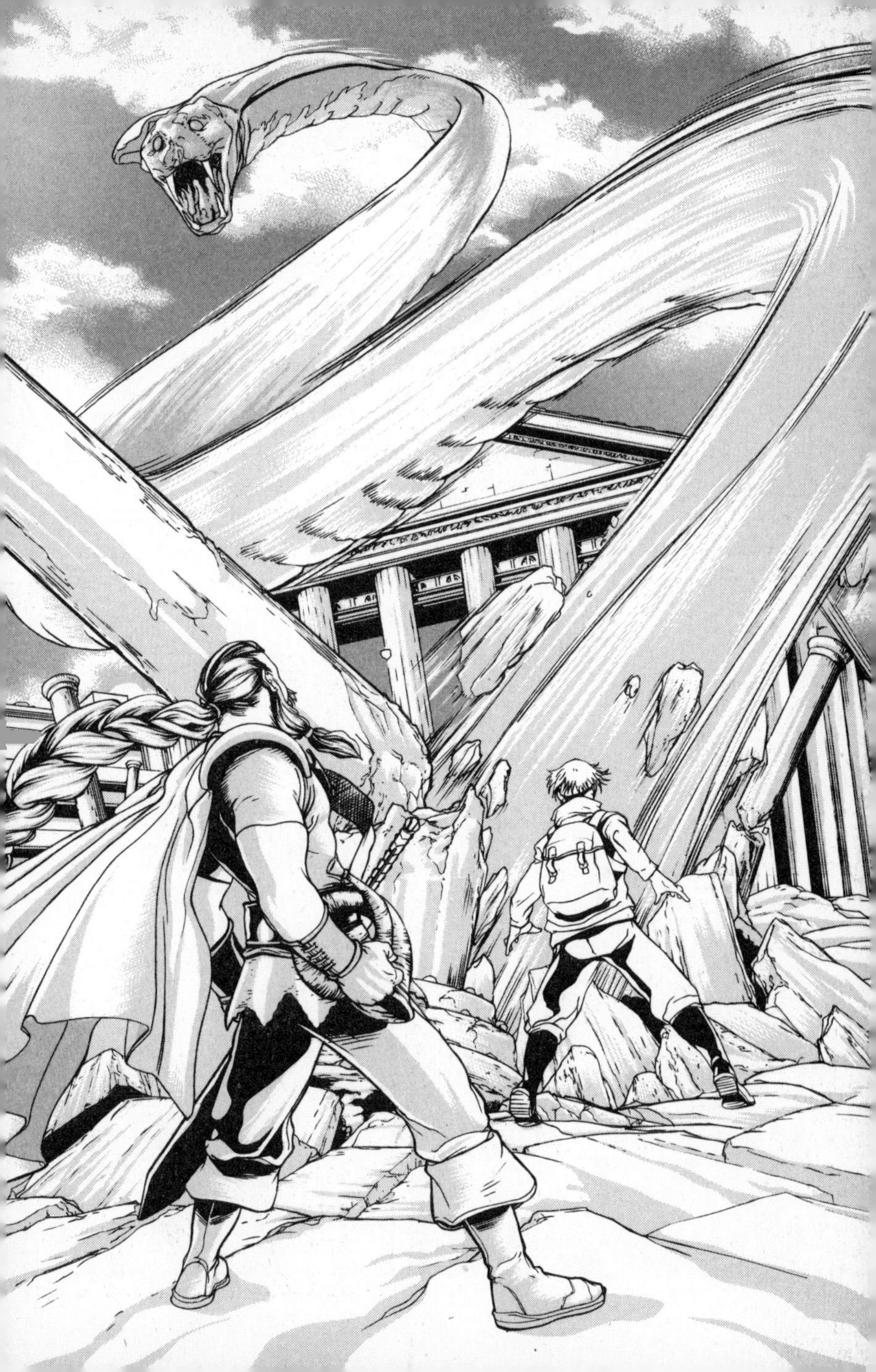

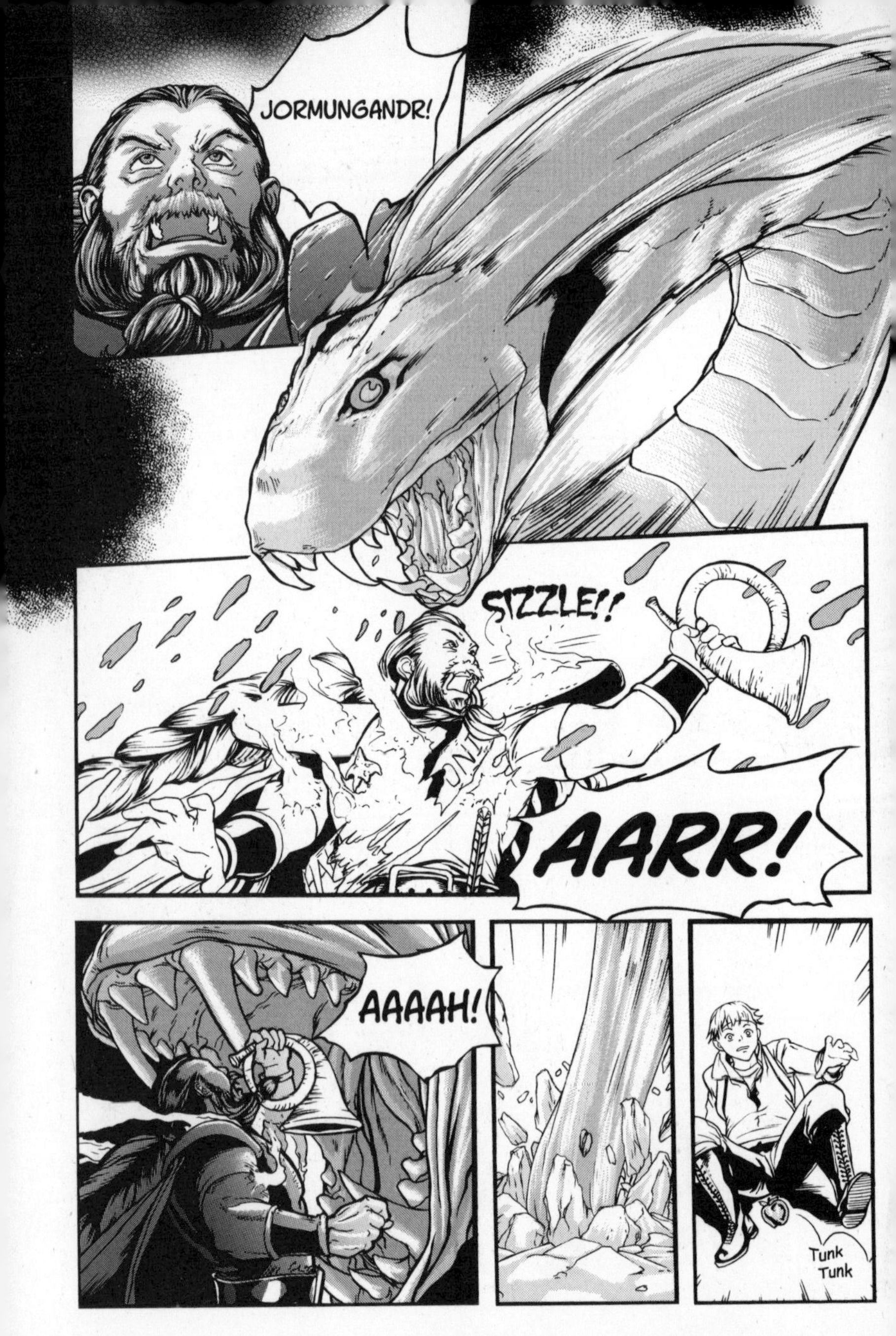
JORMUNGANDR!
SIZZLE!!
AARR!
AAAAH!
Tunk
Tunk

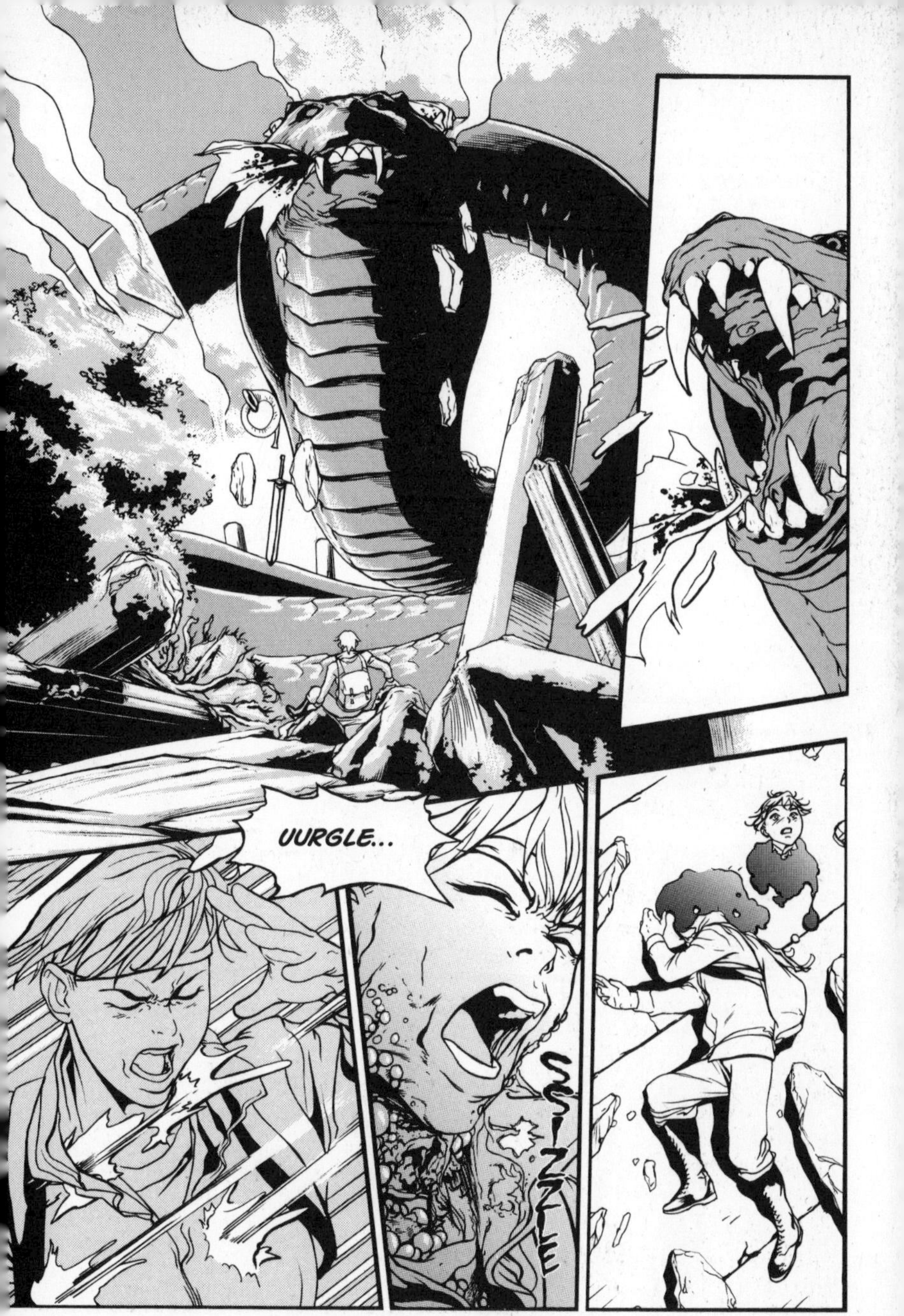
UURGLE...
SSIZZLE

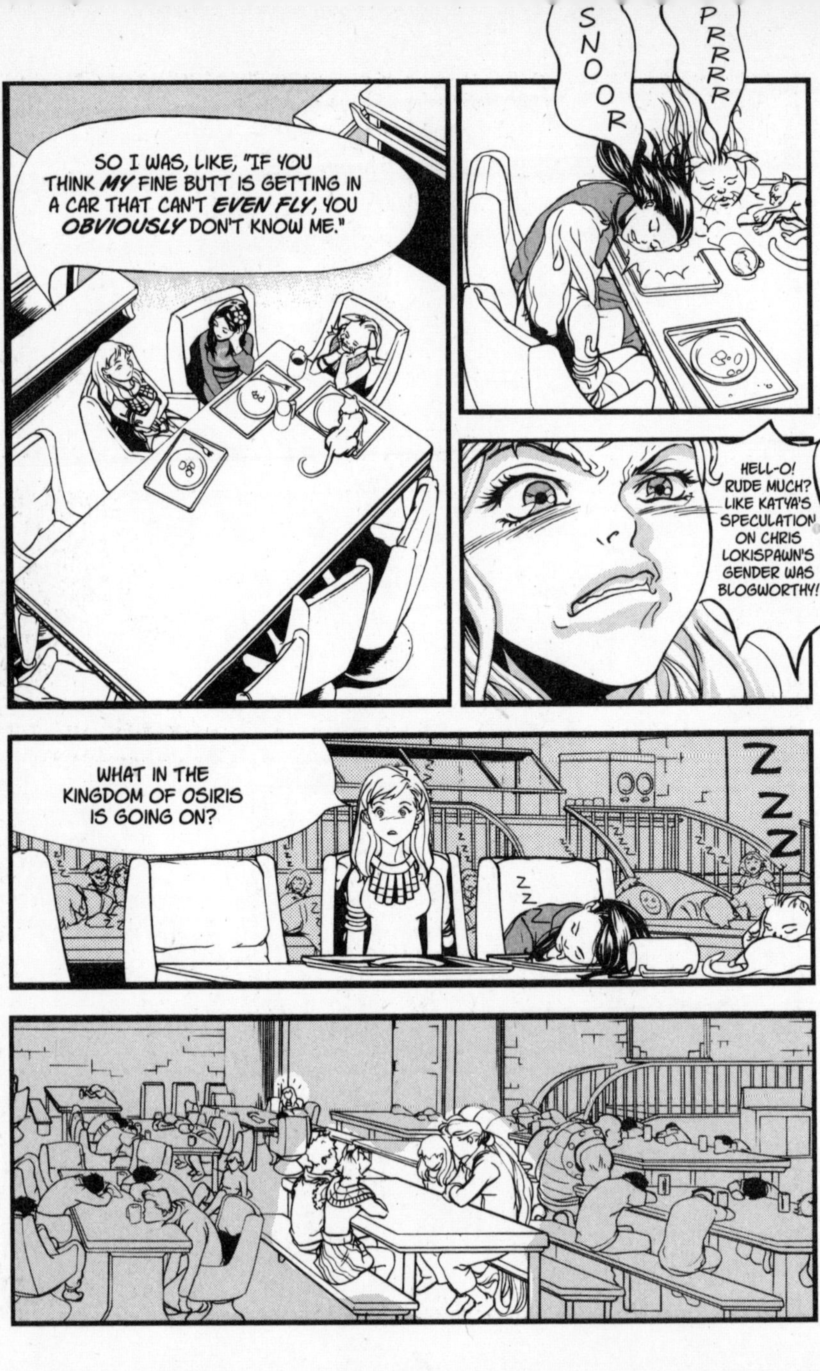
SO I WAS, LIKE, "IF YOU THINK *MY* FINE BUTT IS GETTING IN A CAR THAT CAN'T *EVEN FLY*, YOU *OBVIOUSLY* DON'T KNOW ME."
SNOOR
PRRRR
HELL-O! RUDE MUCH? LIKE KATYA'S SPECULATION ON CHRIS LOKISPAWN'S GENDER WAS BLOGWORTHY!
WHAT IN THE KINGDOM OF OSIRIS IS GOING ON?
ZZZ

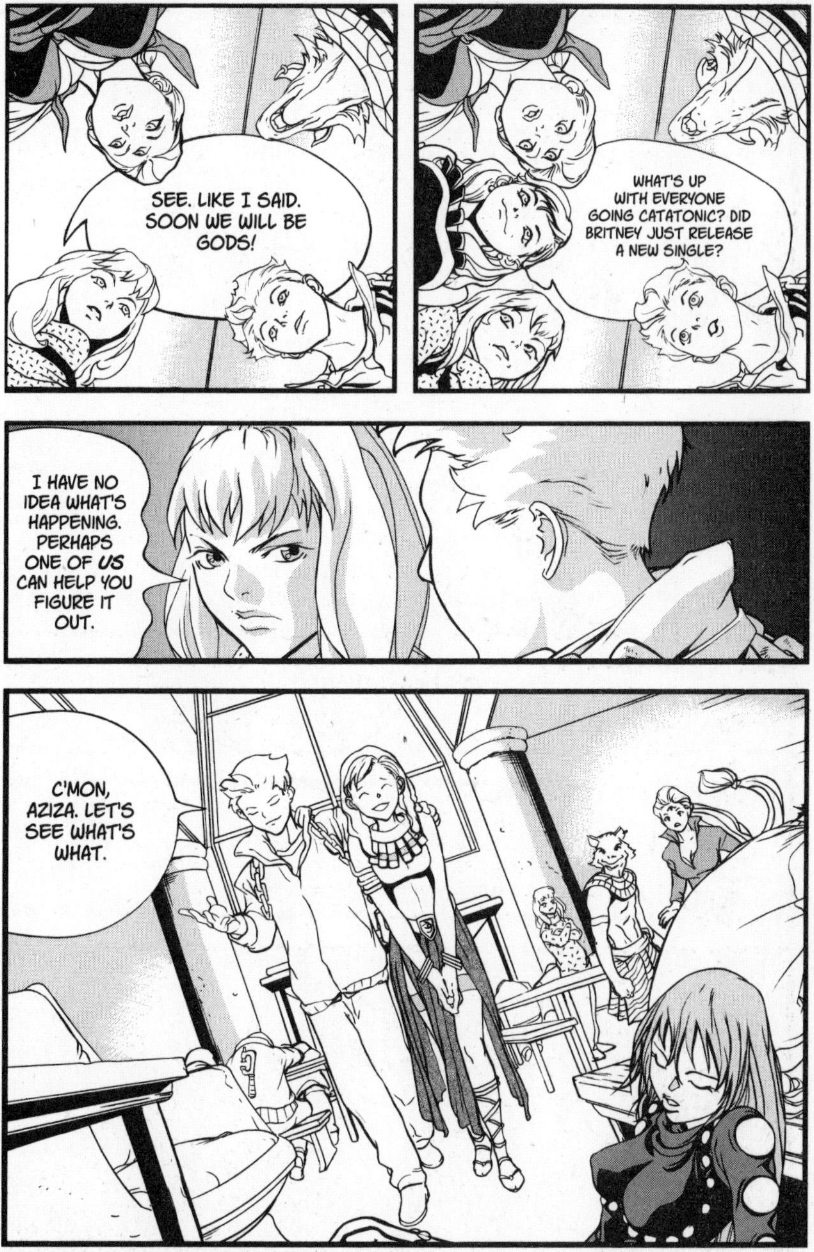
SEE. LIKE I SAID. SOON WE WILL BE GODS!
WHAT'S UP WITH EVERYONE GOING CATATONIC? DID BRITNEY JUST RELEASE A NEW SINGLE?
I HAVE NO IDEA WHAT'S HAPPENING. PERHAPS ONE OF US CAN HELP YOU FIGURE IT OUT.
C'MON, AZIZA. LET'S SEE WHAT'S WHAT.

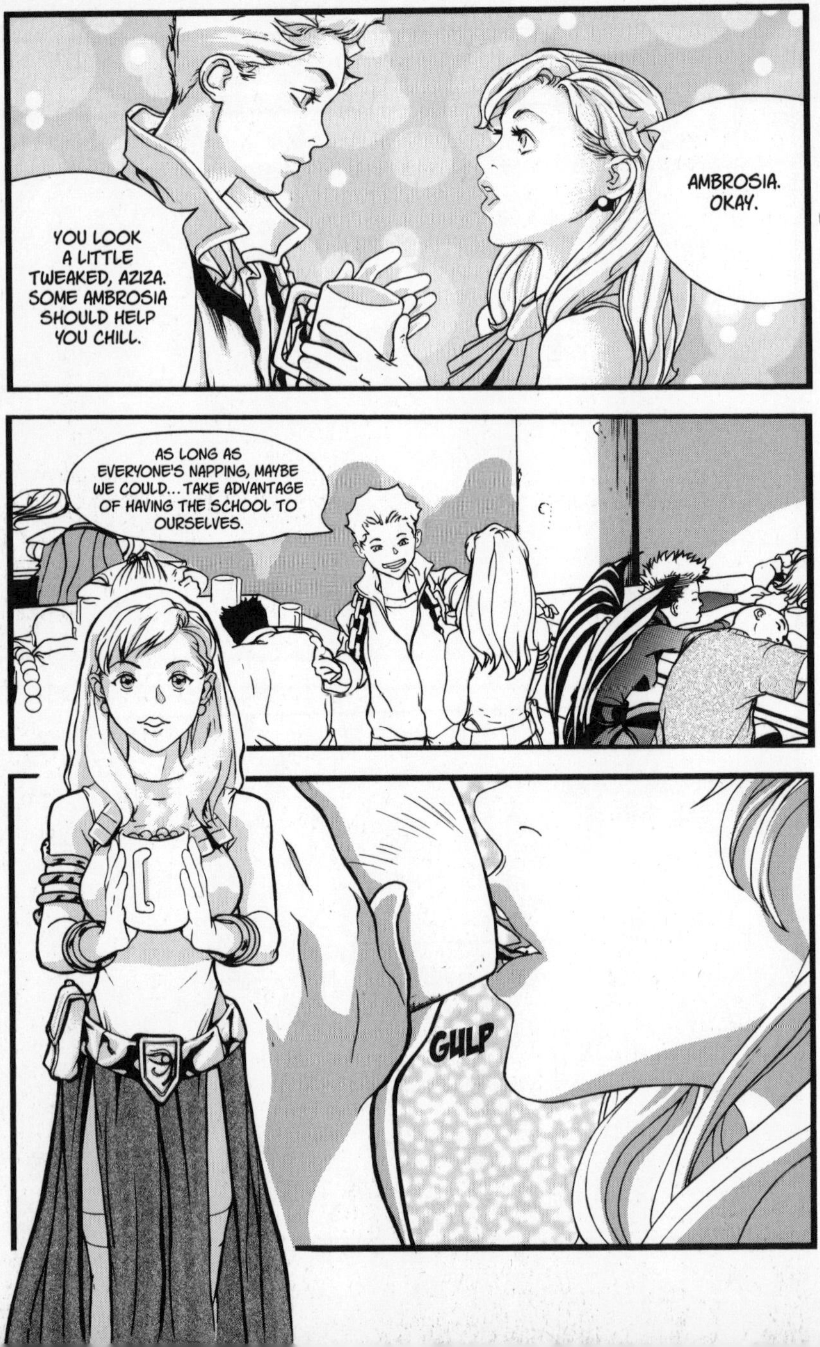
YOU LOOK A LITTLE TWEAKED, AZIZA. SOME AMBROSIA SHOULD HELP YOU CHILL.
AMBROSIA. OKAY.
AS LONG AS EVERYONE'S NAPPING, MAYBE WE COULD... TAKE ADVANTAGE OF HAVING THE SCHOOL TO OURSELVES.
GULP

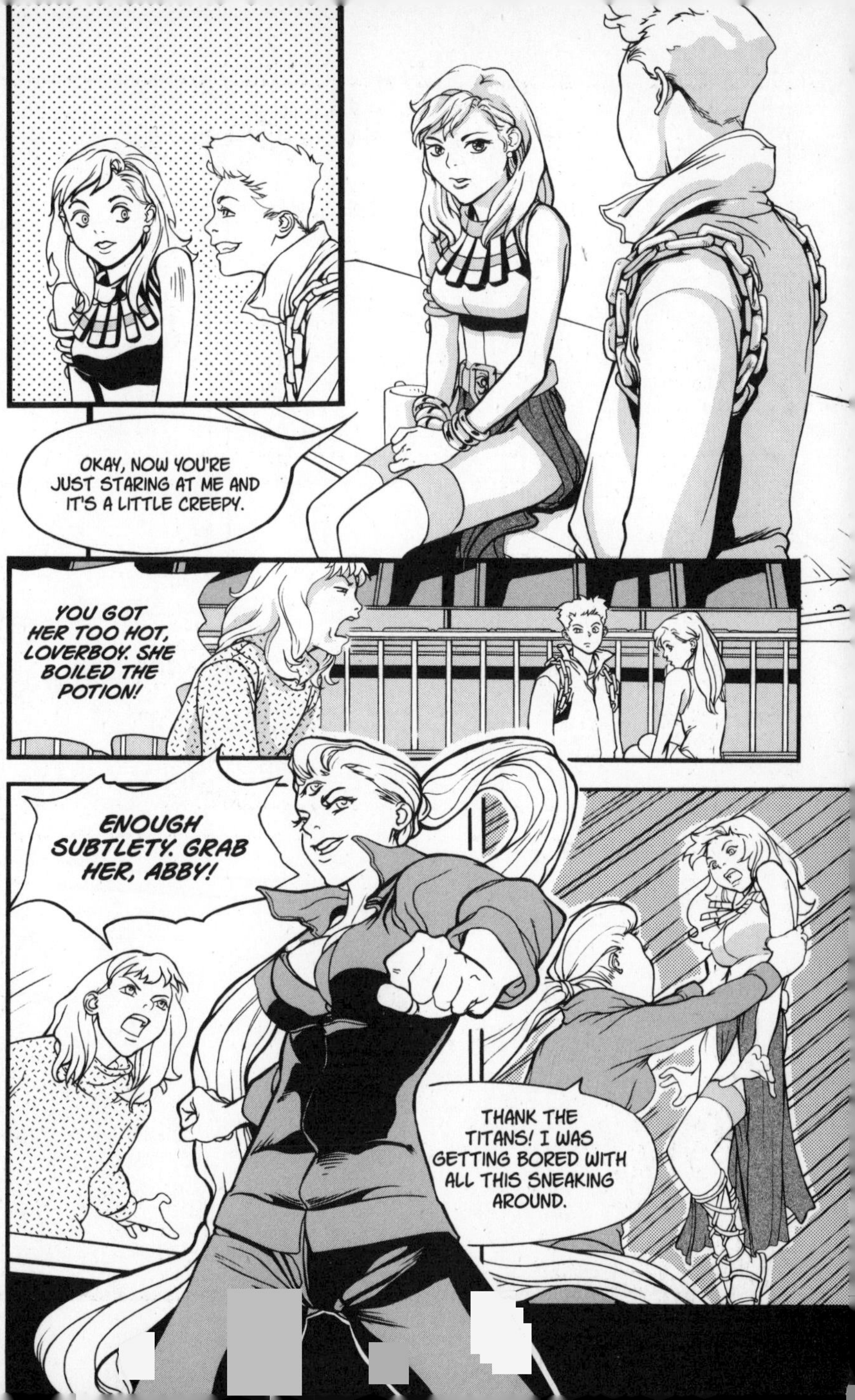
OKAY, NOW YOU'RE JUST STARING AT ME AND IT'S A LITTLE CREEPY.
YOU GOT HER TOO HOT, LOVERBOY. SHE BOILED THE POTION!
ENOUGH SUBTLETY. GRAB HER, ABBY!
THANK THE TITANS! I WAS GETTING BORED WITH ALL THIS SNEAKING AROUND.

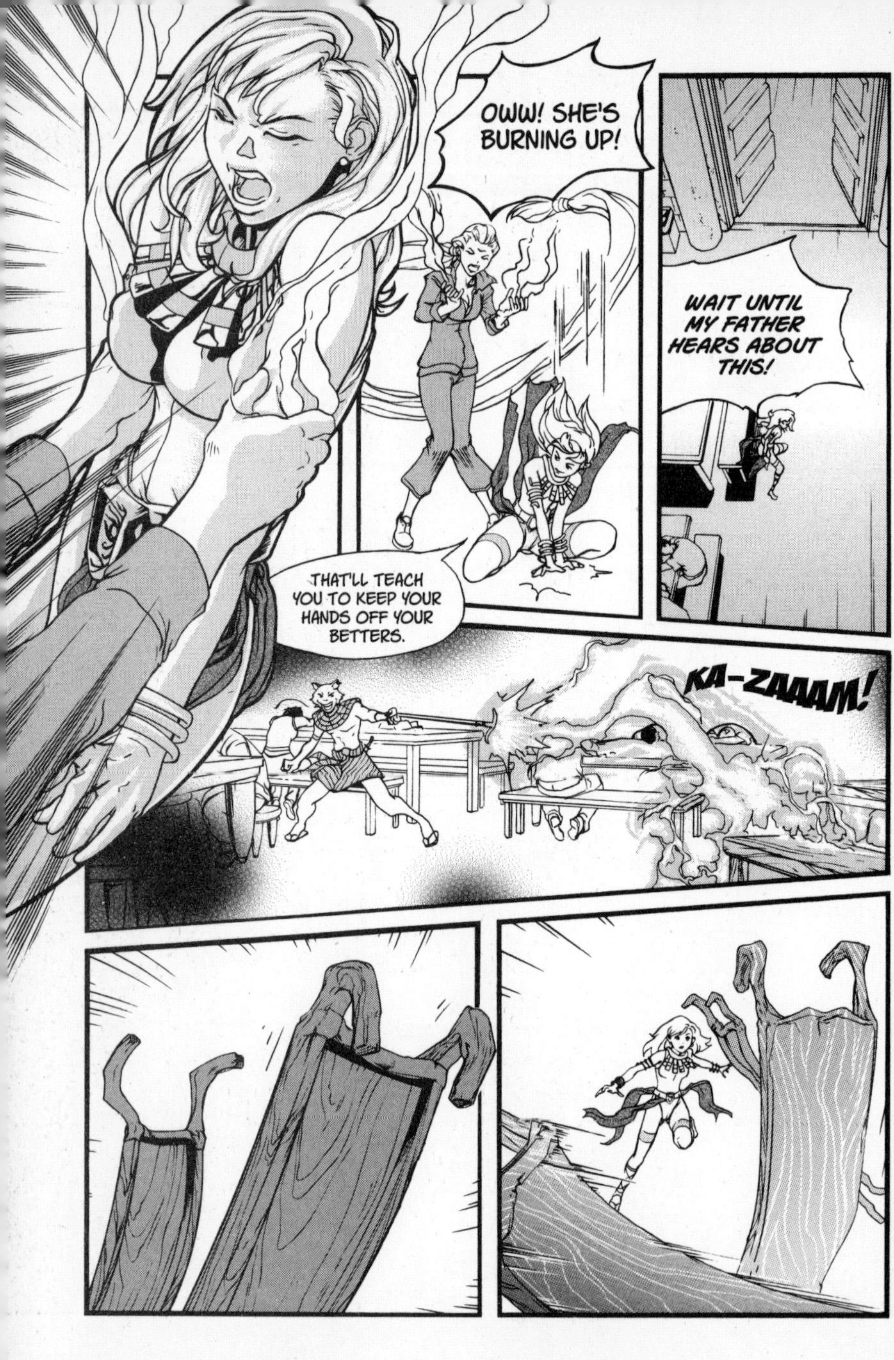
OWW! SHE'S BURNING UP!
THAT'LL TEACH YOU TO KEEP YOUR HANDS OFF YOUR BETTERS.
WAIT UNTIL MY FATHER HEARS ABOUT THIS!
KA-ZAAAM!

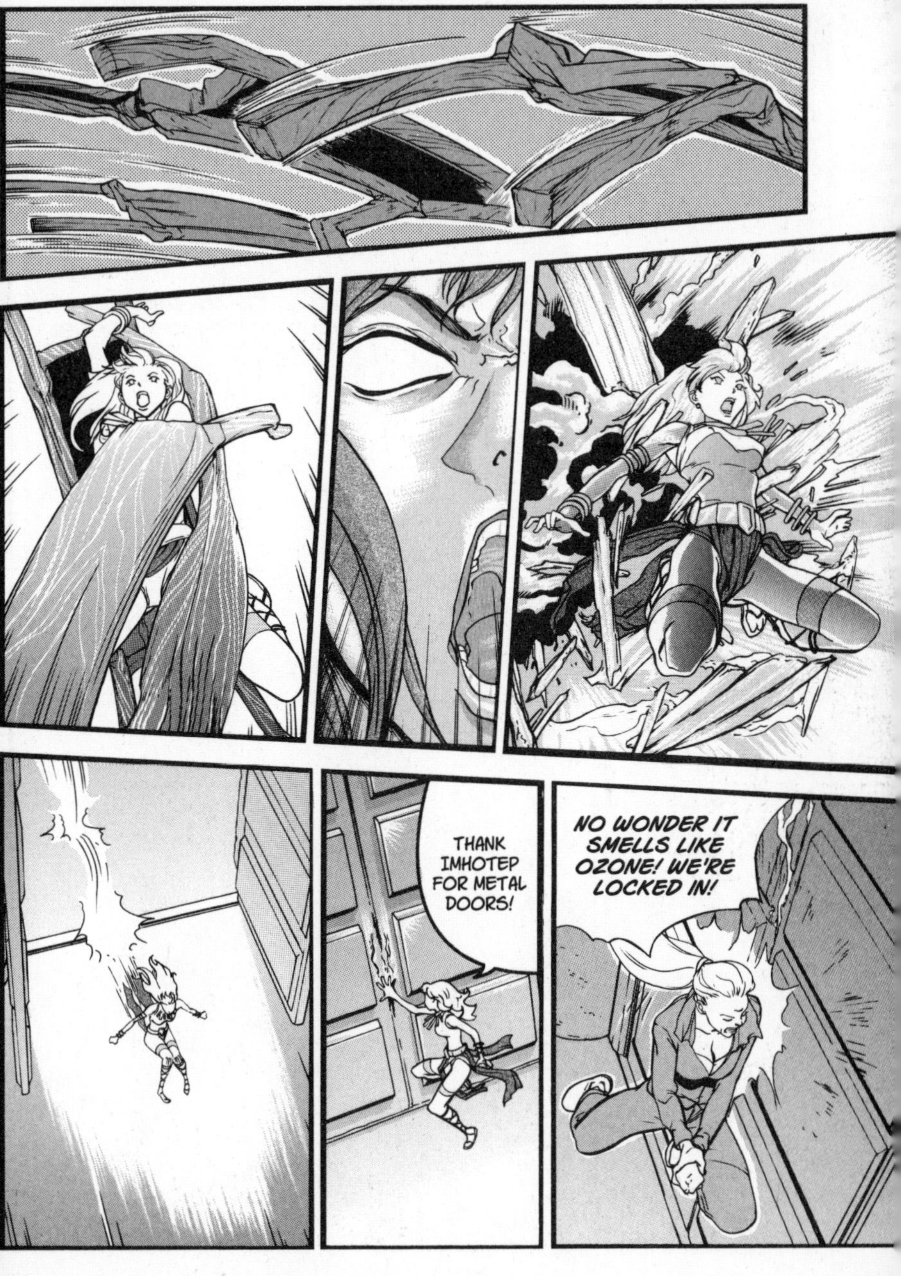
THANK IMHOTEP FOR METAL DOORS!
NO WONDER IT SMELLS LIKE OZONE! WE'RE LOCKED IN!

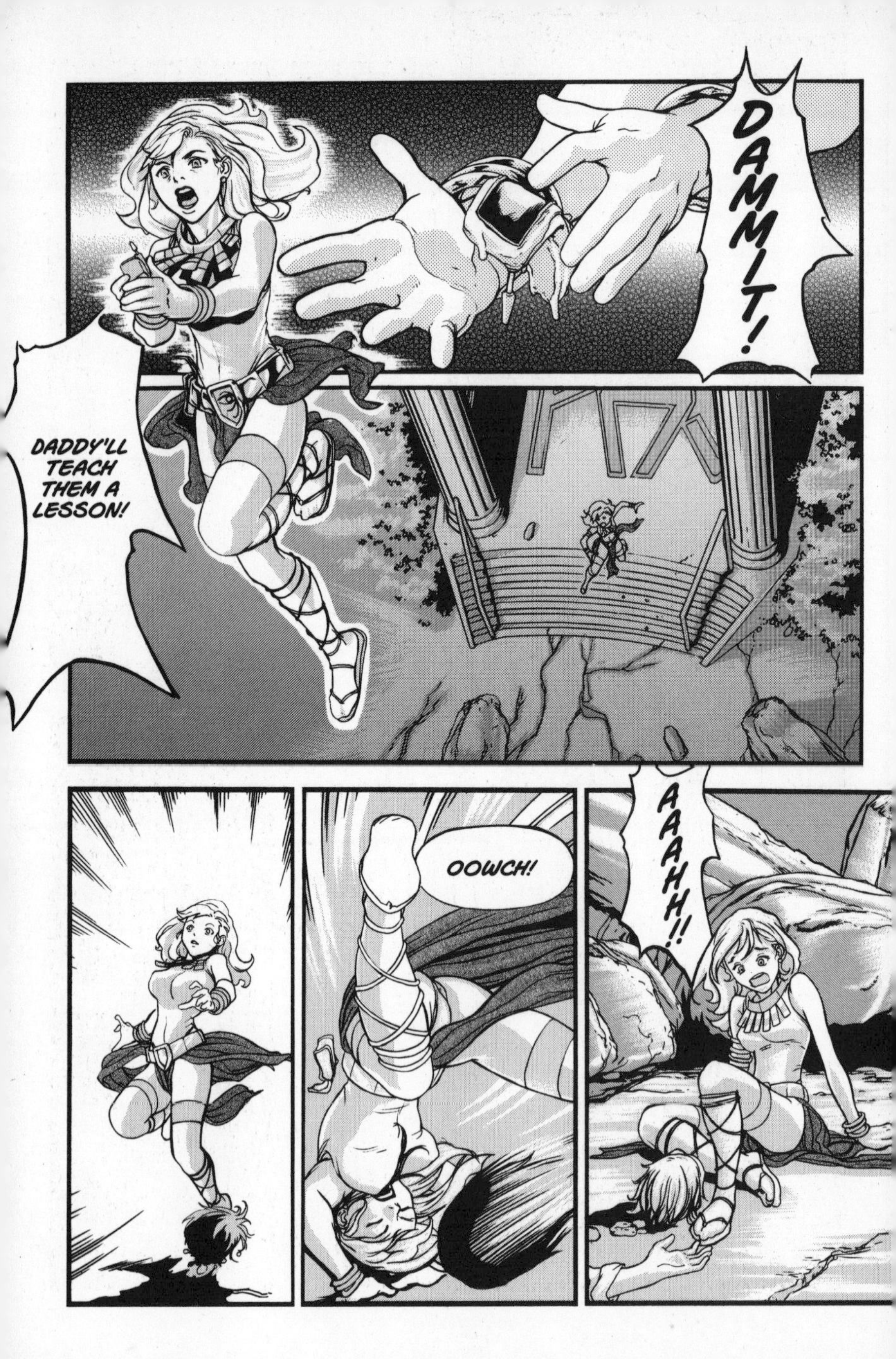
DAMMIT!
DADDY'LL TEACH THEM A LESSON!
OOWCH!
AAAHH!!

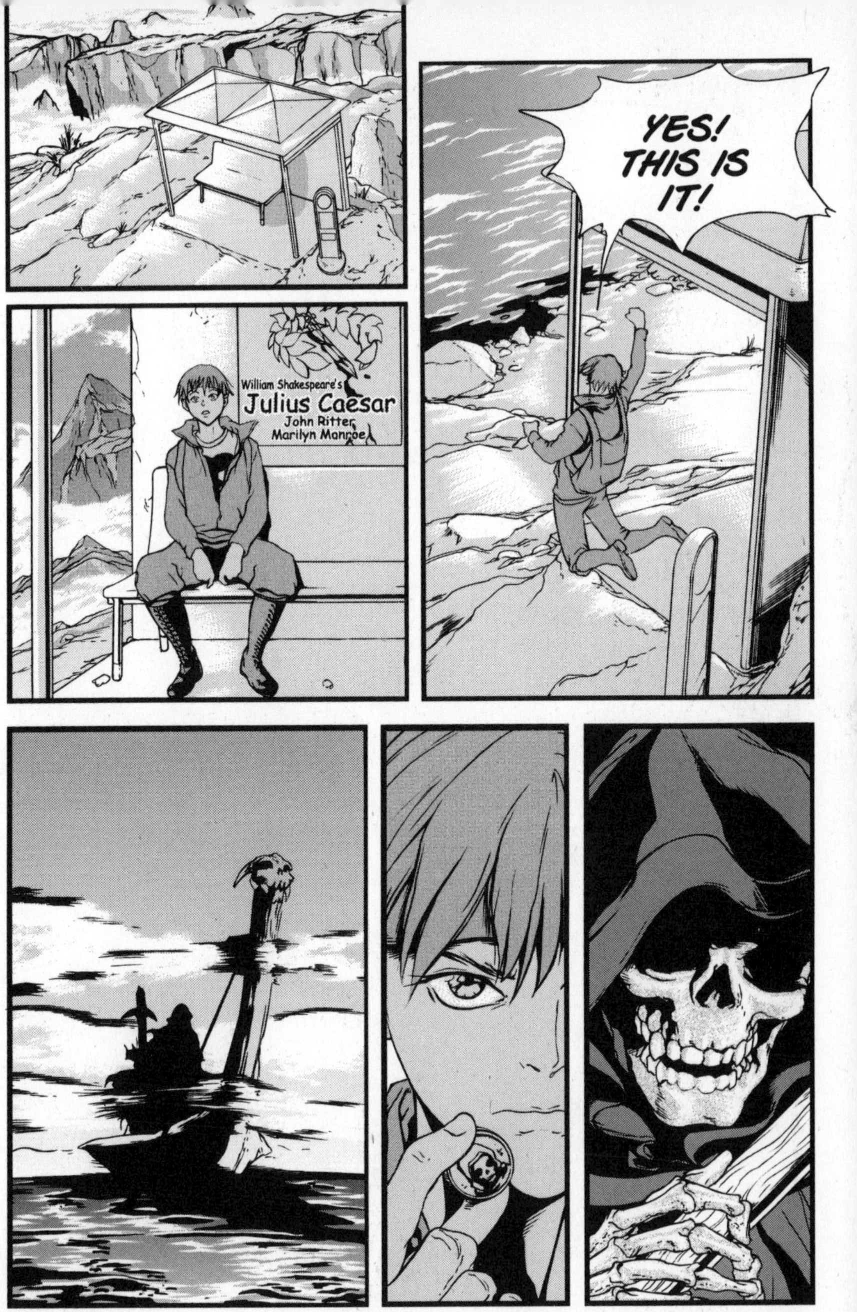
William Shakespeare's
Julius Caesar
John Ritter, Marilyn Monroe
YES! THIS IS IT!

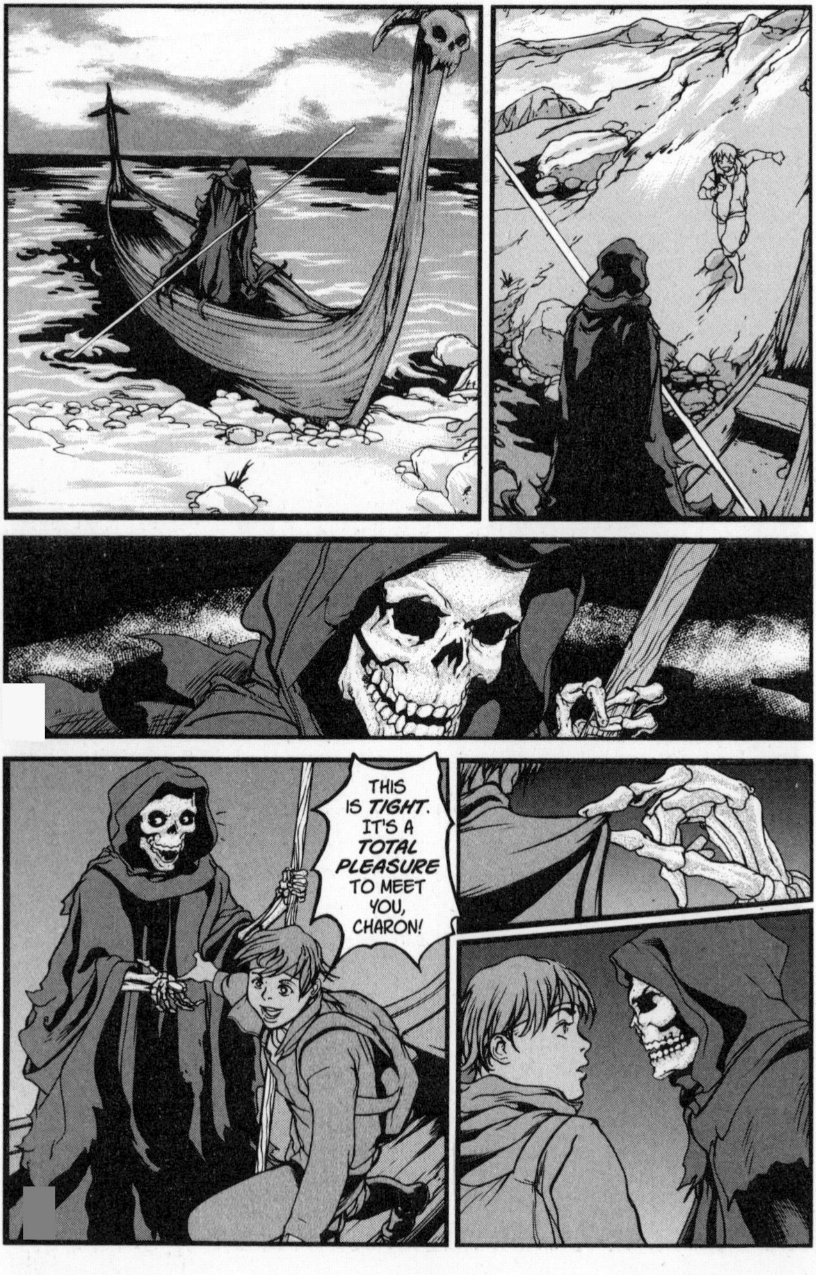
THIS IS TIGHT. IT'S A TOTAL PLEASURE TO MEET YOU, CHARON!

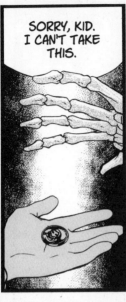

SORRY, KID. I CAN'T TAKE THIS.

IT'S YOUR *JOB* TO TAKE IT. LET'S HIT THE STYX.

NO CAN DO. *I'VE GOT MY ORDERS.*

SCREW YOUR ORDERS! DO YOU *KNOW* WHO I AM?

I KNOW *EXACTLY* WHO YOU ARE. *THAT'S* WHY I CAN'T LET YOU INTO HADES.

BUT I JUST WANT TO BE WITH MY PARENTS.

LOOK, KID, I'M SORRY. YOUR DAD'S A TOUGH BOSS AND I CAN'T AFFORD TO LOSE THIS GIG.

GOOD LUCK UP THERE.

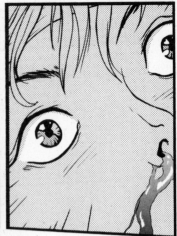

EWWW! GROSS MUCH?

LEAVE ME ALONE.

I DON'T THINK LEAVING'S AN OPTION...

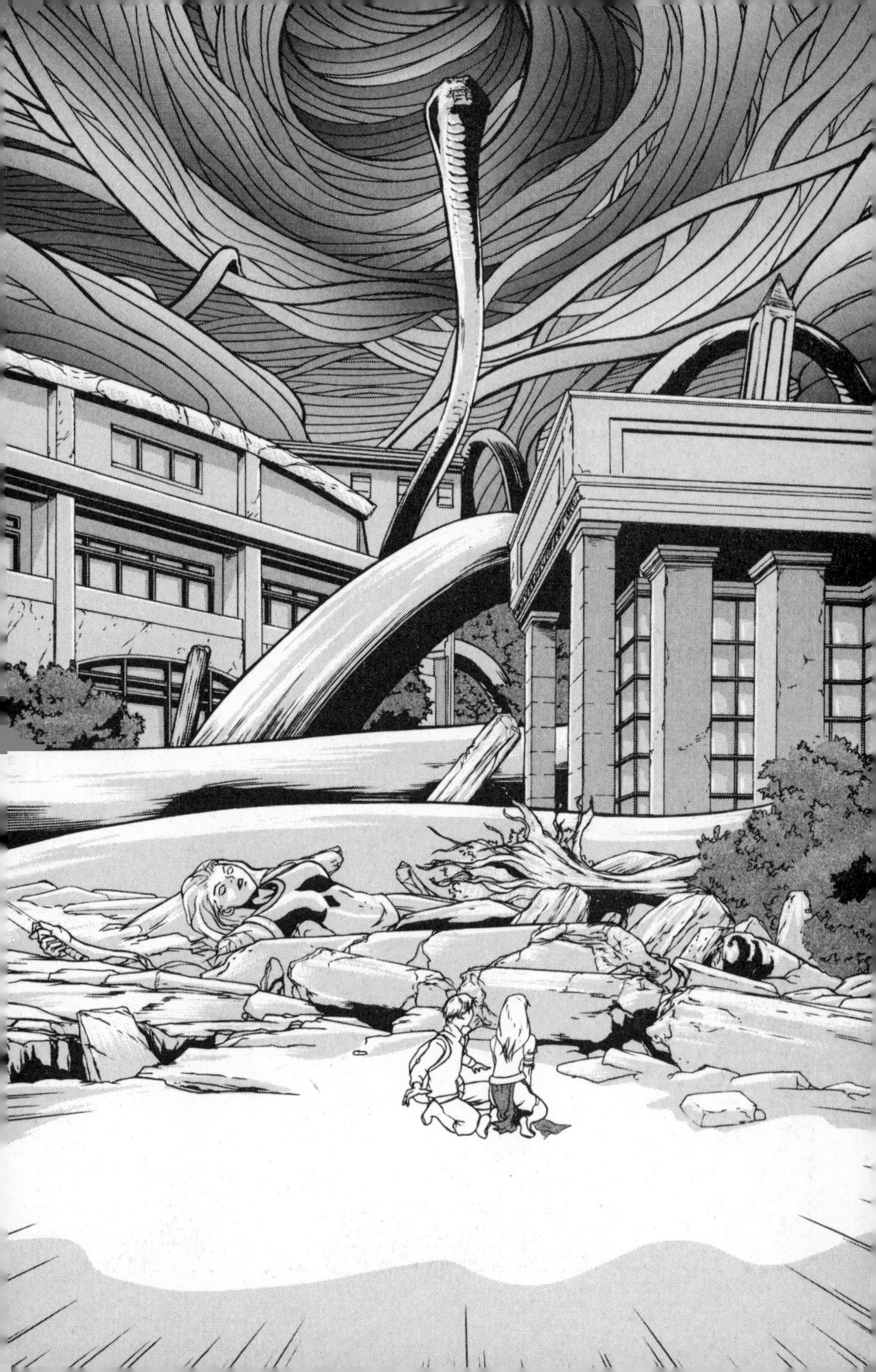

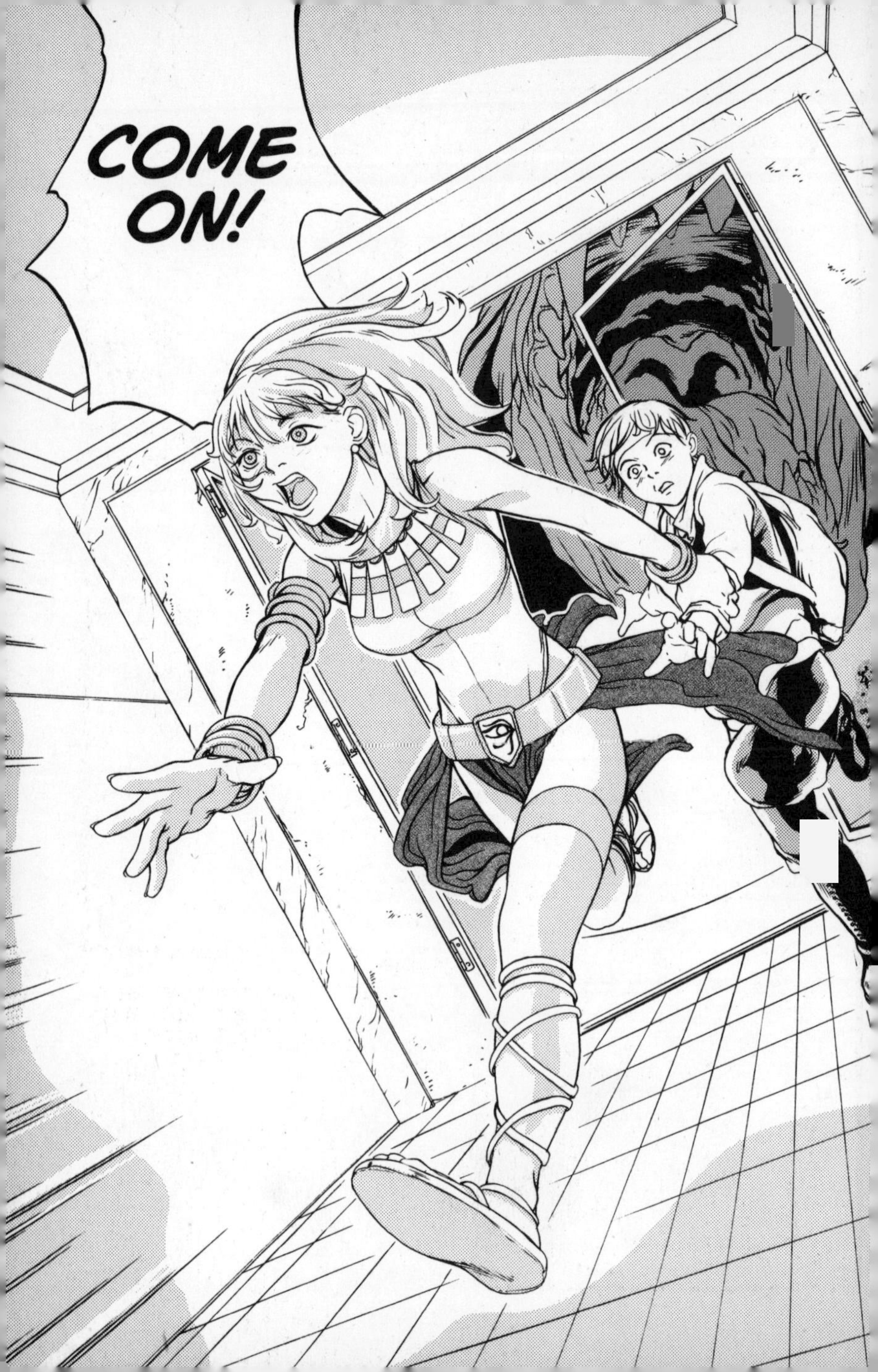
COME ON!

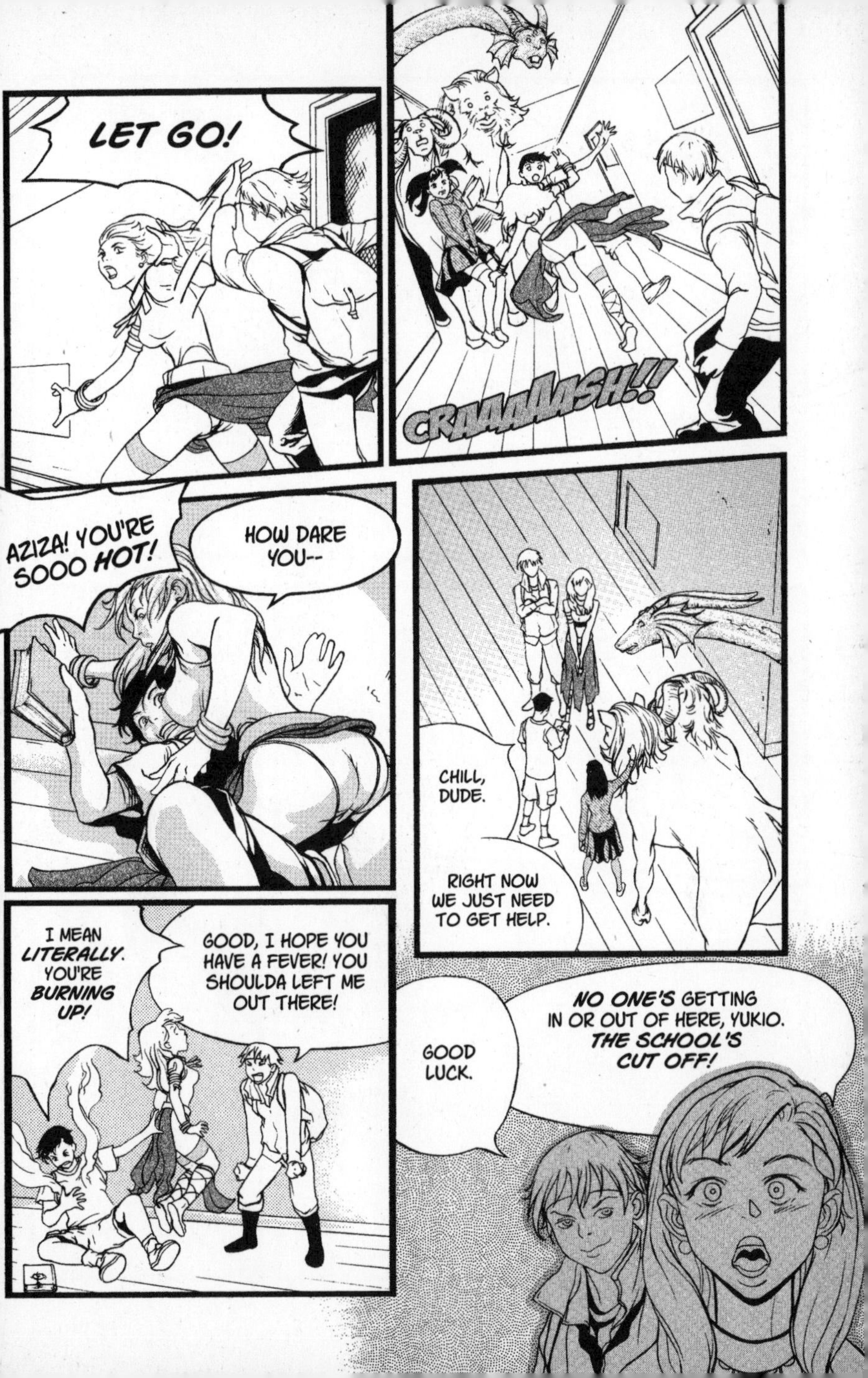
LET GO!
CRAAAAASH!!
AZIZA! YOU'RE SOOO HOT!
HOW DARE YOU--
I MEAN LITERALLY. YOU'RE BURNING UP!
GOOD, I HOPE YOU HAVE A FEVER! YOU SHOULDA LEFT ME OUT THERE!
CHILL, DUDE.
RIGHT NOW WE JUST NEED TO GET HELP.
NO ONE'S GETTING IN OR OUT OF HERE, YUKIO. THE SCHOOL'S CUT OFF!
GOOD LUCK.

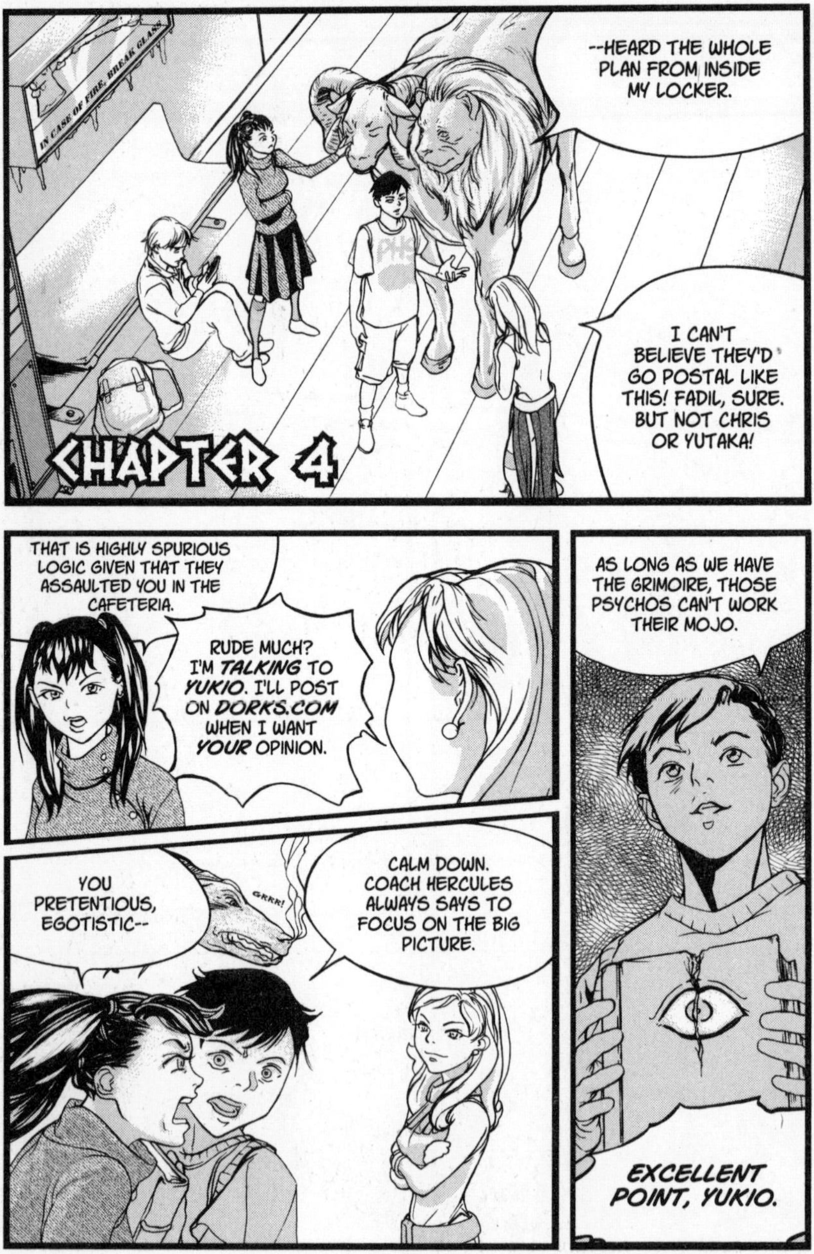
IN CASE OF FIRE, BREAK GLAS
CHAPTER 4
--HEARD THE WHOLE PLAN FROM INSIDE MY LOCKER.
I CAN'T BELIEVE THEY'D GO POSTAL LIKE THIS! FADIL, SURE. BUT NOT CHRIS OR YUTAKA!
THAT IS HIGHLY SPURIOUS LOGIC GIVEN THAT THEY ASSAULTED YOU IN THE CAFETERIA.
RUDE MUCH? I'M *TALKING* TO *YUKIO*. I'LL POST ON *DORKS.COM* WHEN I WANT *YOUR* OPINION.
YOU PRETENTIOUS, EGOTISTIC--
GRRR!
CALM DOWN. COACH HERCULES ALWAYS SAYS TO FOCUS ON THE BIG PICTURE.
AS LONG AS WE HAVE THE GRIMOIRE, THOSE PSYCHOS CAN'T WORK THEIR MOJO.
EXCELLENT POINT, YUKIO.

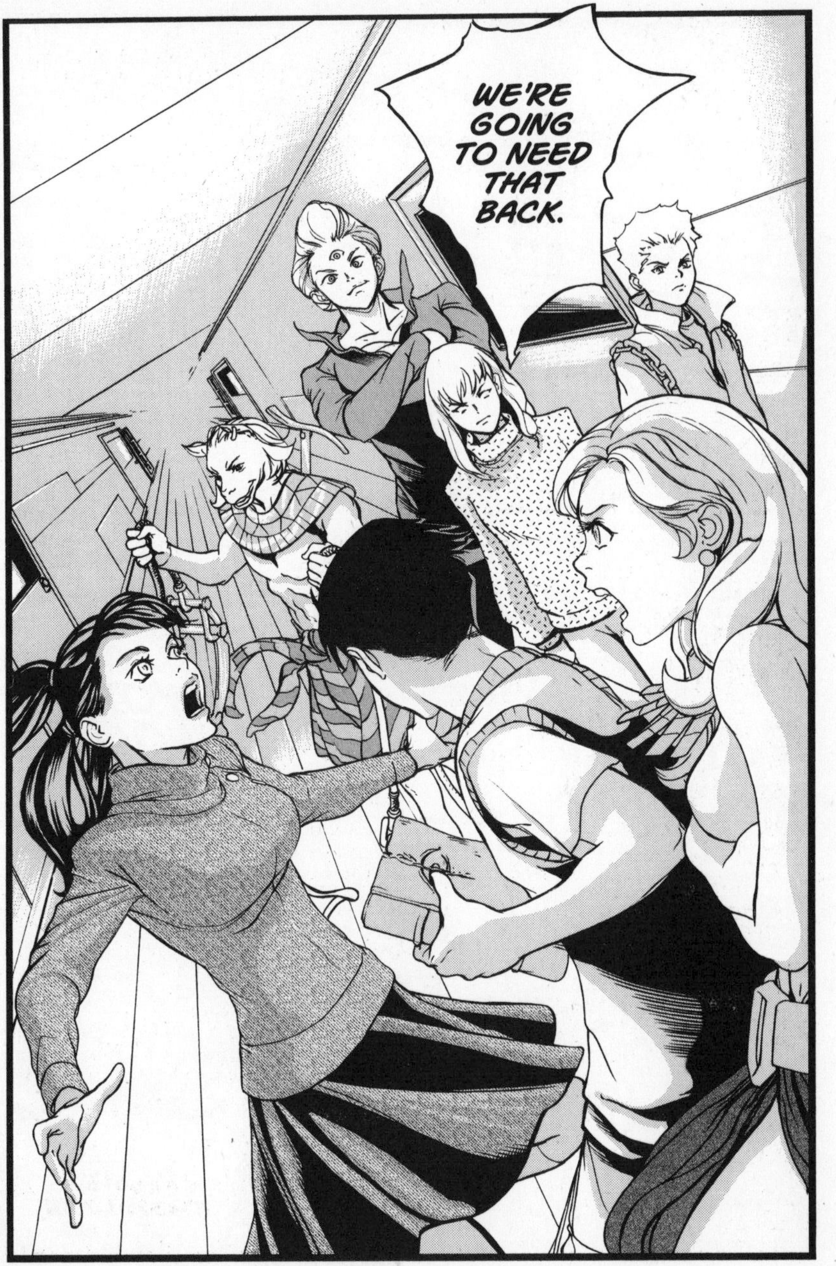
WE'RE GOING TO NEED THAT BACK.

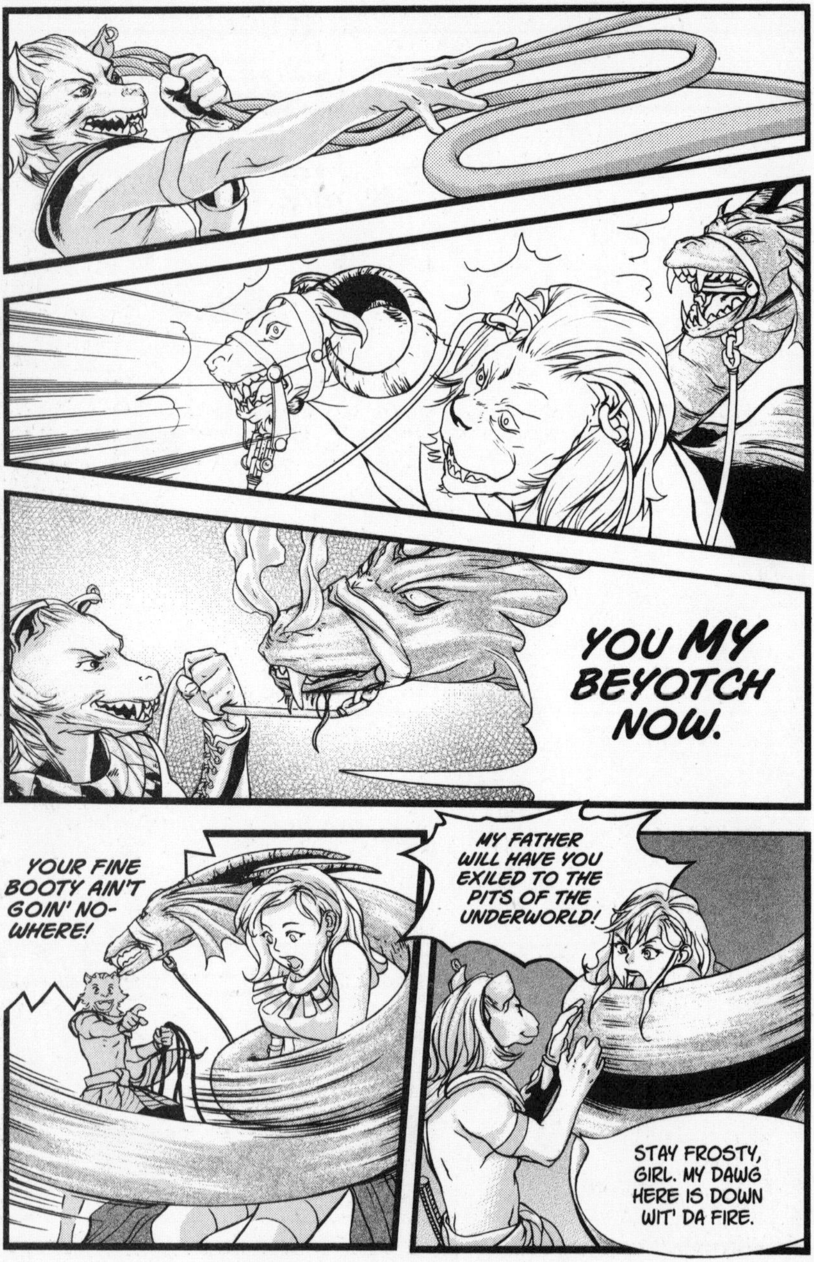
YOU MY BEYOTCH NOW.
YOUR FINE BOOTY AIN'T GOIN' NO-WHERE!
MY FATHER WILL HAVE YOU EXILED TO THE PITS OF THE UNDERWORLD!
STAY FROSTY, GIRL. MY DAWG HERE IS DOWN WIT' DA FIRE.

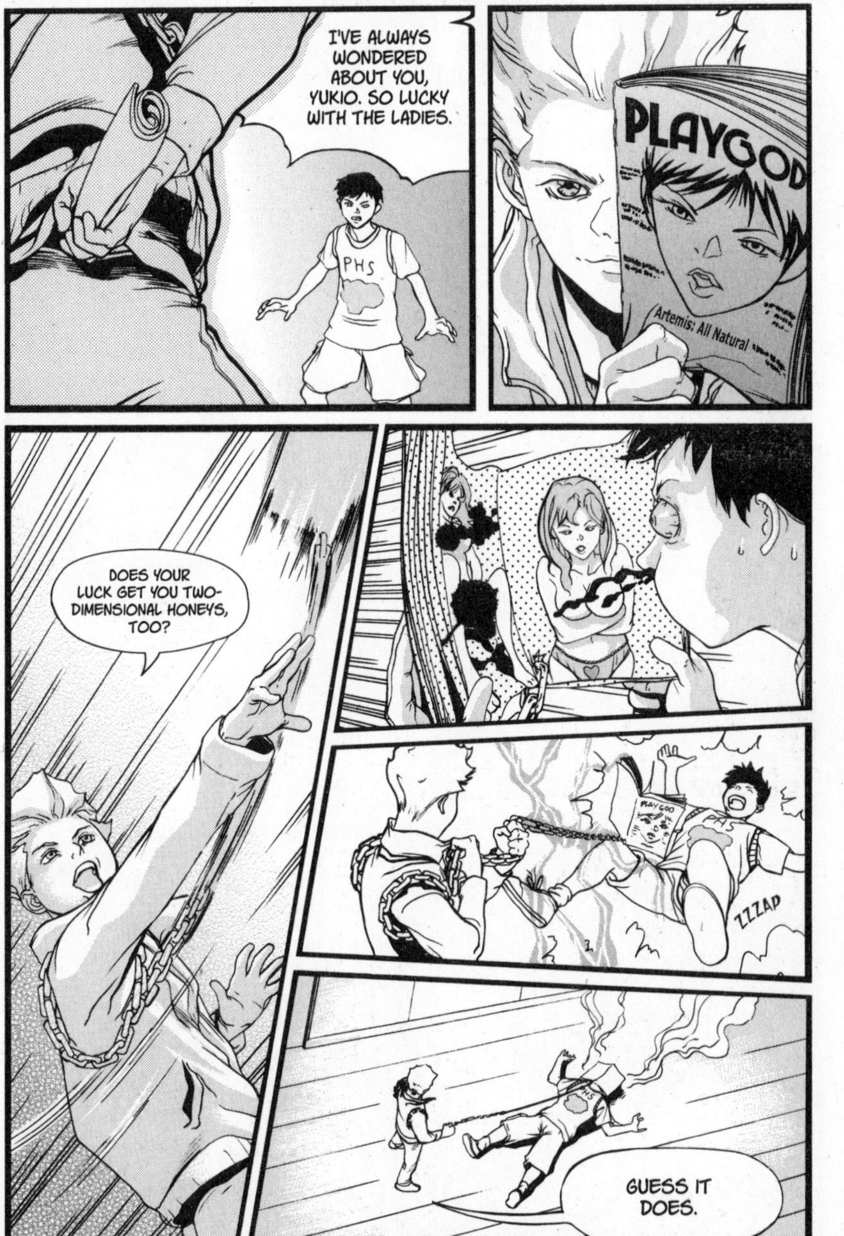
I'VE ALWAYS WONDERED ABOUT YOU, YUKIO. SO LUCKY WITH THE LADIES.
PLAYGOD
Artemis: All Natural
DOES YOUR LUCK GET YOU TWO-DIMENSIONAL HONEYS, TOO?
ZZZAP
GUESS IT DOES.

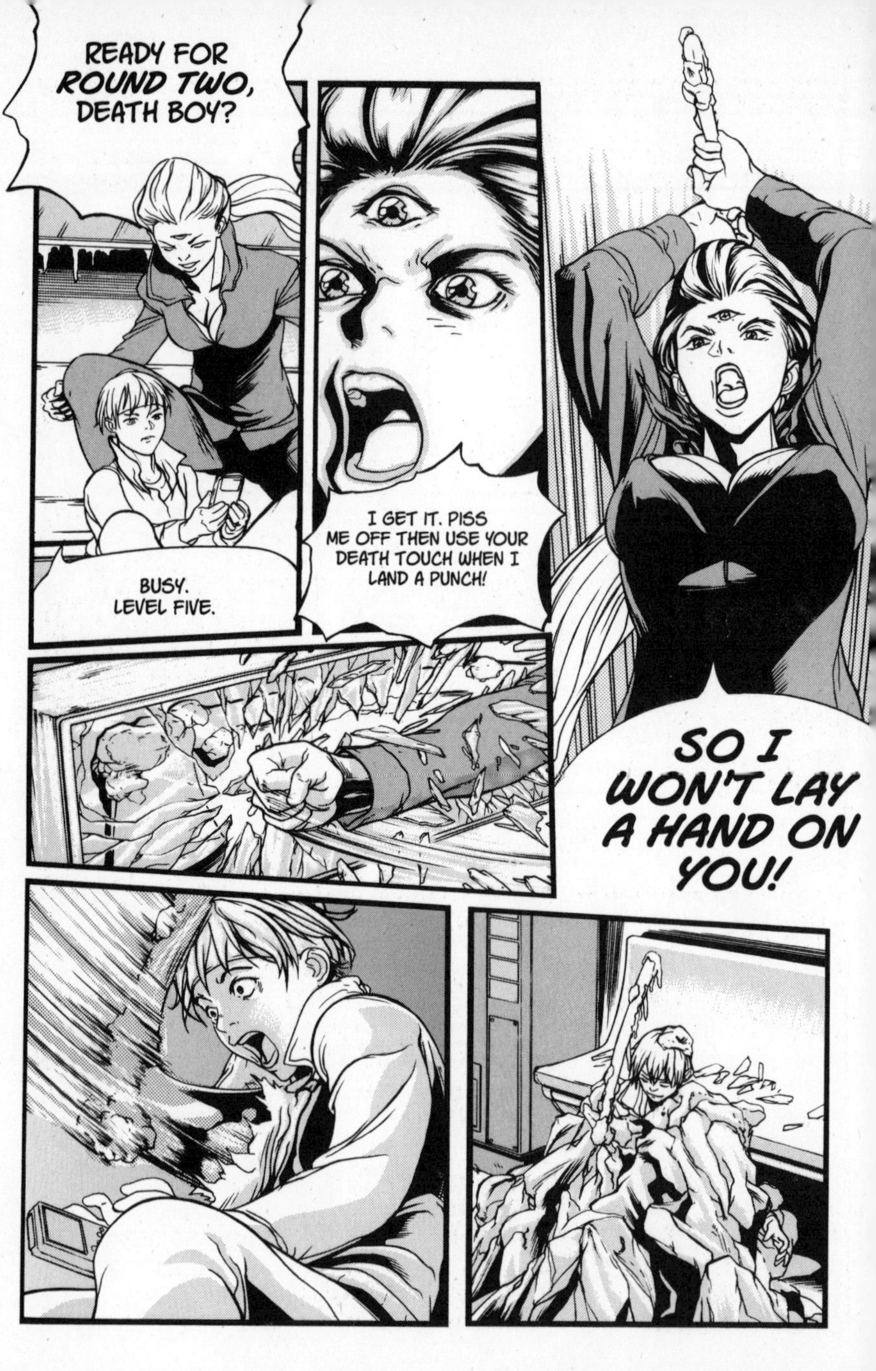
READY FOR ROUND TWO, DEATH BOY?
BUSY. LEVEL FIVE.
I GET IT. PISS ME OFF THEN USE YOUR DEATH TOUCH WHEN I LAND A PUNCH!
SO I WON'T LAY A HAND ON YOU!

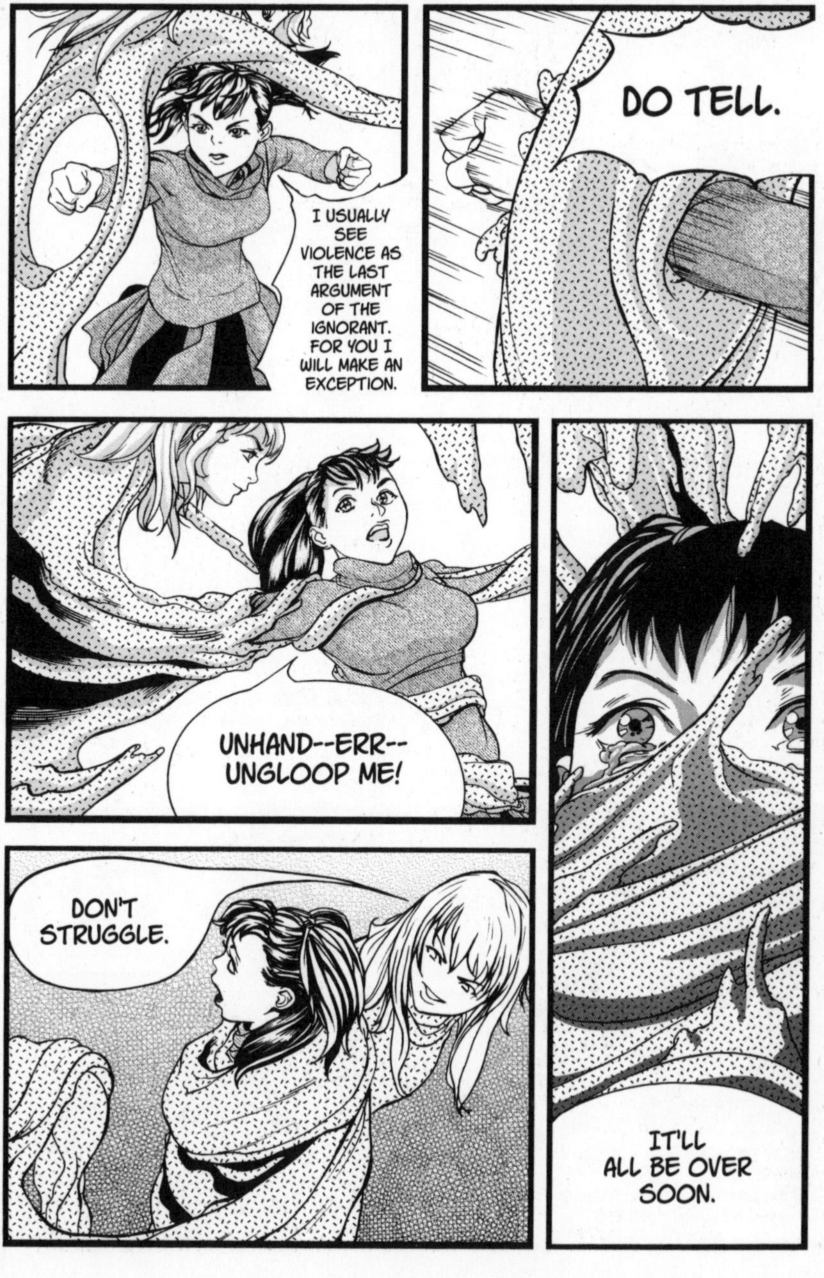
I USUALLY SEE VIOLENCE AS THE LAST ARGUMENT OF THE IGNORANT. FOR YOU I WILL MAKE AN EXCEPTION.
DO TELL.
UNHAND--ERR--UNGLOOP ME!
DON'T STRUGGLE.
IT'LL ALL BE OVER SOON.

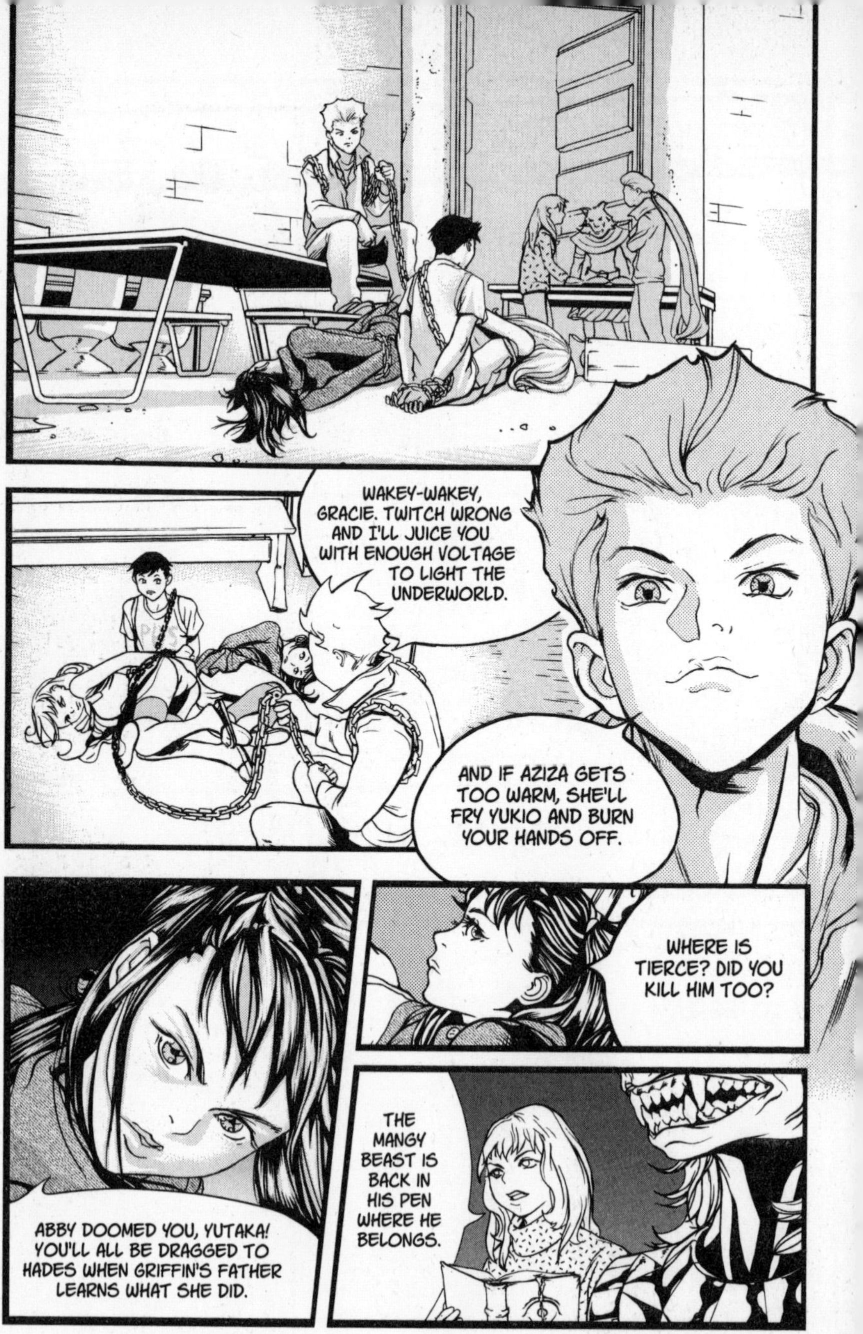
WAKEY-WAKEY, GRACIE. TWITCH WRONG AND I'LL JUICE YOU WITH ENOUGH VOLTAGE TO LIGHT THE UNDERWORLD.
AND IF AZIZA GETS TOO WARM, SHE'LL FRY YUKIO AND BURN YOUR HANDS OFF.
ABBY DOOMED YOU, YUTAKA! YOU'LL ALL BE DRAGGED TO HADES WHEN GRIFFIN'S FATHER LEARNS WHAT SHE DID.
WHERE IS TIERCE? DID YOU KILL HIM TOO?
THE MANGY BEAST IS BACK IN HIS PEN WHERE HE BELONGS.

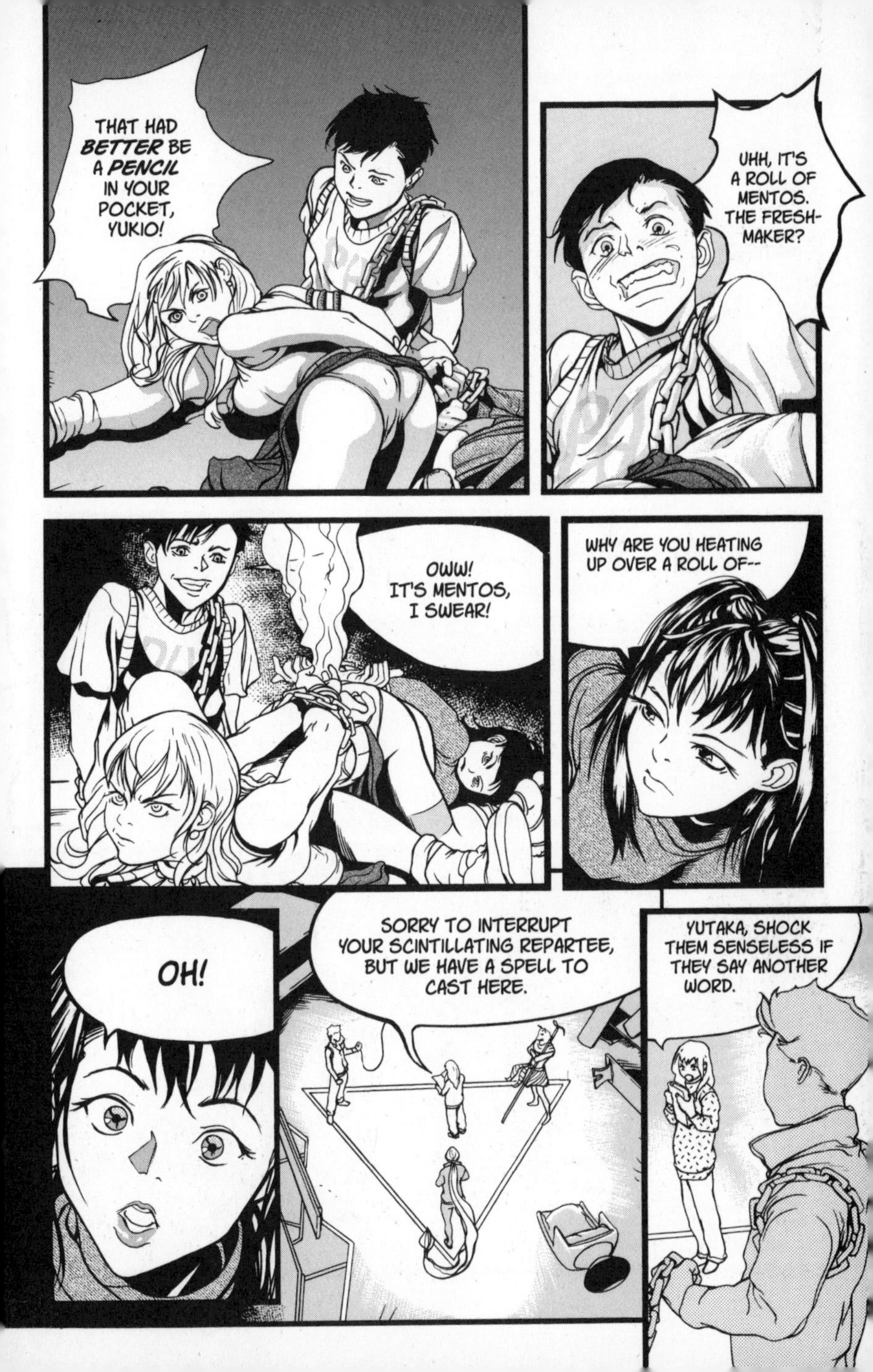
THAT HAD BETTER BE A PENCIL IN YOUR POCKET, YUKIO!
UHH, IT'S A ROLL OF MENTOS. THE FRESH-MAKER?
OWW! IT'S MENTOS, I SWEAR!
WHY ARE YOU HEATING UP OVER A ROLL OF--
OH!
SORRY TO INTERRUPT YOUR SCINTILLATING REPARTEE, BUT WE HAVE A SPELL TO CAST HERE.
YUTAKA, SHOCK THEM SENSELESS IF THEY SAY ANOTHER WORD.

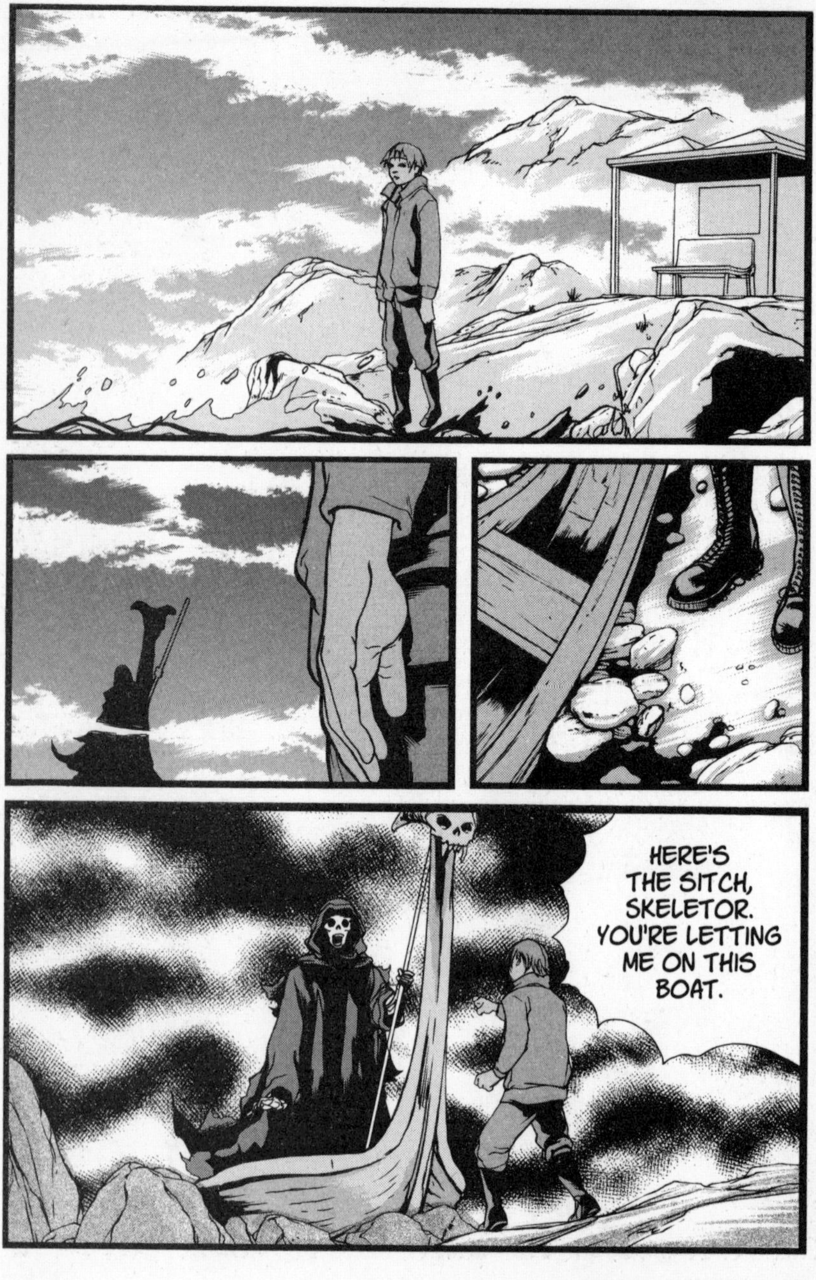
HERE'S THE SITCH, SKELETOR. YOU'RE LETTING ME ON THIS BOAT.

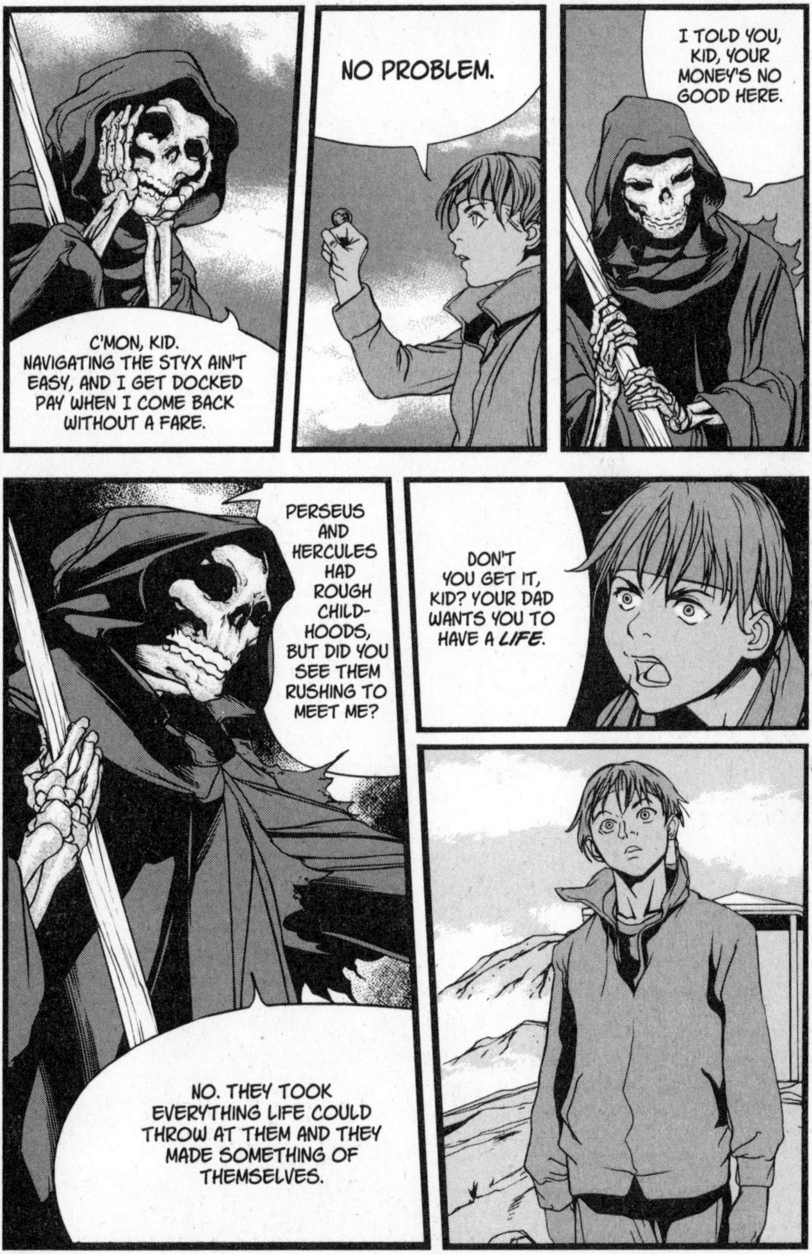
C'MON, KID. NAVIGATING THE STYX AIN'T EASY, AND I GET DOCKED PAY WHEN I COME BACK WITHOUT A FARE.
NO PROBLEM.
I TOLD YOU, KID, YOUR MONEY'S NO GOOD HERE.
PERSEUS AND HERCULES HAD ROUGH CHILD-HOODS, BUT DID YOU SEE THEM RUSHING TO MEET ME?
NO. THEY TOOK EVERYTHING LIFE COULD THROW AT THEM AND THEY MADE SOMETHING OF THEMSELVES.
DON'T YOU GET IT, KID? YOUR DAD WANTS YOU TO HAVE A *LIFE*.

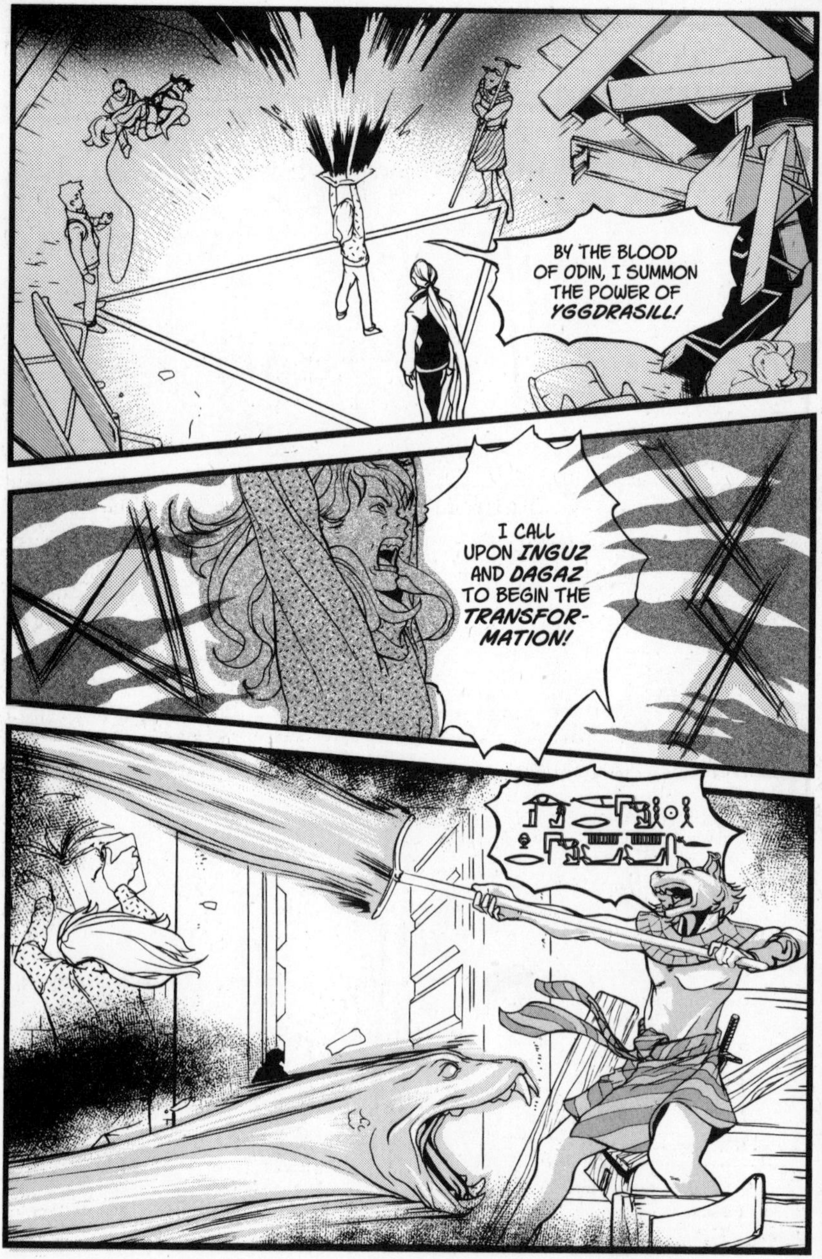
BY THE BLOOD OF ODIN, I SUMMON THE POWER OF *YGGDRASILL!*
I CALL UPON *INGUZ* AND *DAGAZ* TO BEGIN THE *TRANSFORMATION!*

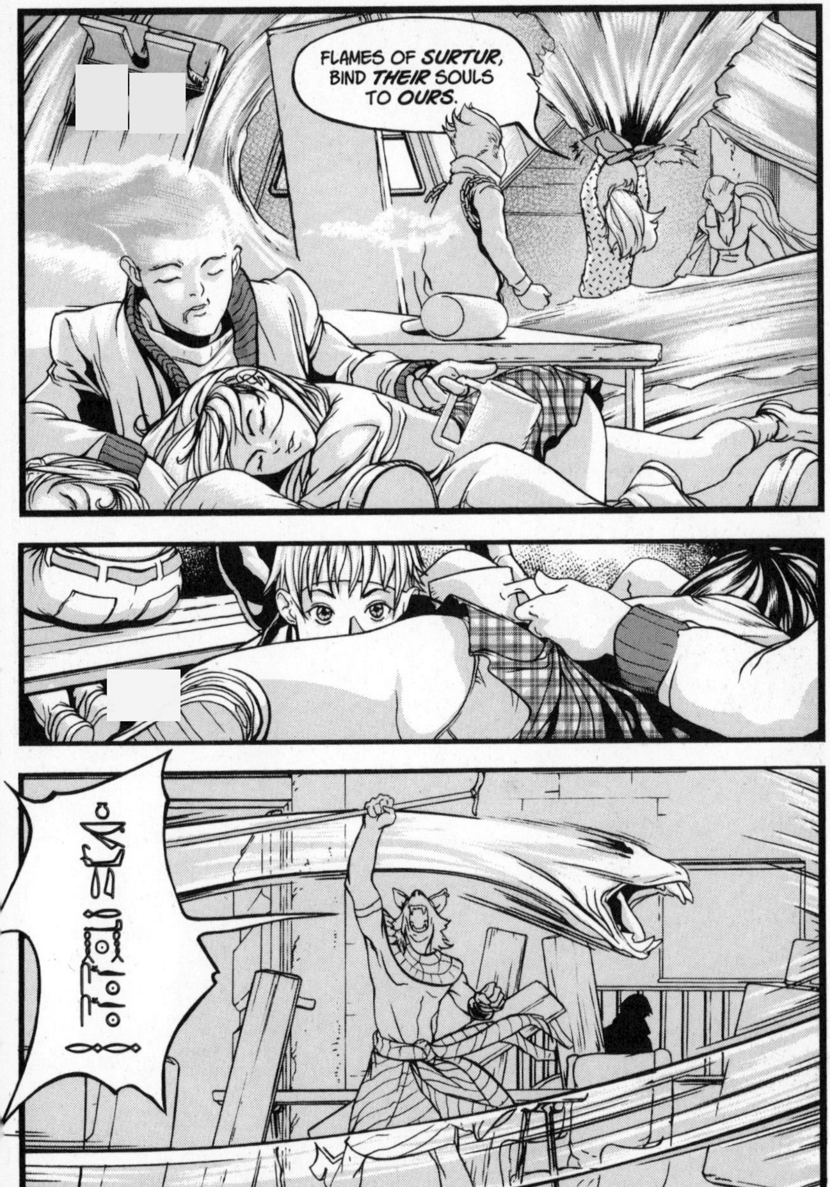
FLAMES OF SURTUR, BIND THEIR SOULS TO OURS.

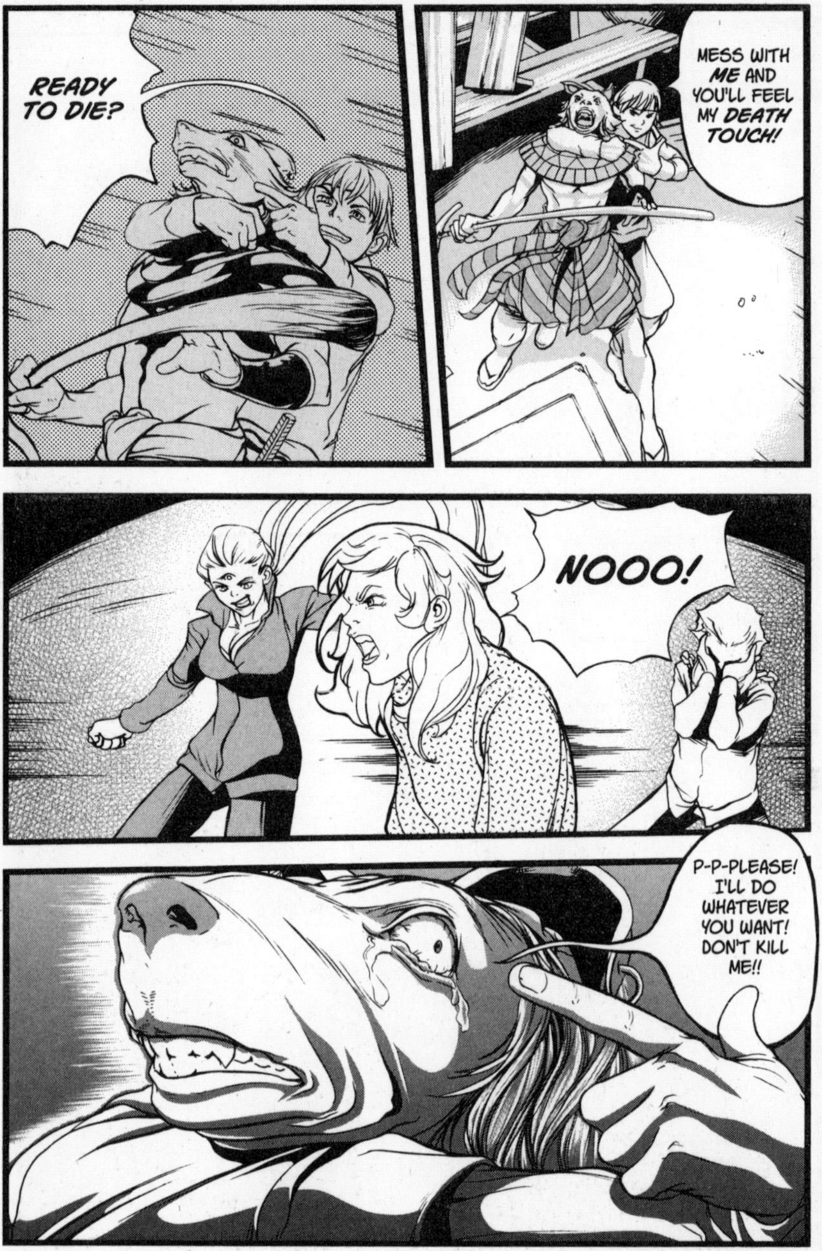
READY TO DIE?
MESS WITH ME AND YOU'LL FEEL MY DEATH TOUCH!
NOOO!
P-P-PLEASE! I'LL DO WHATEVER YOU WANT! DON'T KILL ME!!

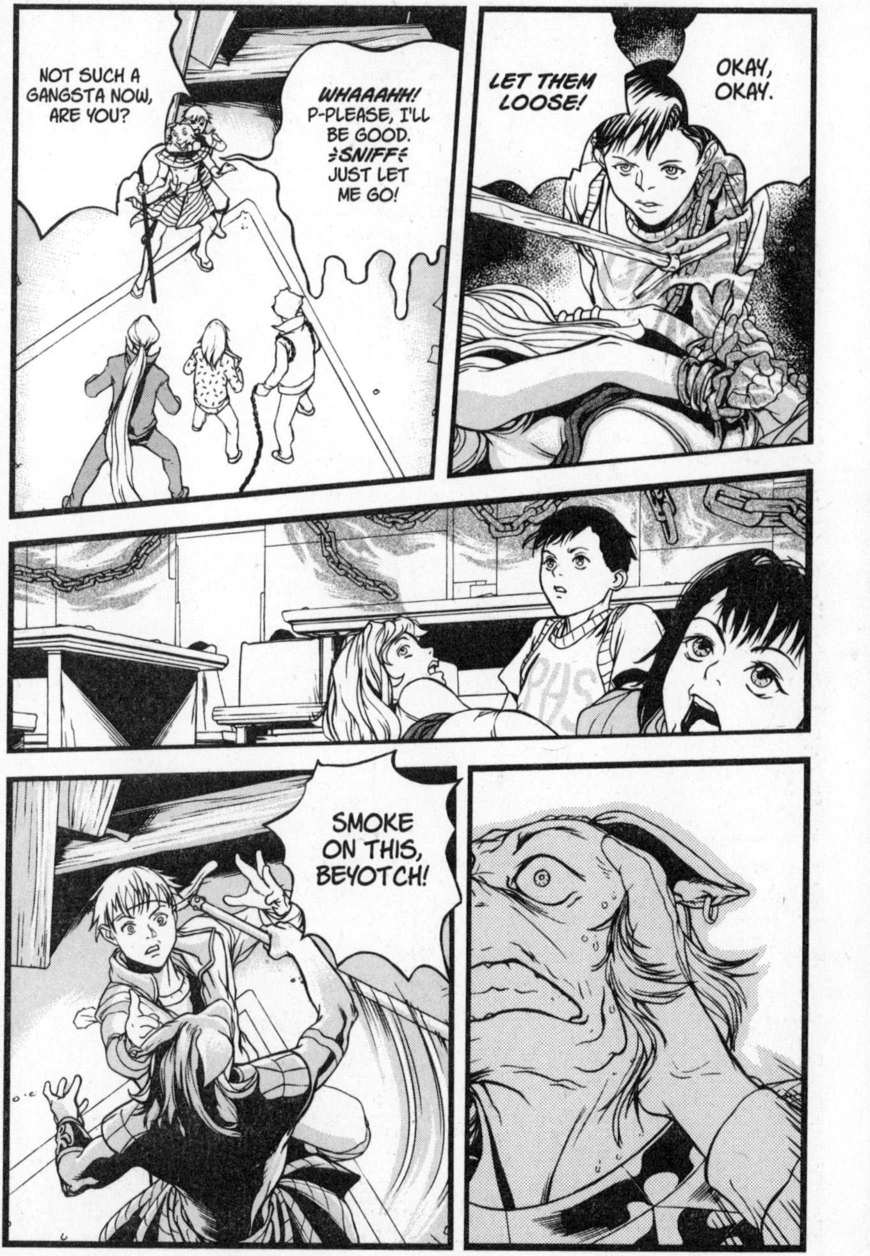

NOT SUCH A GANGSTA NOW, ARE YOU?
WHAAAHH! P-PLEASE, I'LL BE GOOD. SNIFF JUST LET ME GO!
LET THEM LOOSE!
OKAY, OKAY.
SMOKE ON THIS, BEYOTCH!

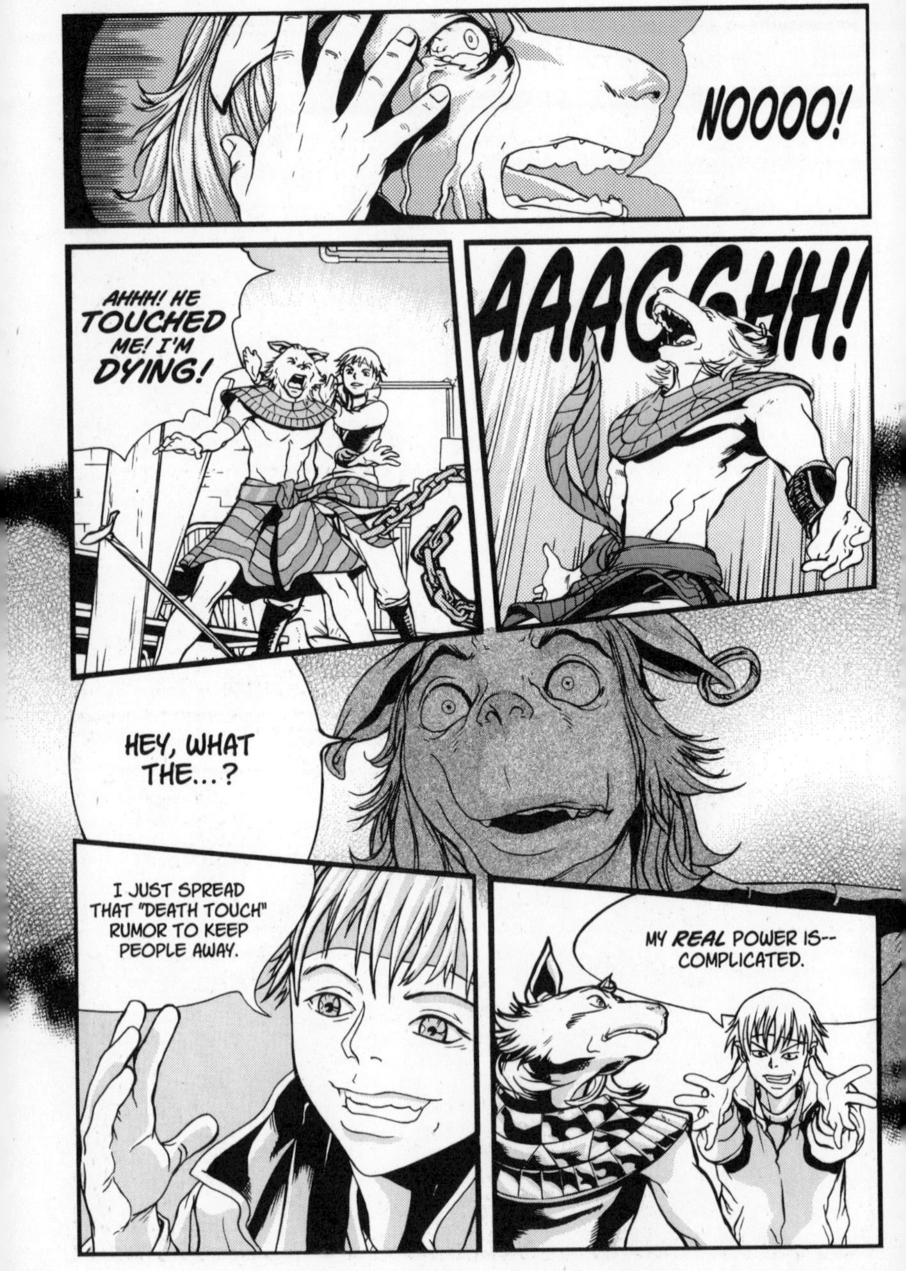
NOOOO!
AHHH! HE TOUCHED ME! I'M DYING!
AAAGGHH!
HEY, WHAT THE...?
I JUST SPREAD THAT "DEATH TOUCH" RUMOR TO KEEP PEOPLE AWAY.
MY REAL POWER IS-- COMPLICATED.

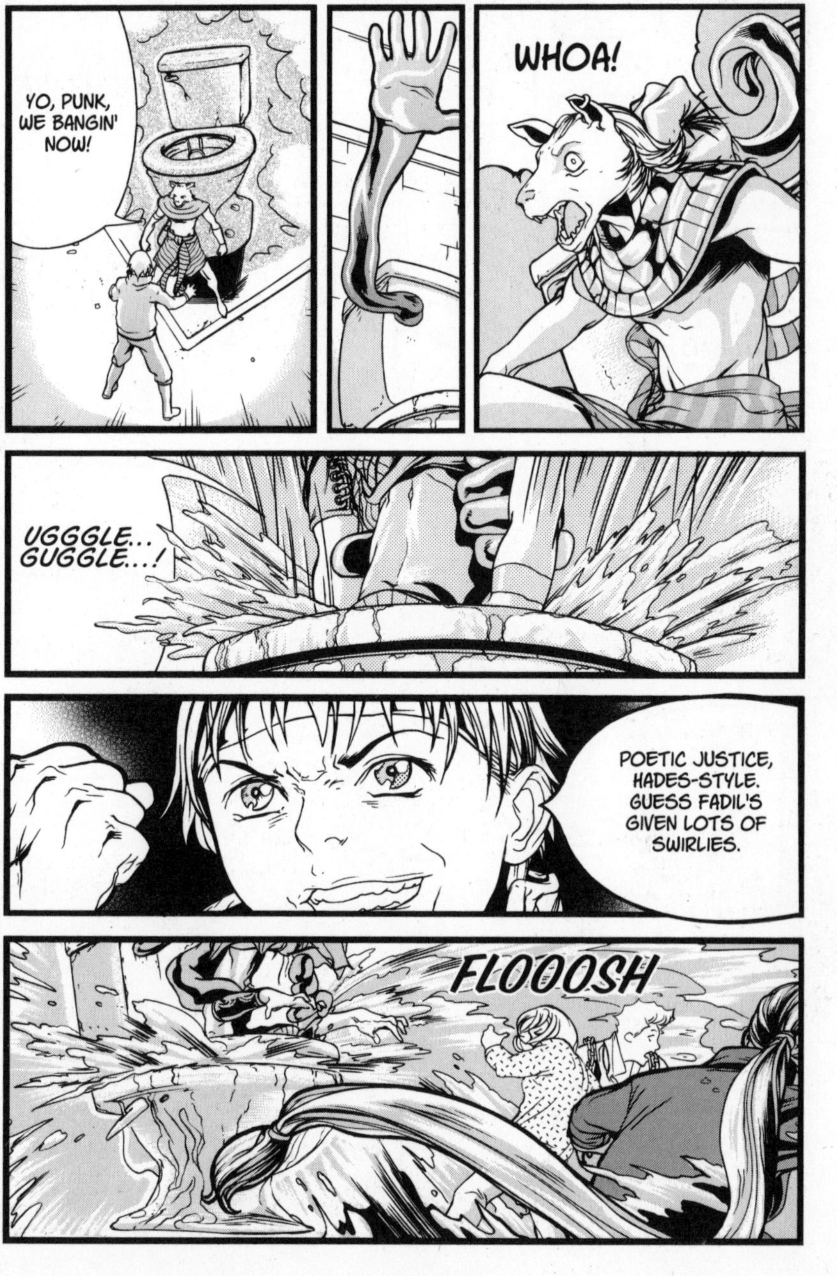
YO, PUNK, WE BANGIN' NOW!
WHOA!
UGGGLE... GUGGLE...!
POETIC JUSTICE, HADES-STYLE. GUESS FADIL'S GIVEN LOTS OF SWIRLIES.
FLOOOSH

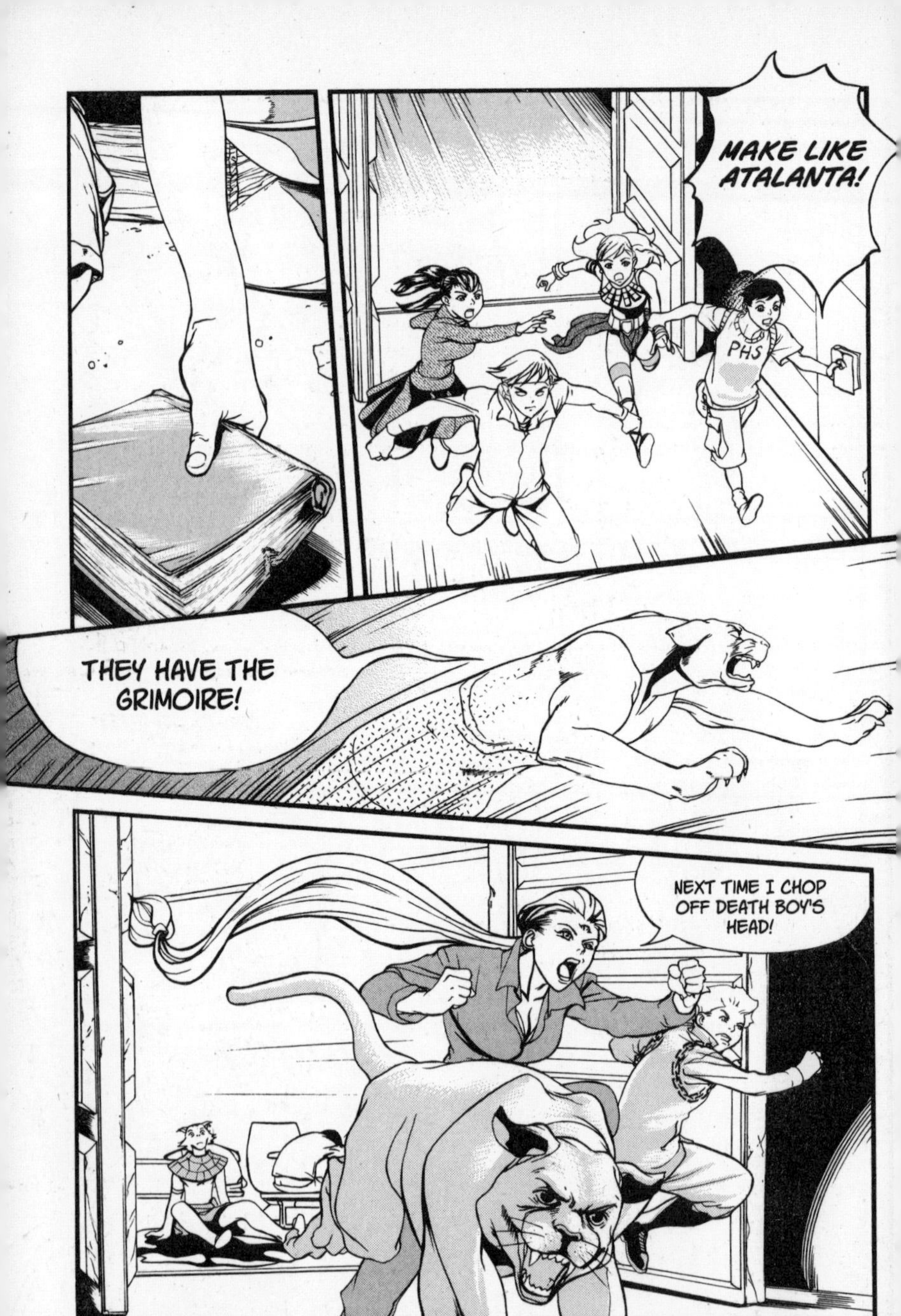

MAKE LIKE ATALANTA!
THEY HAVE THE GRIMOIRE!
NEXT TIME I CHOP OFF DEATH BOY'S HEAD!
PHS

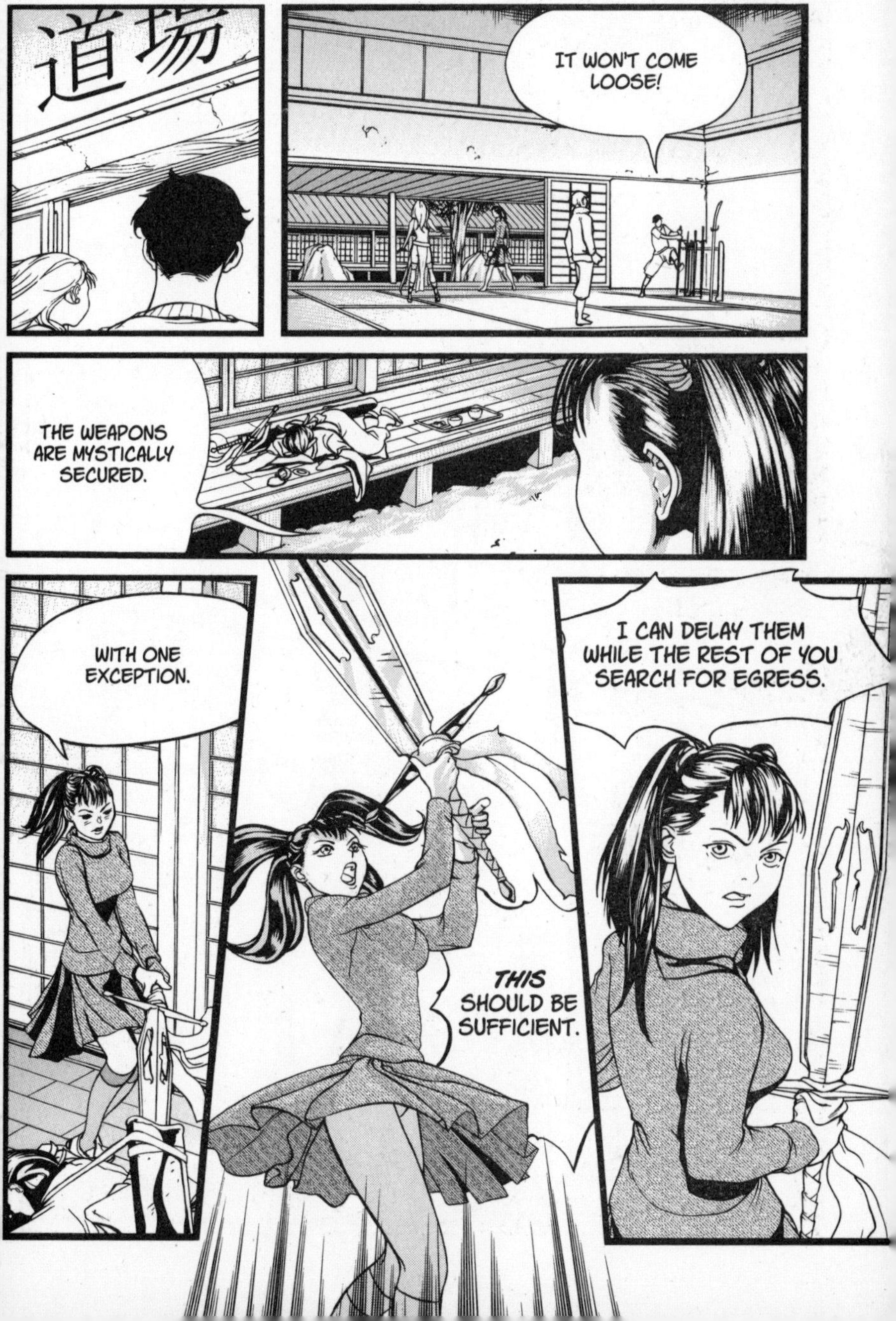
道場
IT WON'T COME LOOSE!
THE WEAPONS ARE MYSTICALLY SECURED.
WITH ONE EXCEPTION.
THIS SHOULD BE SUFFICIENT.
I CAN DELAY THEM WHILE THE REST OF YOU SEARCH FOR EGRESS.

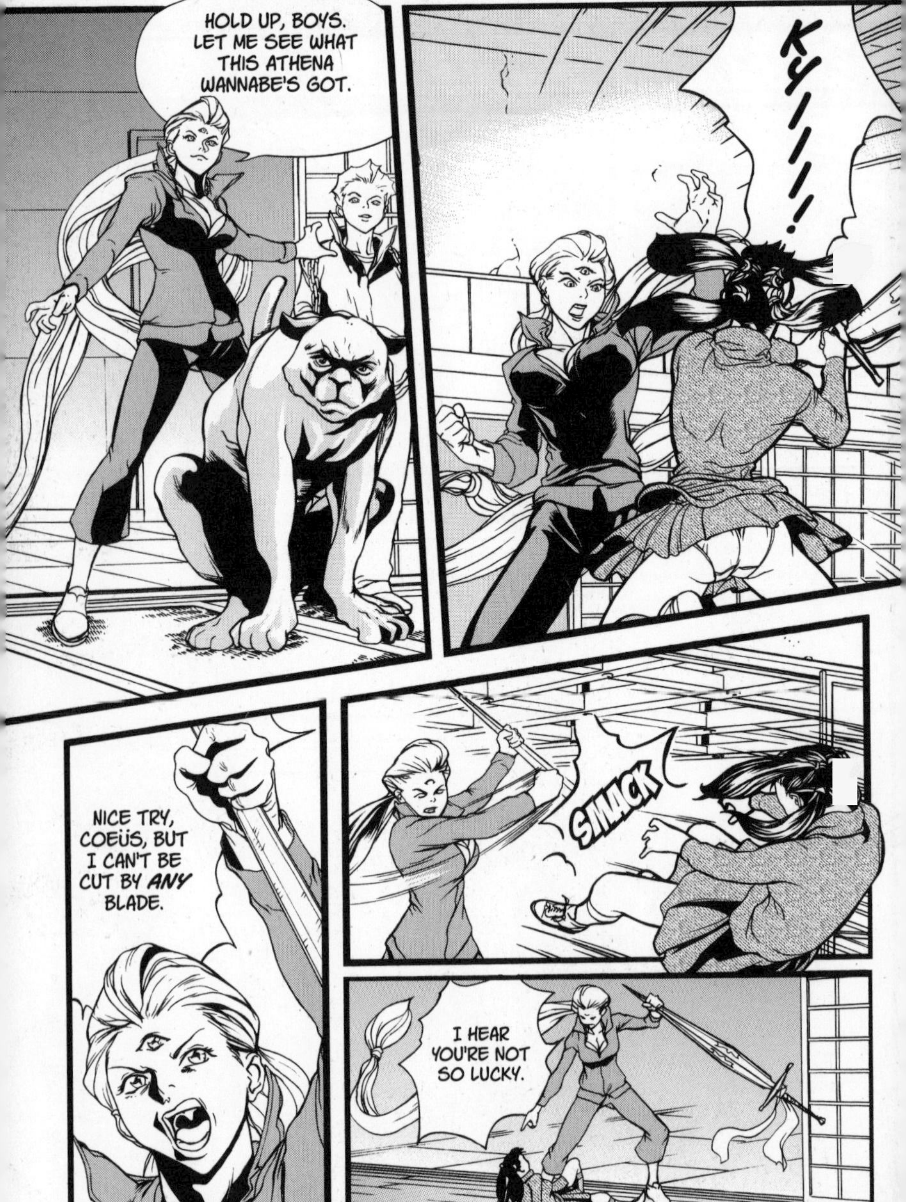
HOLD UP, BOYS. LET ME SEE WHAT THIS ATHENA WANNABE'S GOT.
KYIIII!
NICE TRY, COEÜS, BUT I CAN'T BE CUT BY *ANY* BLADE.
SMACK
I HEAR YOU'RE NOT SO LUCKY.

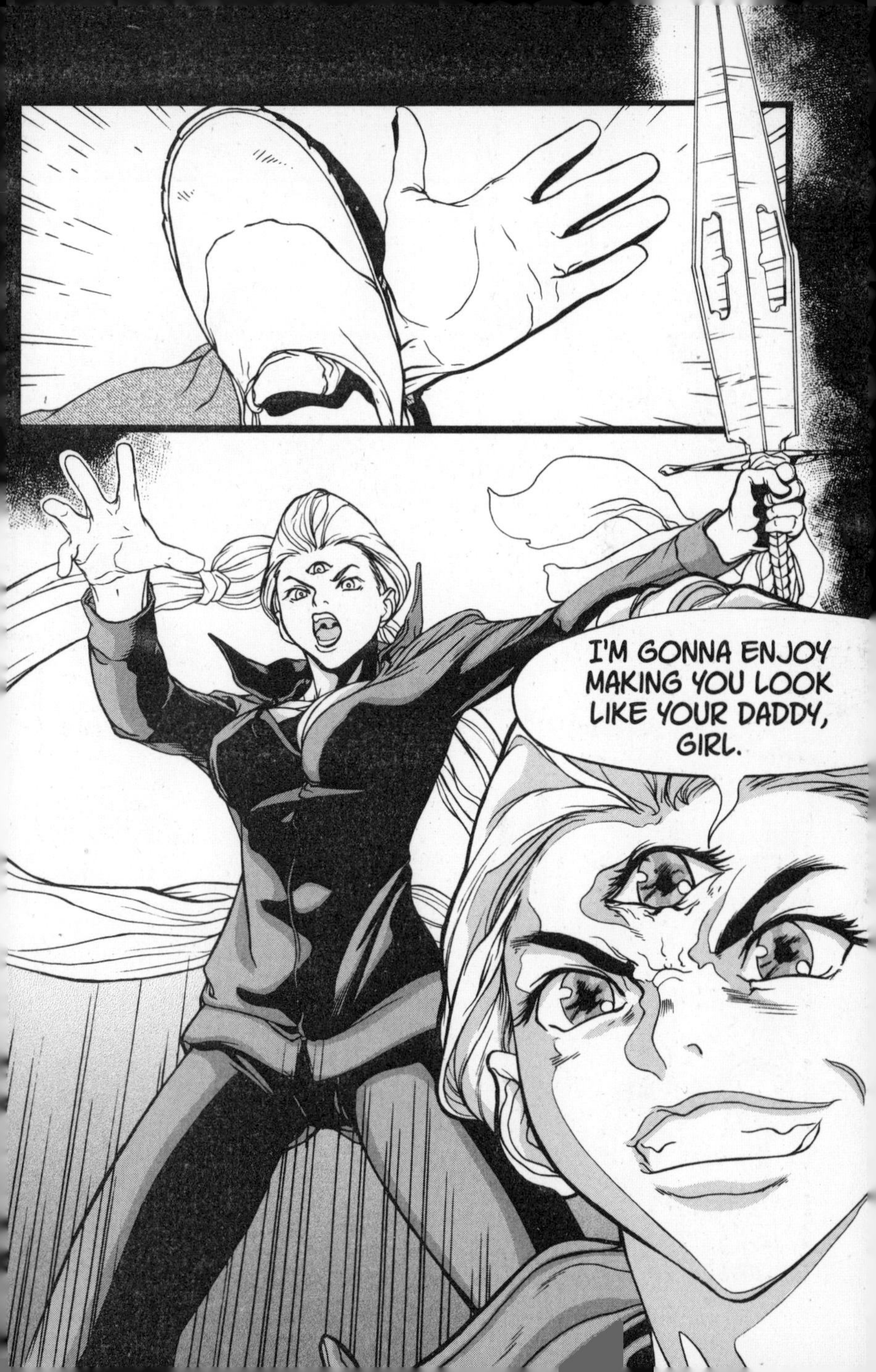
I'M GONNA ENJOY MAKING YOU LOOK LIKE YOUR DADDY, GIRL.

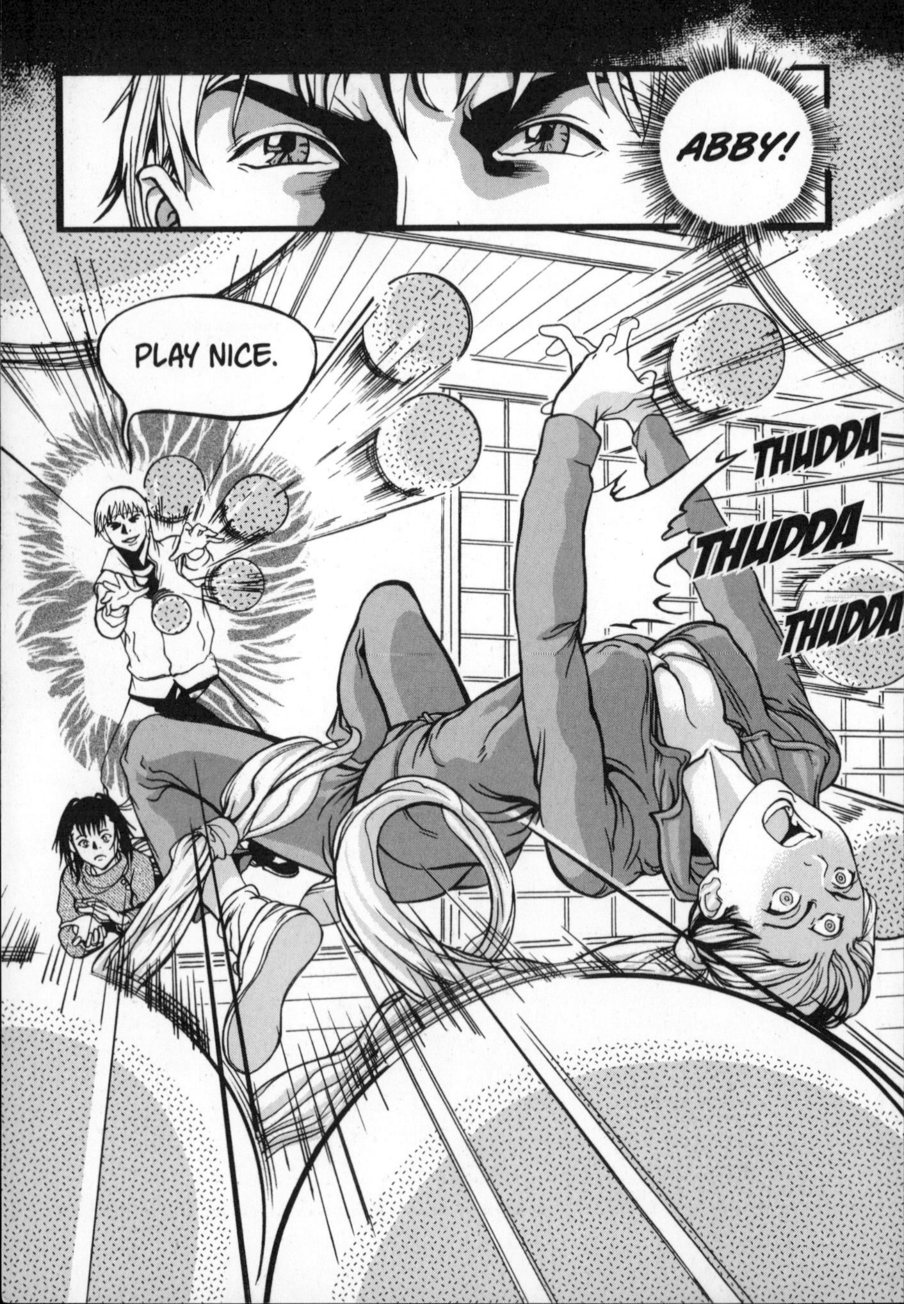
ABBY!
PLAY NICE.
THUDDA
THUDDA
THUDDA

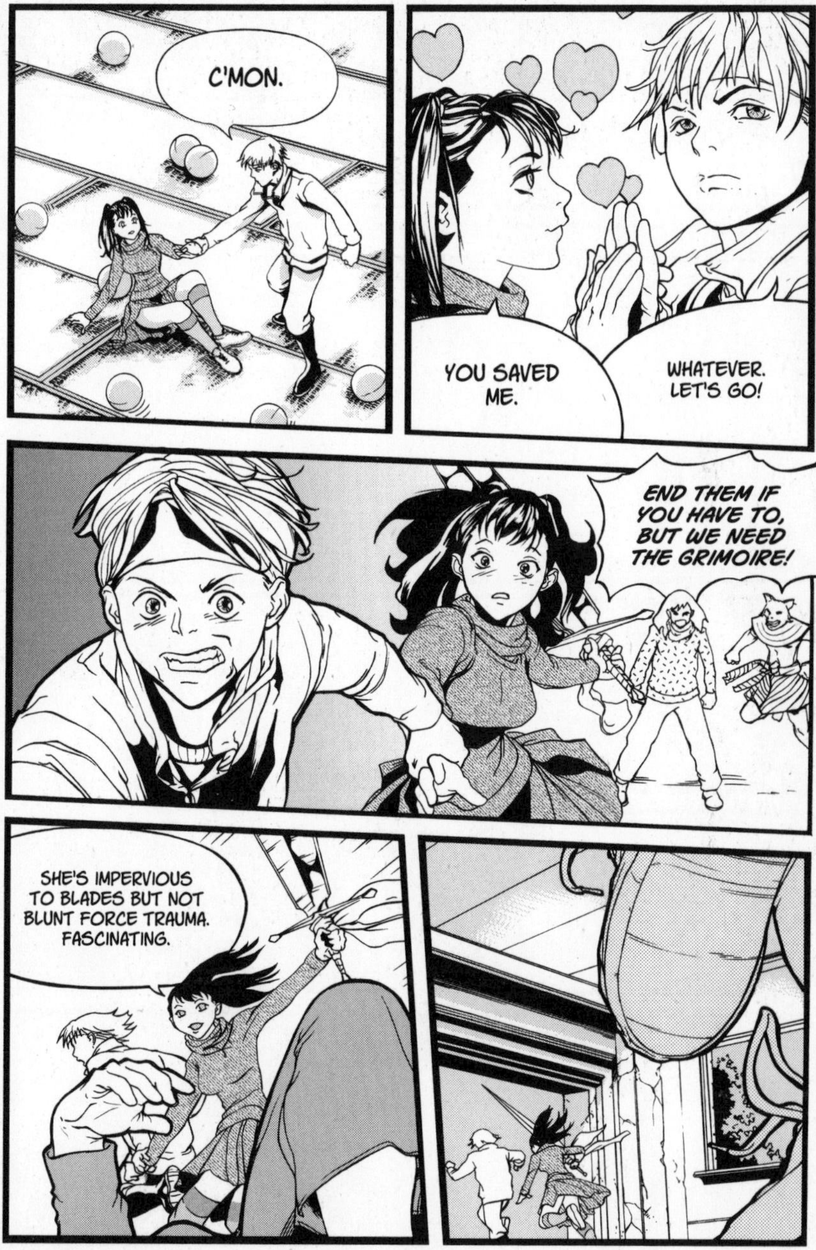
C'MON.
YOU SAVED ME.
WHATEVER. LET'S GO!
END THEM IF YOU HAVE TO, BUT WE NEED THE GRIMOIRE!
SHE'S IMPERVIOUS TO BLADES BUT NOT BLUNT FORCE TRAUMA. FASCINATING.

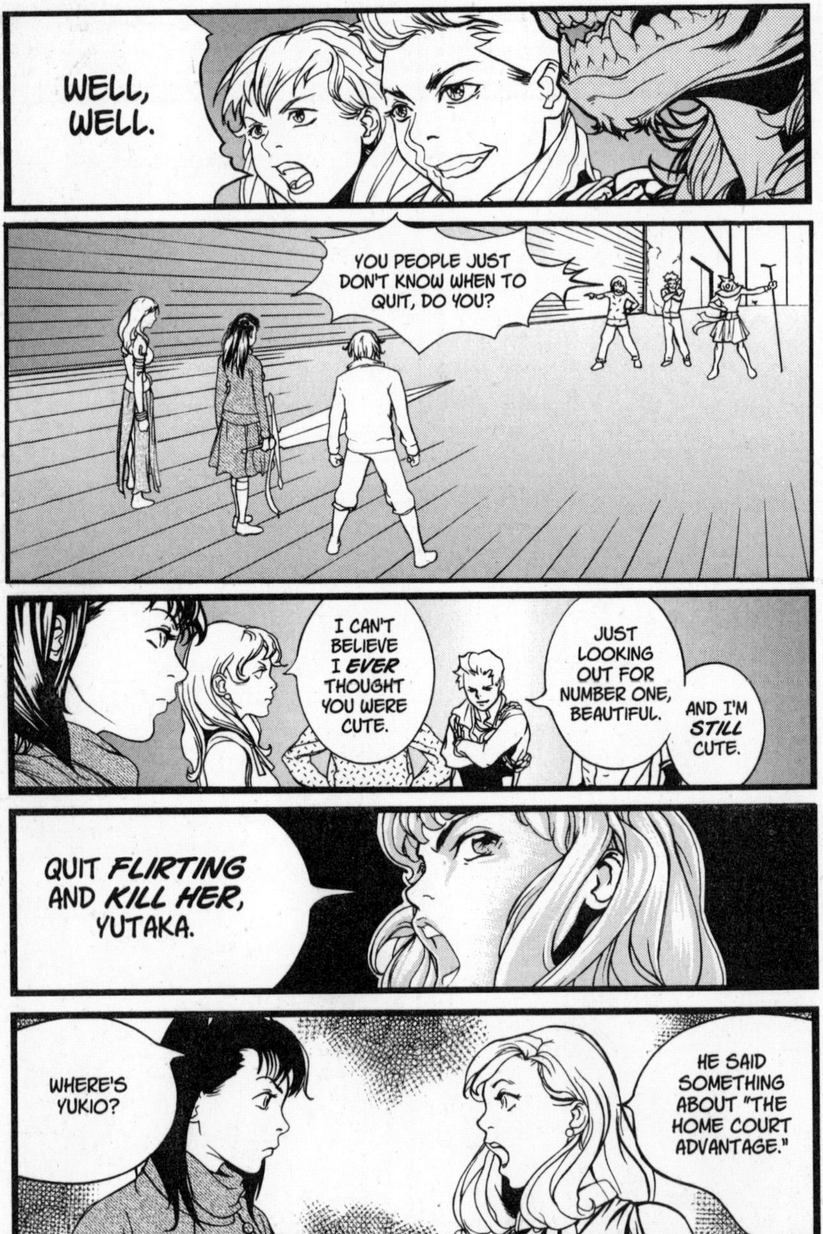
WELL, WELL.
YOU PEOPLE JUST DON'T KNOW WHEN TO QUIT, DO YOU?
I CAN'T BELIEVE I *EVER* THOUGHT YOU WERE CUTE.
JUST LOOKING OUT FOR NUMBER ONE, BEAUTIFUL.
AND I'M *STILL* CUTE.
QUIT *FLIRTING* AND *KILL HER*, YUTAKA.
WHERE'S YUKIO?
HE SAID SOMETHING ABOUT "THE HOME COURT ADVANTAGE."

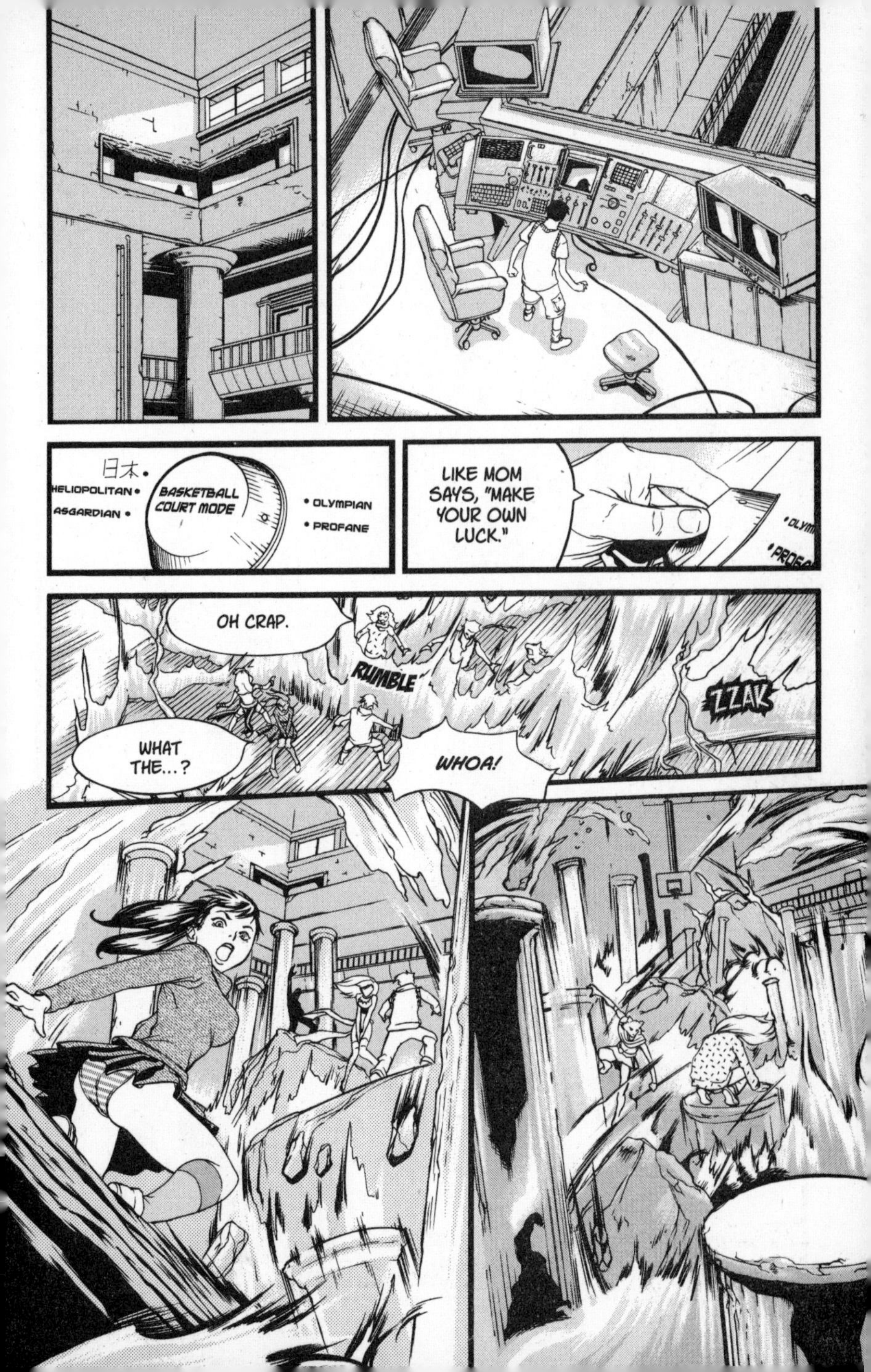
日本
HELIOPOLITAN
ASGARDIAN
BASKETBALL COURT MODE
OLYMPIAN
PROFANE
LIKE MOM SAYS, "MAKE YOUR OWN LUCK."
OH CRAP.
RUMBLE
ZZAK
WHAT THE...?
WHOA!

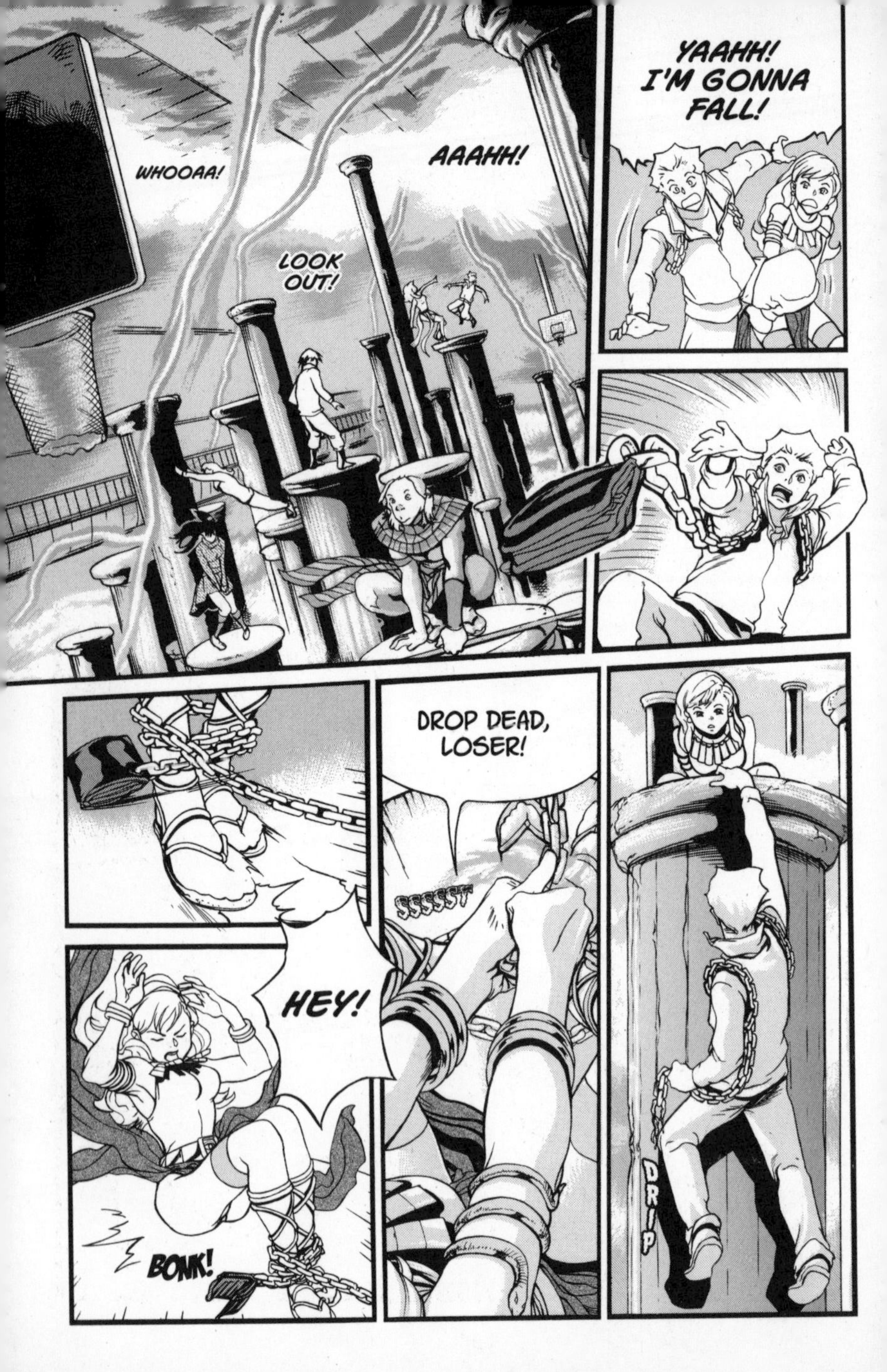
WHOOAA!
AAAHH!
LOOK OUT!
YAAHH! I'M GONNA FALL!
HEY!
BONK!
DROP DEAD, LOSER!
SSSSST
DRIP

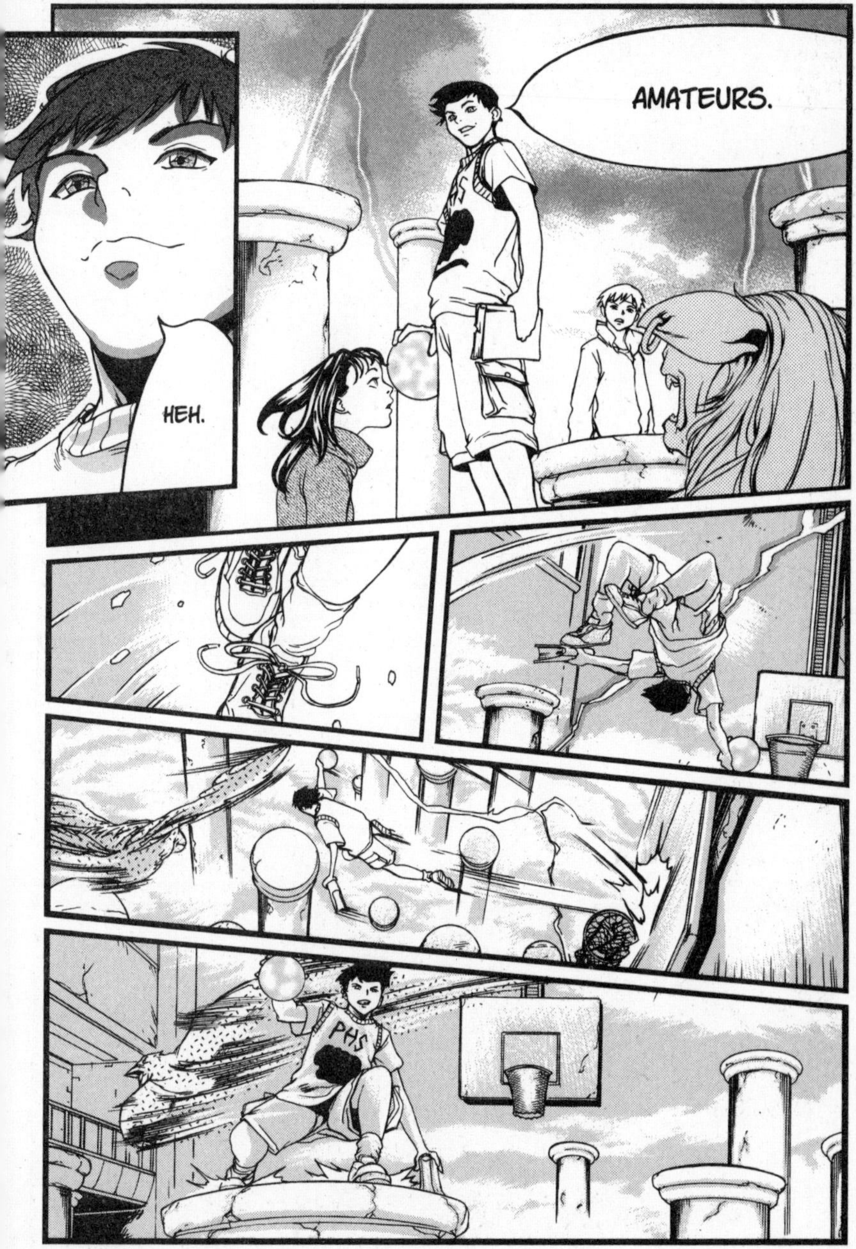
AMATEURS.
HEH.

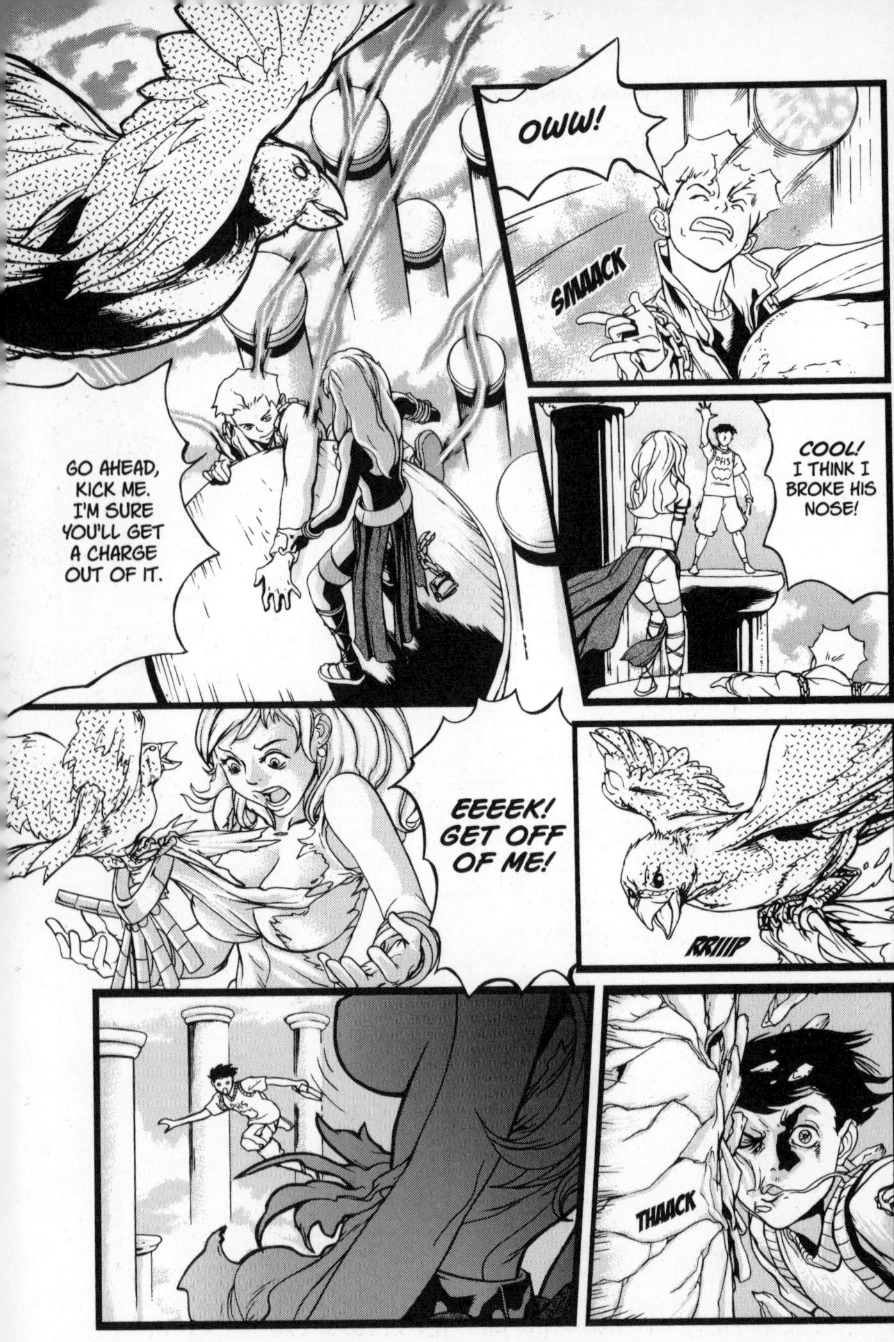
GO AHEAD, KICK ME. I'M SURE YOU'LL GET A CHARGE OUT OF IT.
OWW!
SMAACK
COOL! I THINK I BROKE HIS NOSE!
EEEEK! GET OFF OF ME!
RRIIP
THAACK

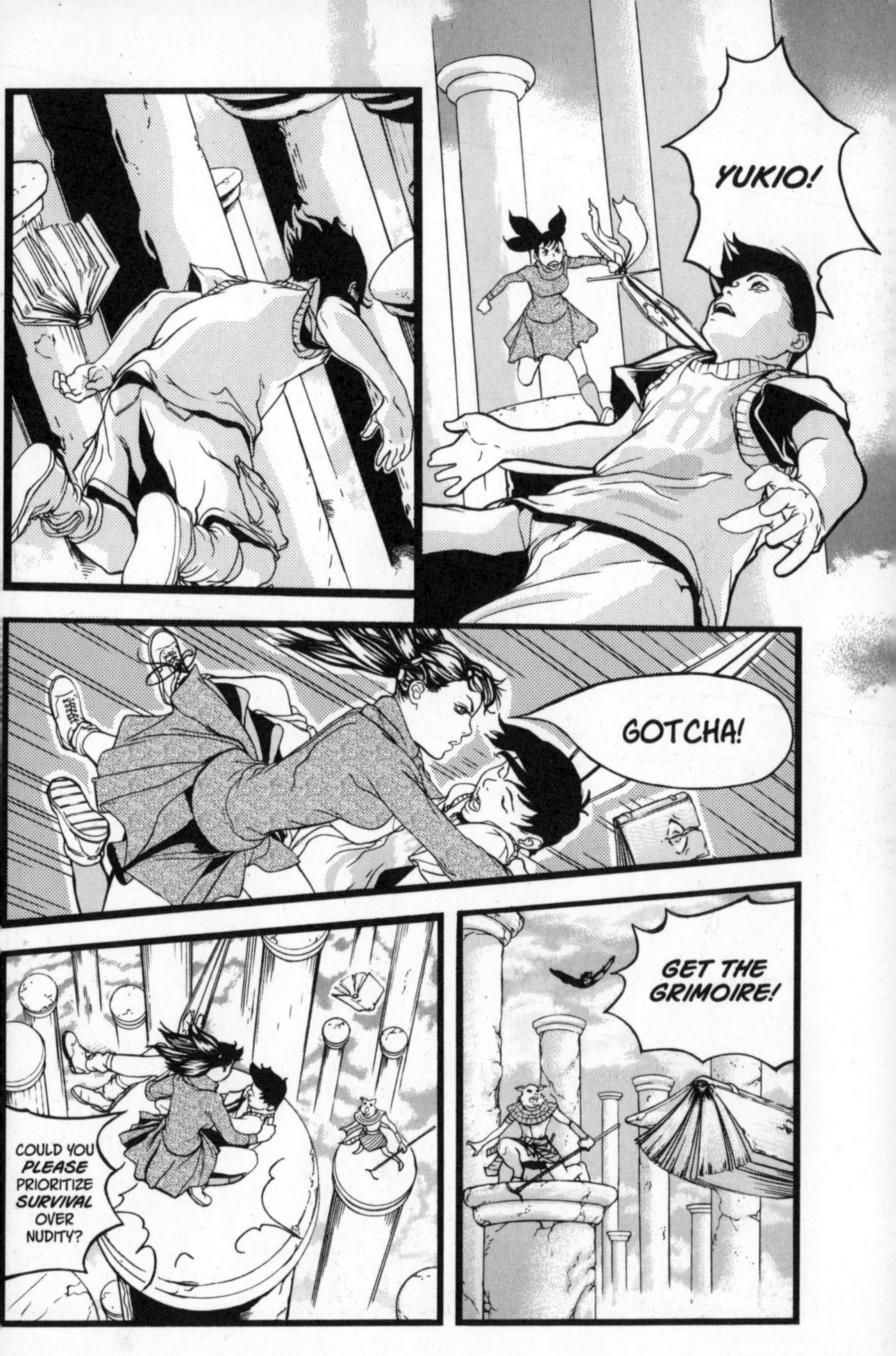
YUKIO!
GOTCHA!
COULD YOU *PLEASE* PRIORITIZE *SURVIVAL* OVER NUDITY?
GET THE GRIMOIRE!

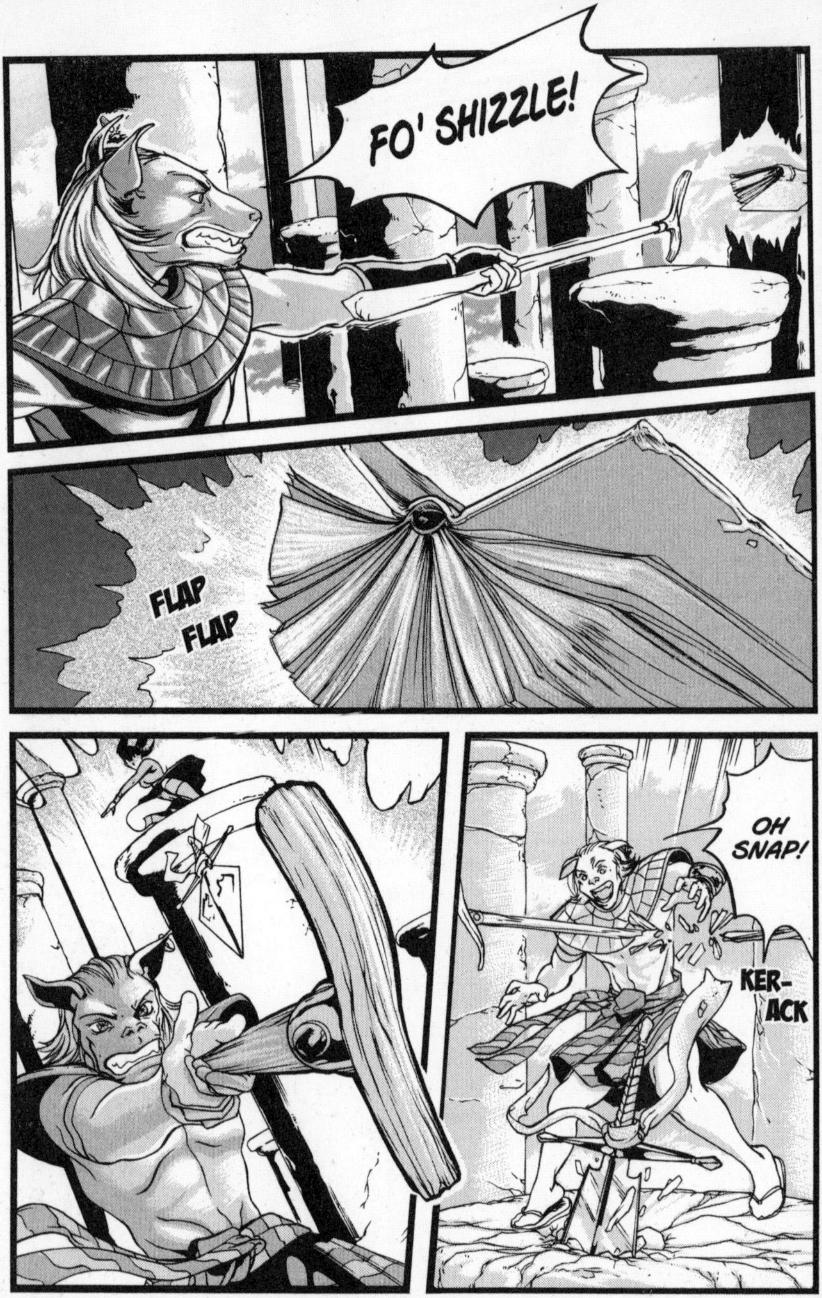
FO' SHIZZLE!
FLAP
FLAP
OH SNAP!
KER-
ACK

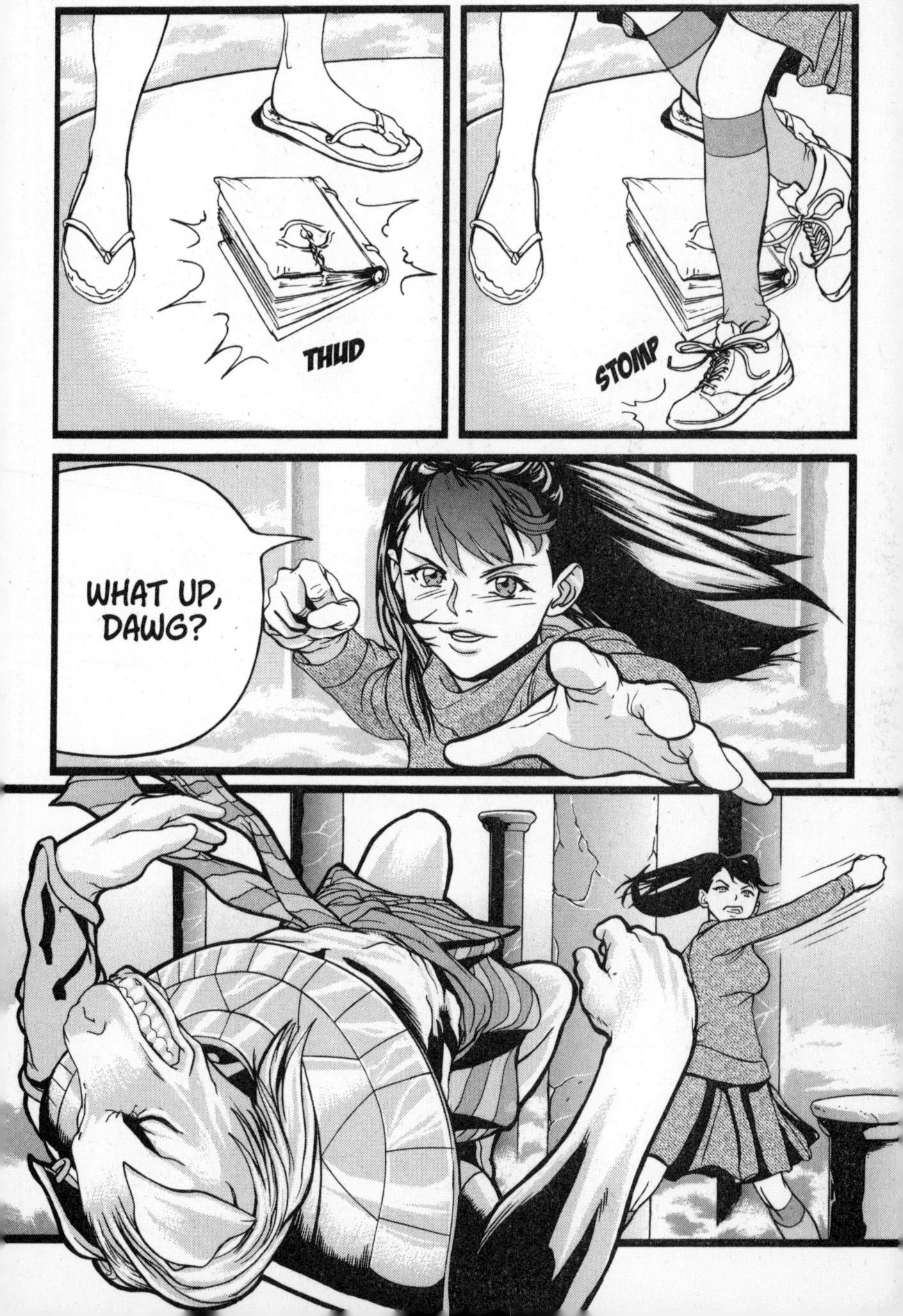
THUD
STOMP
WHAT UP, DAWG?

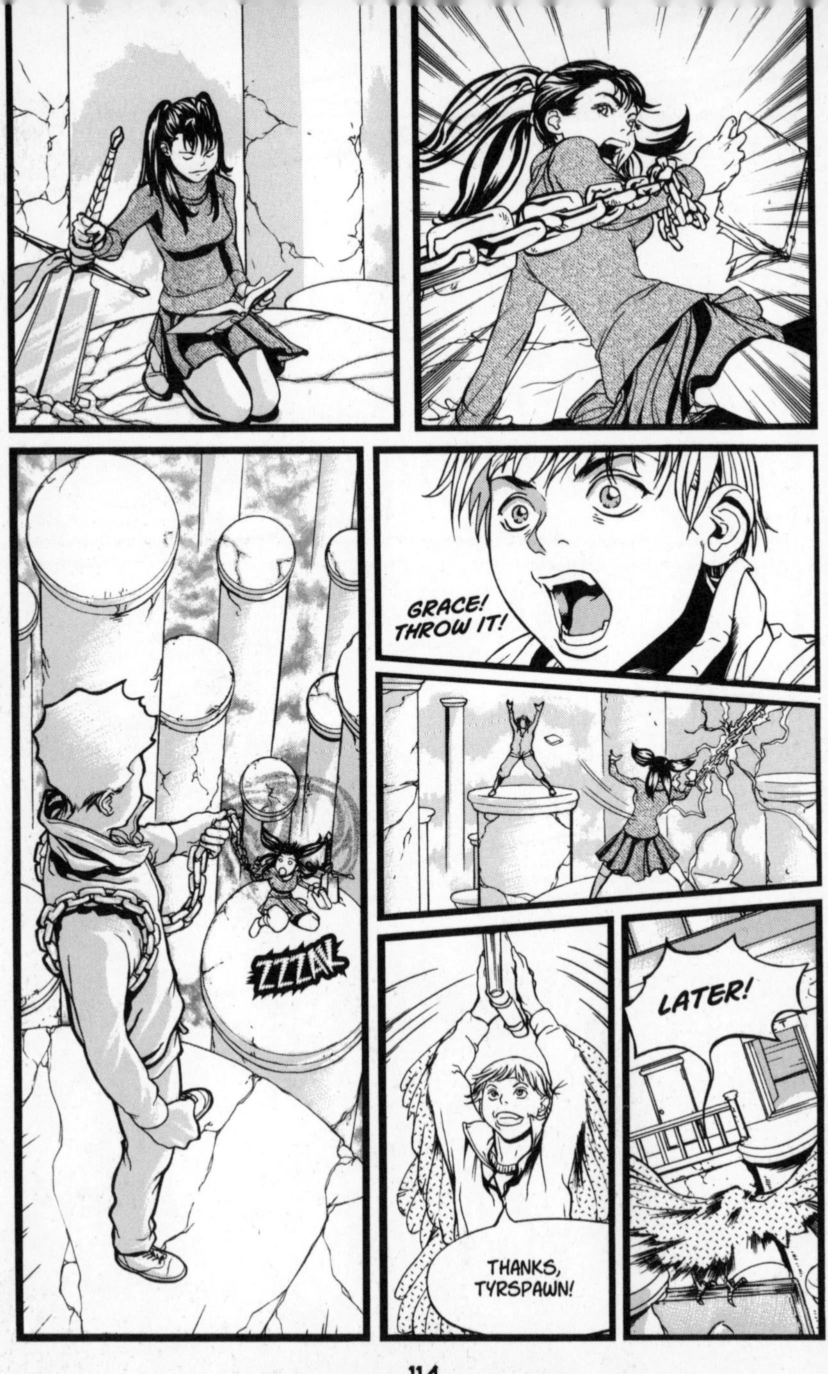
GRACE! THROW IT!
ZZZAK
THANKS, TYRSPAWN!
LATER!

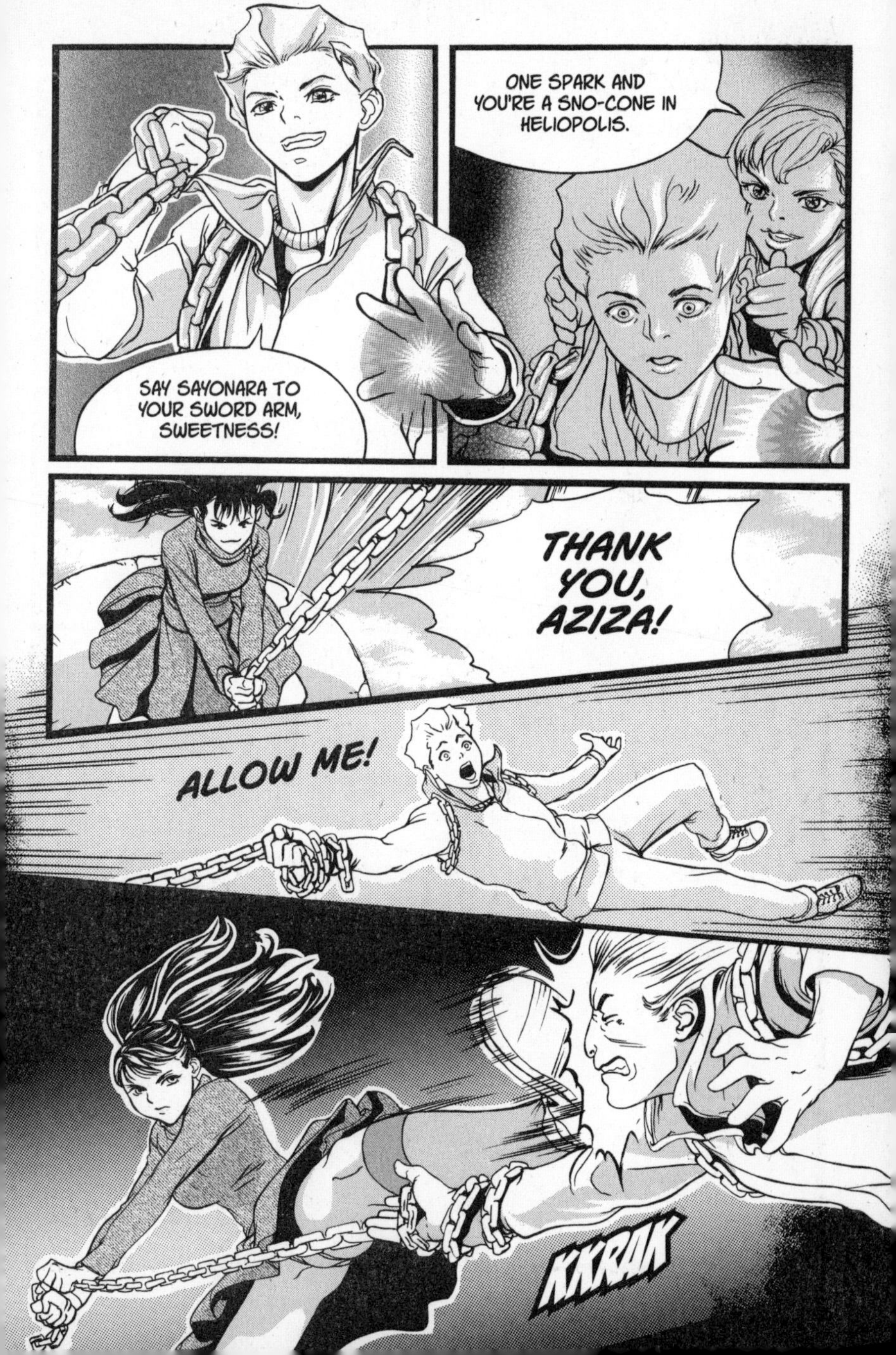
SAY SAYONARA TO YOUR SWORD ARM, SWEETNESS!
ONE SPARK AND YOU'RE A SNO-CONE IN HELIOPOLIS.
THANK YOU, AZIZA!
ALLOW ME!
KKRAK

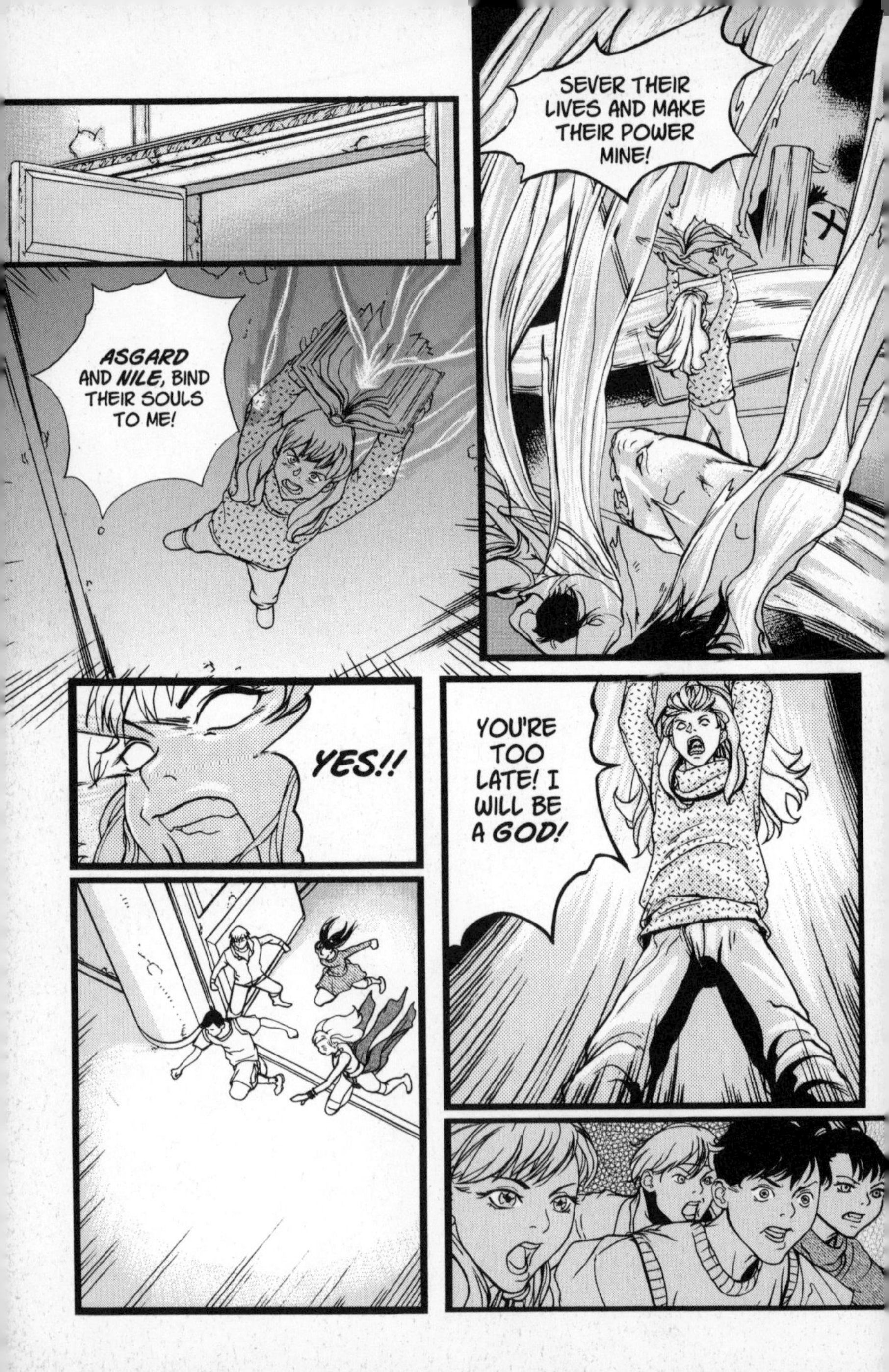
ASGARD AND NILE, BIND THEIR SOULS TO ME!
SEVER THEIR LIVES AND MAKE THEIR POWER MINE!
YES!!
YOU'RE TOO LATE! I WILL BE A GOD!

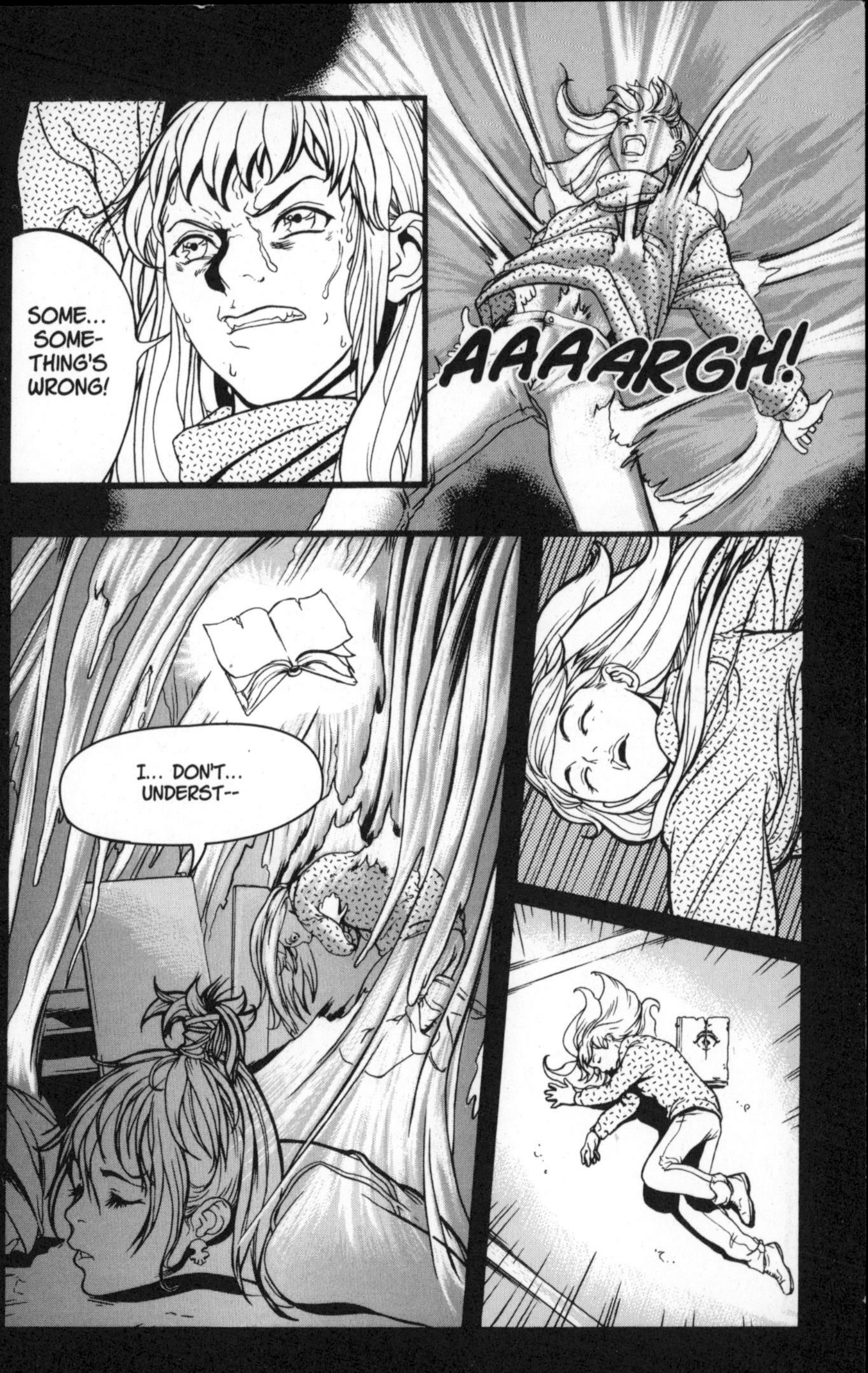
SOME... SOME-THING'S WRONG!
AAAAARGH!
I... DON'T... UNDERST--

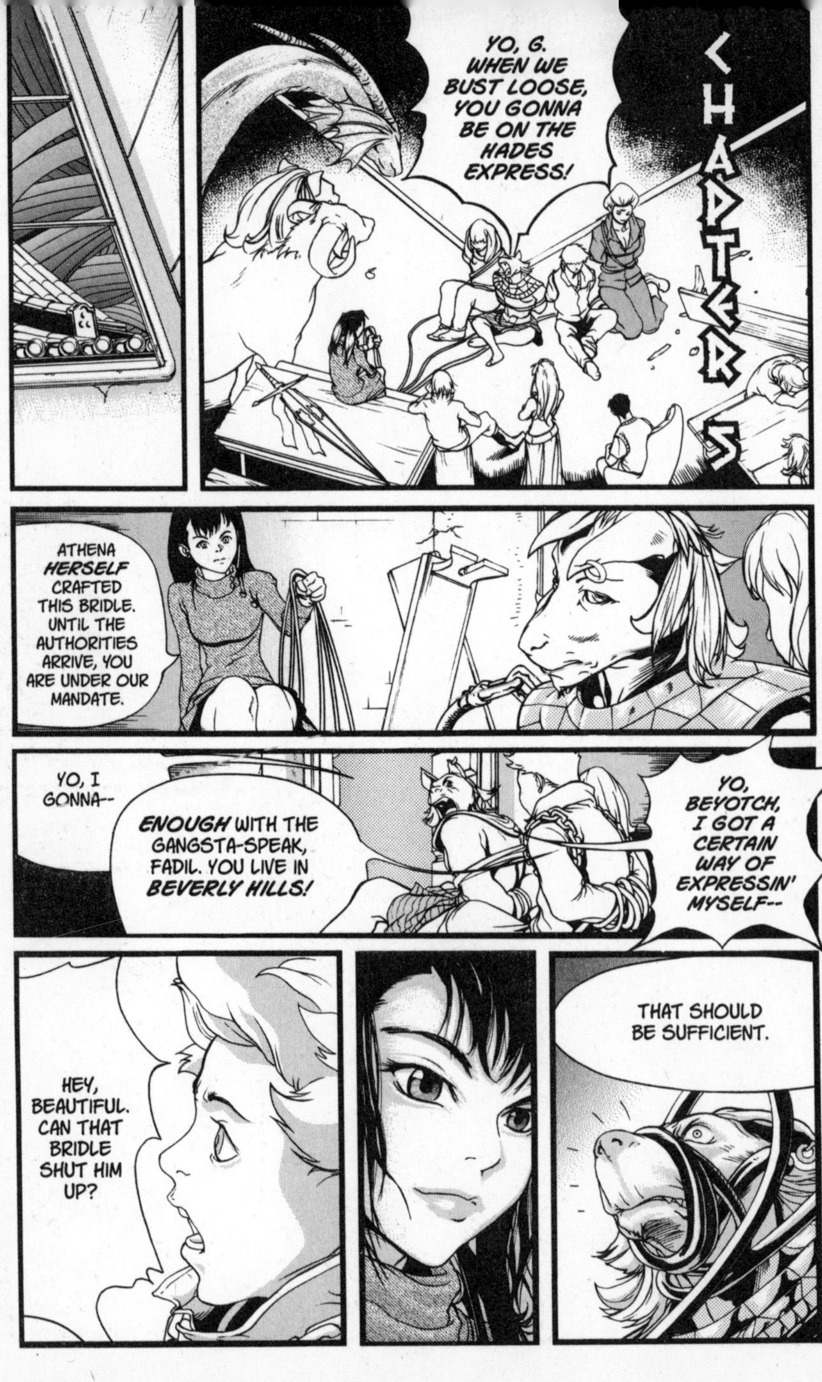
YO, G. WHEN WE BUST LOOSE, YOU GONNA BE ON THE HADES EXPRESS!
CHAPTER 5
ATHENA HERSELF CRAFTED THIS BRIDLE. UNTIL THE AUTHORITIES ARRIVE, YOU ARE UNDER OUR MANDATE.
YO, I GONNA--
ENOUGH WITH THE GANGSTA-SPEAK, FADIL. YOU LIVE IN BEVERLY HILLS!
YO, BEYOTCH, I GOT A CERTAIN WAY OF EXPRESSIN' MYSELF--
HEY, BEAUTIFUL. CAN THAT BRIDLE SHUT HIM UP?
THAT SHOULD BE SUFFICIENT.

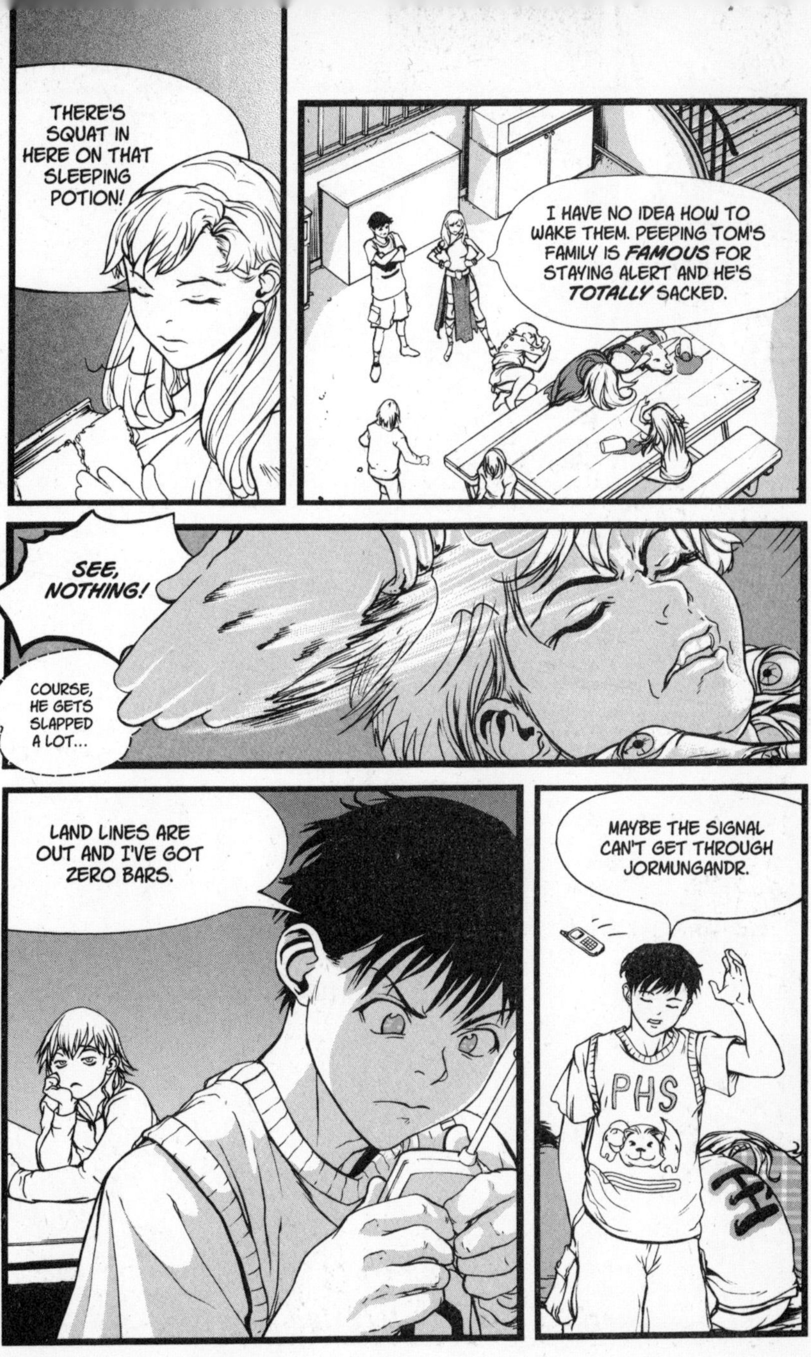

THERE'S SQUAT IN HERE ON THAT SLEEPING POTION!
I HAVE NO IDEA HOW TO WAKE THEM. PEEPING TOM'S FAMILY IS *FAMOUS* FOR STAYING ALERT AND HE'S *TOTALLY* SACKED.
SEE, NOTHING!
COURSE, HE GETS SLAPPED A LOT...
LAND LINES ARE OUT AND I'VE GOT ZERO BARS.
MAYBE THE SIGNAL CAN'T GET THROUGH JORMUNGANDR.
PHS

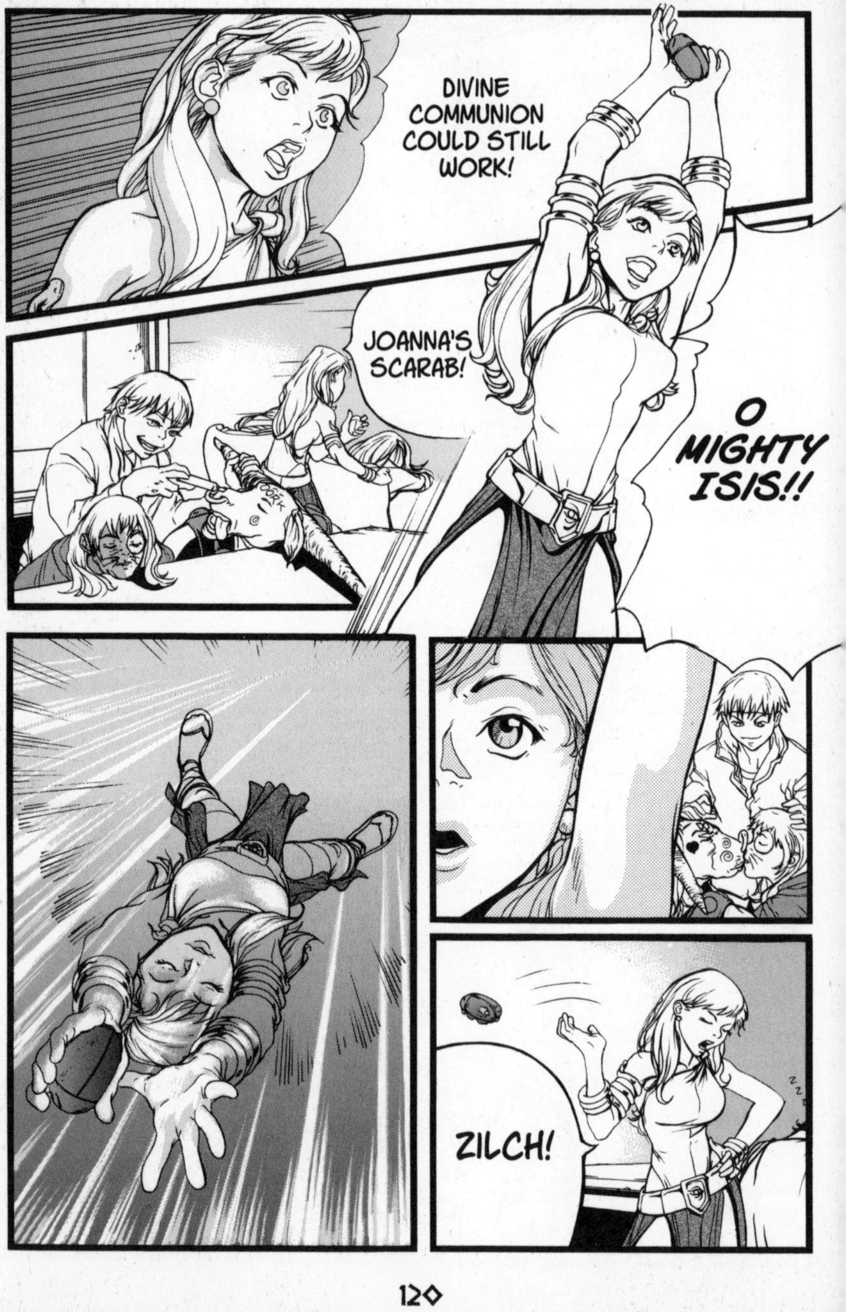
DIVINE COMMUNION COULD STILL WORK!
JOANNA'S SCARAB!
O MIGHTY ISIS!!
ZILCH!

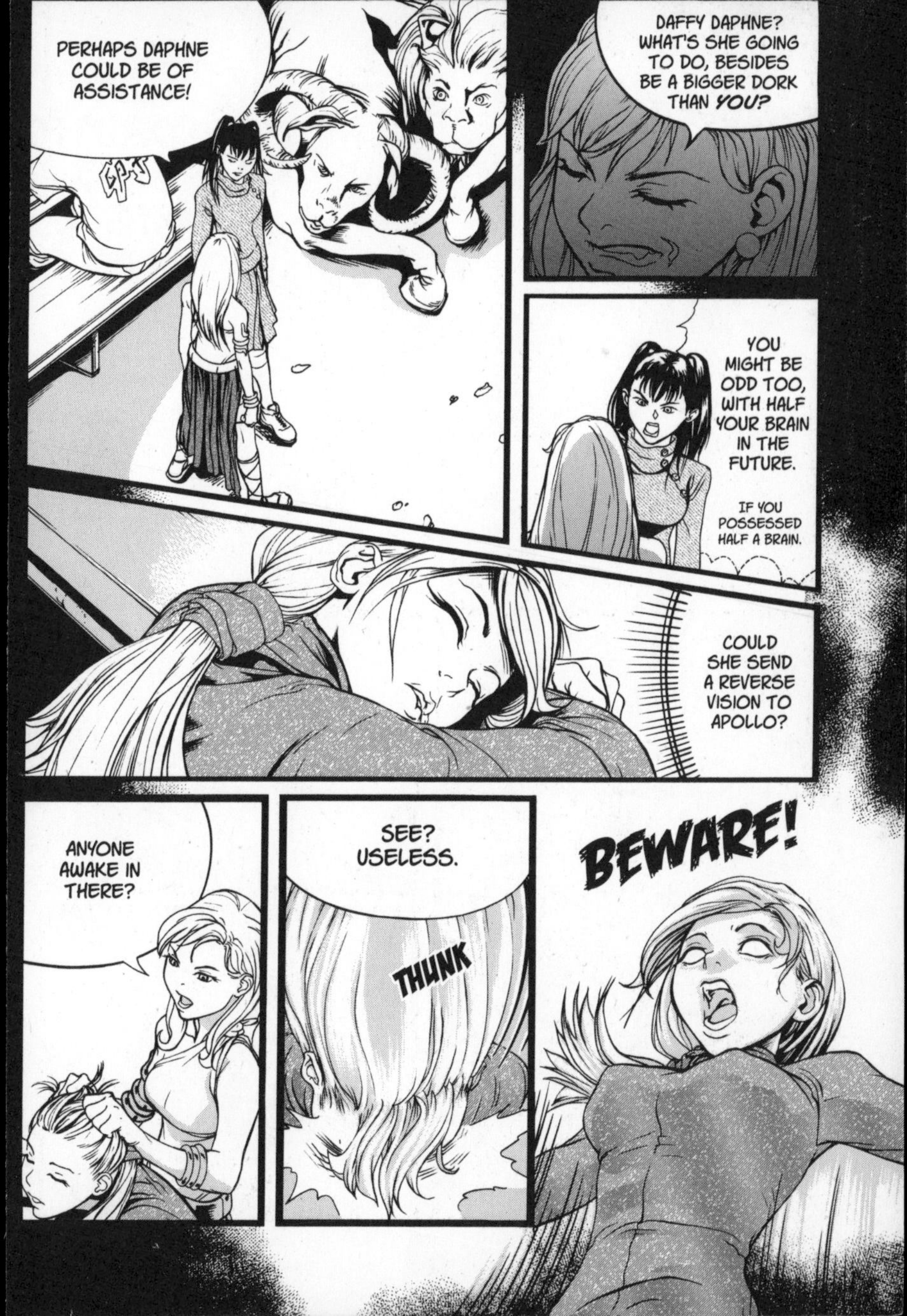

PERHAPS DAPHNE COULD BE OF ASSISTANCE!
DAFFY DAPHNE? WHAT'S SHE GOING TO DO, BESIDES BE A BIGGER DORK THAN *YOU?*
YOU MIGHT BE ODD TOO, WITH HALF YOUR BRAIN IN THE FUTURE.
IF YOU POSSESSED HALF A BRAIN.
COULD SHE SEND A REVERSE VISION TO APOLLO?
ANYONE AWAKE IN THERE?
SEE? USELESS.
THUNK
BEWARE!

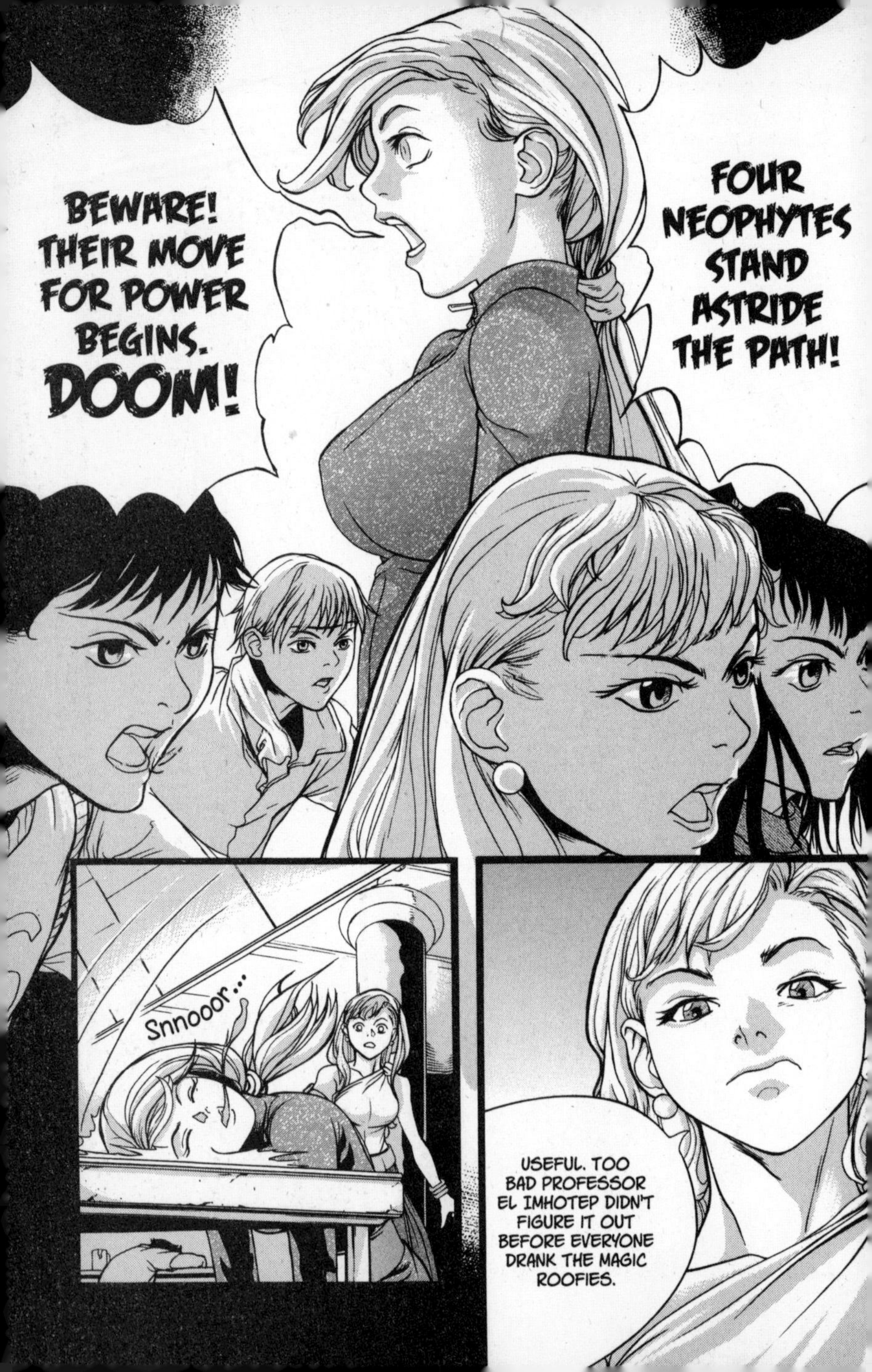
BEWARE! THEIR MOVE FOR POWER BEGINS. DOOM!
FOUR NEOPHYTES STAND ASTRIDE THE PATH!
Snnooor...
USEFUL. TOO BAD PROFESSOR EL IMHOTEP DIDN'T FIGURE IT OUT BEFORE EVERYONE DRANK THE MAGIC ROOFIES.

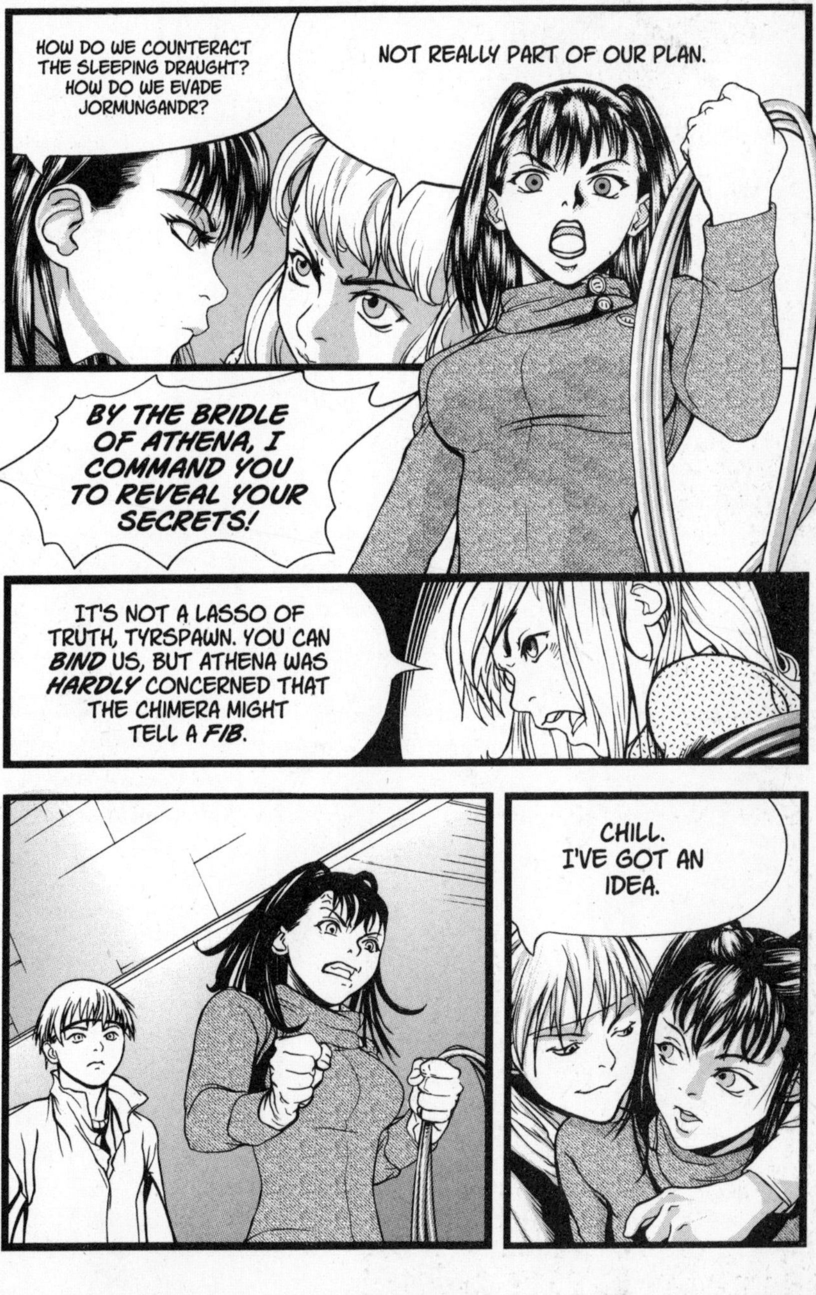
HOW DO WE COUNTERACT THE SLEEPING DRAUGHT? HOW DO WE EVADE JORMUNGANDR?
NOT REALLY PART OF OUR PLAN.
BY THE BRIDLE OF ATHENA, I COMMAND YOU TO REVEAL YOUR SECRETS!
IT'S NOT A LASSO OF TRUTH, TYRSPAWN. YOU CAN BIND US, BUT ATHENA WAS HARDLY CONCERNED THAT THE CHIMERA MIGHT TELL A FIB.
CHILL. I'VE GOT AN IDEA.

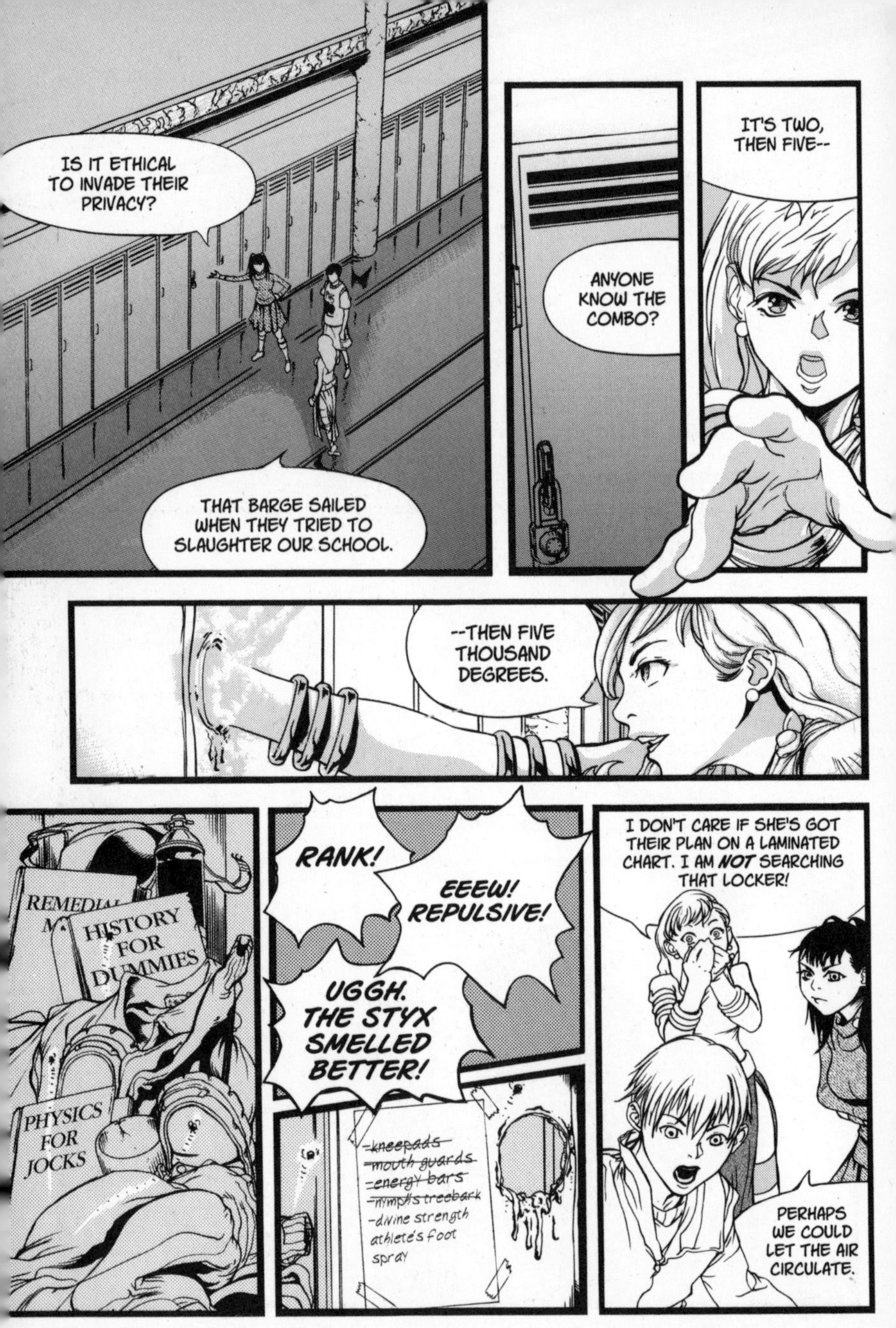

IS IT ETHICAL TO INVADE THEIR PRIVACY?
THAT BARGE SAILED WHEN THEY TRIED TO SLAUGHTER OUR SCHOOL.
ANYONE KNOW THE COMBO?
IT'S TWO, THEN FIVE--
--THEN FIVE THOUSAND DEGREES.
HISTORY FOR DUMMIES
PHYSICS FOR JOCKS
RANK!
EEEW! REPULSIVE!
UGGH. THE STYX SMELLED BETTER!
-kneepads
-mouth guards
-energy bars
-nymph's treebark
-divine strength athlete's foot spray
I DON'T CARE IF SHE'S GOT THEIR PLAN ON A LAMINATED CHART. I AM NOT SEARCHING THAT LOCKER!
PERHAPS WE COULD LET THE AIR CIRCULATE.

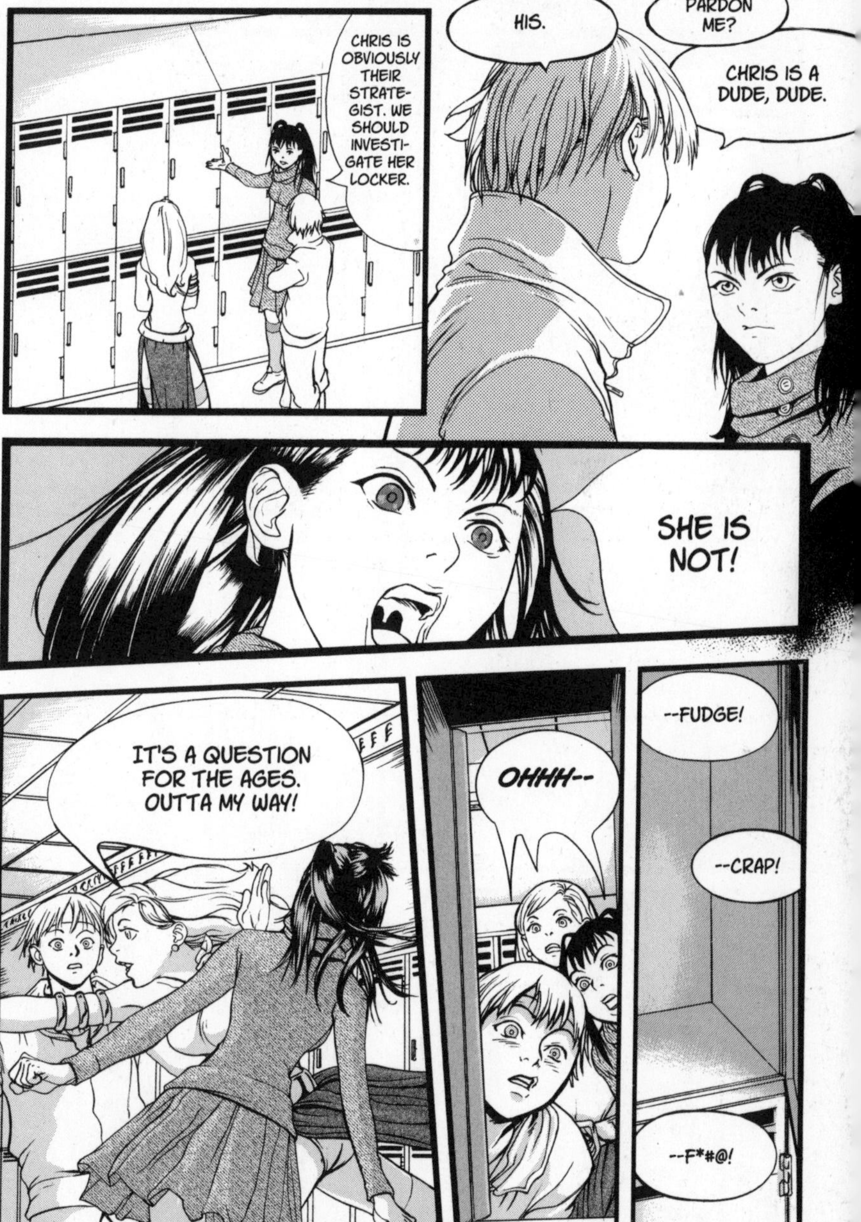
CHRIS IS OBVIOUSLY THEIR STRATE-GIST. WE SHOULD INVESTI-GATE HER LOCKER.
HIS.
PARDON ME?
CHRIS IS A DUDE, DUDE.
SHE IS NOT!
IT'S A QUESTION FOR THE AGES. OUTTA MY WAY!
OHHH--
--FUDGE!
--CRAP!
--F*#@!

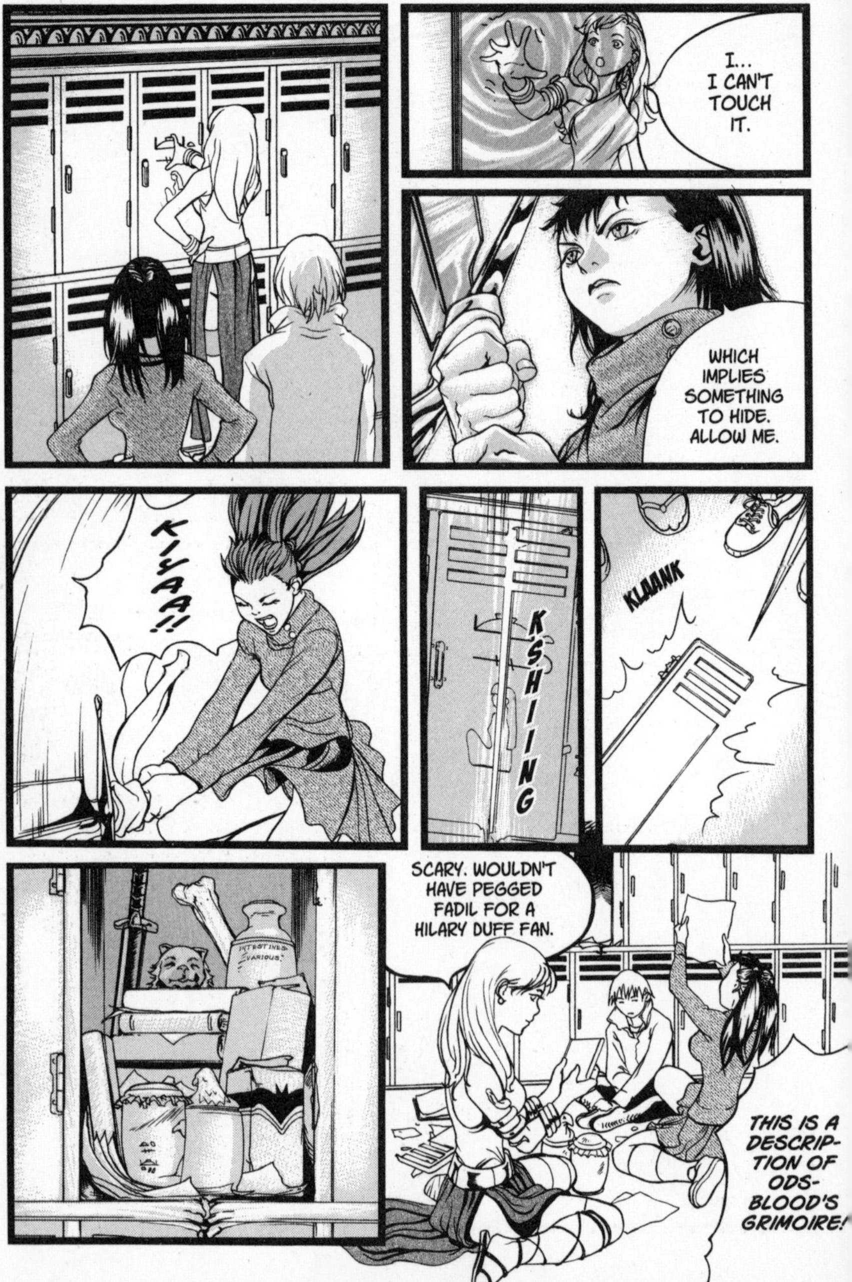
I... I CAN'T TOUCH IT.
WHICH IMPLIES SOMETHING TO HIDE. ALLOW ME.
KIYAA!!
K'SHIIING
KLAANK
INTESTINES VARIOUS
SCARY. WOULDN'T HAVE PEGGED FADIL FOR A HILARY DUFF FAN.
THIS IS A DESCRIPTION OF ODS-BLOOD'S GRIMOIRE!

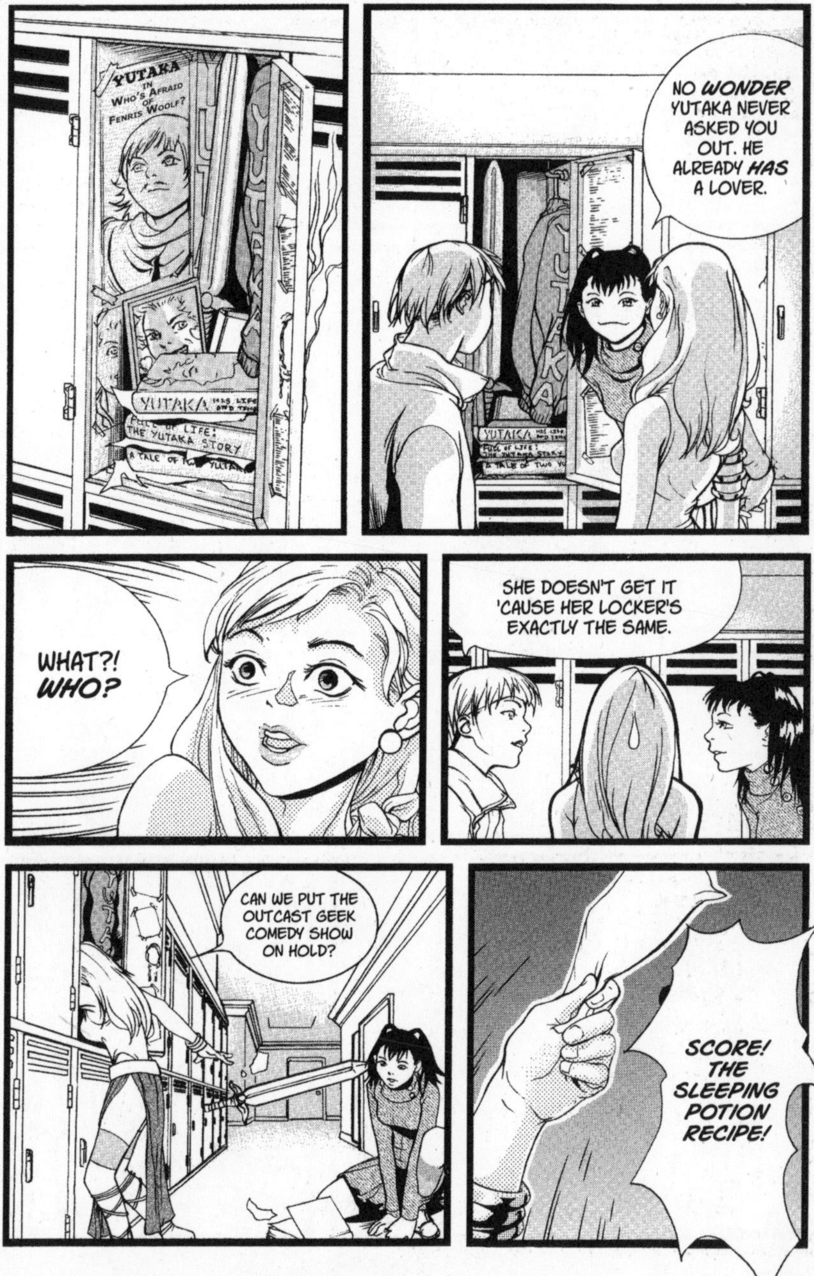
YUTAKA IN WHO'S AFRAID OF FENRIS WOOLF?
YUTAKA
FULL OF LIFE: THE YUTAKA STORY
NO WONDER YUTAKA NEVER ASKED YOU OUT. HE ALREADY HAS A LOVER.
WHAT?! WHO?
SHE DOESN'T GET IT 'CAUSE HER LOCKER'S EXACTLY THE SAME.
CAN WE PUT THE OUTCAST GEEK COMEDY SHOW ON HOLD?
SCORE! THE SLEEPING POTION RECIPE!

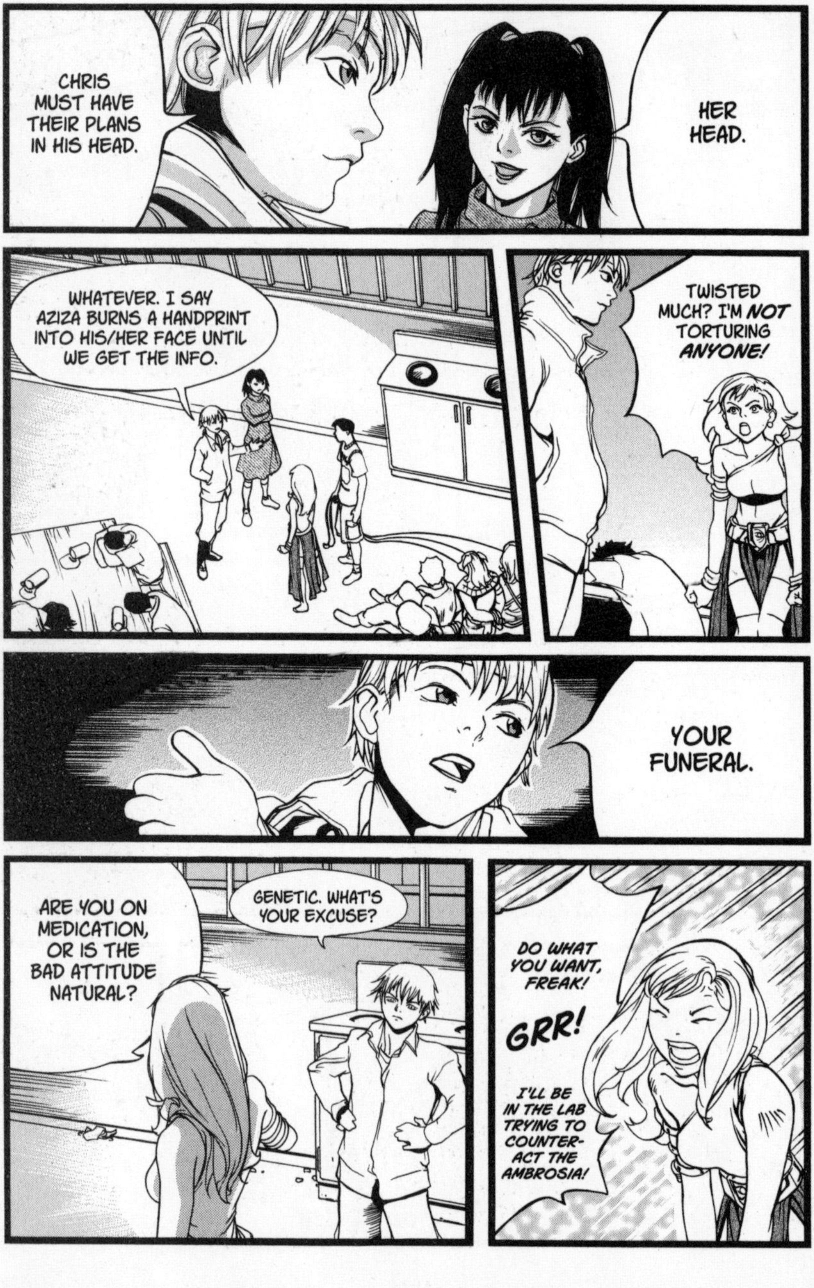
CHRIS MUST HAVE THEIR PLANS IN HIS HEAD.
HER HEAD.
WHATEVER. I SAY AZIZA BURNS A HANDPRINT INTO HIS/HER FACE UNTIL WE GET THE INFO.
TWISTED MUCH? I'M *NOT* TORTURING *ANYONE!*
YOUR FUNERAL.
ARE YOU ON MEDICATION, OR IS THE BAD ATTITUDE NATURAL?
GENETIC. WHAT'S YOUR EXCUSE?
DO WHAT YOU WANT, FREAK!
GRR!
I'LL BE IN THE LAB TRYING TO COUNTER-ACT THE AMBROSIA!

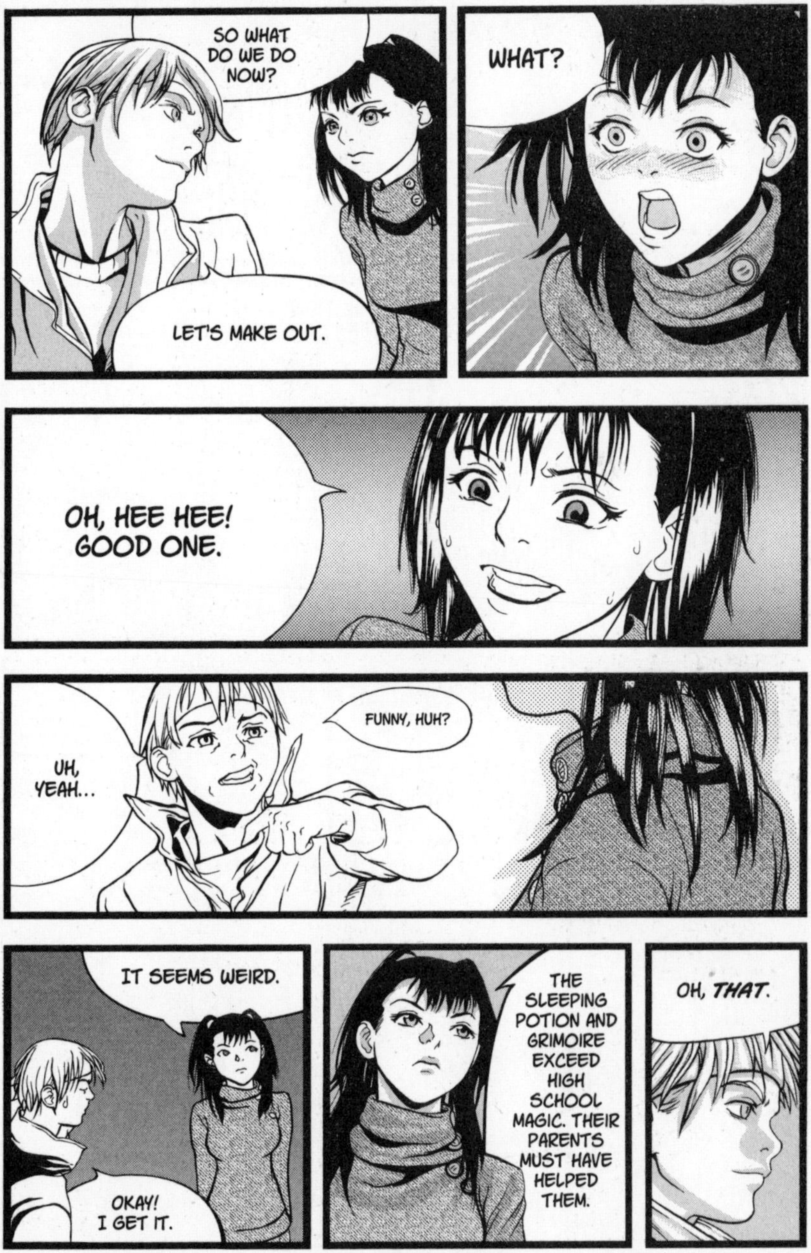
SO WHAT DO WE DO NOW?
LET'S MAKE OUT.
WHAT?
OH, HEE HEE! GOOD ONE.
FUNNY, HUH?
UH, YEAH...
IT SEEMS WEIRD.
OKAY! I GET IT.
THE SLEEPING POTION AND GRIMOIRE EXCEED HIGH SCHOOL MAGIC. THEIR PARENTS MUST HAVE HELPED THEM.
OH, *THAT*.

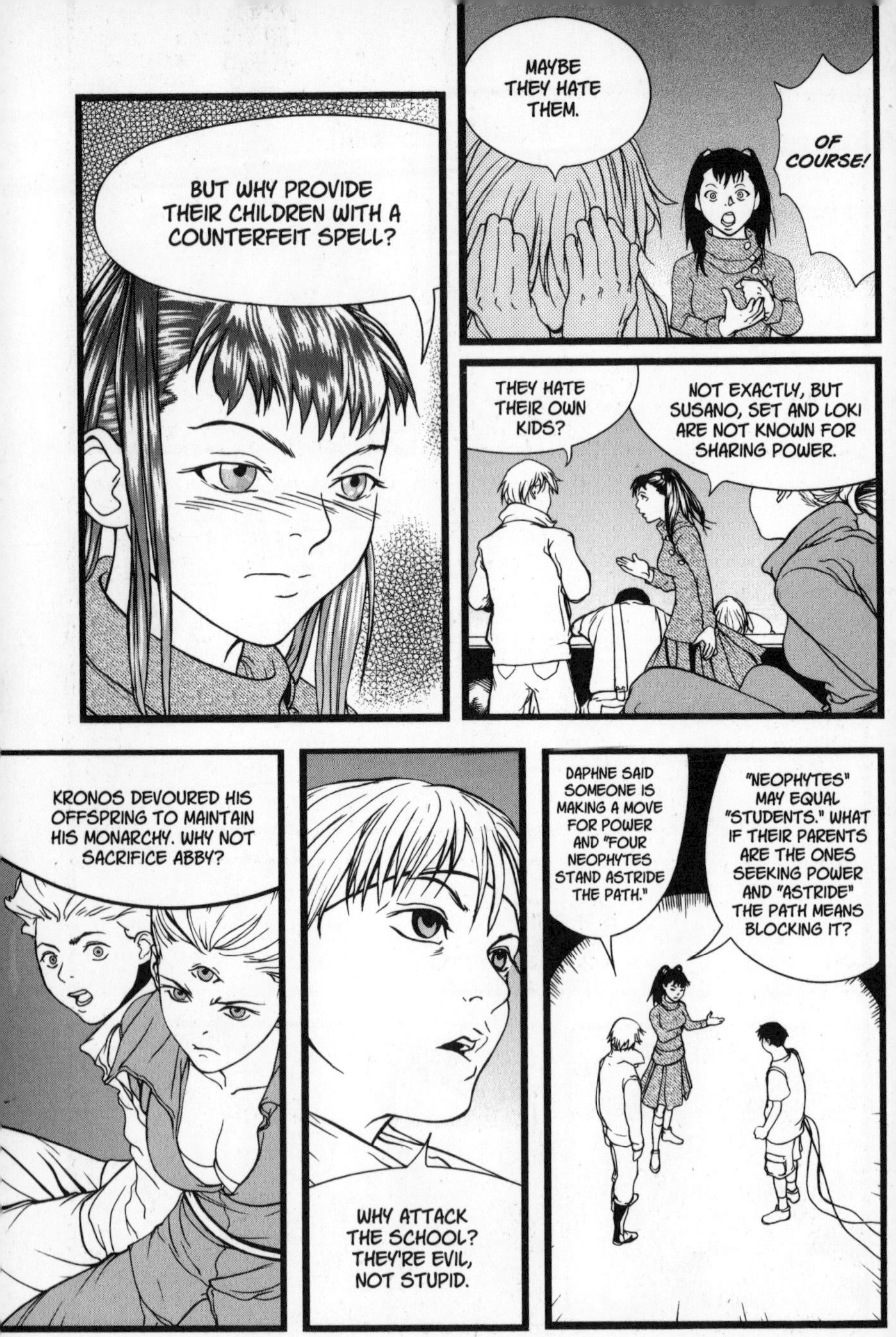
BUT WHY PROVIDE THEIR CHILDREN WITH A COUNTERFEIT SPELL?
MAYBE THEY HATE THEM.
OF COURSE!
THEY HATE THEIR OWN KIDS?
NOT EXACTLY, BUT SUSANO, SET AND LOKI ARE NOT KNOWN FOR SHARING POWER.
KRONOS DEVOURED HIS OFFSPRING TO MAINTAIN HIS MONARCHY. WHY NOT SACRIFICE ABBY?
WHY ATTACK THE SCHOOL? THEY'RE EVIL, NOT STUPID.
DAPHNE SAID SOMEONE IS MAKING A MOVE FOR POWER AND "FOUR NEOPHYTES STAND ASTRIDE THE PATH."
"NEOPHYTES" MAY EQUAL "STUDENTS." WHAT IF THEIR PARENTS ARE THE ONES SEEKING POWER AND "ASTRIDE" THE PATH MEANS BLOCKING IT?

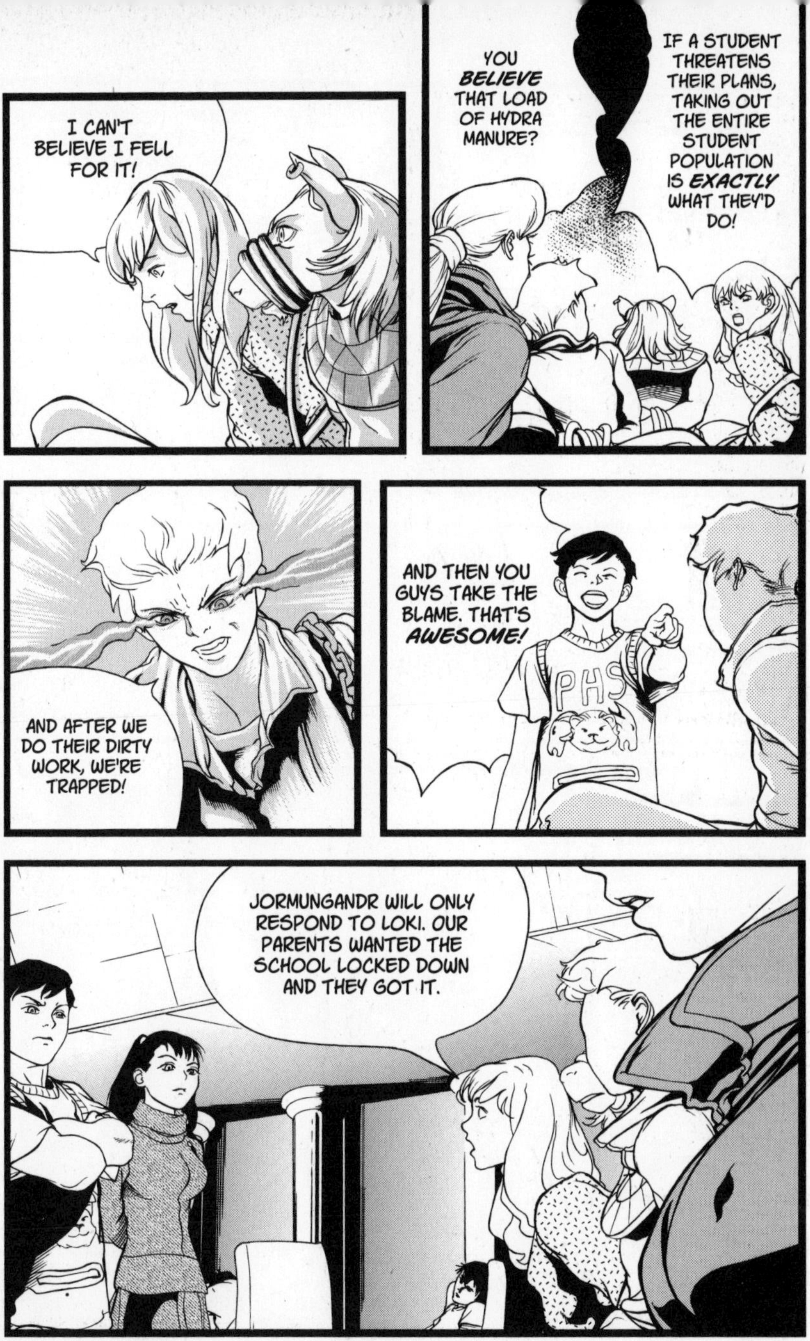

I CAN'T BELIEVE I FELL FOR IT!
YOU *BELIEVE* THAT LOAD OF HYDRA MANURE?
IF A STUDENT THREATENS THEIR PLANS, TAKING OUT THE ENTIRE STUDENT POPULATION IS *EXACTLY* WHAT THEY'D DO!
AND AFTER WE DO THEIR DIRTY WORK, WE'RE TRAPPED!
AND THEN YOU GUYS TAKE THE BLAME. THAT'S *AWESOME!*
PHS
JORMUNGANDR WILL ONLY RESPOND TO LOKI. OUR PARENTS WANTED THE SCHOOL LOCKED DOWN AND THEY GOT IT.

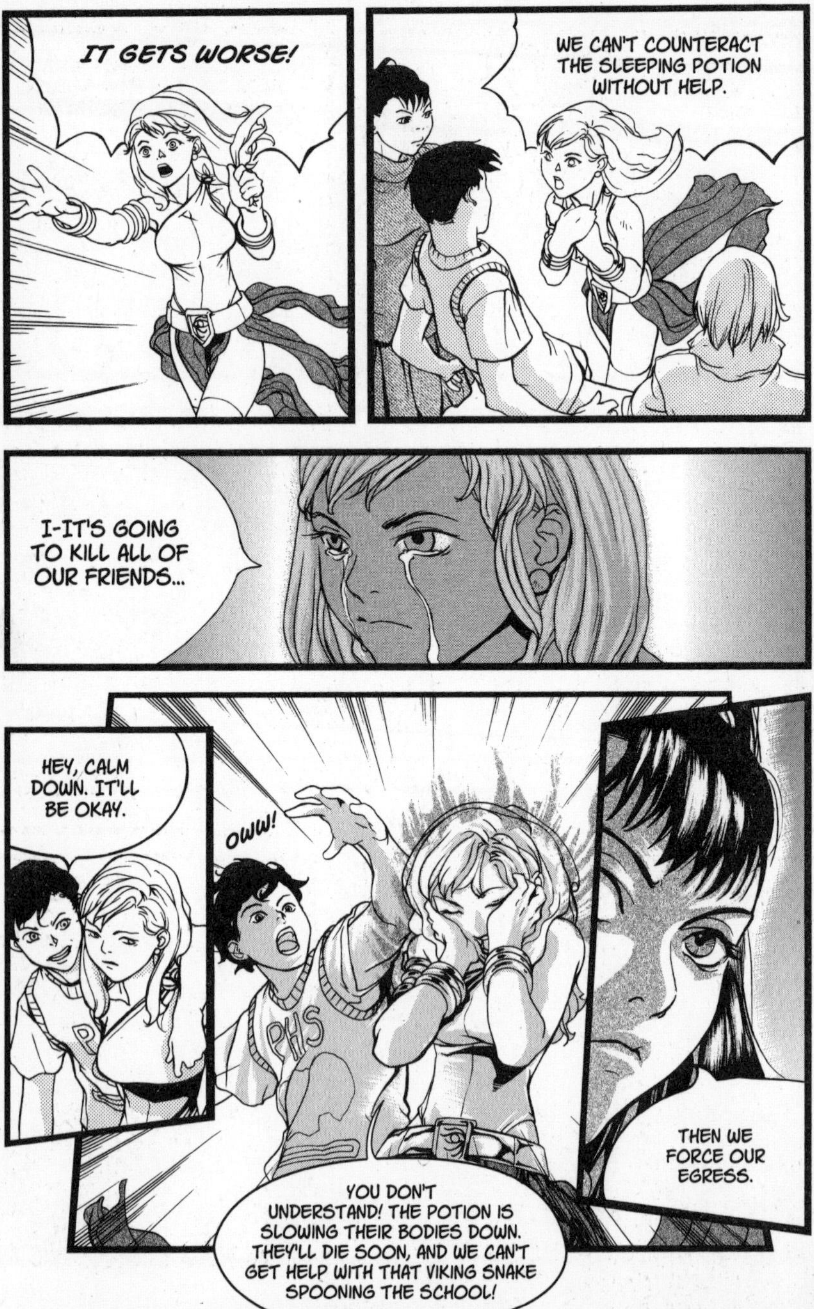
IT GETS WORSE!
WE CAN'T COUNTERACT THE SLEEPING POTION WITHOUT HELP.
I-IT'S GOING TO KILL ALL OF OUR FRIENDS...
HEY, CALM DOWN. IT'LL BE OKAY.
OWW!
YOU DON'T UNDERSTAND! THE POTION IS SLOWING THEIR BODIES DOWN. THEY'LL DIE SOON, AND WE CAN'T GET HELP WITH THAT VIKING SNAKE SPOONING THE SCHOOL!
THEN WE FORCE OUR EGRESS.

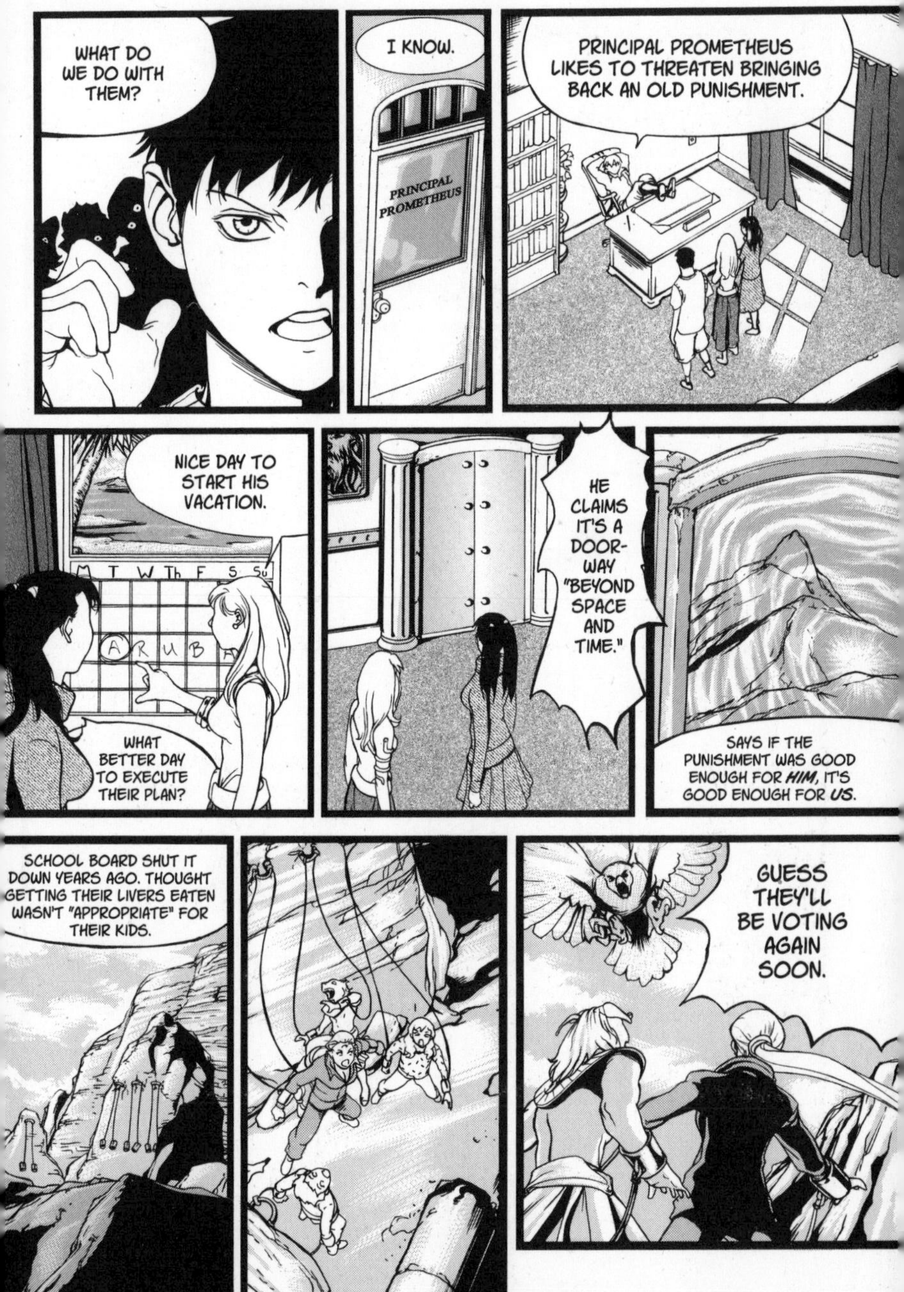
WHAT DO WE DO WITH THEM?
I KNOW.
PRINCIPAL PROMETHEUS
PRINCIPAL PROMETHEUS LIKES TO THREATEN BRINGING BACK AN OLD PUNISHMENT.
NICE DAY TO START HIS VACATION.
M T W Th F S Su
A R U B A
WHAT BETTER DAY TO EXECUTE THEIR PLAN?
HE CLAIMS IT'S A DOOR-WAY "BEYOND SPACE AND TIME."
SAYS IF THE PUNISHMENT WAS GOOD ENOUGH FOR ***HIM***, IT'S GOOD ENOUGH FOR ***US***.
SCHOOL BOARD SHUT IT DOWN YEARS AGO. THOUGHT GETTING THEIR LIVERS EATEN WASN'T "APPROPRIATE" FOR THEIR KIDS.
GUESS THEY'LL BE VOTING AGAIN SOON.

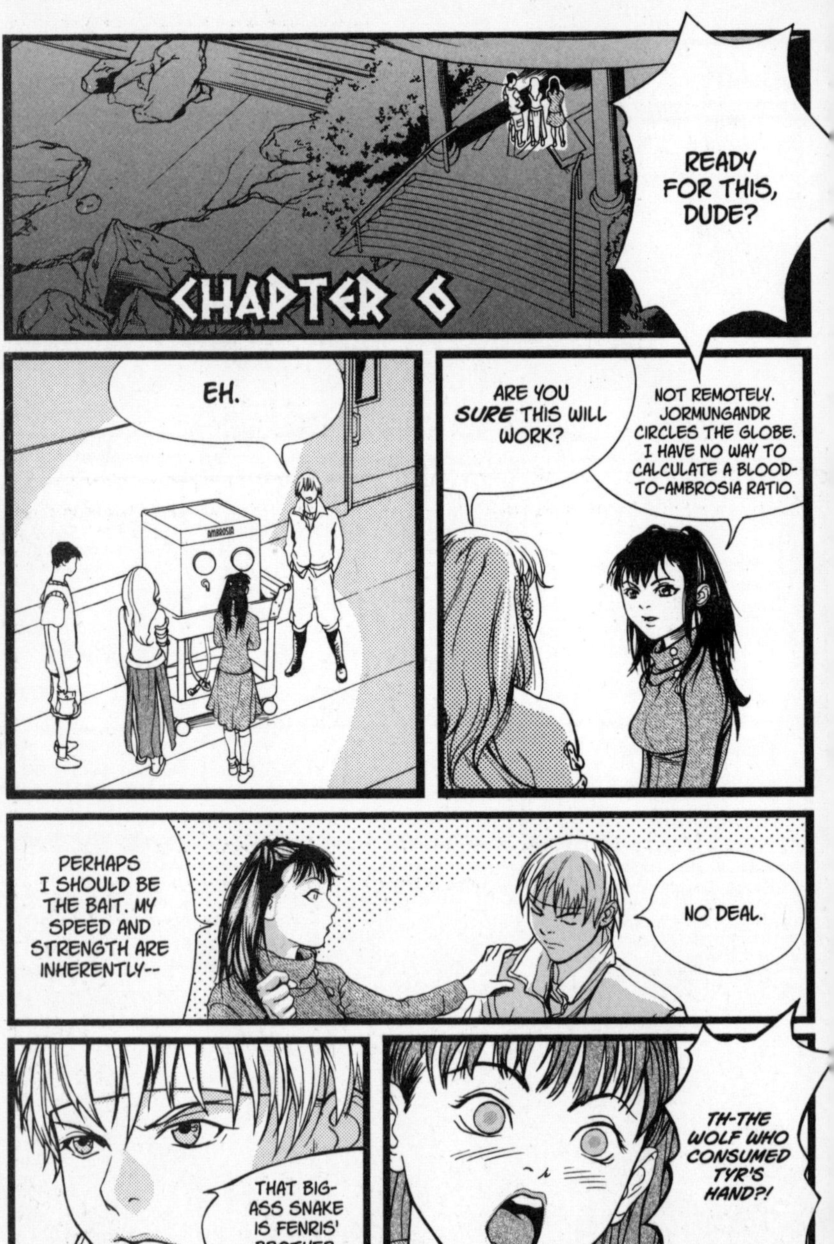
CHAPTER 6
READY FOR THIS, DUDE?
EH.
ARE YOU *SURE* THIS WILL WORK?
NOT REMOTELY. JORMUNGANDR CIRCLES THE GLOBE. I HAVE NO WAY TO CALCULATE A BLOOD-TO-AMBROSIA RATIO.
PERHAPS I SHOULD BE THE BAIT. MY SPEED AND STRENGTH ARE INHERENTLY--
NO DEAL.
THAT BIG-ASS SNAKE IS FENRIS' BROTHER.
TH-THE WOLF WHO CONSUMED TYR'S HAND?!

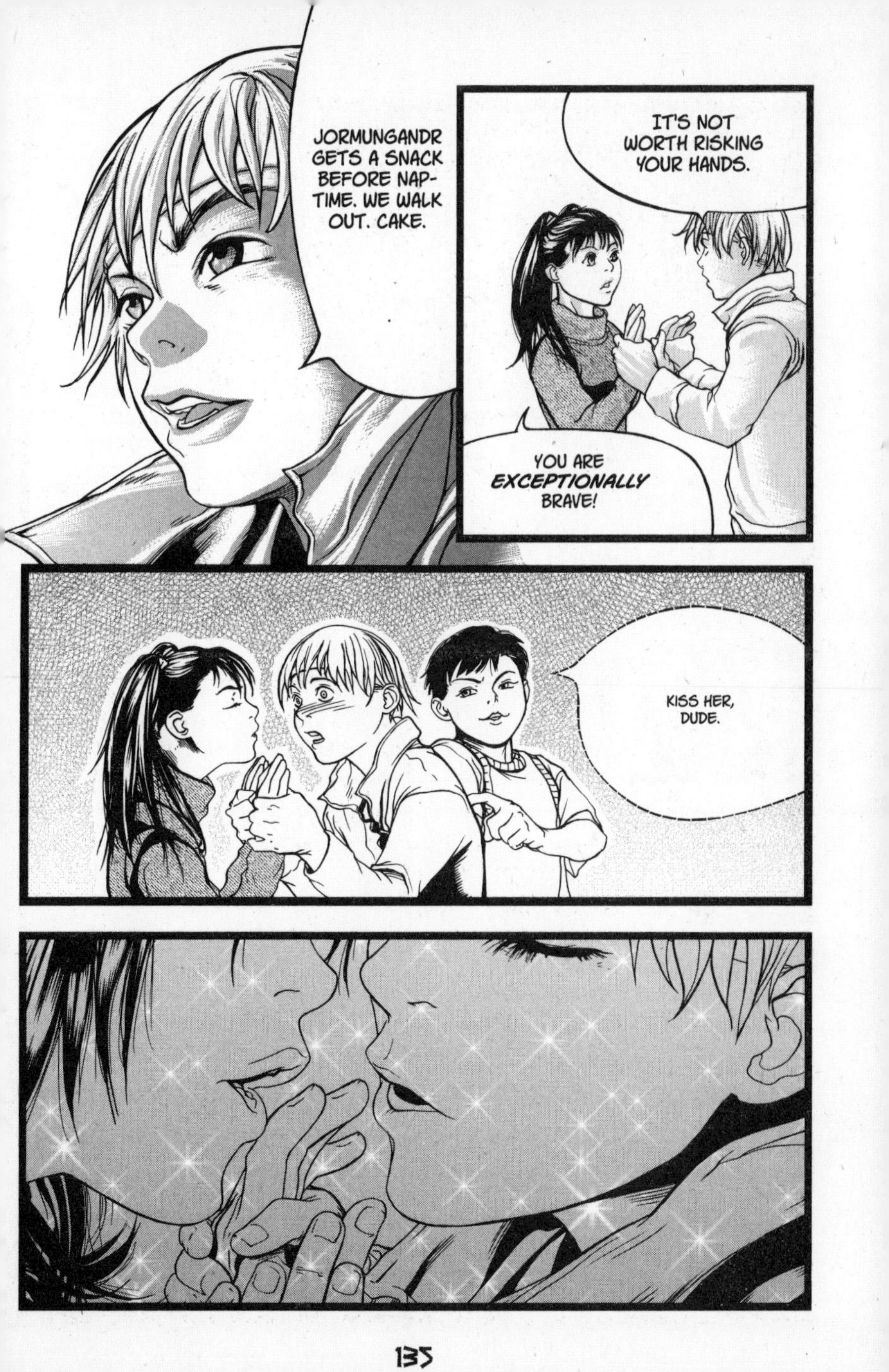
JORMUNGANDR GETS A SNACK BEFORE NAP-TIME. WE WALK OUT. CAKE.
IT'S NOT WORTH RISKING YOUR HANDS.
YOU ARE EXCEPTIONALLY BRAVE!
KISS HER, DUDE.

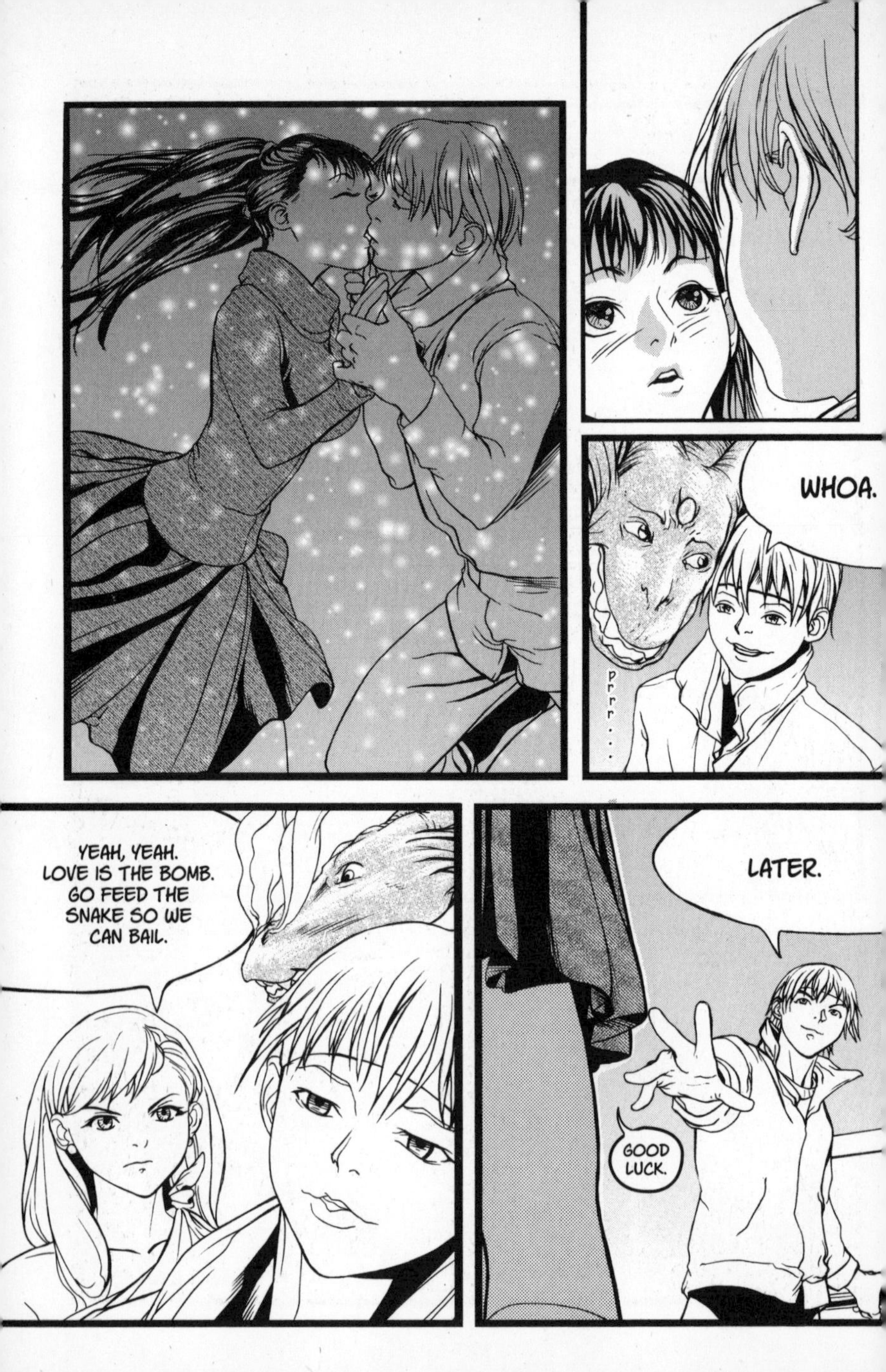
WHOA.
prrr...
YEAH, YEAH. LOVE IS THE BOMB. GO FEED THE SNAKE SO WE CAN BAIL.
LATER.
GOOD LUCK.

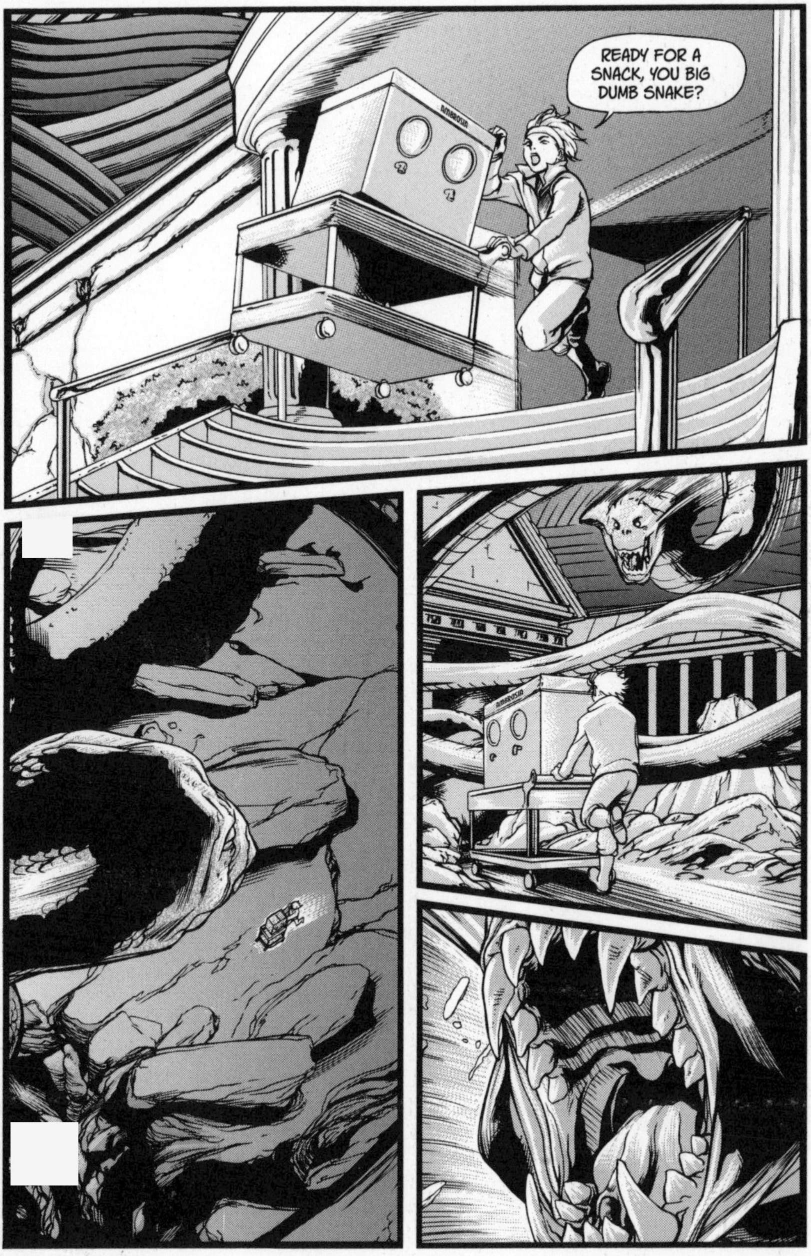
READY FOR A SNACK, YOU BIG DUMB SNAKE?
AMBROSIA

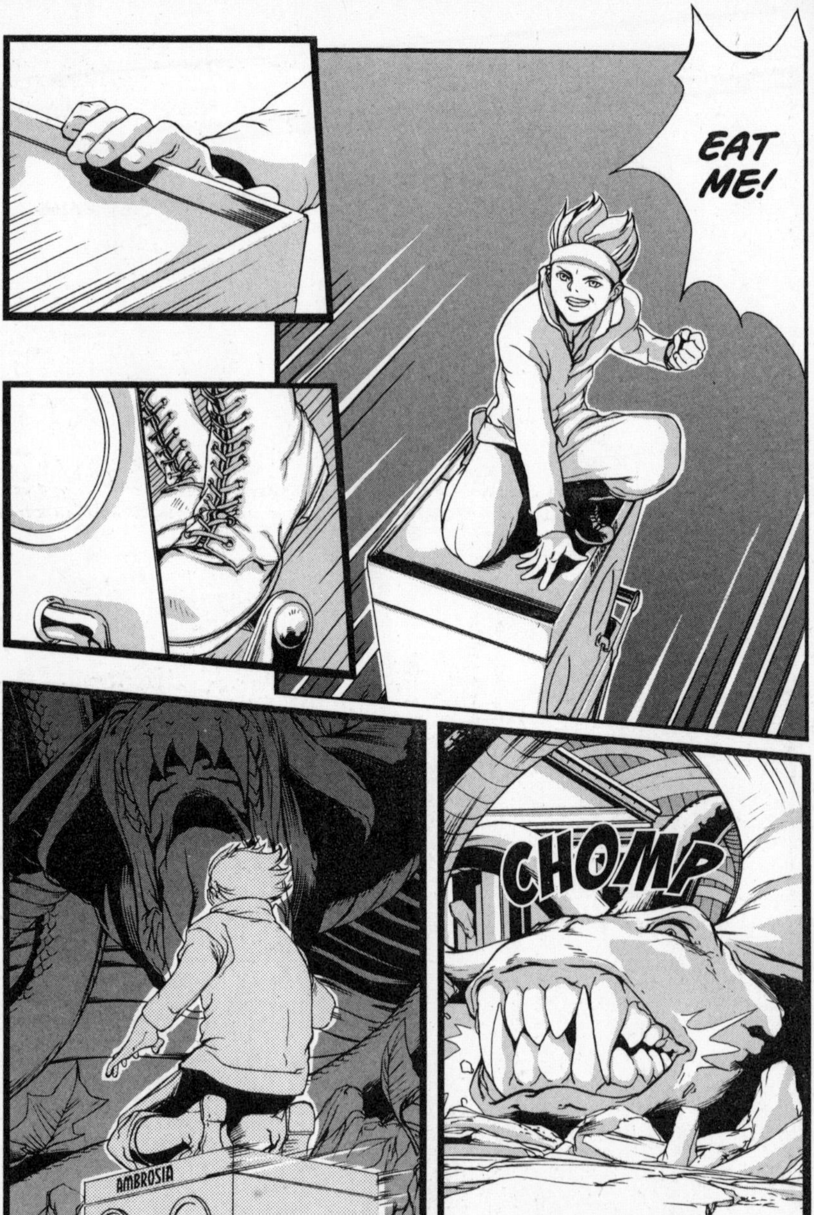
EAT ME!
CHOMP
AMBROSIA

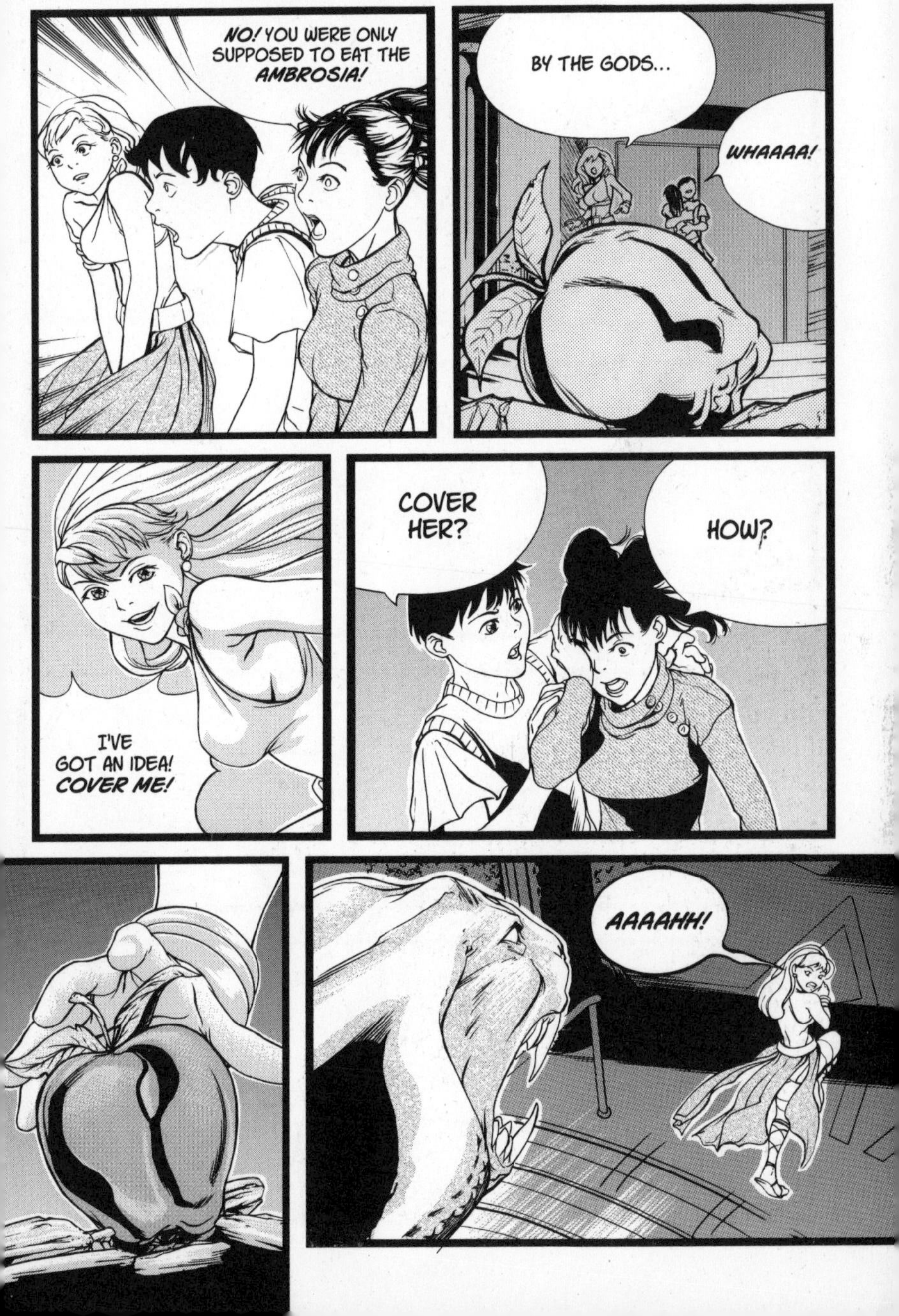
NO! YOU WERE ONLY SUPPOSED TO EAT THE AMBROSIA!
BY THE GODS...
WHAAAA!
I'VE GOT AN IDEA! COVER ME!
COVER HER?
HOW?
AAAAHH!

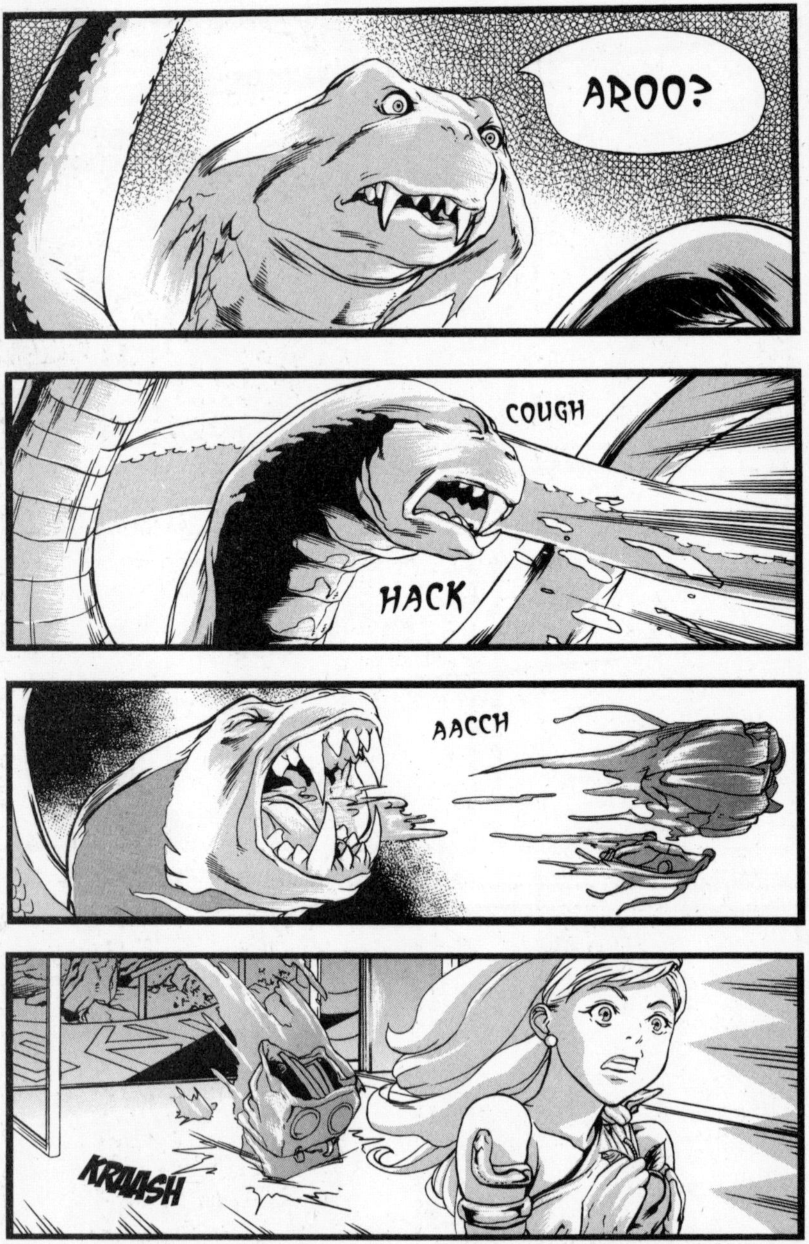
AROO?
COUGH
HACK
AACCH
KRAASH

POOR GRIFFIN.

IT'S NOT OVER YET.

CHECK *THIS* OUT.

WHAT IS IT?

ONE OF IDUN'S GOLDEN APPLES. NORSE GODS EAT THEM DAILY TO STAY *IMMORTAL!*

WHAT IF THEY'RE ON VACATION? OR A BUSINESS TRIP?

WHAT?

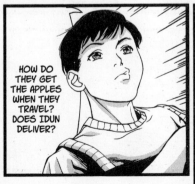

HOW DO THEY GET THE APPLES WHEN THEY TRAVEL? DOES IDUN DELIVER?

NOT... THE... POINT!

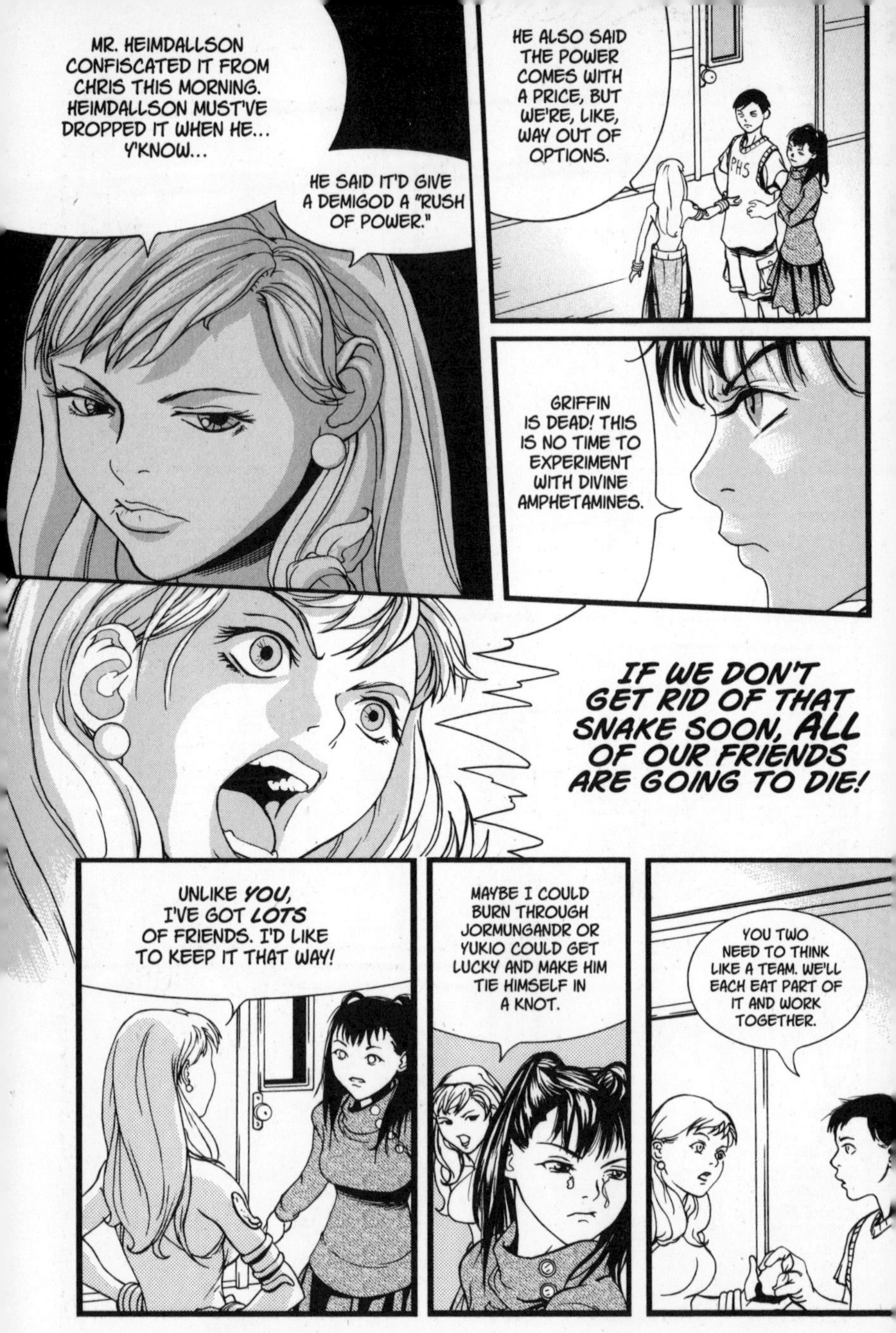
MR. HEIMDALLSON CONFISCATED IT FROM CHRIS THIS MORNING. HEIMDALLSON MUST'VE DROPPED IT WHEN HE... Y'KNOW...
HE SAID IT'D GIVE A DEMIGOD A "RUSH OF POWER."
HE ALSO SAID THE POWER COMES WITH A PRICE, BUT WE'RE, LIKE, WAY OUT OF OPTIONS.
PHS
GRIFFIN IS DEAD! THIS IS NO TIME TO EXPERIMENT WITH DIVINE AMPHETAMINES.
IF WE DON'T GET RID OF THAT SNAKE SOON, ALL OF OUR FRIENDS ARE GOING TO DIE!
UNLIKE *YOU*, I'VE GOT *LOTS* OF FRIENDS. I'D LIKE TO KEEP IT THAT WAY!
MAYBE I COULD BURN THROUGH JORMUNGANDR OR YUKIO COULD GET LUCKY AND MAKE HIM TIE HIMSELF IN A KNOT.
YOU TWO NEED TO THINK LIKE A TEAM. WE'LL EACH EAT PART OF IT AND WORK TOGETHER.

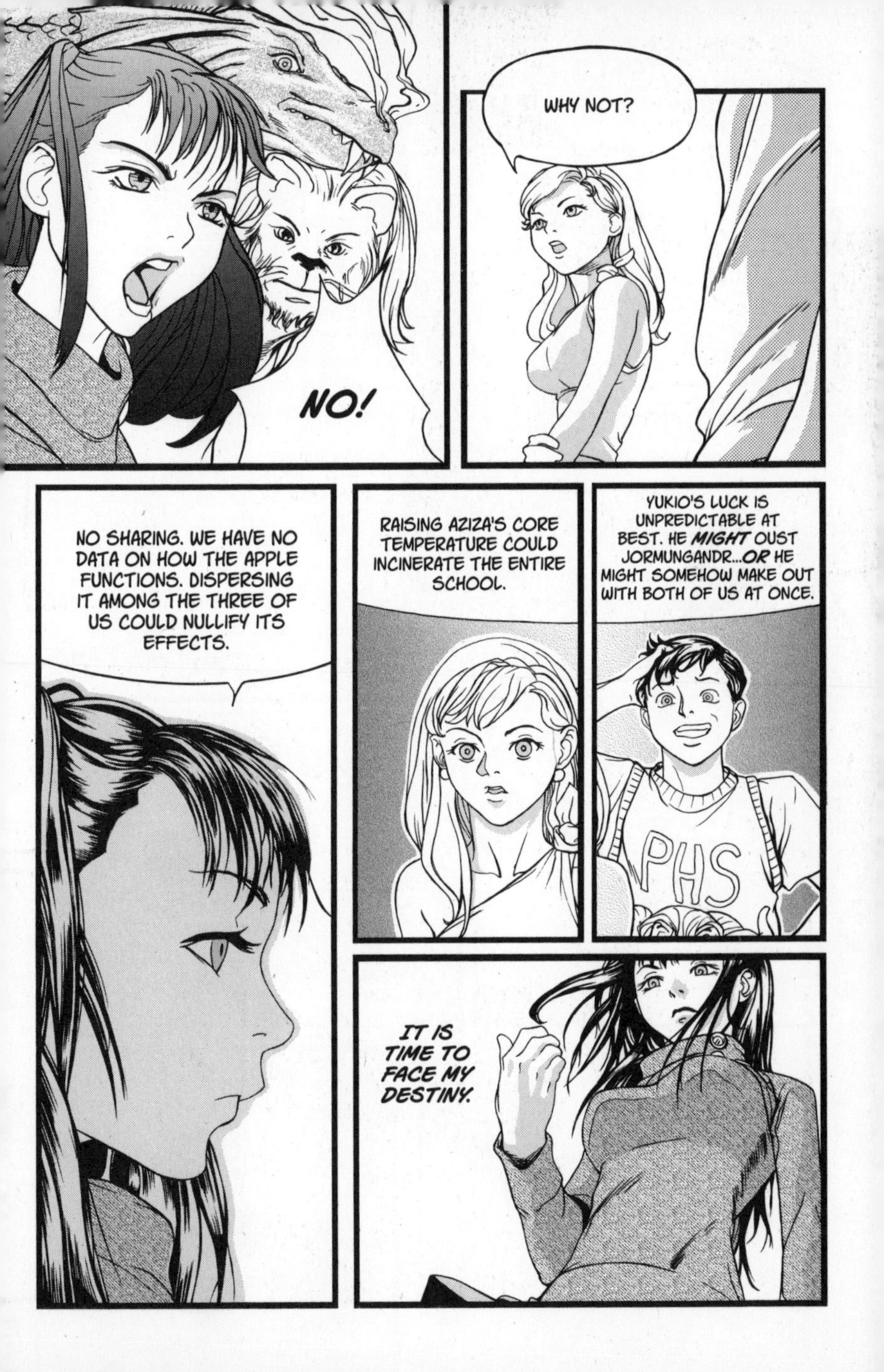
NO!
WHY NOT?
NO SHARING. WE HAVE NO DATA ON HOW THE APPLE FUNCTIONS. DISPERSING IT AMONG THE THREE OF US COULD NULLIFY ITS EFFECTS.
RAISING AZIZA'S CORE TEMPERATURE COULD INCINERATE THE ENTIRE SCHOOL.
YUKIO'S LUCK IS UNPREDICTABLE AT BEST. HE *MIGHT* OUST JORMUNGANDR...*OR* HE MIGHT SOMEHOW MAKE OUT WITH BOTH OF US AT ONCE.
PHS
IT IS TIME TO FACE MY DESTINY.

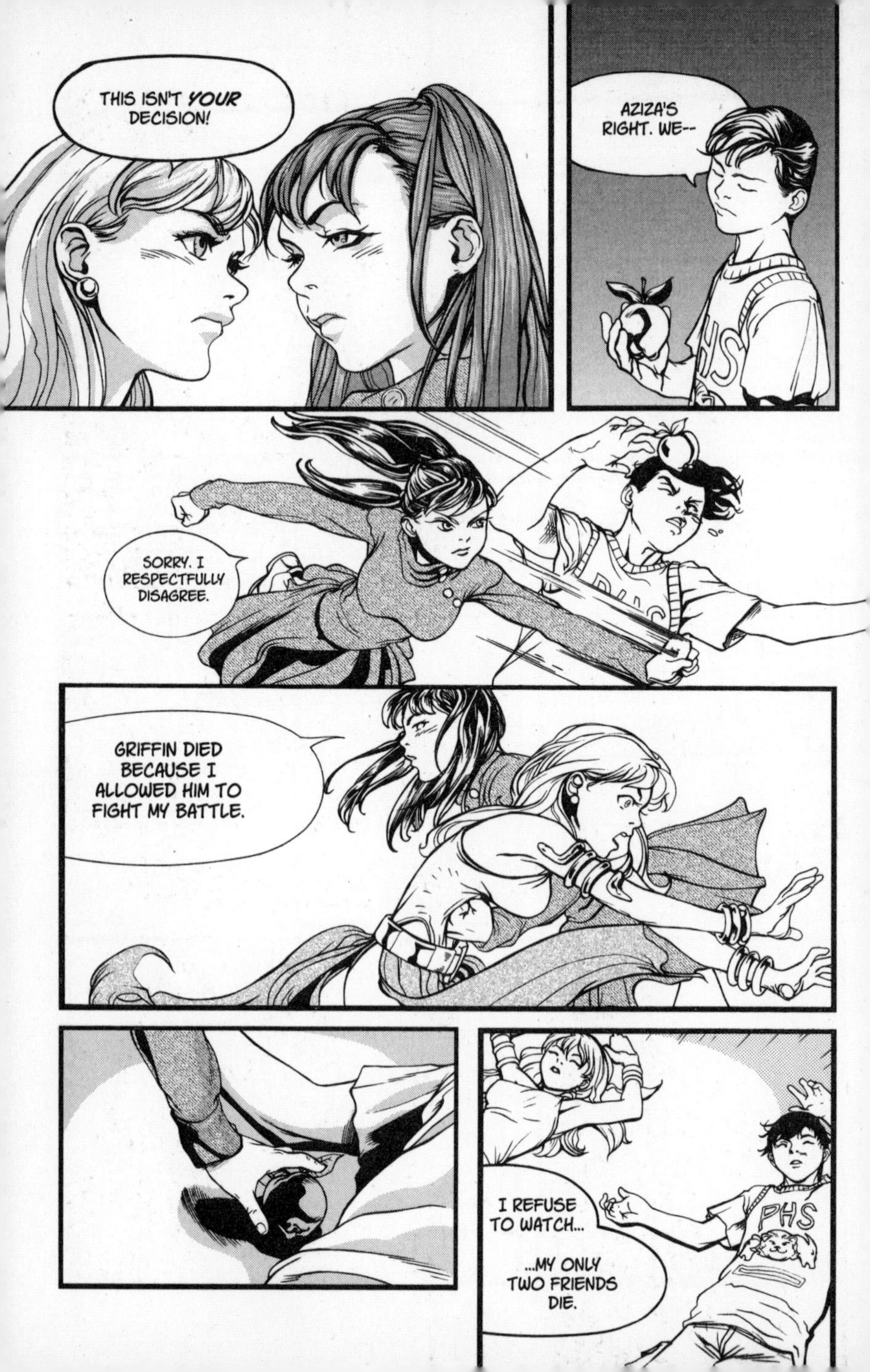
THIS ISN'T YOUR DECISION!
AZIZA'S RIGHT. WE--
SORRY. I RESPECTFULLY DISAGREE.
GRIFFIN DIED BECAUSE I ALLOWED HIM TO FIGHT MY BATTLE.
I REFUSE TO WATCH...
...MY ONLY TWO FRIENDS DIE.

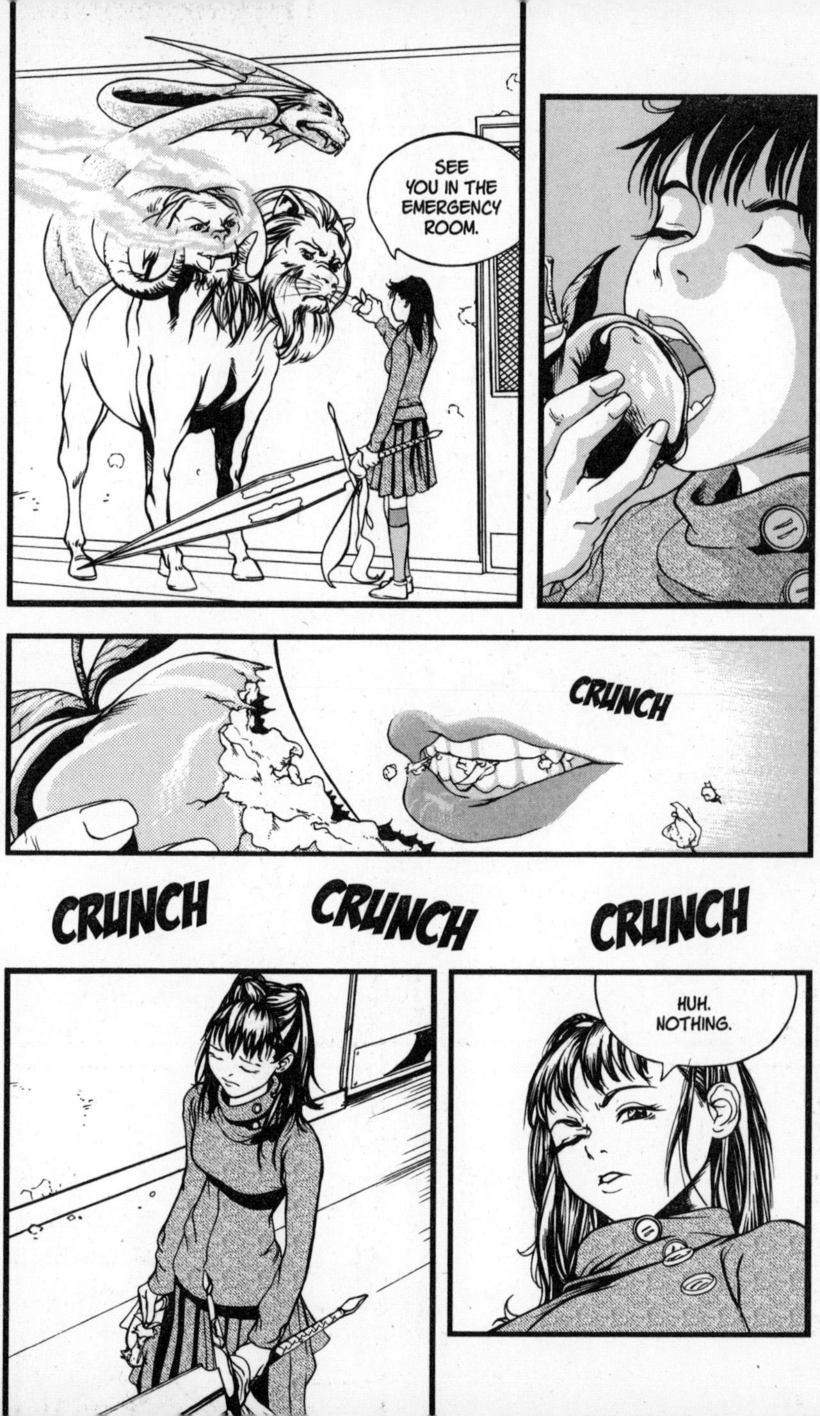
SEE YOU IN THE EMERGENCY ROOM.
CRUNCH
CRUNCH
CRUNCH
CRUNCH
HUH. NOTHING.

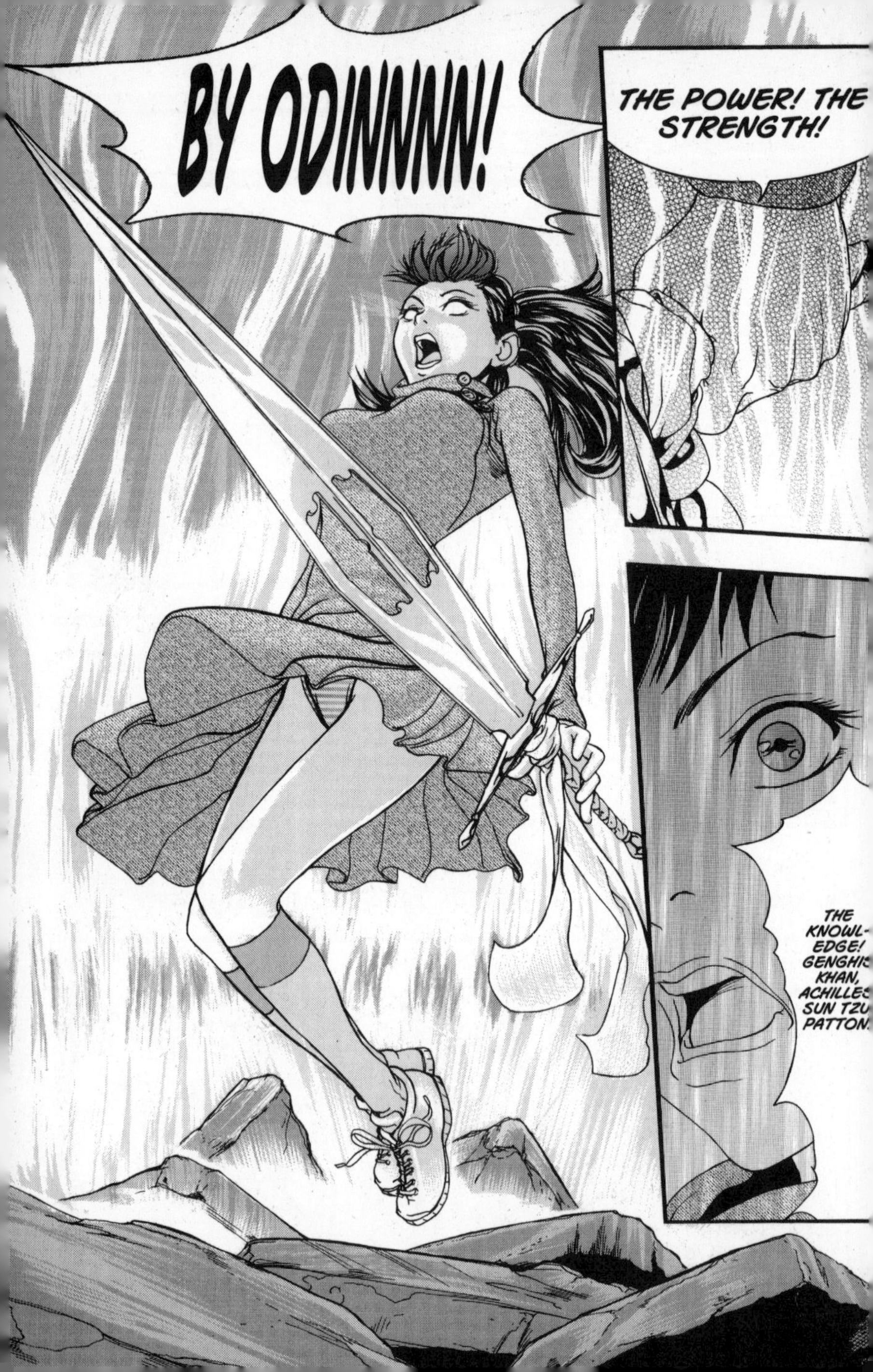
BY ODINNNNN!
THE POWER! THE STRENGTH!
THE KNOWL-EDGE! GENGHIS KHAN, ACHILLES SUN TZU PATTON!

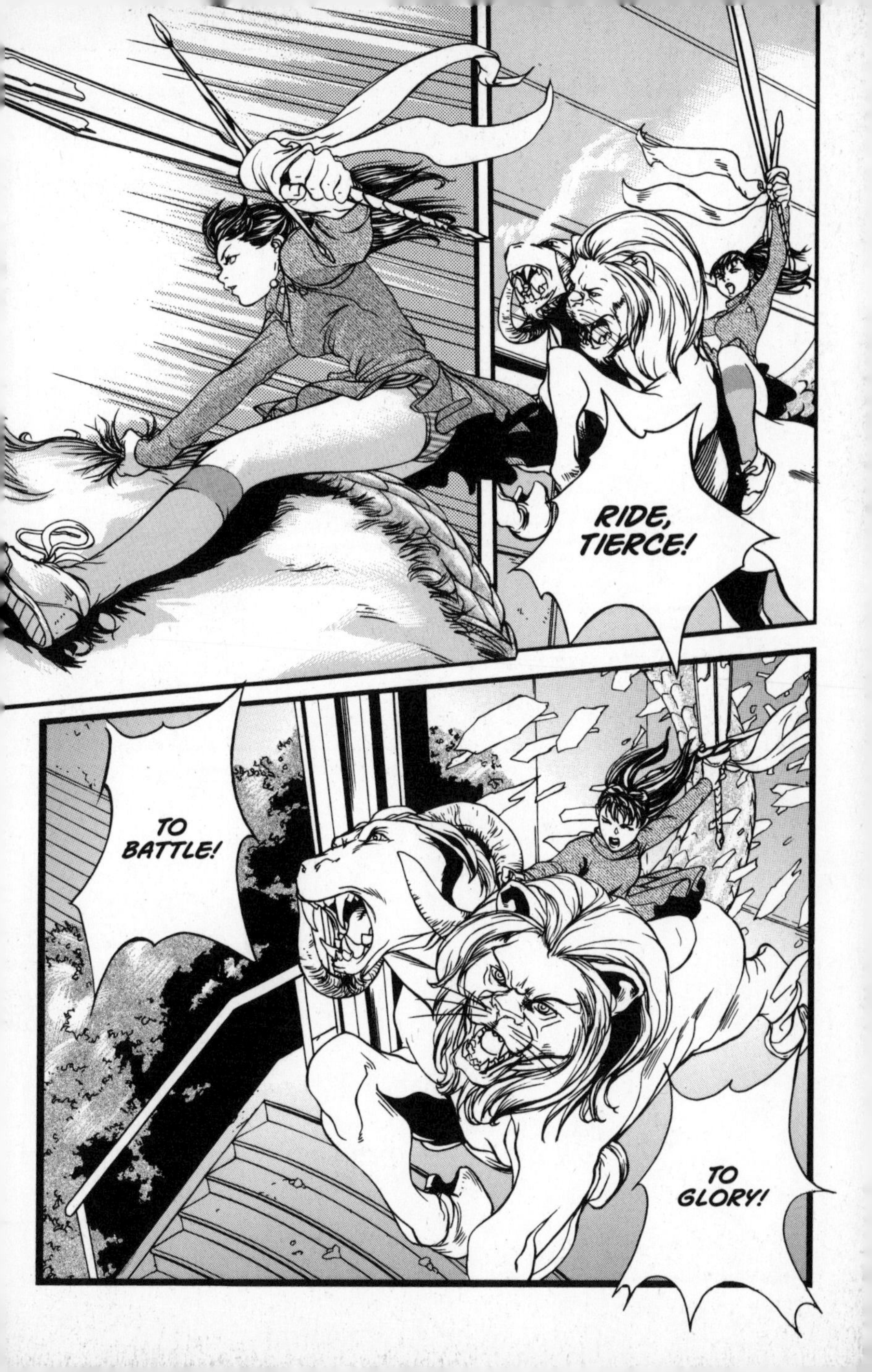
RIDE, TIERCE!
TO BATTLE!
TO GLORY!

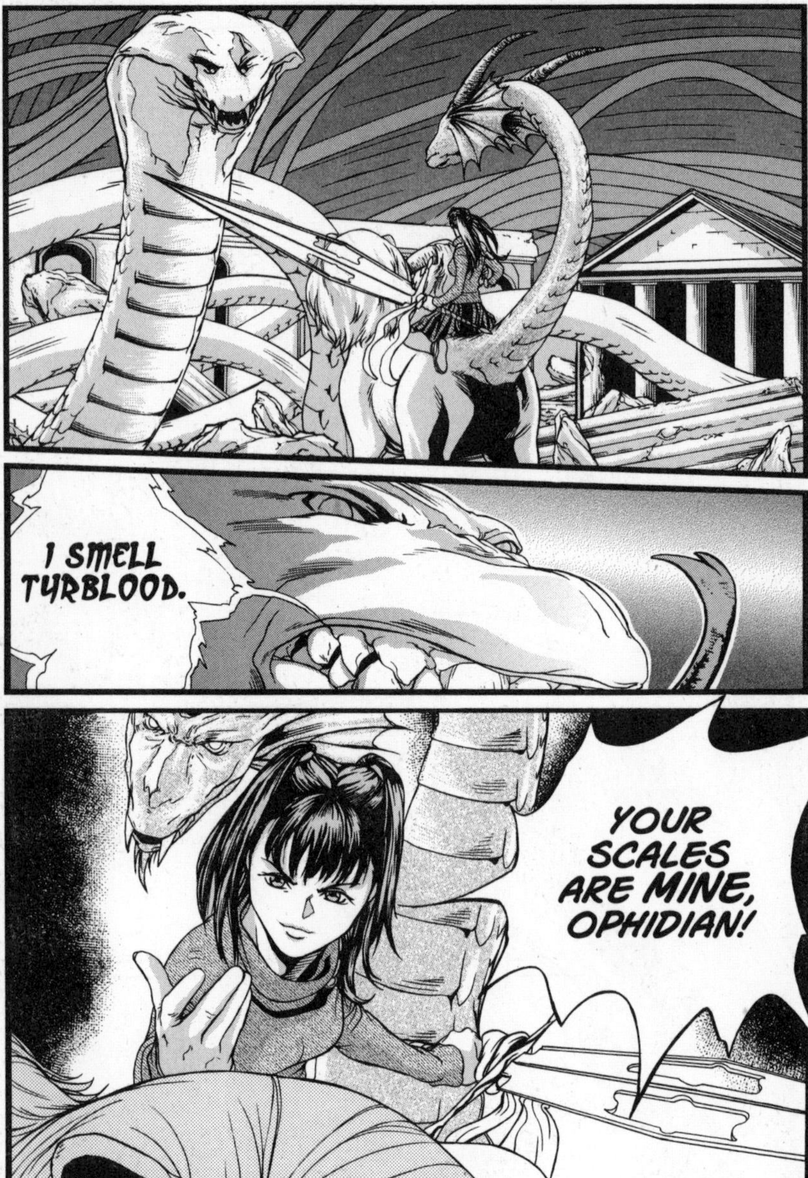
I SMELL TYRBLOOD.
YOUR SCALES ARE MINE, OPHIDIAN!

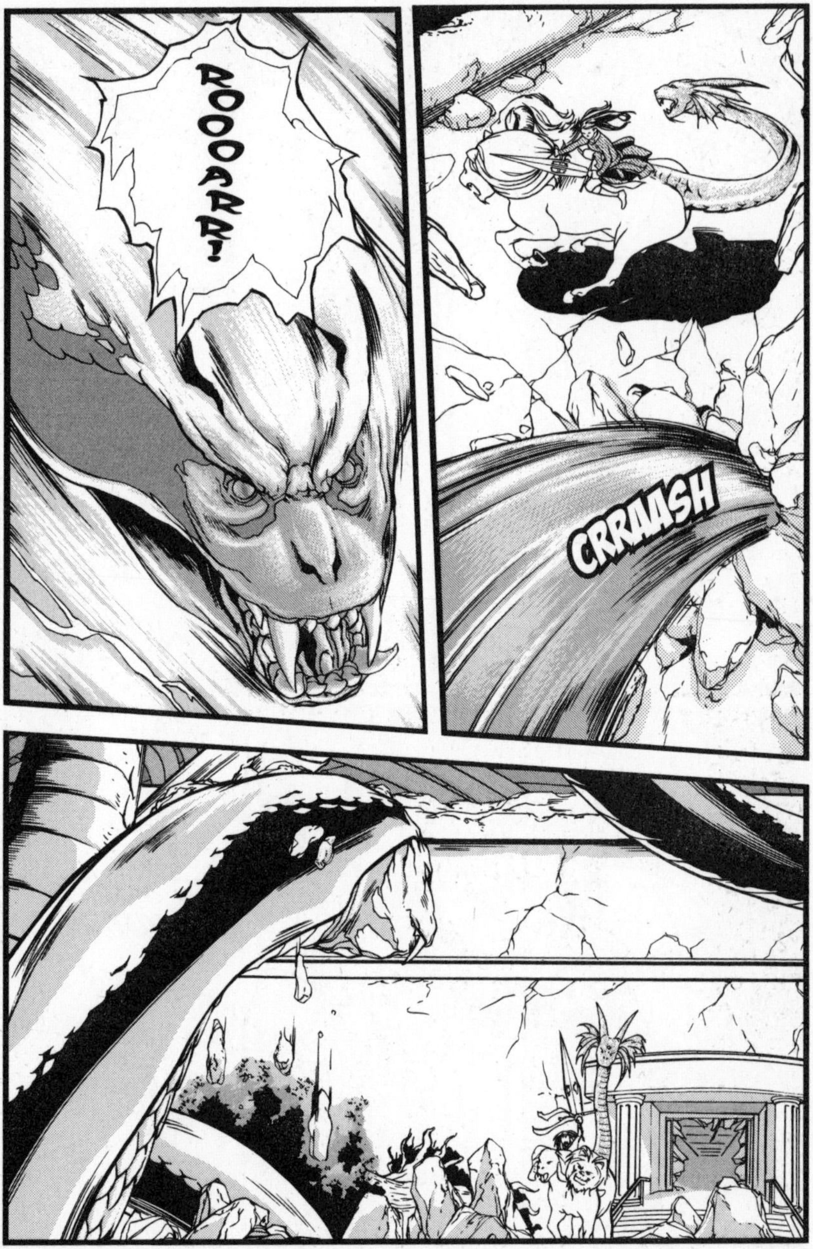

ROOOOARRR!
CRRAASH

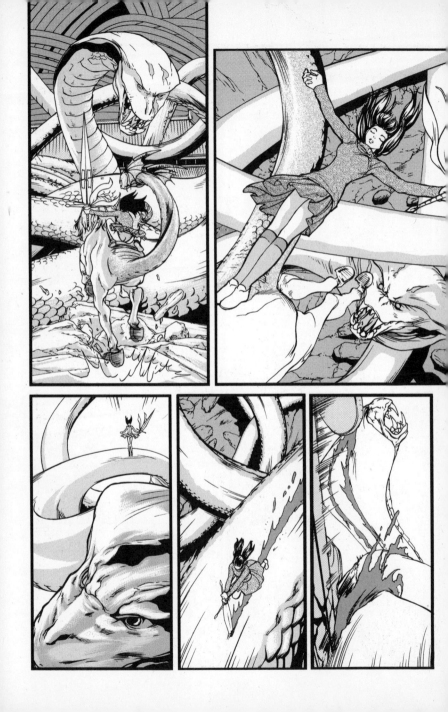

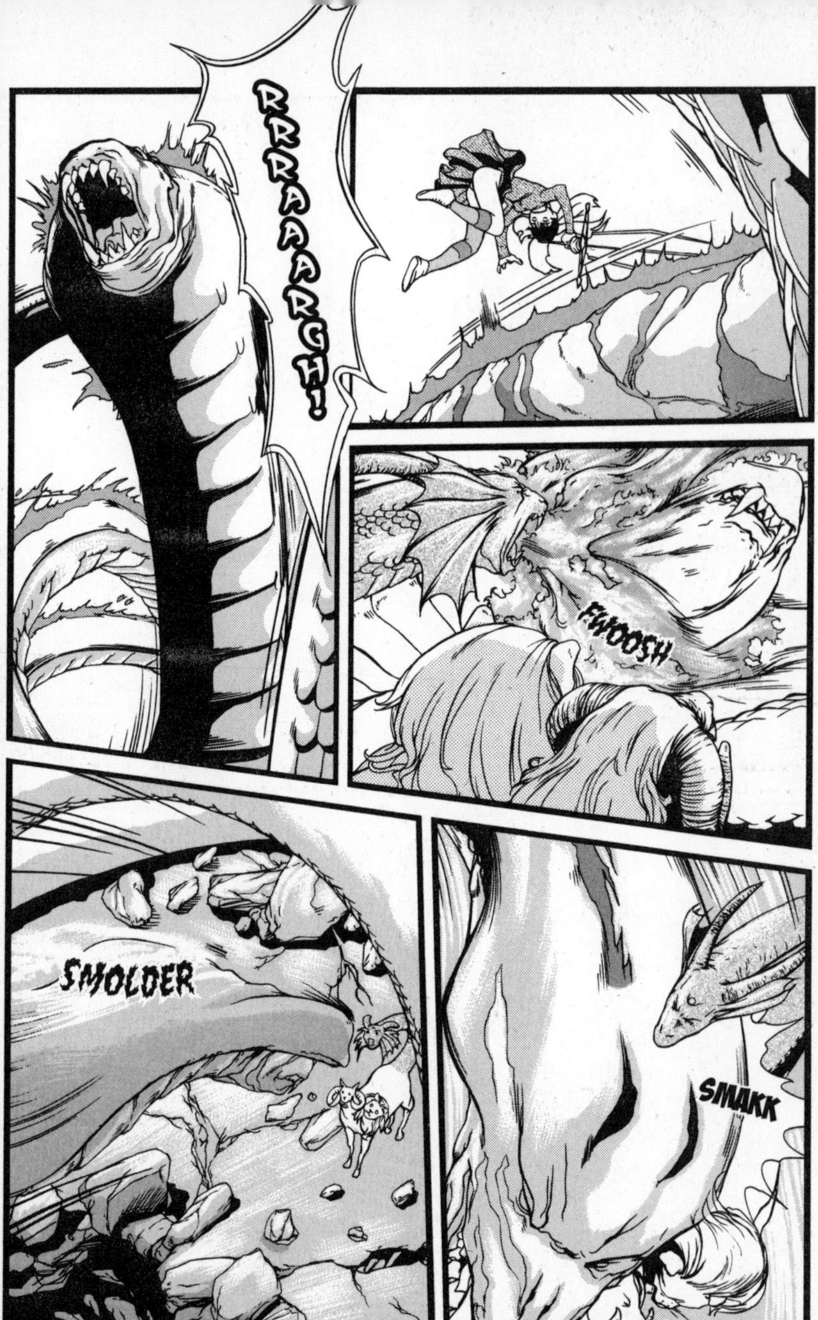
RRRAAARGH!
FWOOSH
SMOLDER
SMAKK

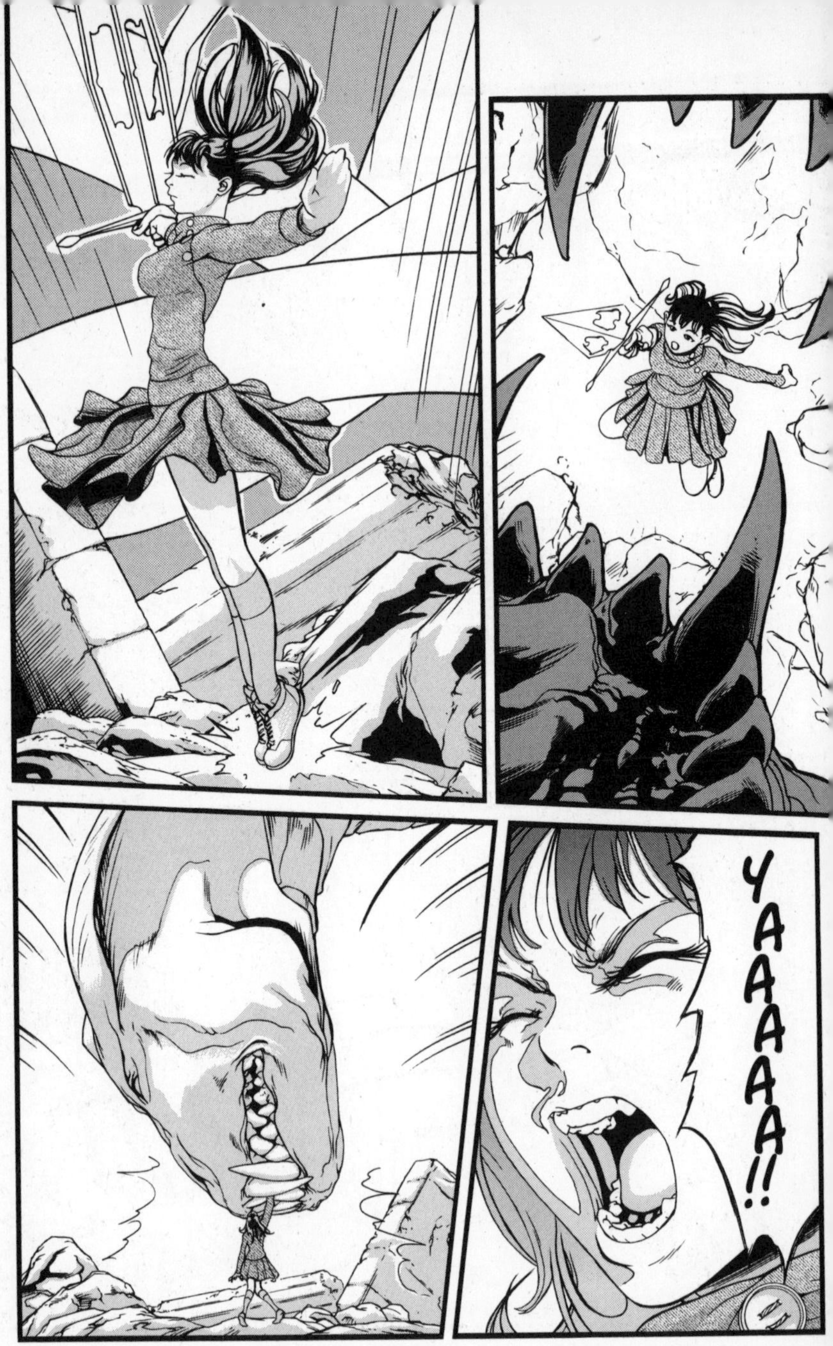
YAAAAA!!

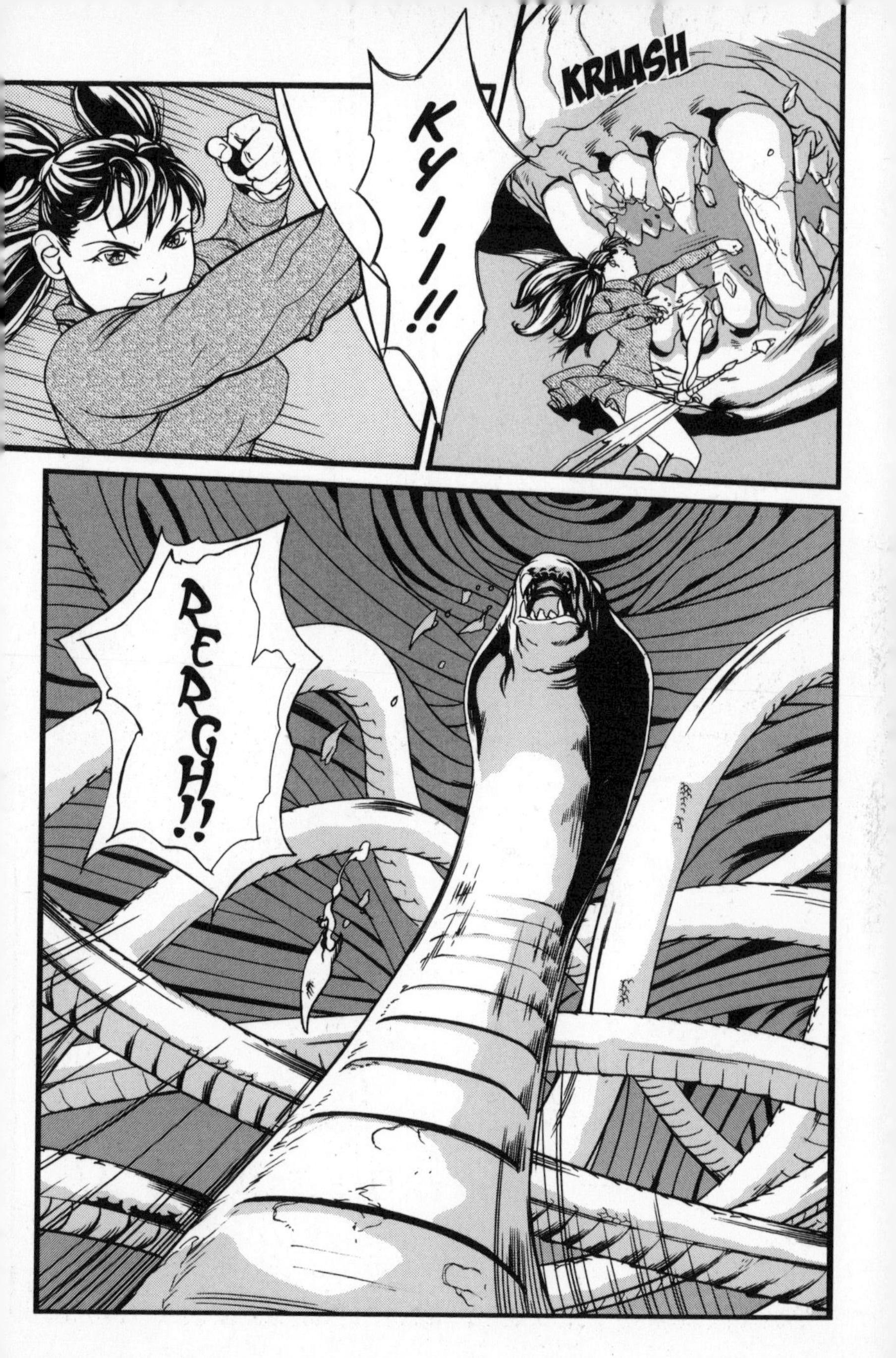
KY--!!
KRAASH
RERGH!!

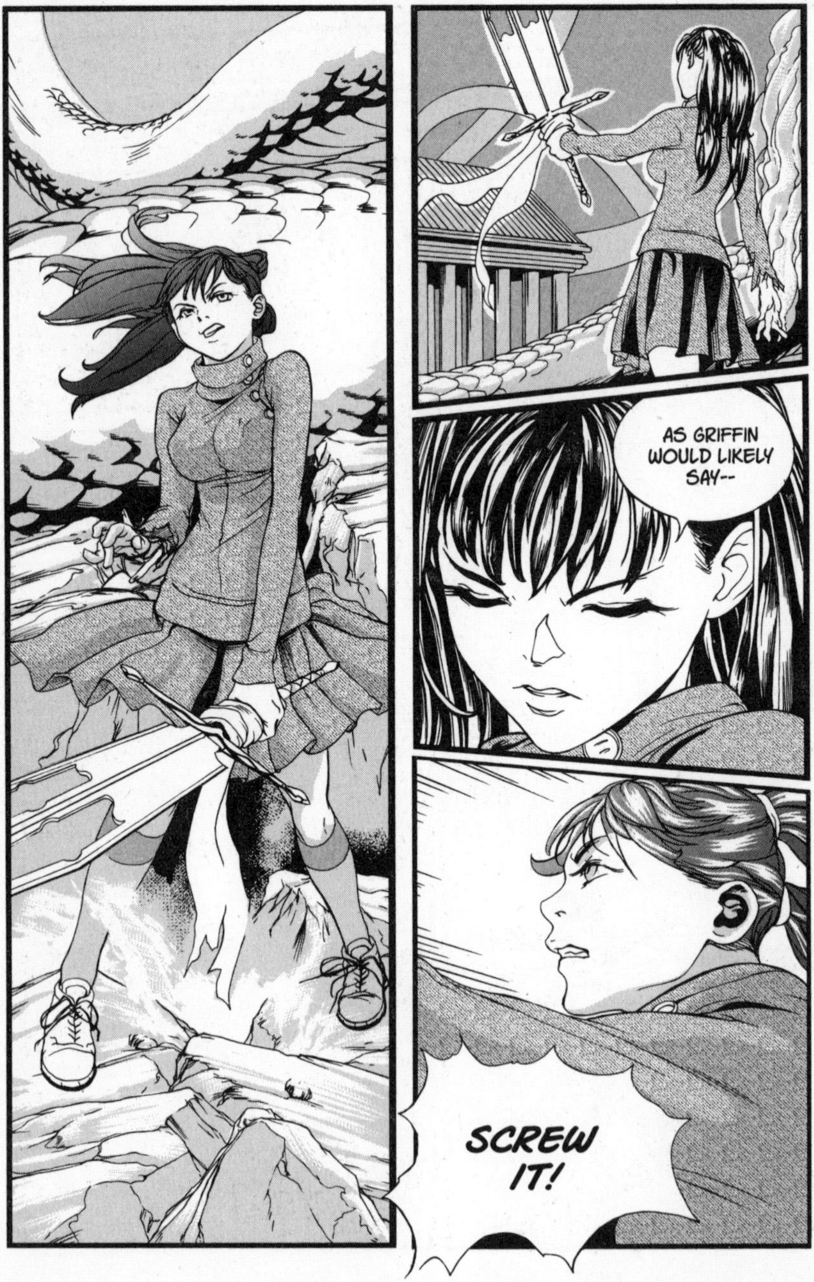
AS GRIFFIN WOULD LIKELY SAY--
SCREW IT!

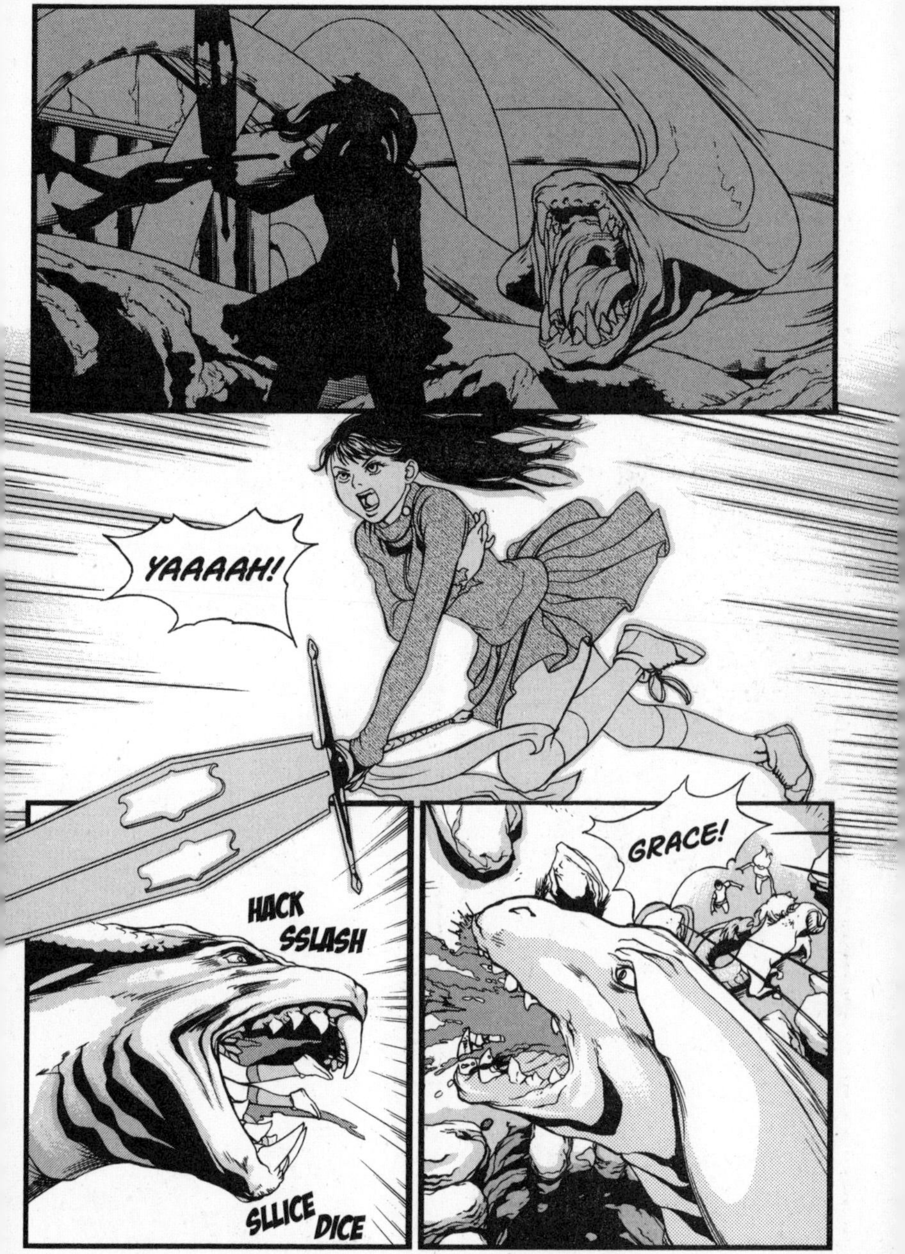
YAAAAH!
HACK
SSLASH
SLLICE
DICE
GRACE!

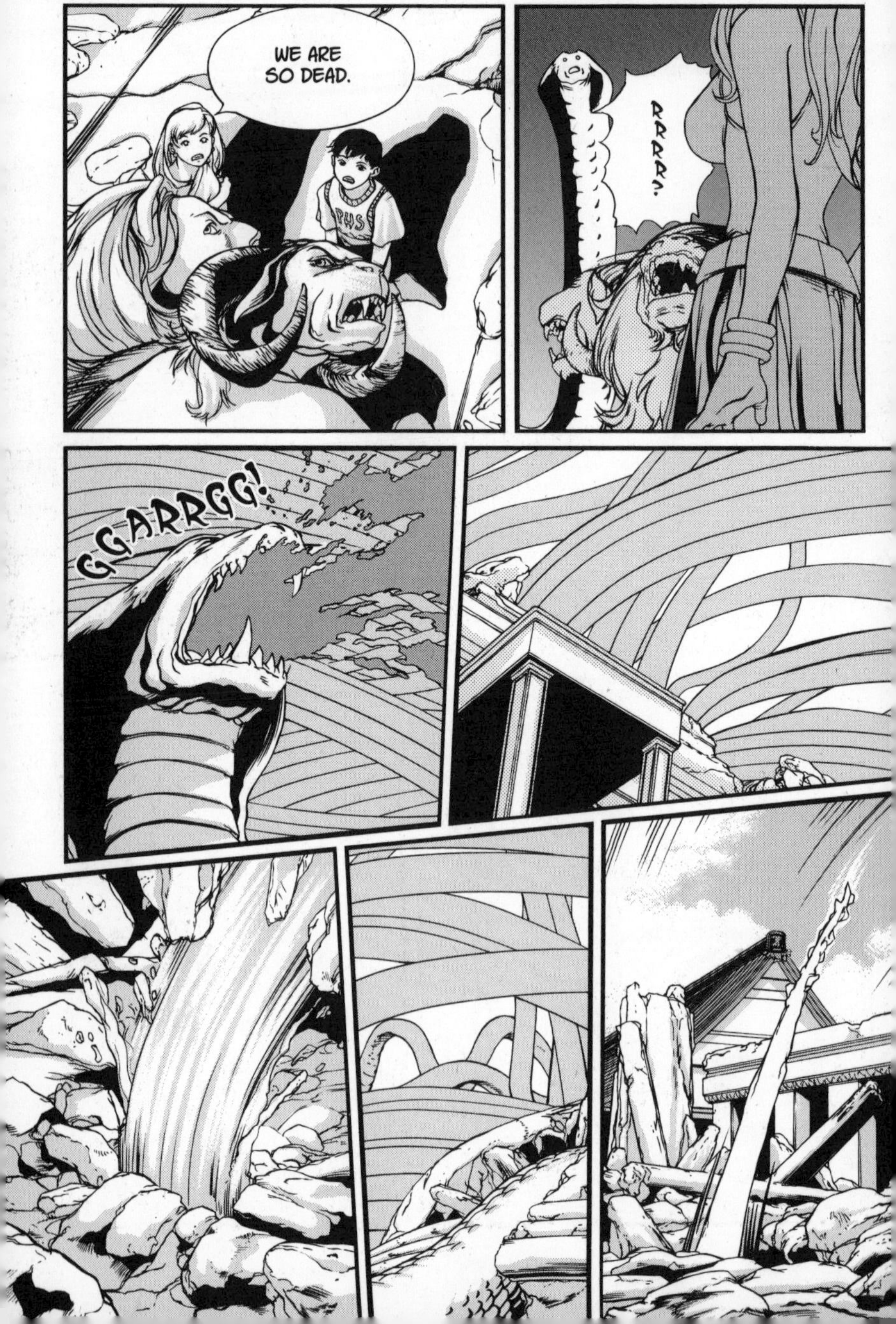
WE ARE SO DEAD.
RRRRR?
GGARRGG!

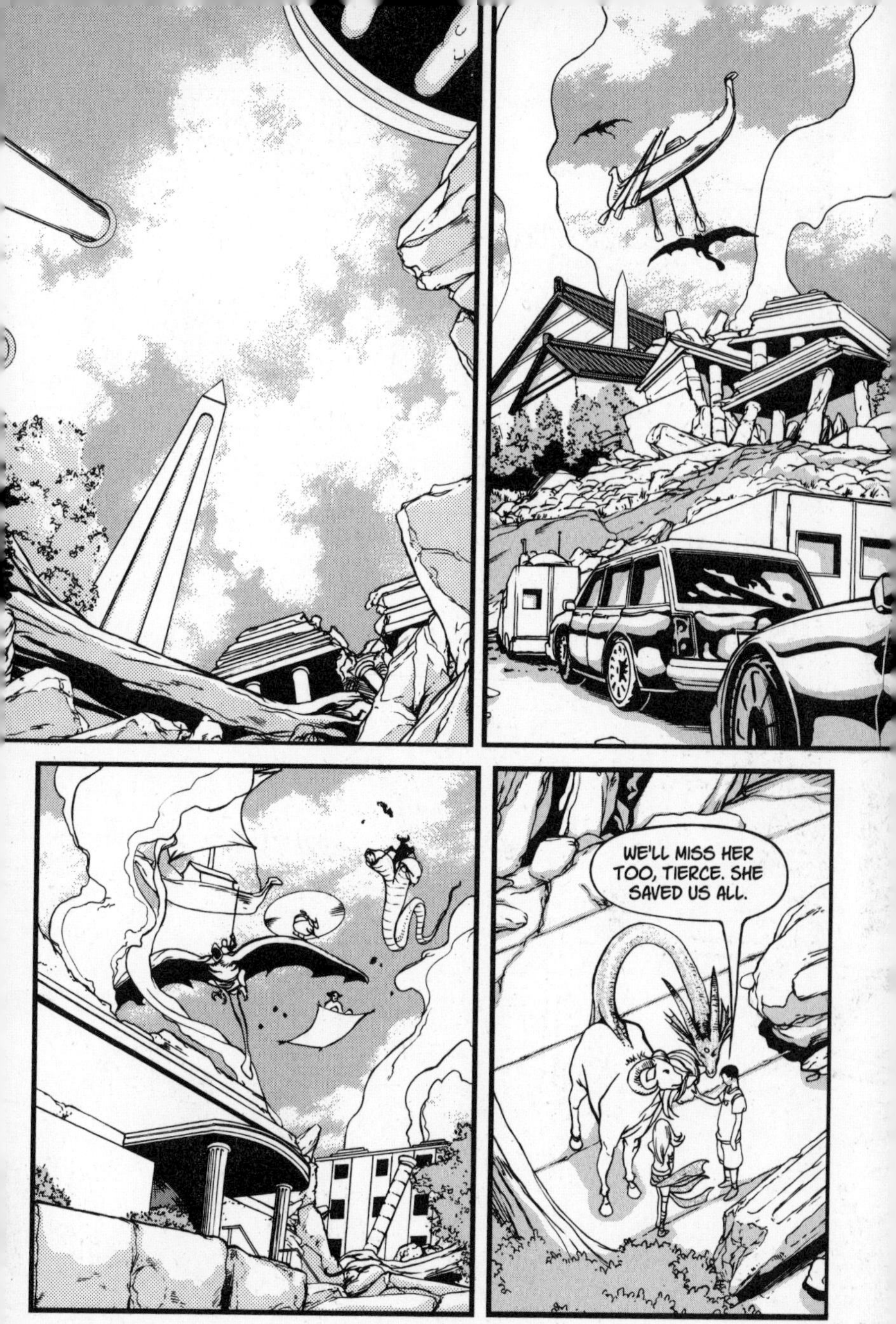
WE'LL MISS HER TOO, TIERCE. SHE SAVED US ALL.

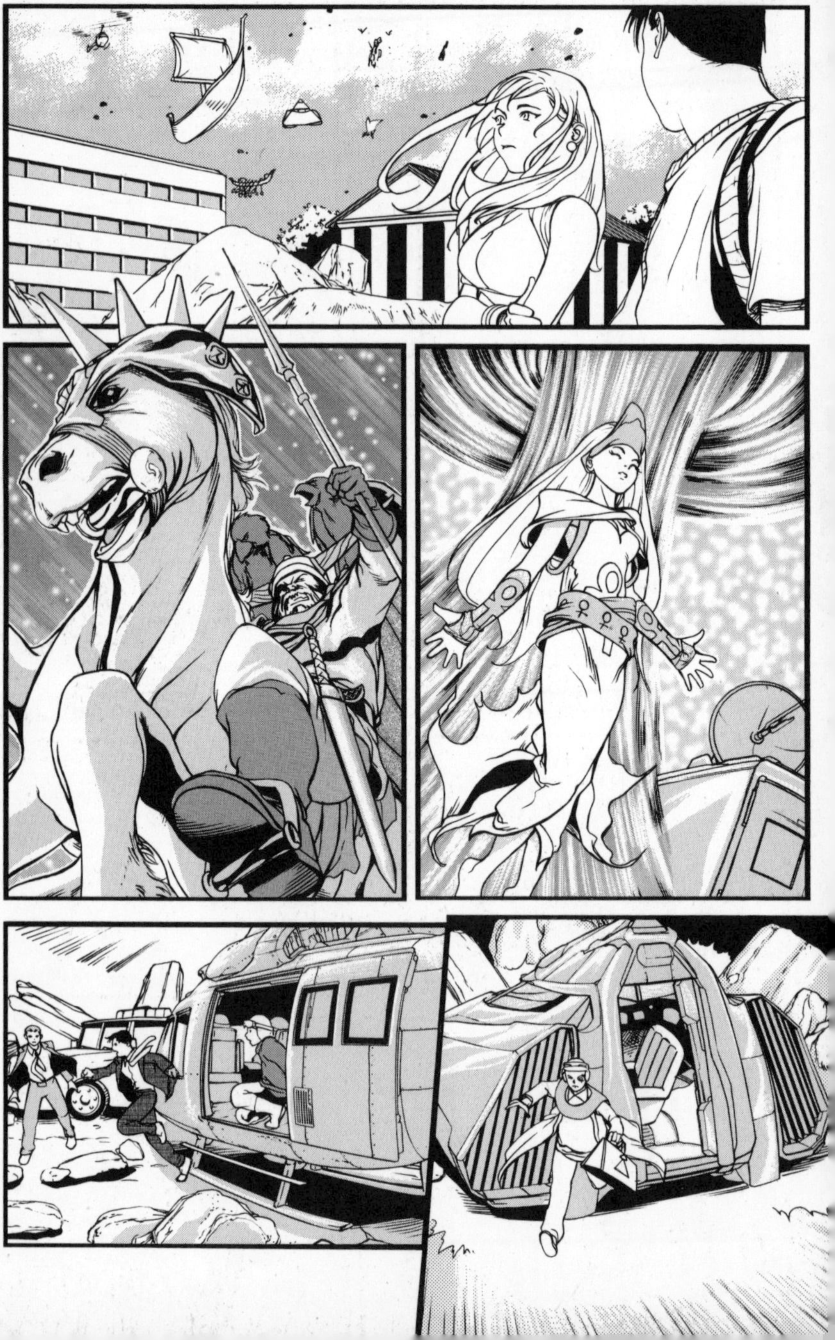

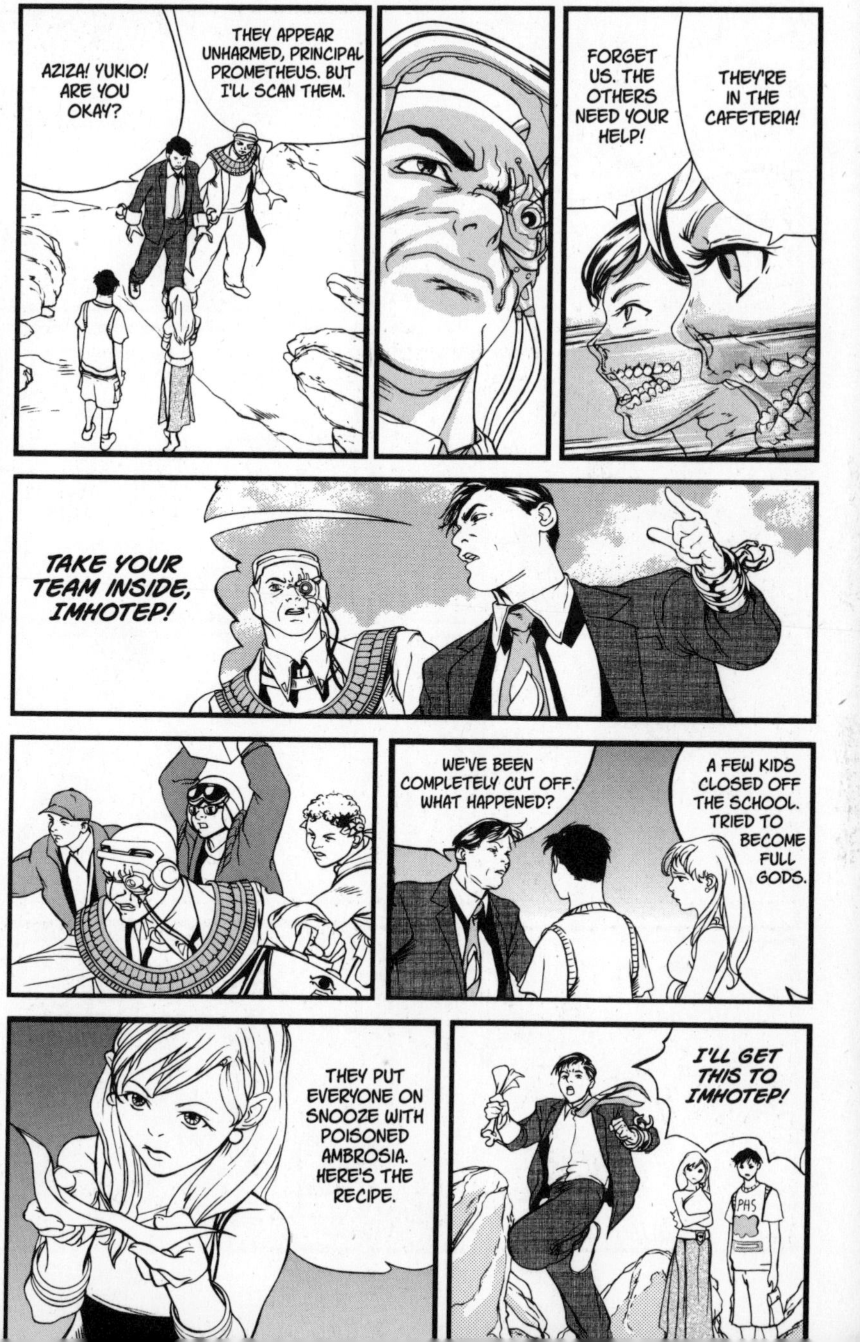
AZIZA! YUKIO! ARE YOU OKAY?
THEY APPEAR UNHARMED, PRINCIPAL PROMETHEUS. BUT I'LL SCAN THEM.
FORGET US. THE OTHERS NEED YOUR HELP!
THEY'RE IN THE CAFETERIA!
TAKE YOUR TEAM INSIDE, IMHOTEP!
WE'VE BEEN COMPLETELY CUT OFF. WHAT HAPPENED?
A FEW KIDS CLOSED OFF THE SCHOOL. TRIED TO BECOME FULL GODS.
THEY PUT EVERYONE ON SNOOZE WITH POISONED AMBROSIA. HERE'S THE RECIPE.
I'LL GET THIS TO IMHOTEP!
PHS

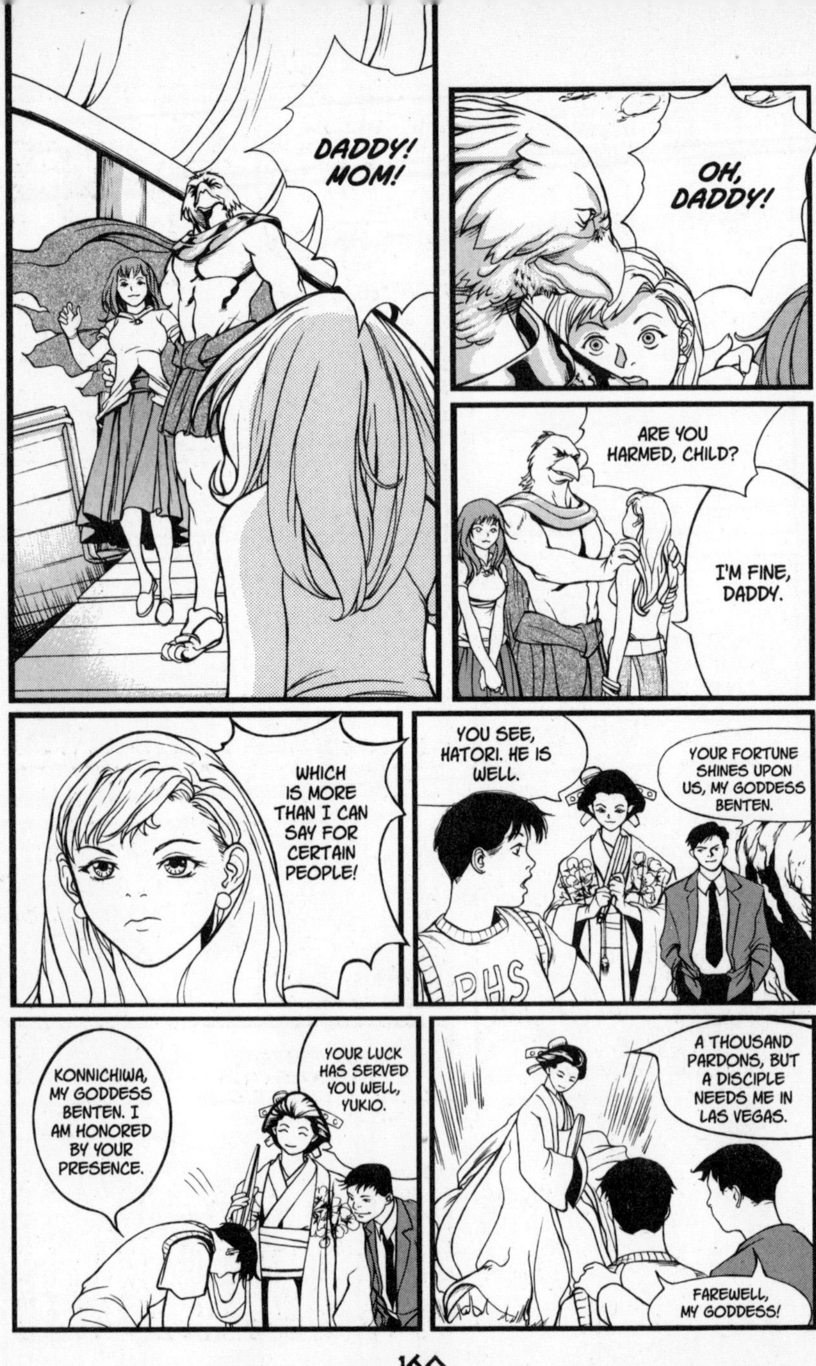
DADDY! MOM!
OH, DADDY!
ARE YOU HARMED, CHILD?
I'M FINE, DADDY.
WHICH IS MORE THAN I CAN SAY FOR CERTAIN PEOPLE!
YOU SEE, HATORI. HE IS WELL.
YOUR FORTUNE SHINES UPON US, MY GODDESS BENTEN.
PHS
KONNICHIWA, MY GODDESS BENTEN. I AM HONORED BY YOUR PRESENCE.
YOUR LUCK HAS SERVED YOU WELL, YUKIO.
A THOUSAND PARDONS, BUT A DISCIPLE NEEDS ME IN LAS VEGAS.
FAREWELL, MY GODDESS!

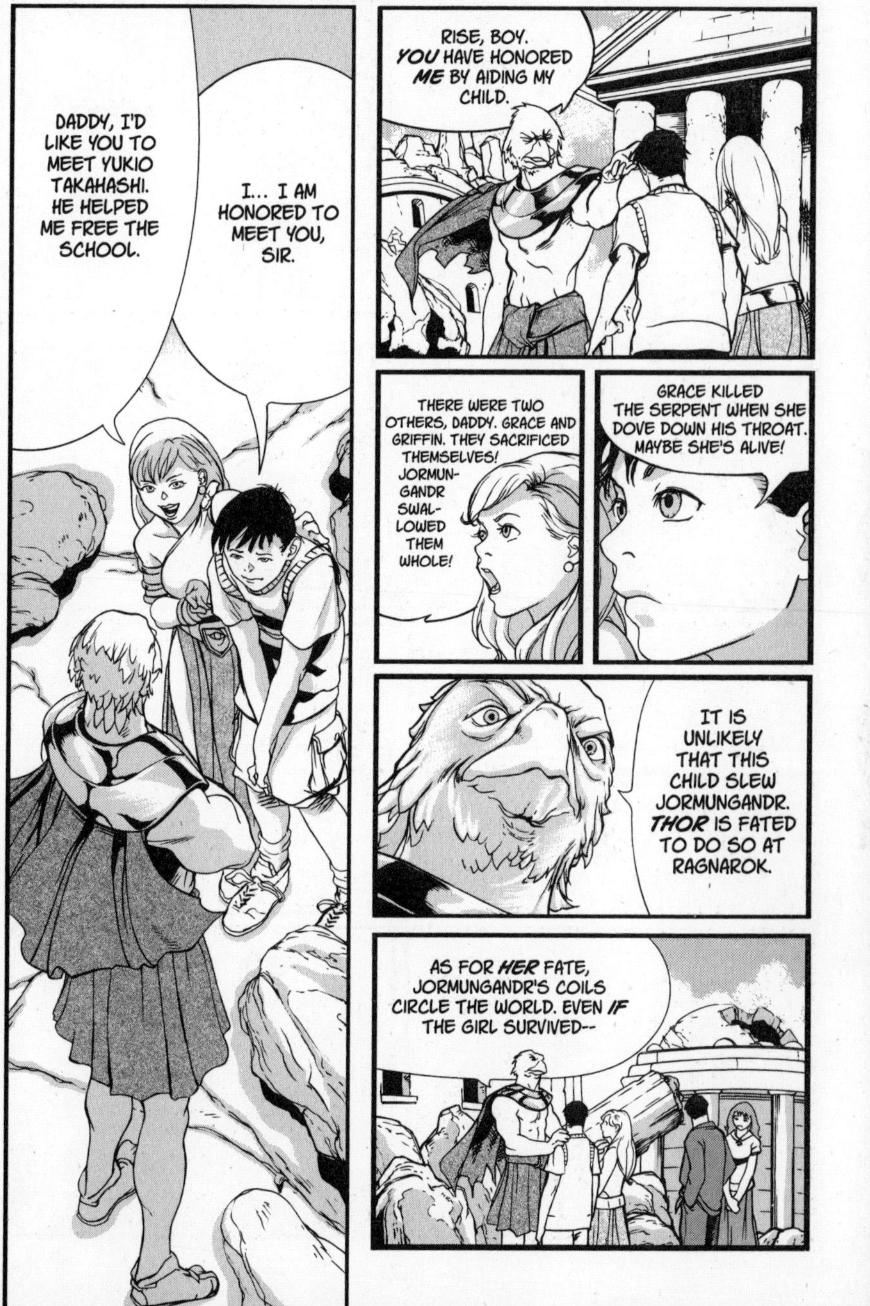
DADDY, I'D LIKE YOU TO MEET YUKIO TAKAHASHI. HE HELPED ME FREE THE SCHOOL.
I... I AM HONORED TO MEET YOU, SIR.
RISE, BOY. ***YOU*** HAVE HONORED ***ME*** BY AIDING MY CHILD.
THERE WERE TWO OTHERS, DADDY. GRACE AND GRIFFIN. THEY SACRIFICED THEMSELVES! JORMUNGANDR SWALLOWED THEM WHOLE!
GRACE KILLED THE SERPENT WHEN SHE DOVE DOWN HIS THROAT. MAYBE SHE'S ALIVE!
IT IS UNLIKELY THAT THIS CHILD SLEW JORMUNGANDR. ***THOR*** IS FATED TO DO SO AT RAGNAROK.
AS FOR ***HER*** FATE, JORMUNGANDR'S COILS CIRCLE THE WORLD. EVEN ***IF*** THE GIRL SURVIVED--

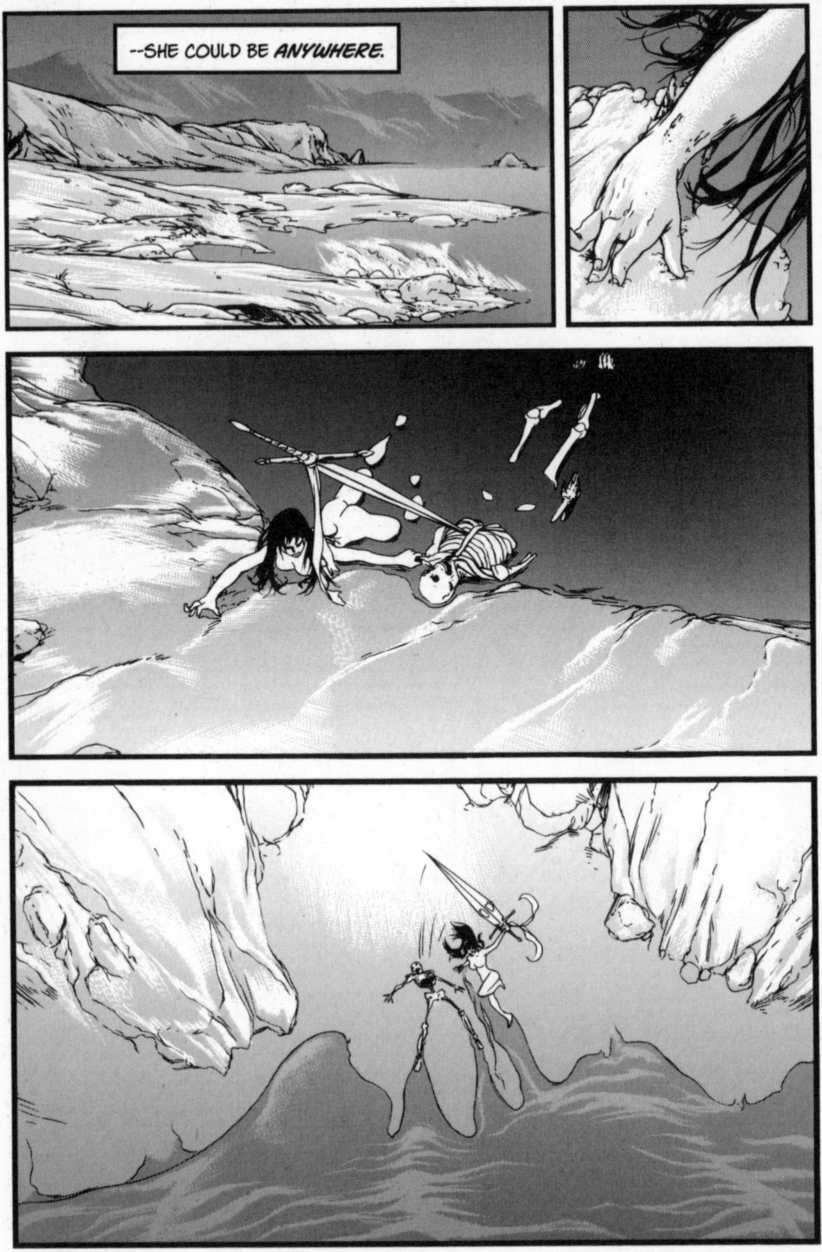
--SHE COULD BE ANYWHERE.

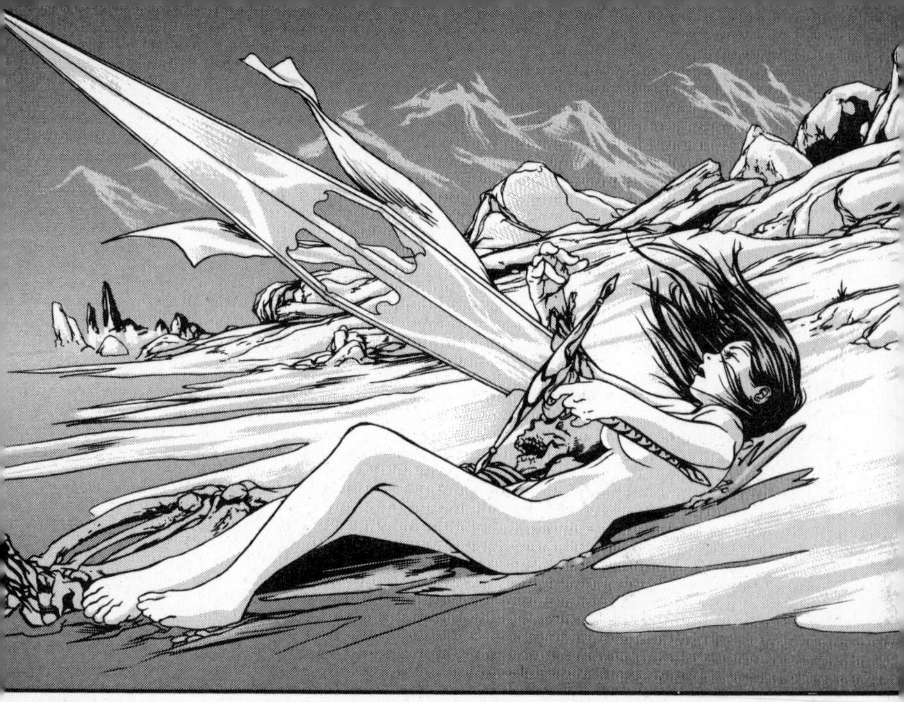
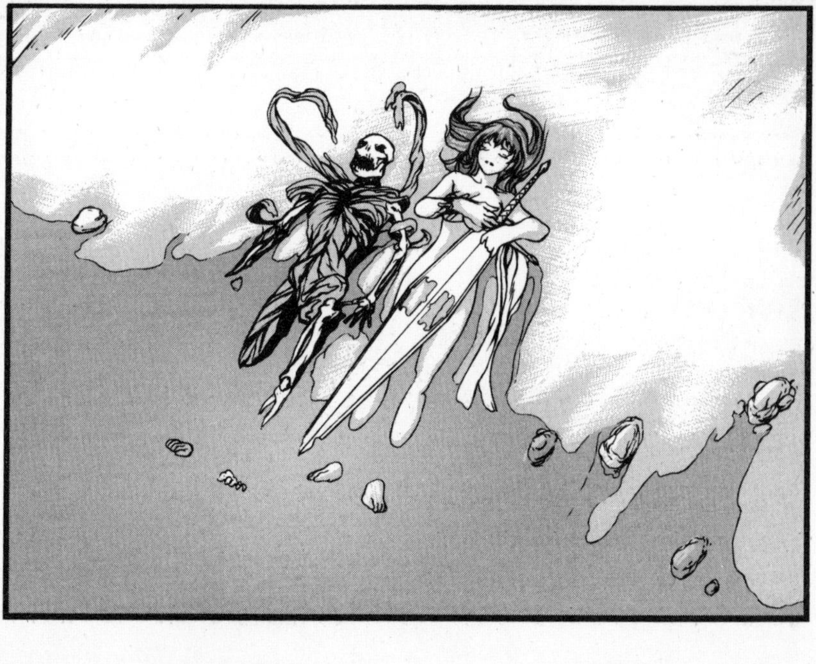

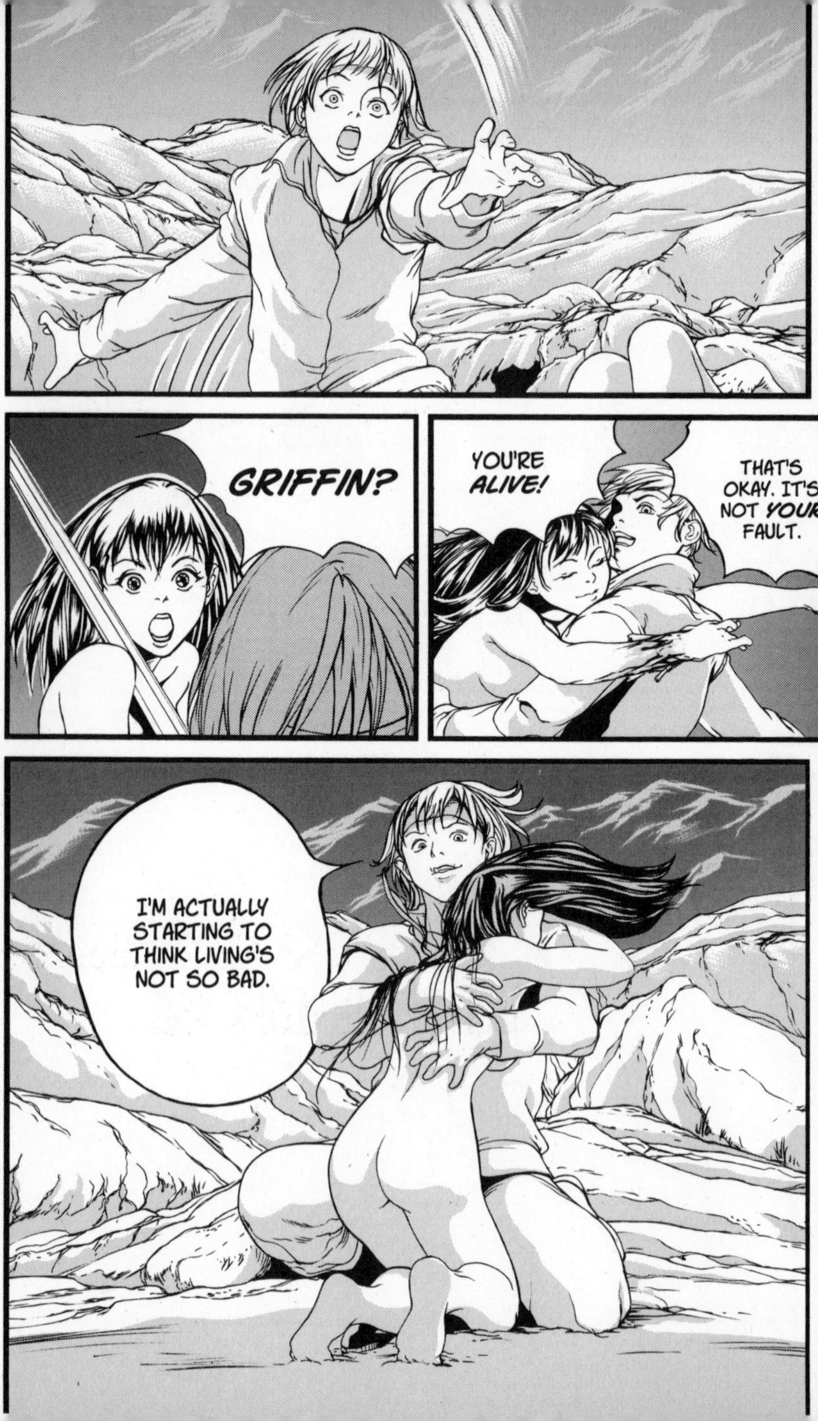
GRIFFIN?
YOU'RE ALIVE!
THAT'S OKAY. IT'S NOT YOUR FAULT.
I'M ACTUALLY STARTING TO THINK LIVING'S NOT SO BAD.

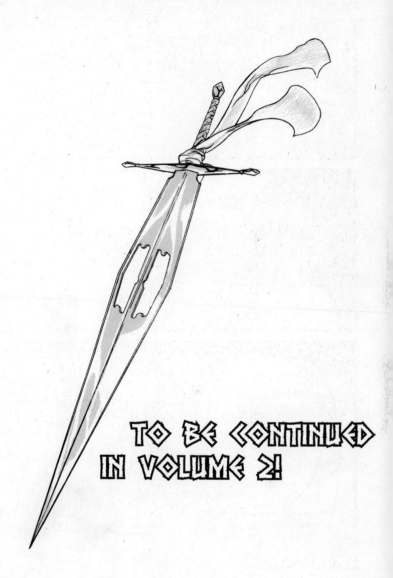

TO BE CONTINUED
IN VOLUME 2!

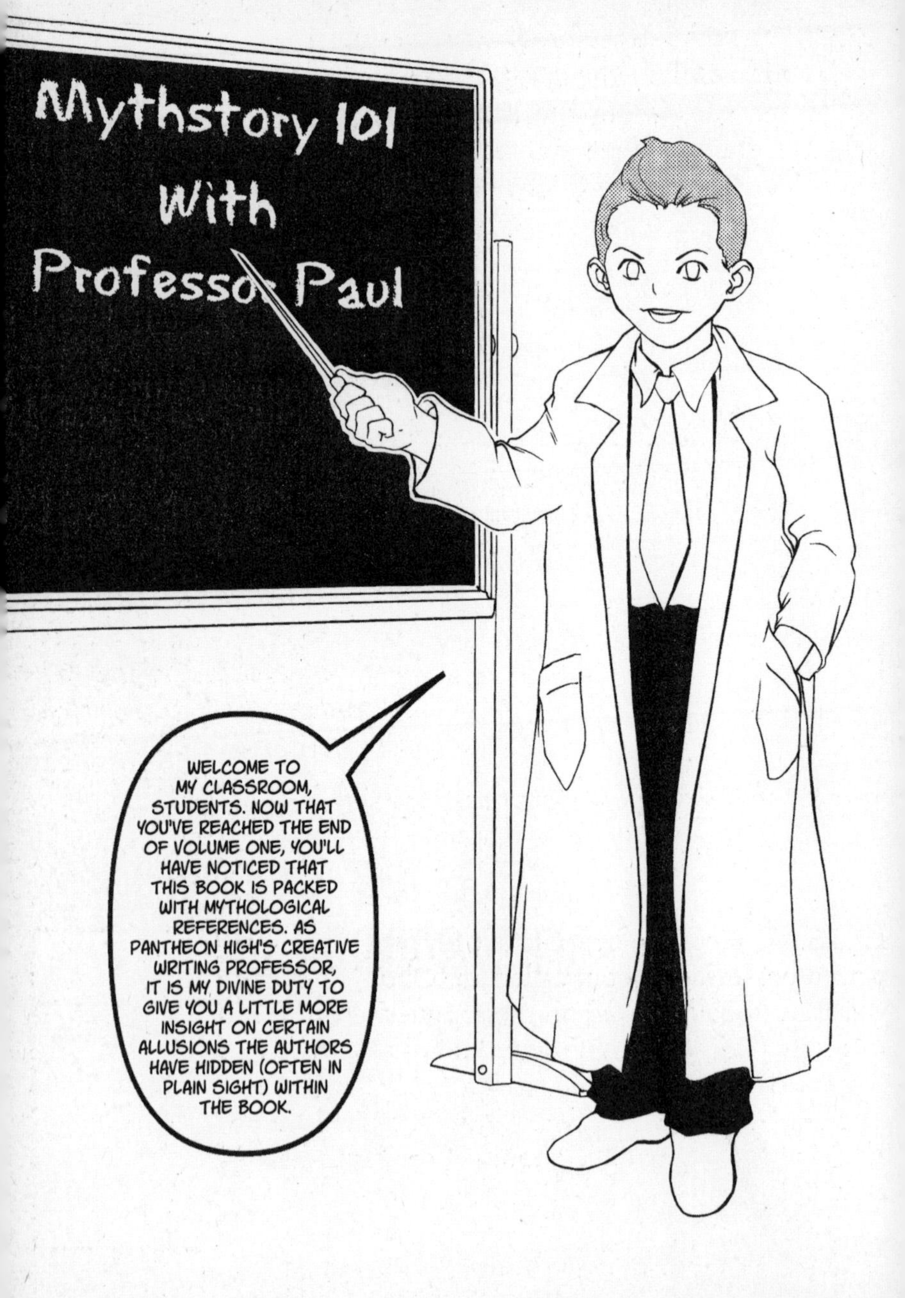
Mythstory 101 With Professor Paul
WELCOME TO MY CLASSROOM, STUDENTS. NOW THAT YOU'VE REACHED THE END OF VOLUME ONE, YOU'LL HAVE NOTICED THAT THIS BOOK IS PACKED WITH MYTHOLOGICAL REFERENCES. AS PANTHEON HIGH'S CREATIVE WRITING PROFESSOR, IT IS MY DIVINE DUTY TO GIVE YOU A LITTLE MORE INSIGHT ON CERTAIN ALLUSIONS THE AUTHORS HAVE HIDDEN (OFTEN IN PLAIN SIGHT) WITHIN THE BOOK.

PAGE 5: Fabulous monuments to the gods exist all over the campus to thank them for supporting the school. From left to right, those are statues of Athena (Greek goddess of wisdom and battle), Thor (Norse god of thunder), and Khons (Egyptian moon god).

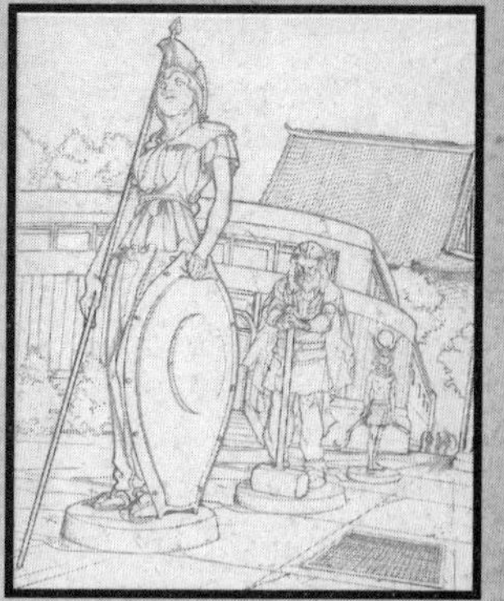

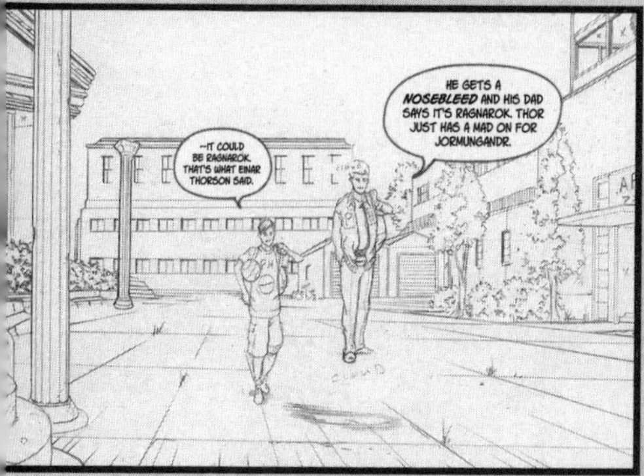
HE GETS A NOSEBLEED AND HIS DAD SAYS IT'S RAGNAROK. THOR JUST HAS A MAD ON FOR JORMUNGANDR.
—IT COULD BE RAGNAROK. THAT'S WHAT EINAR THORSON SAID.

PAGE 9: Todd and Yukio are talking about Jormungandr's role in the battle of Ragnarok. In Norse myth, Ragnarok is the predestined war between the gods and their enemies which will result in the end of the world. It is foretold that Jormungandr and Thor will slay each other in that hideous battle.

PAGE 17: Here we spy Griffin flipping his most prized possession, a coin called an "Obol." The obol was traditionally placed on the tongues of the dead in ancient Greece so that they could pay Charon the ferryman to take their spirit across the river Styx into Hades, the land of the dead. Otherwise their spirit would wander the shores of the river for all eternity.

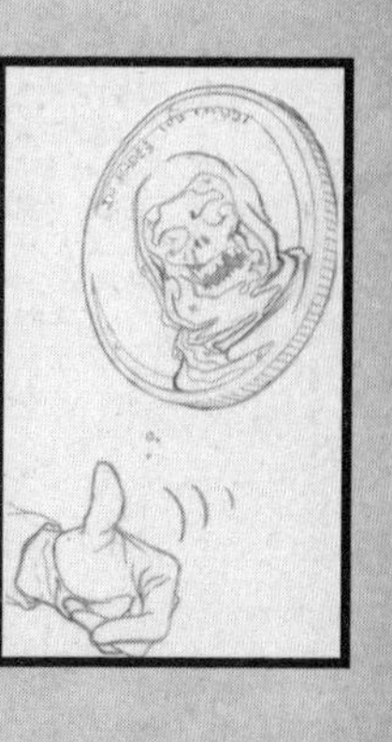

PAGE 19: In that last panel, Katya el Bastet is chatting with Aziza about Eric Areson's party. Ares is the Greek god of war, so it makes sense that he'd be spending a weekend (or longer) taking care of business in the Middle East. Perhaps one day the world will have changed so much that someone will read this book and wonder why a war god would have any business in that part of the world.

--PARTY AT ERIC ARESON'S. HIS DAD'S GOING TO BE IN THE MIDDLE EAST ALL WEEKEND.

PAGE 20: Aziza's ride is an Egyptian gondola that floats on a portable cloud. Her father, Ra, drives the sun across the sky every day using his solar barge, which allows him to float through Duat (the underworld) each night without letting the sun be extinguished by the river waters in Duat.

PAGE 21: Jake Smith is the son of Hephaestus, the Greek god of the forge. Hephaestus is known for creating many incredible magical items from Zeus' lightning bolts to Hades' helm of invisibility to Pandora's box. Hephaestus has one bad leg and is therefore quite literally lame. So do you think Aziza knew the irony of her own statement when she smarted off to Jake Smith?

HE FORGES ZEUS' LIGHTNING BOLTS!

WHAT-*EVER*. HE'S TOTALLY LAME.

GET PINCHED WITH THOSE AND I DON'T KNOW YOU FROM BURI.

YOU PLANNING A CRADLE HEIST, CHRIS?

PAGE 23: Onela is much older than she appears because her mother is Idun, the Norse goddess of immortality who gives her magical apples to the gods every day to keep them young. When Onela says, "I don't know you from Buri" to Chris, she's referencing the common phrase, "I don't know you from Adam." Buri is the Norse equivalent of the Judeo/Christian bible's first man.

PAGE 26: In Greek mythology, the chimera was a sibling of such famous monsters as Cerberus and the Lernean Hydra. The chimera was slain by the hero Bellerophon who rode Pegasus into battle thanks to an enchanted saddle that let him ride the winged horse. The Bridle of Athena that controls the chimera is based on that saddle which Athena gave to Bellerophon. It is my special duty to mention that if you ever see the film *Clash of the Titans* you'll witness Perseus, not Bellerophon, riding Pegasus. This is highly inaccurate. In the ancient Greek legends, Perseus flew by means of a pair of winged sandals loaned to him by Hermes. Pegasus was born when Perseus decapitated Medusa. The winged horse leapt out of the bloody stump of Medusa's neck. Then again, a flying horse looks a lot cooler in a movie than a pair of sandals with wings on them.

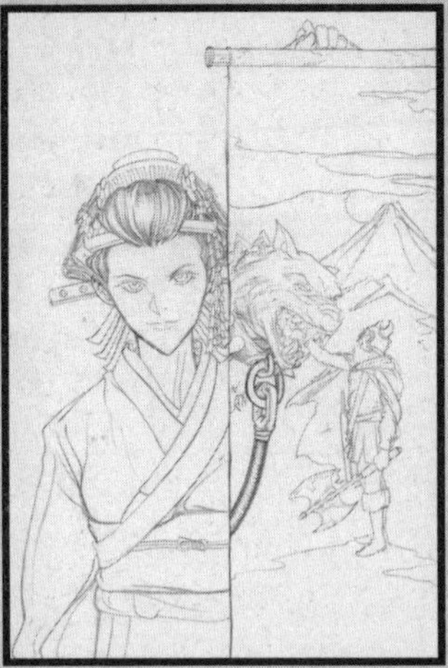

PAGE 30: Tyr is the Norse god of war. Ms. Hachiman already taught this lesson. You'll pay more attention in her class if you want to get into a good divine college.

PAGE 31: Daphne's visions come from Apollo, Greek god of light, the arts and prophecy. Apollo sent visions of the future to the legendary Oracle in the Greek town of Delphi. People traveled from miles around to seek the Oracle's advice. Hopefully her advice back then was more useful than Daphne's visions tend to be.

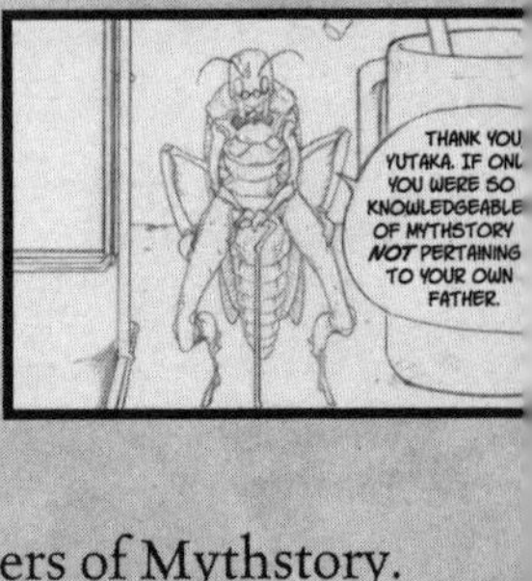
THANK YOU YUTAKA. IF ONL YOU WERE SO KNOWLEDGEABLE OF MYTHSTORY *NOT* PERTAINING TO YOUR OWN FATHER.

PAGE 34: When Eos, Titan goddess of the dawn, fell in love with the mortal Tithonus, she asked Zeus to make him immortal. Unfortunately, she failed to request eternal youth. Over the centuries, Tithonus became so old and shriveled he transformed into a grasshopper. Tithonus may not be the tallest teacher in the school, but with his many thousands of years of study, he is undoubtedly the most knowledgeable in matters of Mythstory.

PAGE 36: As you can see, Coach Hercules wears the skin of the Nemean Lion. It was his first of twelve famous labors to kill the impervious beast. The lion's hide made it invulnerable, but Hercules managed to slay it by choking it to death. He then used the lion's own claws to skin it and wore its hide as armor. Hercules is perhaps the most famous of all the demigods, so it was only natural that he be recruited as staff when Pantheon High first opened. The fact that Hercules was dead at the time was a bit of a roadblock, but thanks to some creative arrangements with Hades, Hercules was allowed back into the land of the living so that he could provide the students of Pantheon High with adequate athletic instruction.

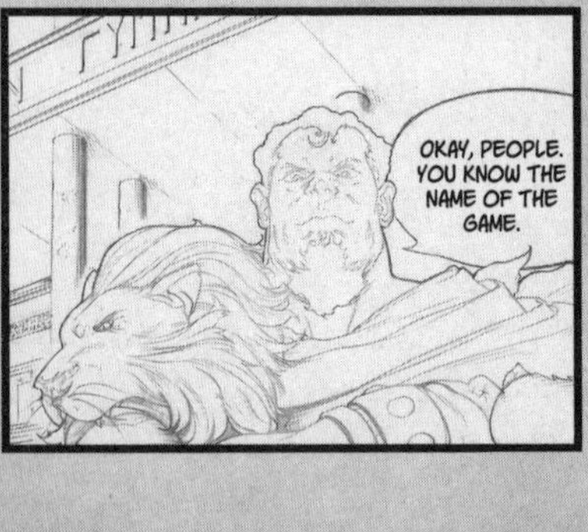
OKAY, PEOPLE. YOU KNOW THE NAME OF THE GAME.

PAGE 45: Canopic jars were used to make mummies in ancient Egypt. Organs were excised from the corpses of the deceased and then each organ was placed in its own jar. Removing the organs from the body helped preserve it.

PAGE 46: The sleeping potion is made by combining various items that either induce sleep or delay the progression of time. Abby provides bark from a Nymph's tree. In Greek myth, nymphs are beautiful female nature spirits. If a nymph bonds her soul to a tree, she will live as long as the tree remains standing. Thus, while nymphs are generally carefree souls, they will go to great lengths to defend their trees.

PAGE 51: In Greek myth, Ambrosia was known as the "nectar of the gods." Some tales described the beverage as having healing properties while others claimed that it was the source of the gods' immortality.

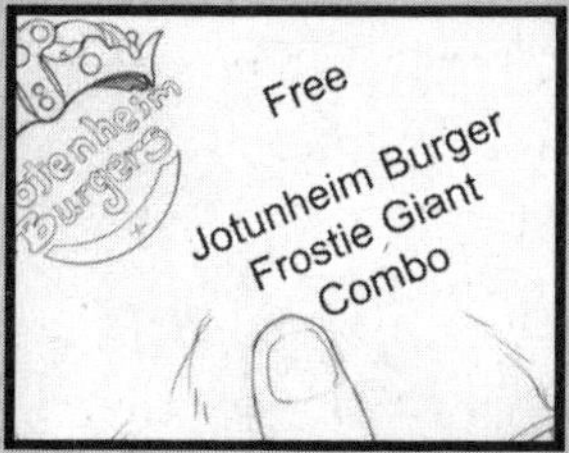
Jotunheim Burgers
Free
Jotunheim Burger
Frostie Giant
Combo

PAGE 54: The giants of Norse legend were the mortal enemies of the gods. Many Norse myths center around the gods' interactions with giants. Though different races of giants lived in different realms, most were said to hail from the frigid lands of Jotunheim.

PAGE 56: The Pantheon High library's Dark Lore section is off-limits to students. A living statue of a Japanese Asura guards the entrance. The Asuras were Buddhist demons of great power who were once cast out of the land of the gods. The gods are ever watchful of the Asuras, wary that they might attempt an invasion at any time.

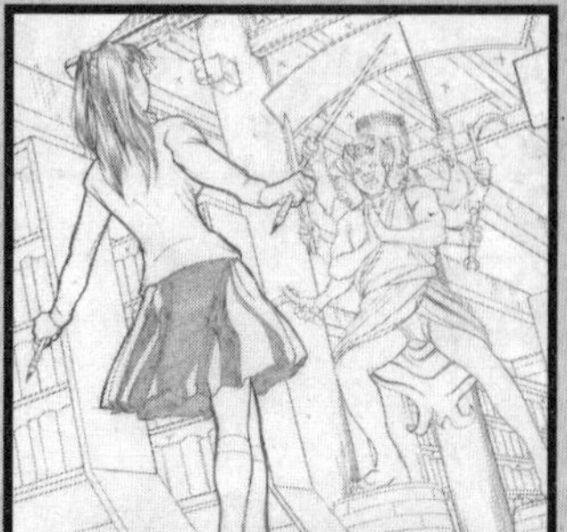

PAGE 59: Natron is a combination of baking soda, salt and a few other elements which were mined from dry lake beds near the Nile River in ancient Egypt. In the mummification process, natron was used to dry out a corpse and prevent tissue decay.

PAGE 73: The Titans were the gods who ruled the ancient Greek world before they were overthrown by Zeus and his siblings. Kronus (Abby's father) was their king. (He was also the father of the cyclopses--hence Abby's good looks). It's no surprise that Abby would swear by her father and his siblings.

PAGE 77: Charon is the ferryman who takes newly departed souls across the river Styx and into Hades. Some scholars argue that in a number of myths Charon ferries souls across the river Acheron, rather than the Styx. However, the most popular belief is that Charon took people across the Styx. In mythology, belief gives legends power, which is why you see Charon on the River Styx in this tale.

PAGE 94: Yggdrasill is also known as the World Tree. It is an enormous ash tree connecting the nine worlds or realms of the Norse cosmology. Asgard, Alfheim (home of the elves) and Vanaheim rested in the high branches. Midgard (our world) and Jotunheim were at the trunk of Yggdrasill with Nidavellir (land of the dwarves) and Svartalheim (land of the dark elves) just below. The roots of the World Tree reach down to Nifelheim (land of mist and ice), Muspelheim (land of the fire giants) and Hel (realm of the dead). The Norse runes are said to be symbols with great power. Rune stones are thrown like dice and read in a certain order to foretell the future or suggest a course of action. The runes Chris calls upon are Inguz, for strength and new beginnings, and Dagaz, for change or a breakthrough.

PAGE 95: Surtur is king of the fire giants and ruler of Muspelheim. He wields an enormous flaming sword and is destined to slay the sun god Frey in the battle of Ragnarok.

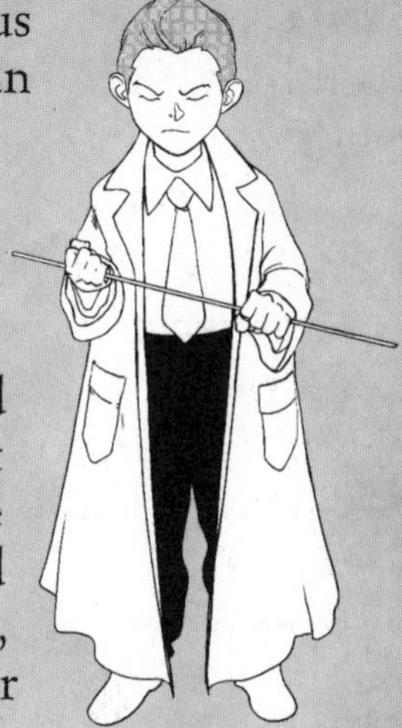

PAGE 99: Griffin's father is Hades, whose name is eponymous with the underworld of Greek myth. In the realm of Hades, people suffer torments that are poetic justice based on the sins they committed in life. The most famous is Sisyphus, a king who tricked the gods again and again. Sisyphus was charged to roll a boulder up a hill for all eternity, but before he reaches the top the boulder always slips from his grasp and rolls down the hill again. This was intended to keep his mind occupied and prevent him from tricking the gods. A task that seems to go on forever no matter how much time you spend on it (like homework) is referred to as a "Sisyphean task."

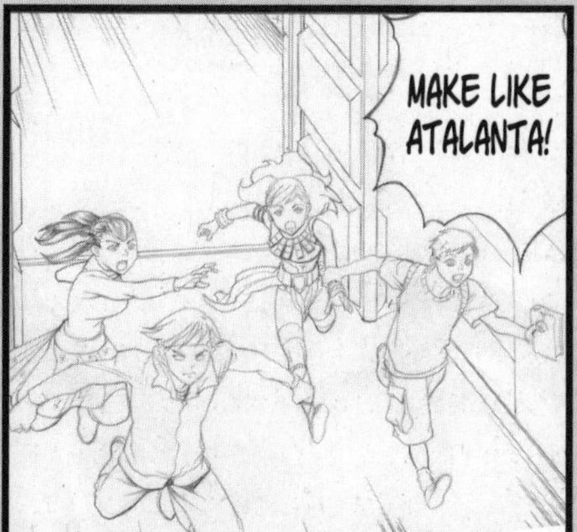
MAKE LIKE ATALANTA!

PAGE 100: Atalanta was a famous huntress in Greek mythology known for being an incredibly fast runner. She was so fast that the only way to win her hand in marriage was to beat her in a race. Even though the losers were executed, Atalanta still had many suitors, for lo, she was a hottie. Hippomenes eventually won his race by distracting Atalanta with golden apples given to him by Aphrodite, goddess of love.

PAGE 102: Athena is the Greek goddess of wisdom and battle. Coeüs is the Titan god of intellect.

PAGE 115: Heliopolis was an ancient city in Egypt and was an important site for those who worshipped the sun. Needless to say, it is really, really hot there.

ONE SPARK AND YOU'RE A SNO-CONE IN HELIOPOLIS.

PAGE 120: Isis, Egyptian goddess of magic, was one of the most powerful of the Nile deities. She was also the wife of Osiris and the mother of Horus.

SCHOOL BOARD SHUT IT DOWN YEARS AGO. THOUGHT GETTING THEIR LIVERS EATEN WASN'T "APPROPRIATE" FOR THEIR KIDS.

PAGE 133: When Zeus and the other Olympian gods rose up against the Titans, Prometheus, a Titan himself, fought at Zeus' side. However, Prometheus always put the interests of mortals above those of the gods, for it was Prometheus who created humankind. When Prometheus stole fire from the gods and bestowed it upon humankind, Zeus was enraged. As punishment, Prometheus was chained to the top of Mount Caucasus where an eagle would fly down and eat his liver. Every night his liver grew back and every day the eagle returned until Zeus' son Hercules freed Prometheus as one of his famous Twelve Labors. Zeus was so proud of his son Hercules that he let Prometheus remain free.

PAGE 146: By eating Idun's apple of immortality, Grace gains the military knowledge of some of the greatest strategists of all time. Ghengis Khan was a real life Mongol warlord who united the Mongol tribes to create the largest contiguous empire in world history. Of all these military leaders, Achilles is the only one who did not truly exist. In Greek myth, young Achilles was dipped in the River Styx to become invulnerable, but he was held by his ankle, and so that part of his body was still subject to harm. Achilles was a great hero of the Trojan War. Sun Tzu was a Chinese general who may have been the creator of what we now know as martial arts. Sun Tzu's ancient book "The Art of War"

THE POWER! THE STRENGTH!

is a famous primer not only for generals but is often used as a tool for modern businesspeople who compare business strategies to warfare. General George S. Patton was a leading general in the US Army during World War II. Patton is generally known as a brilliant military leader and is credited as one of the major factors in the Allied victories in Europe and North Africa.

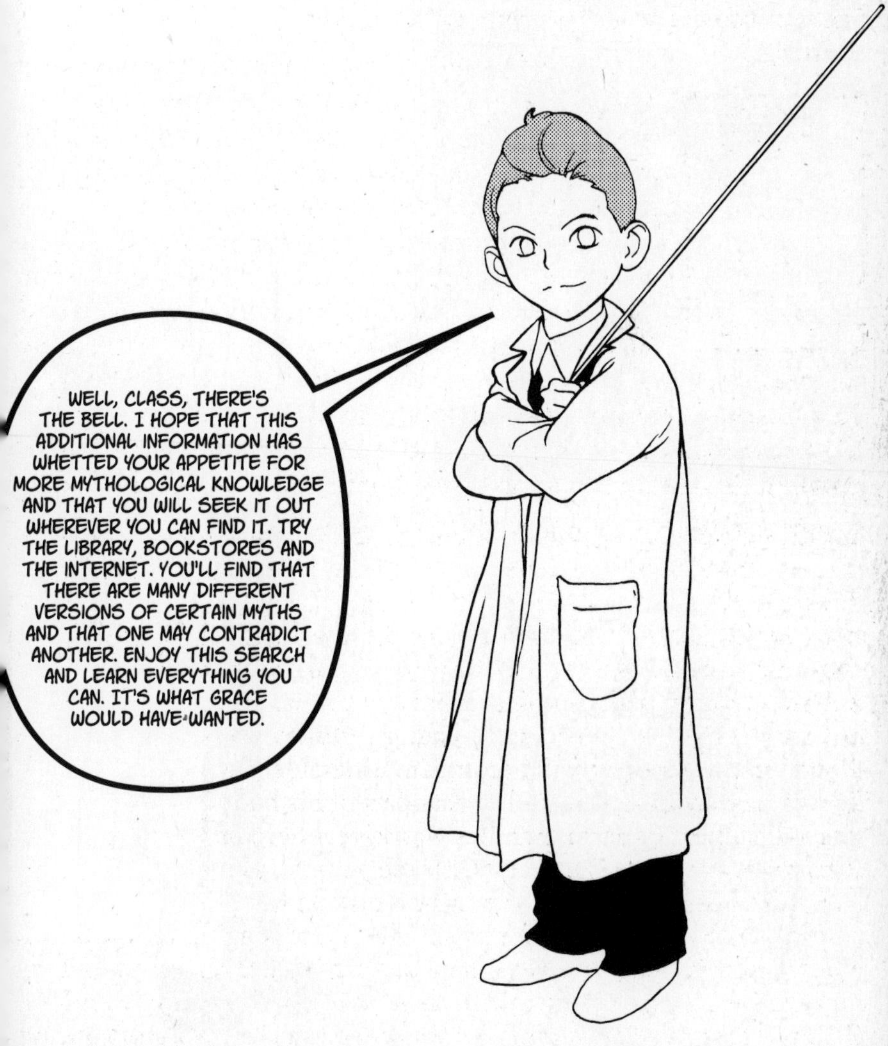
WELL, CLASS, THERE'S THE BELL. I HOPE THAT THIS ADDITIONAL INFORMATION HAS WHETTED YOUR APPETITE FOR MORE MYTHOLOGICAL KNOWLEDGE AND THAT YOU WILL SEEK IT OUT WHEREVER YOU CAN FIND IT. TRY THE LIBRARY, BOOKSTORES AND THE INTERNET. YOU'LL FIND THAT THERE ARE MANY DIFFERENT VERSIONS OF CERTAIN MYTHS AND THAT ONE MAY CONTRADICT ANOTHER. ENJOY THIS SEARCH AND LEARN EVERYTHING YOU CAN. IT'S WHAT GRACE WOULD HAVE WANTED.

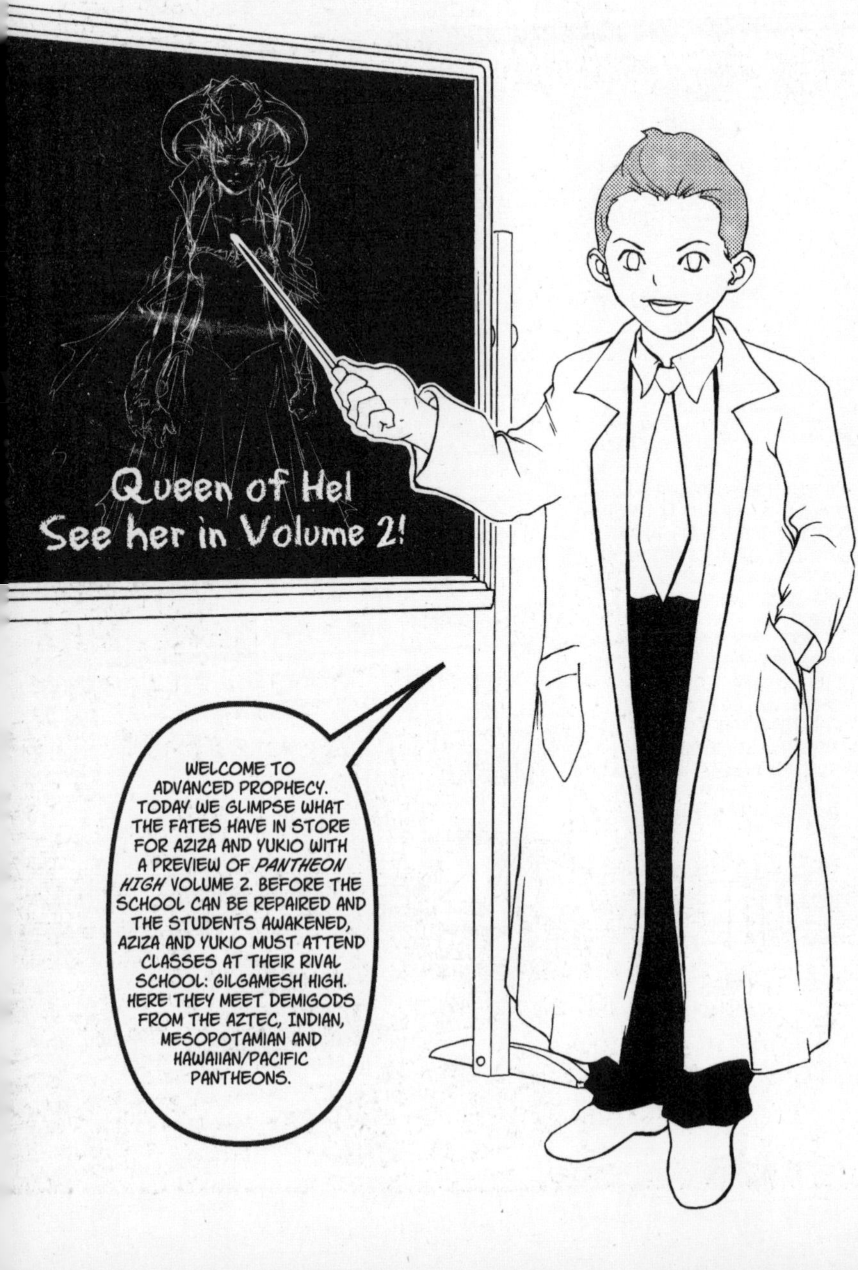
Queen of Hel
See her in Volume 2!
WELCOME TO ADVANCED PROPHECY. TODAY WE GLIMPSE WHAT THE FATES HAVE IN STORE FOR AZIZA AND YUKIO WITH A PREVIEW OF *PANTHEON HIGH* VOLUME 2. BEFORE THE SCHOOL CAN BE REPAIRED AND THE STUDENTS AWAKENED, AZIZA AND YUKIO MUST ATTEND CLASSES AT THEIR RIVAL SCHOOL: GILGAMESH HIGH. HERE THEY MEET DEMIGODS FROM THE AZTEC, INDIAN, MESOPOTAMIAN AND HAWAIIAN/PACIFIC PANTHEONS.

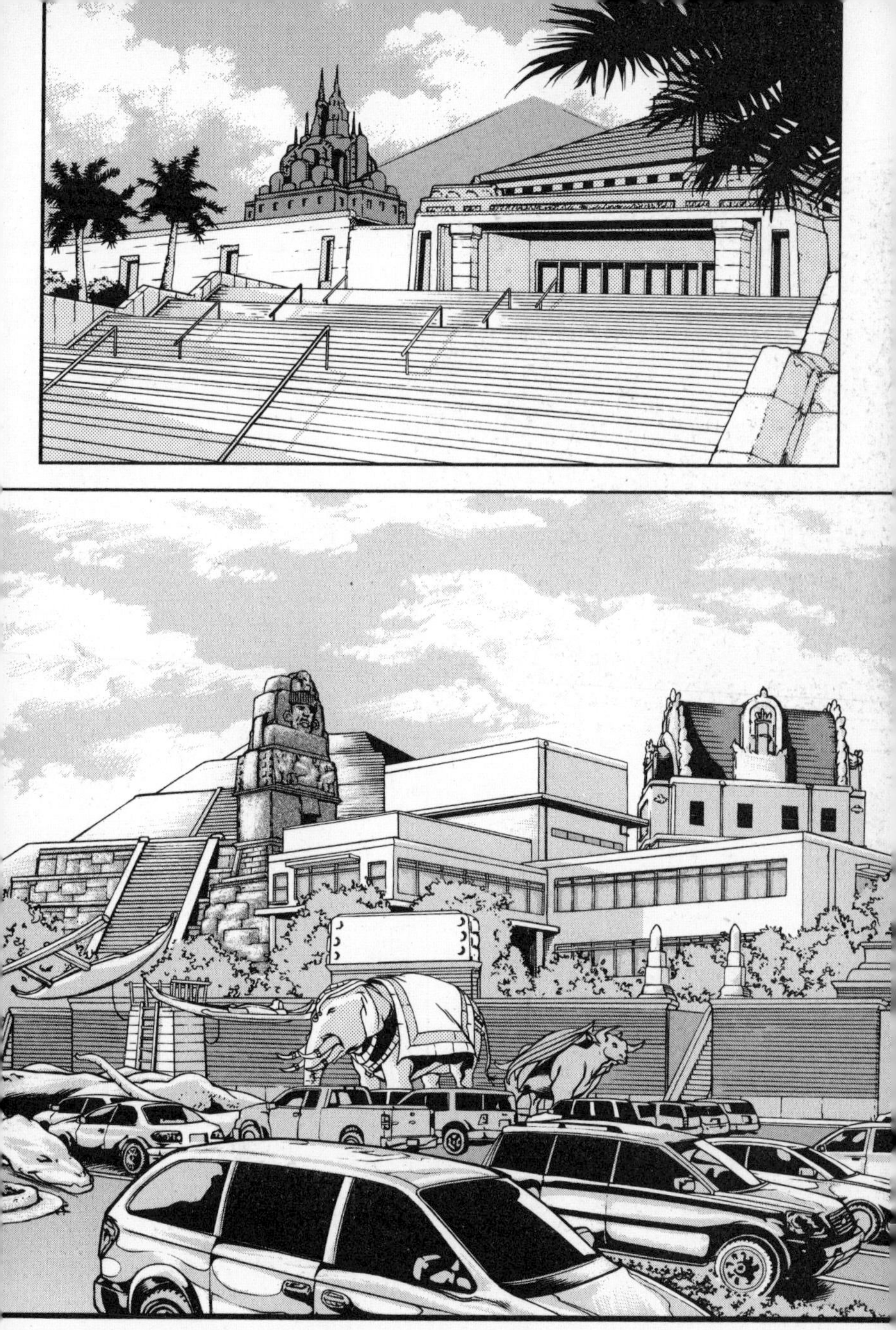

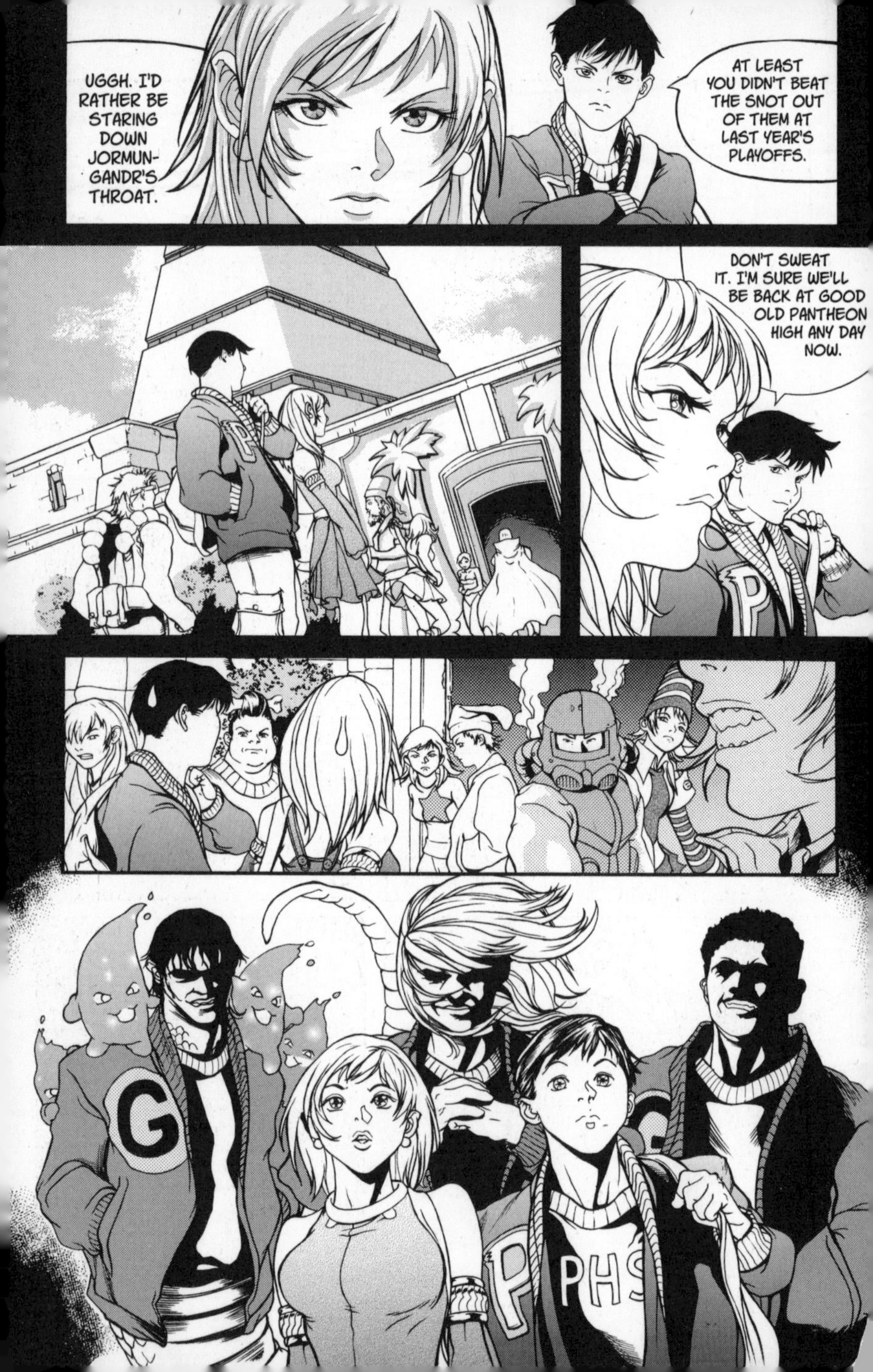
UGGH. I'D RATHER BE STARING DOWN JORMUNGANDR'S THROAT.
AT LEAST YOU DIDN'T BEAT THE SNOT OUT OF THEM AT LAST YEAR'S PLAYOFFS.
DON'T SWEAT IT. I'M SURE WE'LL BE BACK AT GOOD OLD PANTHEON HIGH ANY DAY NOW.
G
P
PHS

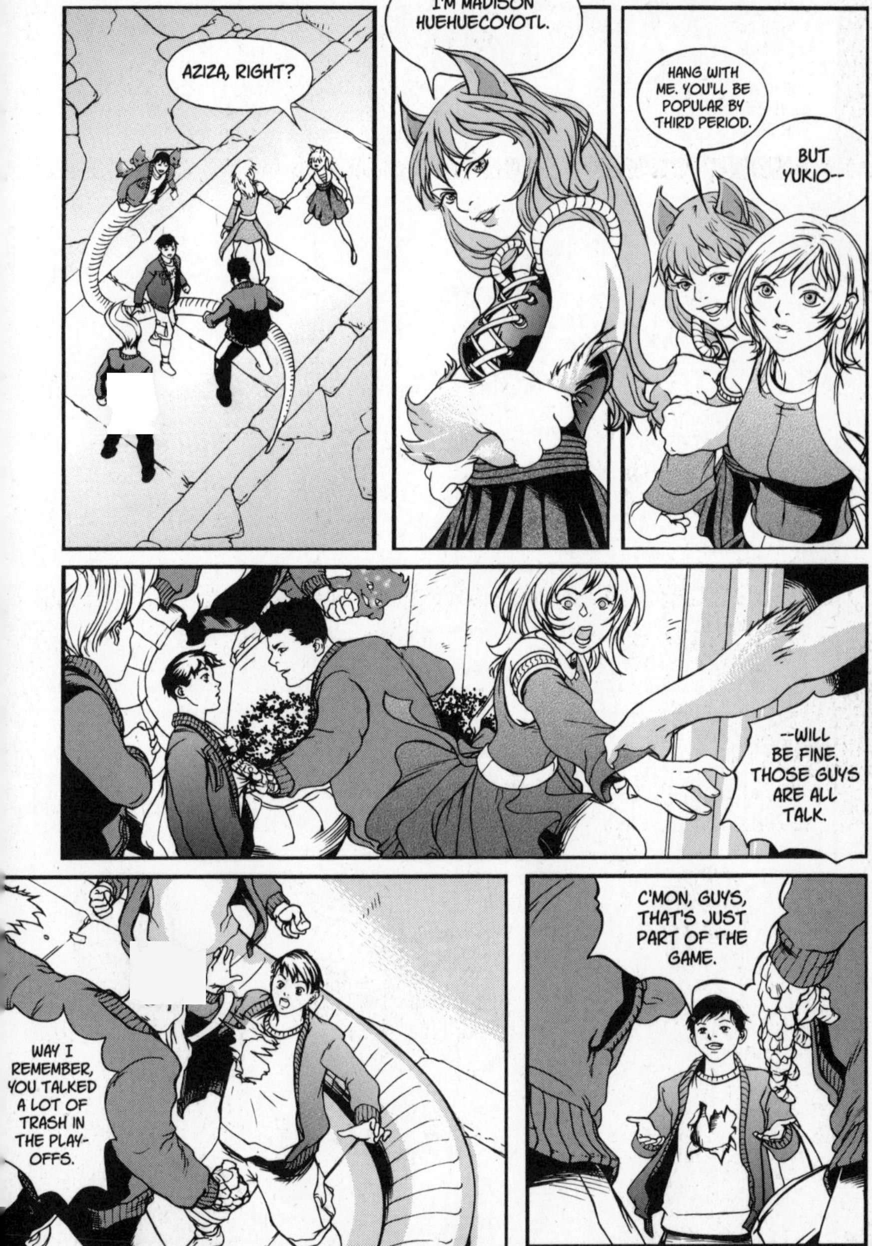
AZIZA, RIGHT?
I'M MADISON HUEHUECOYOTL.
HANG WITH ME. YOU'LL BE POPULAR BY THIRD PERIOD.
BUT YUKIO--
--WILL BE FINE. THOSE GUYS ARE ALL TALK.
WAY I REMEMBER, YOU TALKED A LOT OF TRASH IN THE PLAY-OFFS.
C'MON, GUYS, THAT'S JUST PART OF THE GAME.

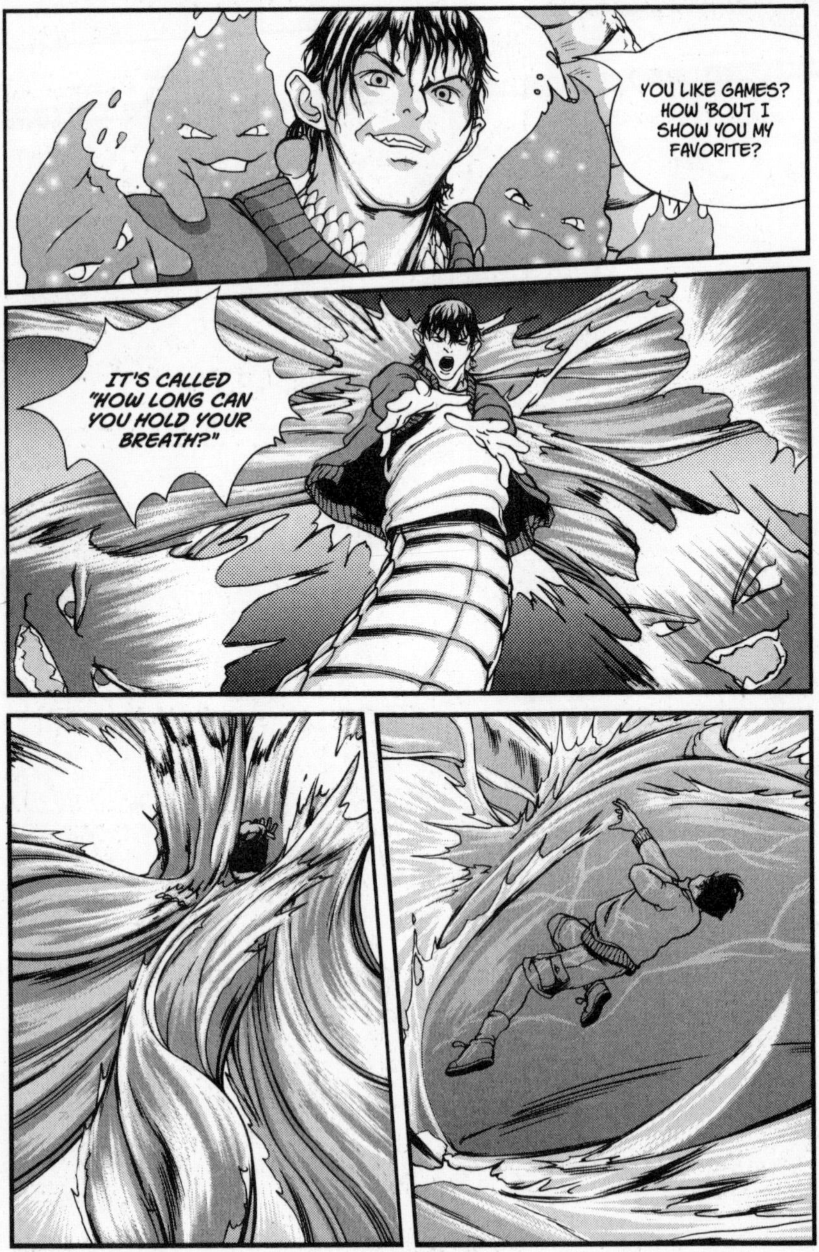
YOU LIKE GAMES? HOW 'BOUT I SHOW YOU MY FAVORITE?
IT'S CALLED "HOW LONG CAN YOU HOLD YOUR BREATH?"

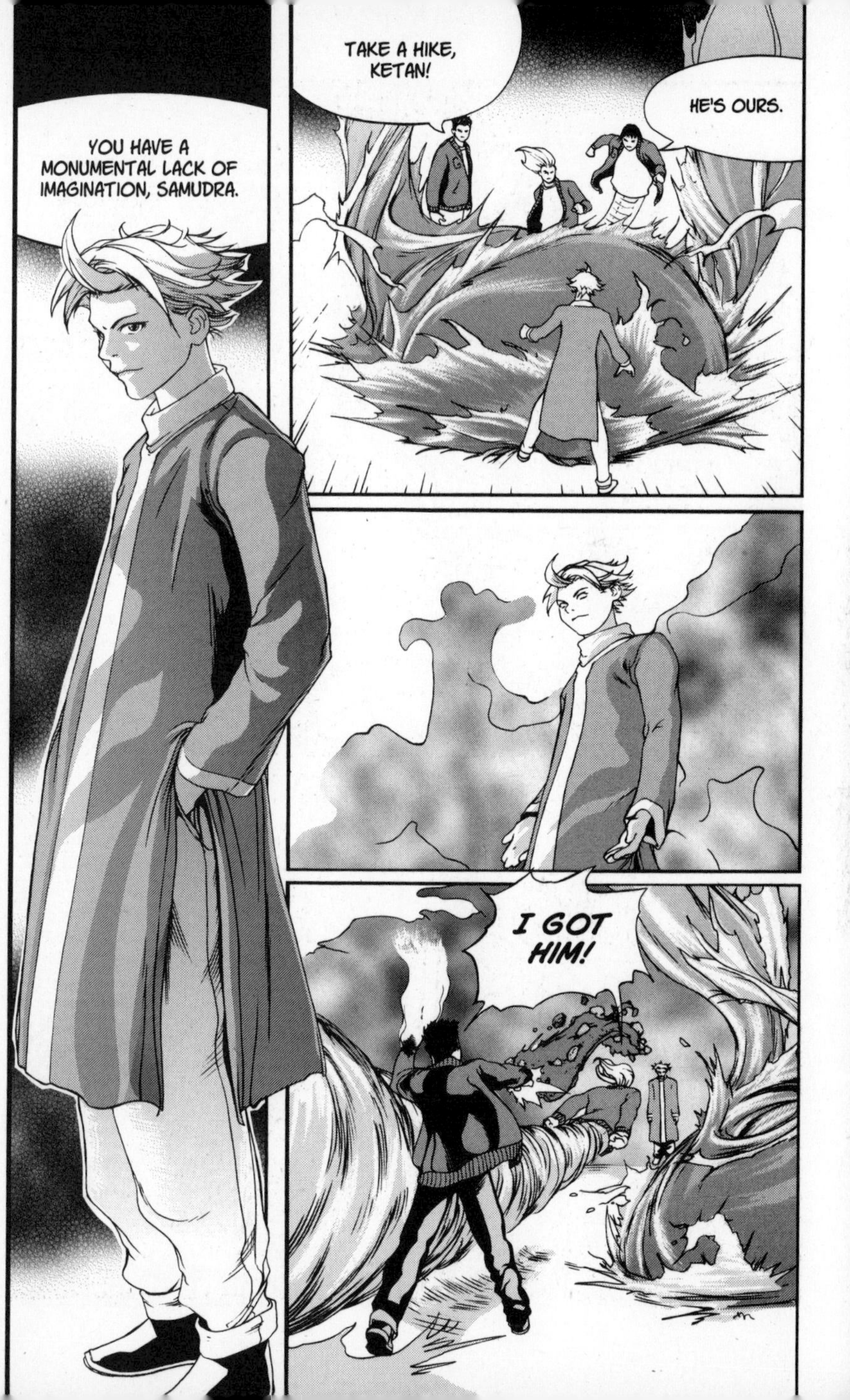
YOU HAVE A MONUMENTAL LACK OF IMAGINATION, SAMUDRA.
TAKE A HIKE, KETAN!
HE'S OURS.
I GOT HIM!

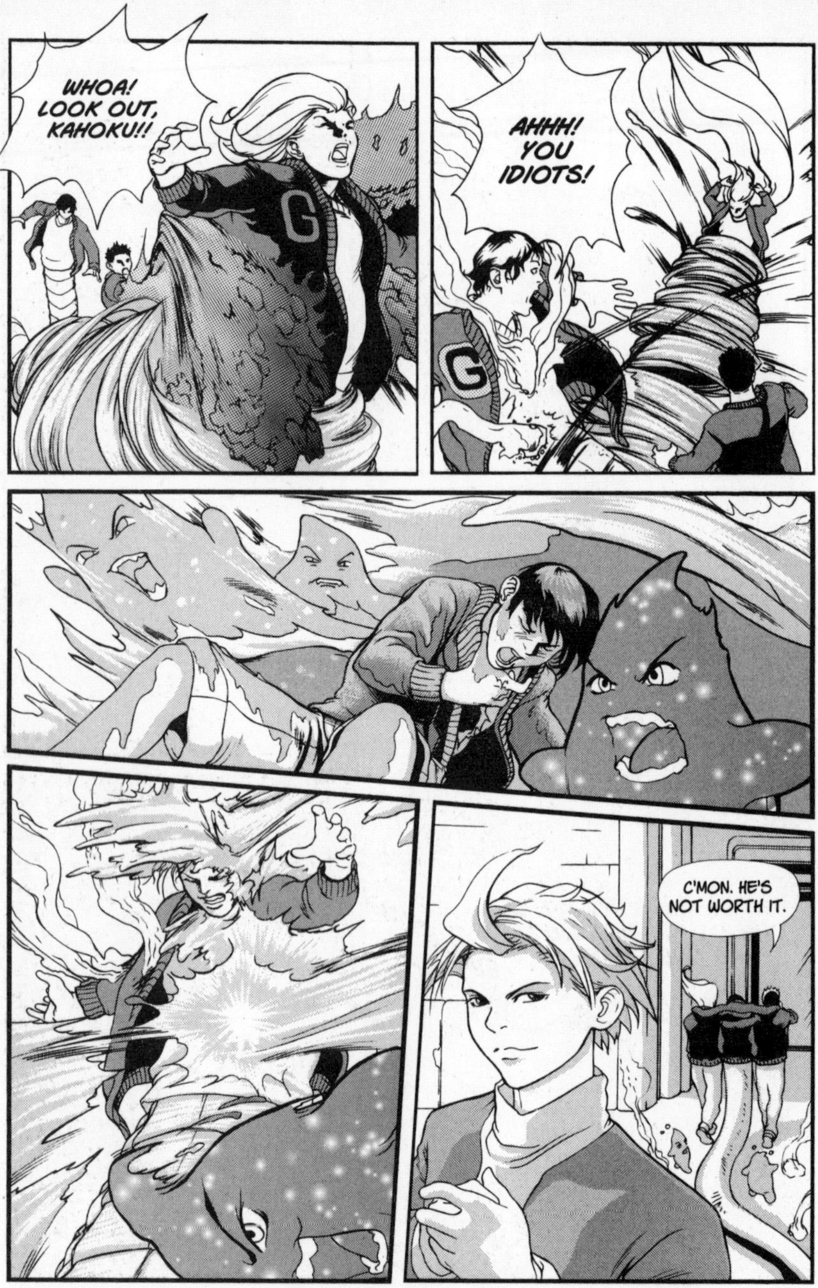
WHOA! LOOK OUT, KAHOKU!!
AHHH! YOU IDIOTS!
C'MON. HE'S NOT WORTH IT.

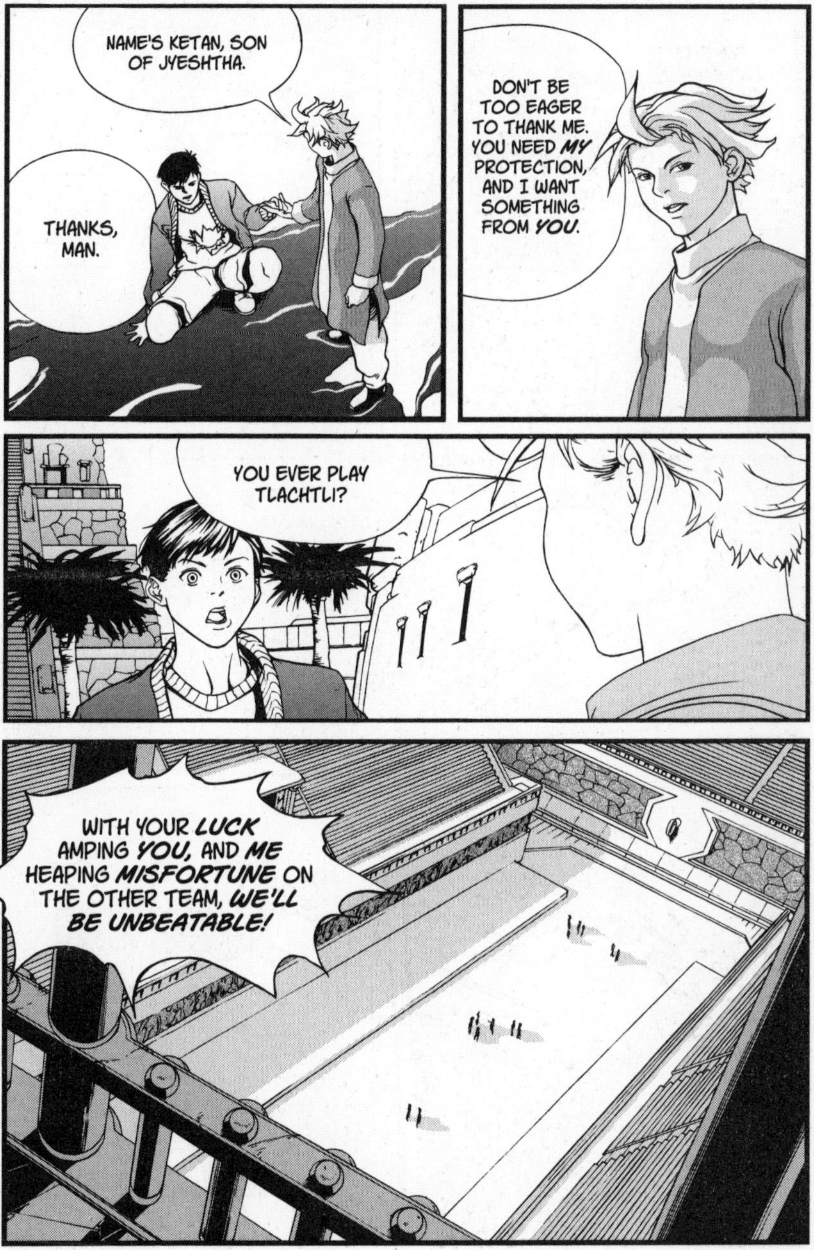
NAME'S KETAN, SON OF JYESHTHA.
THANKS, MAN.
DON'T BE TOO EAGER TO THANK ME. YOU NEED *MY* PROTECTION, AND I WANT SOMETHING FROM *YOU*.
YOU EVER PLAY TLACHTLI?
WITH YOUR *LUCK* AMPING *YOU*, AND *ME* HEAPING *MISFORTUNE* ON THE OTHER TEAM, *WE'LL BE UNBEATABLE!*

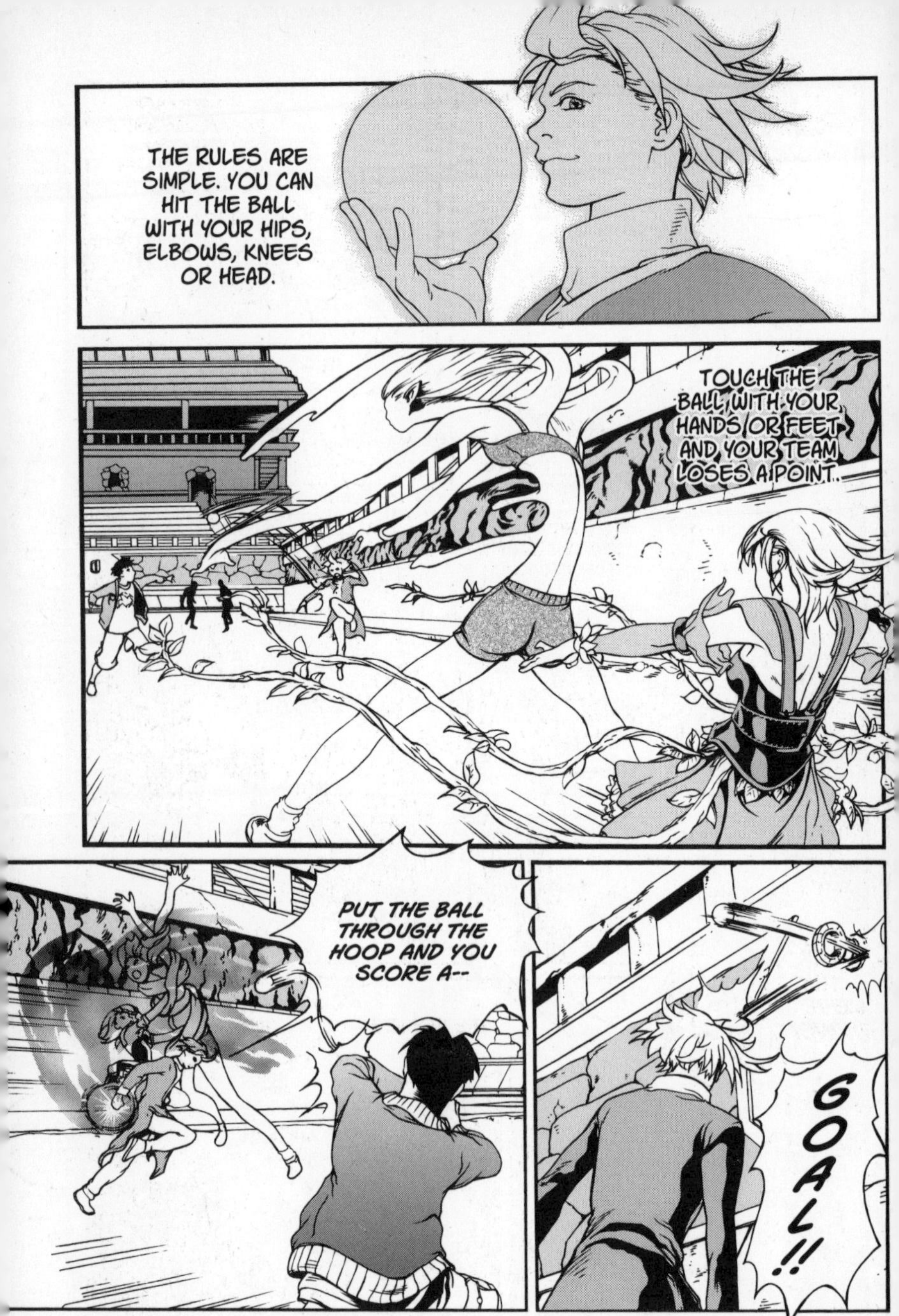
THE RULES ARE SIMPLE. YOU CAN HIT THE BALL WITH YOUR HIPS, ELBOWS, KNEES OR HEAD.
TOUCH THE BALL WITH YOUR HANDS OR FEET AND YOUR TEAM LOSES A POINT.
PUT THE BALL THROUGH THE HOOP AND YOU SCORE A--
GOAL!!

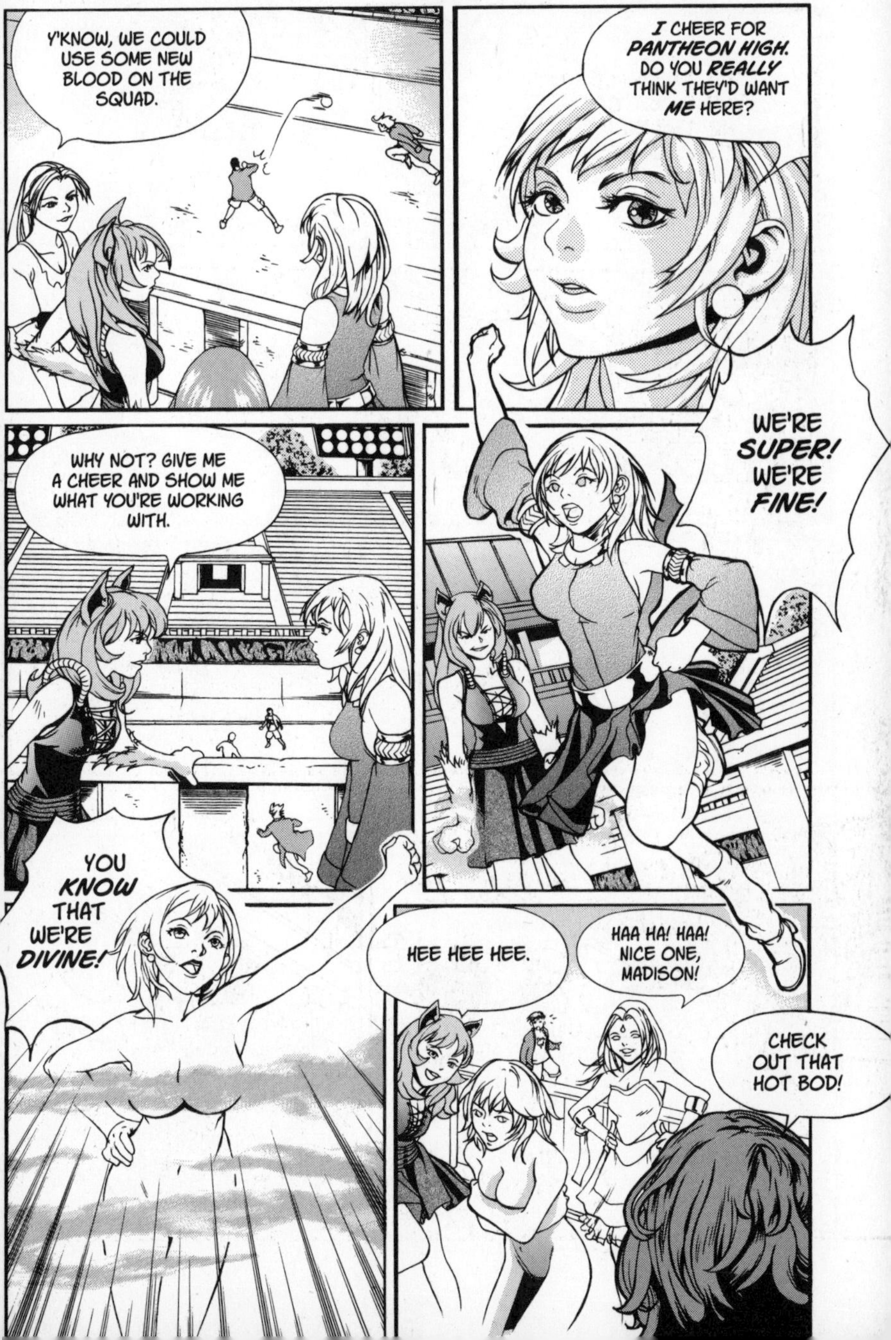
Y'KNOW, WE COULD USE SOME NEW BLOOD ON THE SQUAD.
I CHEER FOR PANTHEON HIGH. DO YOU REALLY THINK THEY'D WANT ME HERE?
WHY NOT? GIVE ME A CHEER AND SHOW ME WHAT YOU'RE WORKING WITH.
WE'RE SUPER! WE'RE FINE!
YOU KNOW THAT WE'RE DIVINE!
HEE HEE HEE.
HAA HA! HAA! NICE ONE, MADISON!
CHECK OUT THAT HOT BOD!

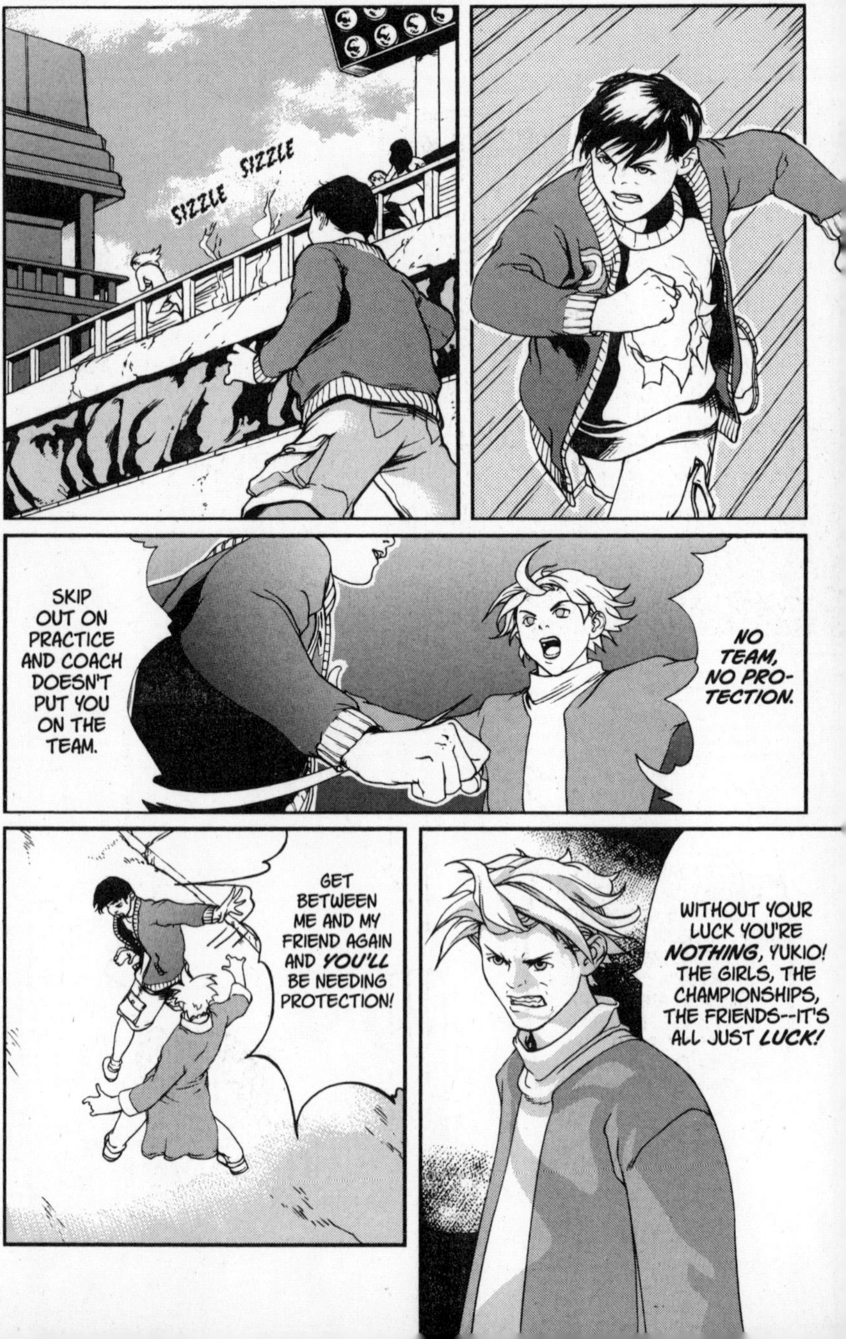
SIZZLE
SIZZLE
SKIP OUT ON PRACTICE AND COACH DOESN'T PUT YOU ON THE TEAM.
NO TEAM, NO PRO-TECTION.
GET BETWEEN ME AND MY FRIEND AGAIN AND YOU'LL BE NEEDING PROTECTION!
WITHOUT YOUR LUCK YOU'RE NOTHING, YUKIO! THE GIRLS, THE CHAMPIONSHIPS, THE FRIENDS--IT'S ALL JUST LUCK!

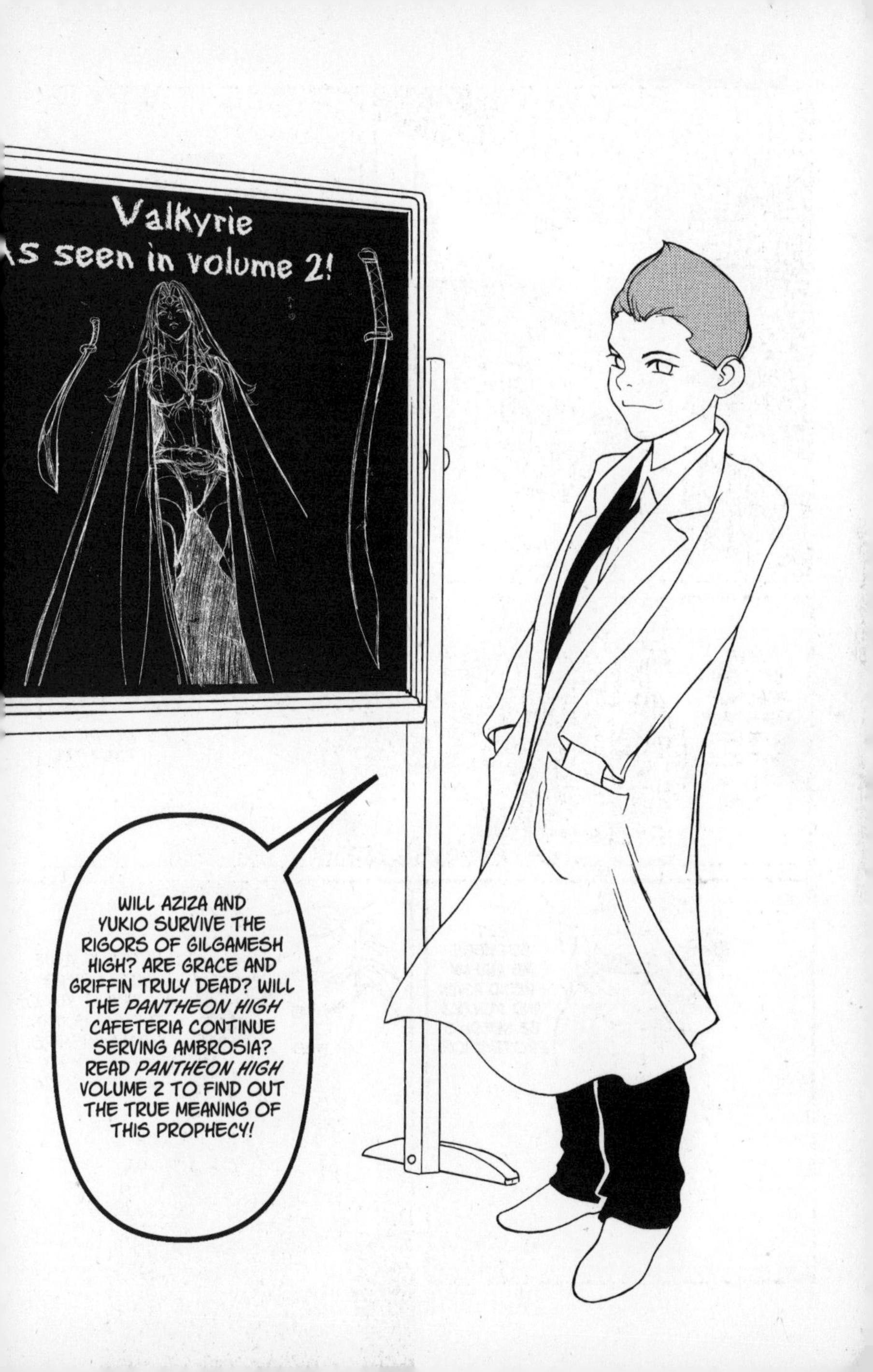
Valkyrie
As seen in volume 2!
WILL AZIZA AND YUKIO SURVIVE THE RIGORS OF GILGAMESH HIGH? ARE GRACE AND GRIFFIN TRULY DEAD? WILL THE *PANTHEON HIGH* CAFETERIA CONTINUE SERVING AMBROSIA? READ *PANTHEON HIGH* VOLUME 2 TO FIND OUT THE TRUE MEANING OF THIS PROPHECY!

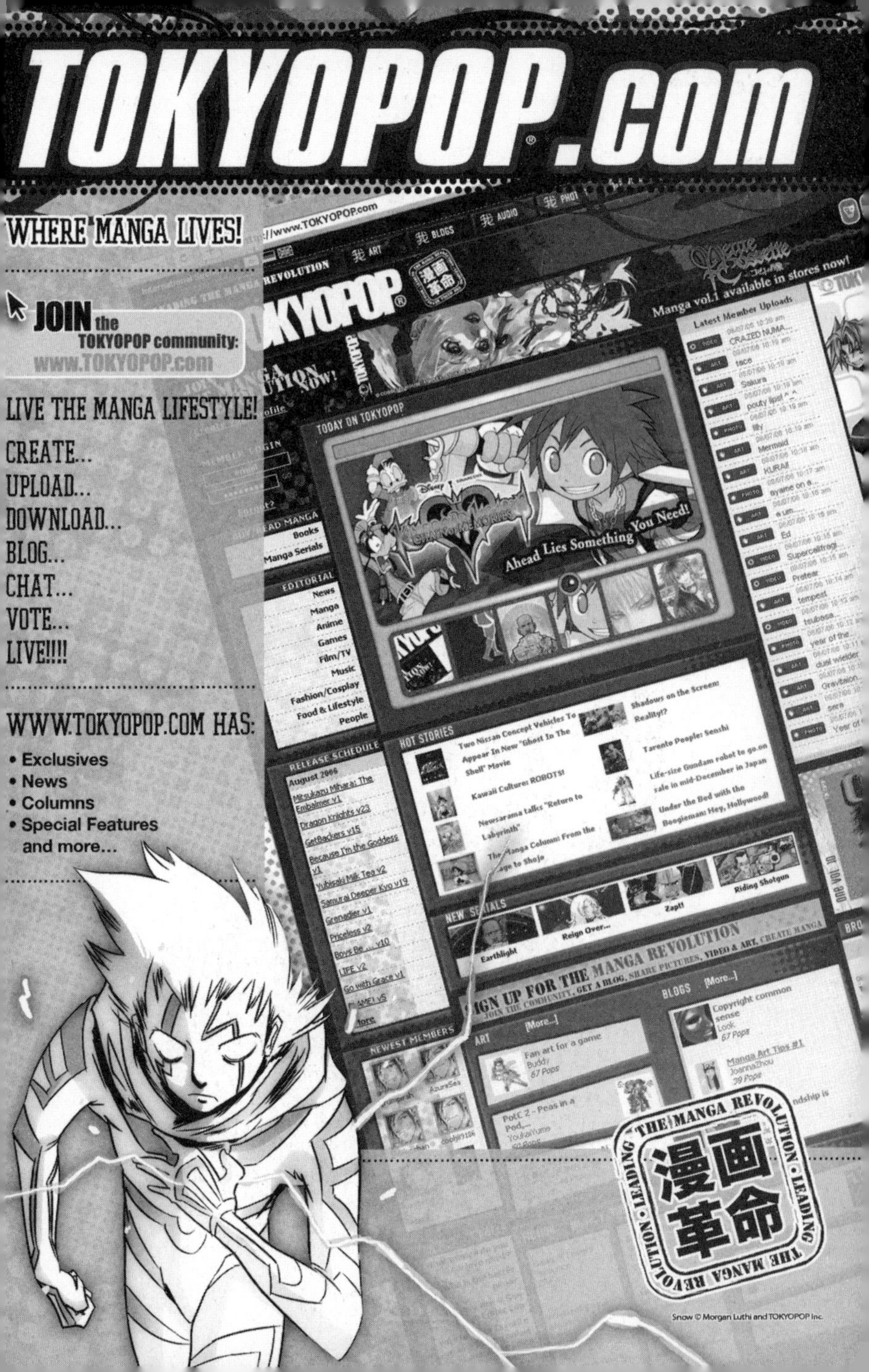
TOKYOPOP®.com
WHERE MANGA LIVES!
JOIN the TOKYOPOP community:
www.TOKYOPOP.com
LIVE THE MANGA LIFESTYLE!
CREATE...
UPLOAD...
DOWNLOAD...
BLOG...
CHAT...
VOTE...
LIVE!!!!
WWW.TOKYOPOP.COM HAS:
• Exclusives
• News
• Columns
• Special Features
and more...
THE MANGA REVOLUTION • LEADING
漫画革命
Snow © Morgan Luthi and TOKYOPOP Inc.